# Global Development and the Environment Series

## Series Editors
## Richard M. Auty and Robert B. Potter

## Approaches to Sustainable Development

Titles previously published in the Global Development and the Environment series, under the Mansell imprint:

*Economic Development and the Environment*
*Agricultural Change, Environment and Economy*
*Economic Development and Industrial Policy*
*Water and the Quest for Sustainable Development in the Ganges Valley*

# Approaches to Sustainable Development

## Edited by
## Richard M. Auty and Katrina Brown

Routledge
Taylor & Francis Group

LONDON AND NEW YORK

First published 1997 by Pinter

2 Park Square, Milton Park, Abingdon, Oxfordshire OX14 4RN
52 Vanderbilt Avenue, New York, NY 10017

*Routledge is an imprint of the Taylor & Francis Group, an informa business*

First issued in paperback 2019

**British Library Cataloguing in Publication Data**
A catalogue record for this book is available from the British Library.

**Library of Congress Cataloging-in-Publication Data**
Approaches to sustainable development / edited by Richard M. Auty and
    Katrina Brown.
       p.   cm. — (Global development and the environment)
    "Rev. and rewritten selection of papers prepared for a special
series of workshop sessions at the Development Studies Association
annual conference, held in Dublin in Sept. 1995"—
    Includes bibliographical references and index.
    ISBN 1-85567-439-4 (hardcover)
    1. Sustainable development—Congresses.  I. Auty, R.M. (Richard
M.)  II. Brown, Katrina. III. Series.
HC79.E5A658   1997
338.9—dc20
                                      96-20532
                                        CIP

Typeset by BookEns Limited, Royston, Herts.

ISBN 13: 978-1-85567-439-4 (hbk)
ISBN 13: 978-1-138-96372-6 (pbk)

# Contents

List of Figures                                                    vii

List of Tables                                                      ix

Contributors                                                      xiii

Foreword                                                           xv

**I Introduction**
1 An Overview of Approaches to Sustainable Development              3
  *Richard M. Auty and Katrina Brown*

**II Approaches to Sustainable Development**
2 Accounting for Sustainability                                    21
  *Kirk Hamilton*
3 Sustainable Management of Water Resources: An Economic View      31
  *James T. Winpenny*
4 Labour Force Analysis as a Means to Understand the Livelihood
  Dimension of Sustainability                                      50
  *John Cameron*
5 Sustainable Utilization: A Grand Illusion?                       83
  *Katrina Brown*

**III Rural Applications of Sustainability**
6 Population and Food in South Asia: Recent Trends and Prospects   103
  *Tim Dyson*
7 Land, Livestock and Livelihoods: Towards Sustainable Pastoral
  Development in Marsabit District, Kenya                          129
  *Oriel Kenny*
8 Annapurna Conservation Area Project: In Pursuit of Sustainable
  Development?                                                     144
  *Sara Parker*
9 Global Processes and the Politics of Sustainable Development
  in Colombia and Costa Rica                                       169
  *Philip J. O'Brien*

**IV Coping with Industrialization and Pollution**

10  Sustaining Mineral-driven Development: Chile and Jamaica       197
    *Richard M. Auty*
11  Pollution Patterns in the Industrialization Process            220
    *Richard M. Auty and Michael Tribe*
12  Industrialization in Vietnam: Social Change and Environment in
    Transitional Developing Countries                             247
    *Tim Forsyth*
13  The International Dimensions of Sustainable Development:
    Rio Reconsidered                                              270
    *Andrew Jordan and Katrina Brown*

14  Sustainable Development: Taking Stock                          296
    *Richard M. Auty and Katrina Brown*

    Name Index                                                    303
    Subject Index                                                 309

# List of Figures

| | | |
|---|---|---|
| 1.1 | Costs and benefits of curbing global warming | 7 |
| 2.1 | Genuine savings rate by region (*Source*: World Bank, 1995) | 24 |
| 2.2 | Malawi: genuine savings rate 1981–90 (*Source*: Hamilton, 1994b) | 26 |
| 5.1 | Royal Bardia National Park | 88 |
| 5.2 | Grass-cutting permits sold in Royal Bardia National Park (*Source*: Royal Bardia National Park) | 91 |
| 6.1 | South Asia's per capita cereal production 1951–91 (*Sources*: FAO, 1987; United Nations, 1992) | 107 |
| 6.2 | Country measures of per capita cereal production 1951–91 (*Sources*: FAO, 1987; United Nations, 1992) | 108 |
| 7.1 | Map of Kenya and Marsabit area | 131 |
| 8.1 | Nepal's protected areas | 145 |
| 8.2 | The Annapurna conservation area (*Source*: ACAP/KMTNC, 1995) | 149 |
| 8.3 | Phased approach and zoning in ACA | 151 |
| 8.4 | The components of the ACAP approach | 153 |
| 10.1 | Location of Jamaican bauxite reserves, mines and alumina refineries | 209 |
| 10.2 | Location of Chilean copper mines and processing plants | 212 |
| 11.1 | Breaking the link between growth in GDP and pollution (*Source*: World Bank, 1992) | 232 |
| 11.2 | Historical trends in the energy-efficiency of GDP (*Source*: Reddy and Goldenberg, 1990) | 236 |
| 11.3 | Structure of value added in manufacturing, by country type (*Source*: Syrquin and Chenery, 1989) | 237 |

# List of Tables

1.1   Perspectives on sustainable development   6
2.1   Genuine saving in sub-Saharan Africa   27
3.1   Economic value of water   44
3.2   Economic value of water   45
4.1   Economically active population/labour force (millions) in 1989 by age and gender with Labour Force Participation Rates (LFPR)   57
4.2   Estimate of hours per week worked by economically active people of 15 years of age or more   58
4.3   Estimate of hours worked and involuntarily idle by the labour force, economically active people of 15 years of age or more, 1989   58
4.4   Education and skill composition of the employed population, 1989   59
4.5   Comparison of employed labour force skills with education/ skill profiles of unemployed and Bangladeshi temporary migrant workers in 1989 (in thousands)   60
4.6   Comparison of narrowly defined Labour Force Participation Rates derived from the 1989 Labour Force Survey with the 1990 projections from the 1983–84 Labour Force Survey   62
4.7   Comparison of educational profile of the whole population in the 1983–84 and 1989 Labour Force Surveys   62
4.8   Economic status profiles of the major sectors in 1989 for those aged 15 or more   64
4.9   Estimate of labour time used by sector in 1989 for those aged 15 or more   64
4.10  Changes in employment in major industries 1983–90   66
4.11  Public and private sector employment in formal manufacturing   67
4.12  Annual migration on official temporary employment contracts (thousands)   68
4.13  The impact of irrigation provision on employment   74
4.14  Sectoral output growth rates (% per annum) and sectoral output growth elasticities of employment   76
4.15  Labour use estimates in millions of person hours per year, 1989–2000   76

4.16   Comparison of high labour use and low labour use simulation
       results with Taskforces' two scenarios results (in millions of
       person years, by the year 2000)                                      77
5.1    Grasses collected from Royal Bardia National Park                    90
5.2    Estimates of biomass production in five southern *phantas* in
       RBNP                                                                 92
6.1    Summary demographic measures and projections, principal
       countries of South Asia, 1950–2020                                  105
6.2    FAO estimates of average per capita daily calorie supply and
       its composition principal countries of South Asia 1988–90           105
6.3    Summary measures of cereal production, area harvested and
       yield, in the principal countries of South Asia 1951–91             109
6.4    FAO indices of food production per capita, principal countries
       of South Asia 1952–91                                               113
6.5    Cereal production, trade and aid, by volume, principal countries
       of South Asia 1987–90                                               114
6.6    Projected demand for cereals, principal countries of South Asia
       2020                                                                116
6.7    Factors affecting the supply of food, principal countries of
       South Asia *c.* 1990                                                118
6.8    Comparison of projected cereal demand and supply calculations
       for 2020, principal countries of South Asia                         121
8.1    The national parks and reserves of Nepal                            146
8.2    Institutions formed in ACA                                          156
8.3    Achievements and problems of the CEEP as perceived by
       the Conservation Education Assistants                               162
10.1   Comparative economic performance, Chile and Jamaica                 199
10.2   Estimated potential and actual rent on Jamaican bauxite, 1990       202
10.3   True income as a percentage of net receipts                         203
10.4   Adjustment to Jamaican national accounts for bauxite depletion,
       1990 (US$million)                                                   204
10.5   Estimated Chilean copper production costs and rents, 1990           204
10.6   Adjustment to Chilean national accounts for ore-depletion,
       1990 (US$billion)                                                   205
11.1   Average variation in industrial structure with level of
       development (Population = 20 million)                               227
11.2   Trends in emission of air pollutants in market economies by
       source, for selected countries, 1970–85 (in thousand metric
       tonnes)                                                             234
11.3   Structure of manufacturing, 1991, selected countries               238
11.4   Typology of industrial development and industrial pollution         243
12.1   Vietnam: average annual growth rate, 1981–93 (%)                    251
12.2   State, co-operative and private industrial activities in Vietnam    253

| 12.3 | Foreign investment in Vietnam 1988–93 | 254 |
| 13.1 | The UNCED agreements | 272 |
| 13.2 | A chronology of climate politics | 279 |

# Contributors

Richard M. Auty
Senior Lecturer in Geography, Lancaster University

Katrina Brown
Lecturer in Environment and Development, University of
East Anglia/Senior Research Fellow, CSERGE

John Cameron
Lecturer in Economics, University of East Anglia

Tim Dyson
Professor in Population Studies, London School of Economics

Tim Forsyth
Lecturer in Geography, London School of Economics

Kirk Hamilton
Environment Department, World Bank

Andrew Jordon
Senior Research Associate, CSERGE

Oriel Kenny
Lecturer, Development Project Planning Centre, Bradford University

Philip J. O'Brien
Lecturer in Latin American Studies, Glasgow University

Sara Parker
Lecturer in Geography, John Moores University

Michael Tribe
Lecturer in Economics, Development Project Planning Centre, Bradford
University

James T. Winpenny
Fellow, Overseas Development Institute, London

# Foreword

The principal aim of the Global Development and the Environment series is to provide an outlet for scholarly work covering important aspects of Third World development and change. The series is aimed at a multidisciplinary audience and it is intended that the issues covered will be treated from a variety of different disciplinary perspectives – economic, social and political, historical and environmental among them. At the same time, we are aware of the need to achieve balance with respect to the various regions of the Third World that are covered by volumes in the series, not least because of the striking heterogeneity that is so characteristic of the nations that make up what we refer to in shorthand terms as the 'developing world'. In essence, we are seeking to promote the publication of works that deal in a rigorous manner with Third World themes and issues that are of topical interest and pressing social importance.

One important objective of the series is to encourage new and bold perspectives on development problems and issues. A second key objective is to develop inter-country comparisons that achieve balanced coverage of the principal regions of the world. It is hoped that such inter-country comparisons will shed new light on the ways in which differing social, cultural, economic, political, ecological and natural resource systems condition responses to global processes of change.

The series is thereby built around two closely related themes: globalization and environmental change. Globalization is a major trend affecting contemporary Third World countries. It is reflected in the diffusion of capital and technology, the evolution of new production systems and the spread of Western life-styles among elites and other groups. It is also witnessed in the increasing importance of multinational corporations. Yet it is clear that the processes of global restructuring and change are affecting various regions and nations at different rates and in a variety of different ways. For example, large income gaps have opened up within countries of Latin America and the Caribbean, while pressures on resources vary markedly among the various rural areas of sub-Saharan Africa. Similarly, rates of economic growth have diverged sharply in East Asia. It is clear that patterns of production are becoming increasingly heterogeneous when viewed at the international level, while patterns of consumption and associated aspirations are frequently converging on what might be described as a global norm.

However, such patterns of consumption are likely to be found to be strongly differentiated when they are examined in different groups and areas at the local scale.

Environmental change is strongly affected by the globalization of development, whether through the clearance and destruction of rainforests, the occurrence of industrial accidents, the despoliation of attractive environments, indigenous cultures and socio-economic landscapes by the demands of international tourism, or the consequences of global warming for sustainable patterns of development and resource use. The examination of the interacting socio-political and environmental causes of these problems, and practical responses, stands as a further major theme of the series.

This strong research-oriented volume fits closely the overall themes of the Global Development and the Environment series. Rick Auty and Katrina Brown have drawn together a revised and rewritten selection of papers that were prepared for a special series of workshop sessions at the Development Studies Association annual conference, held in Dublin in September 1995. The collection initially focuses on conceptualizations of, and approaches to, sustainable development, ranging from orthodox micro- and macro-economic perspectives to more critical and interdisciplinary ones. This sets the scene for examination of the application of sustainablity in both the rural and industrial contexts. A strength of the volume is that it thereby presents empirical materials drawn from Asia, Africa and Central and South America, while the authors are drawn from economics, development studies, demography and geography.

*Rob Potter*
*Rick Auty*

# Introduction

# An Overview of Approaches to Sustainable Development

## Richard M. Auty and Katrina Brown

Sustainable development has dominated the development discourse for some years. It has become the guiding principle of many development agencies and is a primary focus not only within both economic and natural resource debates, but also increasingly in fields such as social development, health and education. However, sustainable development as applied by different perspectives and disciplines is a contested concept, and as pointed out by O'Riordan (1988), it is so widely used precisely because of its 'slippery' nature. Essentially, sustainability lengthens the temporal dimension of development, concerned as it is in its literal definition with the maintenance of something over time.

The idea of development has become contested, in that people concerned with conservation of the natural environment have seen this aspect ignored in the past and point to the role of *economic* development in bringing about undesirable social as well as environmental consequences. The present inequitable distribution of income and wealth at the global scale; the homogenization of societies and the loss of traditional knowledge and culture; and the global environmental changes apparent from the populated parts of the world to the most remote (Turner *et al.*, 1990) are evidence of the unsustainability of 'development' as it has been perceived and practised. To conceive of development which is sustainable requires not only the adoption of a longer time horizon but also some notion of the biophysical and ecological processes involved, as well as some philosophical basis for assessing the social and economic outcomes of development.

The most widely quoted definition of sustainable development is that of the Brundtland Commission: 'development which meets the needs of the current generation without jeopardising the needs of future generations'

(WCED, 1987). This has been utilized by economists in defining criteria for economic development, as discussed in the next section. Yet these economic approaches, however sophisticated in defining limits to the use of 'critical' parts of the natural environment, can only crudely represent the dynamic and evolving nature of the biotic environment – its diversity, its fragility or even its resilience (Holling, 1973; Arrow *et al.*, 1995). Further, the economic approach (with some notable exceptions, e.g. Daly, 1977) leaves the issue of the definition of the goals of, or limits to, economic development largely unresolved. If a sustainability approach leads to defining 'critical natural capital', but implies that this task lies outside the scope of economics, then the ownership and control of such critical resources is paramount, and the role of the expert or scientist in the process of defining 'criticality' is to the fore (see, for example, Owens, 1994). This questioning of the basis of sustainable economic development has resonance in the growing disquiet over the role of the predictive, normative science in driving technological change and economic transformation (see, for example, Wynne, 1992; Wynne and Meyer, 1993; Norgaard, 1994).

The purpose of this introductory chapter is to furnish a context for the contributions in this volume. The overall structure of the chapter is as follows. The next section examines the positive aspects of the economic approach to sustainable development, before turning to critiques and perspectives which address both the social and ecological elements of sustainability. The emphasis of the latter approaches is upon diversity (both social and ecological), resilience and a precautionary approach to human interaction with an uncertain environment. This inevitably leads to recommendations for collective intervention and policy, which is only applicable at a smaller scale than previously attempted. The social and ecological approaches question the more grandiose claims for an overarching blueprint for 'development' by some researchers. The impacts of unmeasurable and uncertain global environmental change have brought with them a realization that global scale management and prescriptions may be neither desirable nor valid (Sachs, 1993).

More specifically, the next (second) section of this chapter outlines two leading and contrasting economic stances, namely strong and weak sustainability. This is in recognition of the key role of economics as a discipline concerned with the allocation of finite resources and the contribution of the discipline to defining the sustainable utilization of these resources. The third section of the chapter then notes the scepticism of some leading economists concerning the value of either approach to sustainable development, but argues that even if such scepticism were to prove well-founded, such research into sustainable development has performed a useful function, and will continue to do so, by drawing attention to the past neglect of environmental capital and how such neglect can be remedied.

The fourth section of the book elaborates on the ecological and social perspectives which affirm that the dynamic and complex nature of ecological systems as well as the political and institutional context of development, need to be encompassed in a broad understanding of the development process. These themes are elaborated on in later chapters. The fifth and final section of this introductory chapter highlights the diversity within the research approaches and the issues addressed by the individual authors in this volume.

## Economic Perspectives: Strong and Weak Sustainability

The focus of this section is the recognition by economists that sustainable development cannot be distilled into one simple definition, and that differing evaluations of risk, variations in the underlying philosophical understandings of the natural environment, as well as contrasting ideological notions of political phenomena will alter the goals of economic development. The scope of the economic discussions of sustainable development can be summarized most conveniently by comparing the weak and strong advocacy of sustainability.

Turner *et al.* (1994) provide a useful summary of the spectrum of views towards the environment which is presented in Table 1.1. They identify four overlapping perspectives which range from the 'cornucopian' view, that natural resource use should be maximized if that is what is required to enhance social welfare, to the spiritual tones of 'deep ecology' in which reverence for nature calls for minimal resource use and sees as an urgent necessity the reduction of both the human population and its burgeoning conspicuous consumption. In extreme cases the advocates of this latter view assert that the environment possesses the right to existence, irrespective of the dictates of human welfare considerations (O'Riordan, 1988). In between these polarized viewpoints are the two stances which are the main focus of this sub-section: strong sustainability and weak sustainability.

Strong sustainability calls for rapid progress towards both the more efficient and the more frugal use of natural resources. It usually posits a timetable of mandatory targets in order to achieve these ends, targets which must be set and enforced by governments. Although some earlier critics of the economic approach such as Lovins (1977) have subsequently developed a deeper appreciation of the role which markets can play, others point to the dubious assumptions of consumer sovereignty when, in the real world, the actors lack perfect information. Moreover, demand can clearly be manipulated to create 'necessities' and 'positional' or status goods which, by their very nature, encourage conspicuous and wasteful consumption but meanwhile can only confer the desired status on an elite minority leaving the majority perpetually dissatisfied (Hirsch, 1977).

The strong sustainability stance also objects to the mainstream orthodox (neo-liberal) economists' relative neglect of critical physical limits on the use

**Table 1.1** Perspectives on sustainable development

| Technocentric (overlapping categories) | | Ecocentric | |
| --- | --- | --- | --- |
| Cornucopian | Accommodating | Communalist | Deep Ecology |
| **Green labels** | | | |
| Resource-exploitative, growth-oriented position | Resource conservationist and 'managerial' position | Resource preservationist position | Extreme preservationist position |
| **Type of economy** | | | |
| Anti-green economy, unfettered free markets | Green economy, green markets guided by economic incentive instruments (EIs) (e.g. pollution charges, etc.) | Deep green economy, steady-state economy regulated by macroenvironmental standards and supplemented by EIs | Very deep green economy, heavily regulated to minimize 'resource-take' |
| **Management strategies** | | | |
| Primary economic policy objective, maximize economic growth (max Gross National Product (GNP)) | Modified economic growth (adjusted green accounting to measure GNP) | Zero economic growth; zero population growth | Reduced scale of economy and population |
| Taken as axiomatic that unfettered free markets in conjunction with technical progress will ensure infinite substitution possibilities capable of mitigating all 'scarcity/limits' constraints (environmental sources and sinks) | Decoupling important but infinite substitution rejected. Substitution rules: constant capital rule. Therefore some scale changes | Decoupling plus no increase in scale. 'Systems' perspective – 'health' of whole ecosystem very important; Gaia hypothesis and implications | Scale reduction imperative; at the extreme for some there is a literal interpretation of Gaia as a personalized agent to which moral obligations are owed |
| **Ethics** | | | |
| Support for traditional ethical reasoning: rights and interests of contemporary individual humans; instrumental value (i.e. of recognized value to humans) in nature | Extension of ethical reasoning: 'caring for others' motive – intragenerational and intergenerational equity (i.e. contemporary poor and future people); instrumental value in nature | Further extension of ethical reasoning: interests of the collective take precedence over those of the individual; primary value of ecosystems and secondary value of component functions and services | Acceptance of bioethics (i.e. moral rights/interests conferred on all non-human species and even the abiotic parts of the environment); intrinsic value in nature (i.e. valuable in its own right regardless of human experience) |
| **Sustainability labels** | | | |
| Very weak sustainability | Weak sustainability | Strong sustainability | Very strong sustainability |

*Source: Turner et al. (1994)*

of environmental capital and the services which it provides. In particular, the strong sustainability view opposes the application of conventional discount rates to environmental problems. The discount rate is used by mainstream economists to compare the value of streams of benefits and costs for investments which are incurred at different points in time. It does so by expressing these costs and benefit streams in terms of their net present value. Strong sustainability advocates argue that such discounting gives greater weight to the *costs* of measures to protect the environment (which typically occur through the short- and medium-term) than it does to the *benefits* of environmental improvement (which are typically deferred and cumulate over the very long-term, thereby being subjected to greater discounting than the cost stream). For example, applying a fairly typical private discount rate of 8 per cent implies that the present value of £1 in one hundred years is only 0.45 pence in today's money.

A specific example will illustrate how conventional discount rates tend to place a very low value upon long-term future uses. In the case of global warming, calculations undertaken by the economist William Cline (1992) show the benefits of curbing global warming occurring far into the future and therefore being very heavily discounted (Figure 1.1) whereas the costs of the required pollution abatement are incurred much earlier and so are weighed much more heavily in present value terms. The strong sustainability case argues that conventional discounting is myopic and tends to place negligible value on long-term environmental improvements. The conventional approach therefore carries a high risk of crossing a critical environmental threshold and incurring irreversible damage.

Strong sustainability also demands a bolder attitude towards poverty

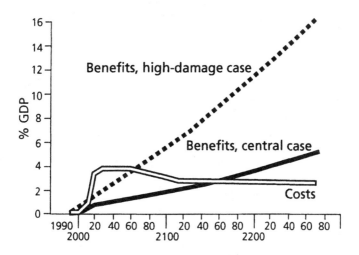

**Figure 1.1** Costs and benefits of curbing global warming

alleviation. It makes the achievement of intra-generational equity a prime goal on the grounds that the natural resource consumption of the richer nations is excessive. It assumes that transfers (subsidies) from rich nations to poor ones will simultaneously confer three important benefits. First, it will reduce rich-country resource use. Second, it will help to alleviate global poverty. Third, it will retard environmental degradation in poor countries.

The weak sustainability approach adopts a more pragmatic stance towards natural resource use and looks to economic growth rather than income transfers to equalize wealth. A central objective is to at least maintain, if not enhance, the *total* capital stock passed on to future generations (Daly and Cobb, 1989). Total capital stock is usually regarded as comprising three main elements: man-made (or 'produced') capital, natural (or environmental) capital and human capital. While accepting the strong sustainability view that there may be critical thresholds beyond which specific natural capital assets (such as the ozone layer) should not be reduced, weak sustainability assumes that much natural capital (such as mineral resources) may be consumed provided there are sufficiently close substitutes available. Summers (1992) argues, for example, that future generations may be helped as much by educating children (expanding human capital) as by leaving oil unexploited; or by improving infrastructure (enhancing man-made capital) as much as by preserving rainforest; or by expanding scientific knowledge as much as by reducing carbon dioxide. Put another way, to the extent that such consumption of environmental capital is instrumental in the creation of additional human or produced capital, it does not represent a simple loss to the total capital stock.

Advocates of weak sustainability oppose the suspension of discount rates, or the application of lower rates, for environmental issues. They argue that the key test of an investment is the net present value and that projects should be chosen in order to yield a higher return than the next best alternative use of scarce capital resources. This implies that those projects (carefully costed to encompass all social costs including appropriate values for environmental damage) are selected which maximize social welfare. The strong sustainability assumption that higher welfare now, based on the consumption of (non-global) natural resources, is at the expense of future generations is rejected. Rather, it is argued that resources exploited now will raise welfare and that, especially in the developing countries, higher living standards now are the key to slowing population growth and limiting the environmental damage caused by the short time horizons associated with extreme poverty.

Two examples will help to illustrate the case. The very poor in developing countries effectively deploy remarkably high rates of discount. For example, Indian peasant farmers may seek a 30 to 40 per cent return in order to make investments to reduce soil erosion. This is because such investment is at the cost of present consumption which, because they already subsist on the margin of existence, peasant farmers are reluctant to forgo. A second illustration may be drawn from the rich countries. West Europeans are seven times better off today than they were 60 years ago, and this is in large part because they have attempted to maximize the net present value of the investments made. In effect, it is argued that the more effectively capital is used (i.e. the higher its social return) the faster the improvement in welfare and the greater the financial resources available to future generations. This in turn enhances the capacity of future generations to research and implement solutions to environmental problems and also engenders a greater willingness by them to incur the expenditures required for environmental defence.

Basically, weak sustainability argues that rigid rules which seek to protect the environment over all other considerations by, for example, applying special discount rates to environmental problems, are mistaken. Such an approach is held to be inferior to the weak sustainability alternative of the careful incorporation of environmental costs into investment decisions. Provided *all* costs and benefits are properly considered, it is not in the best interest of human welfare maximization to undertake investments which do not yield the best (highest) return. As a consequence of this, the weak sustainability approach tends to give lower priority to long-term problems (such as biodiversity conservation and global warming) than to medium-term ones (such as soil erosion, contaminated water, cleaner air).

Peskin (1993) argues that the weak sustainability approach is a more humanitarian one than that of strong sustainability because it seeks to maximize human welfare rather than to assign overall priority to the environment. It can be argued, for example, that giving priority to medium-term environmental problems is likely to benefit the poorest people most. This is because soil erosion, impure water supplies and polluted air are the immediate problems of such people. Scarce state resources can be concentrated on the alleviation of such problems for the poor because the rich within the developing countries are in a position to protect themselves from water-borne disease and air pollution (by, for example, selecting the safest places to live). Such principles applied to the developed countries have substantially reduced pollution since 1970 (World Bank, 1992).

## Is Sustainable Development a Redundant Concept?

Not all economists are persuaded, however, that sustainable development is a useful concept and this is not because they espouse the cornucopian stance summarized in Table 1.1. Nordhaus (1992), for example, challenges even the weak sustainability stance as unnecessarily restrictive. His basic thesis is that the 'reification' of any objective (such as natural resource conservation) is likely to prove both unnecessarily cumbersome and ultimately impractical. For example, technological change provides at least the possibility of increasing welfare from a shrinking (but increasingly productive) capital stock.

Nordhaus regards standard economic growth theory as a superior vehicle to sustainable development for achieving the optimal use of natural resources and for coping with the inter-generational issues which environmental concerns raise. Mankiw (1995) has recently made a careful and positive re-appraisal of growth theory which he also regards as more than flexible enough to absorb most of the criticisms levelled at it over the past two decades. Nordhaus considers weak sustainable development to be redundant. For example, recent research suggests that a central concept in weak sustainability, the depletion component for natural resource capital like minerals (see Chapters 2 and 10), may approximate to the long-established Hicksian concept of depreciation (Nordhaus, 1992; Hartwick and Hageman, 1993).

Another environmental economist, Dasgupta (1995), has also expressed some reservations about the sophistication of the sustainable development literature. He points out that environmental resources provide an example of capital theory which was substantially developed by himself and others in the 1960s and 1970s. Consequently, the insights generated into inter-generational justice by that earlier literature have much to teach those presently concerned with sustainable development.

Adopting a less technical approach, Mikesell (1994) has some sympathy for the stance of Nordhaus. Mikesell provides an eminently sensible overall context for the debate on the need for sustainable development. He notes that the elements embodied in sustaining social welfare are wide-ranging and often non-quantifiable: they include per capita consumption, equity of income distribution, individual security and political freedom. He adds that their attainment depends not only on the legacy of produced (man-made) capital, natural resources and human capital, but also on technology and socio-economic structure as well as on the effort expended by future generations themselves. In other words, concern for natural resources is a part only of a much wider set of issues.

Nevertheless, even if one accepts such sceptical views, it can still be argued that the concept of sustainable development is performing a useful function because it has many assumptions in common with standard growth theory. For example, Nordhaus considers the superiority of economic growth theory to lie in the greater flexibility which that approach engenders. This is because many environmental problems can be usefully conceptualized as market failures which require for their correction either the recreation of effective markets (by valuing environmental services through contingent valuation techniques for example) or practical command and control measures. But the idea of market failure is also at the heart of weak sustainability.

Consequently, to the extent that weak sustainability directs attention to the incorporation of environmental issues into development economics (Mikesell, 1992) and may become redundant when that has been achieved, weak sustainability plays a useful transitional role. Moreover, strong sustainability options also merit careful analysis and monitoring because the more orthodox assumptions about natural resource substitution and the pollution absorptive capacity of the environmental sinks may prove too sanguine. Meanwhile, more fundamental attacks on the economic approaches to sustainable development have come from outside that discipline.

## Competing Perspectives on Sustainable Development

This section highlights some of the emerging themes from other perspectives on sustainable development and sustainability. It does not review or cover the full diversity of these different views, but it summarizes some of the current debates within the environmental sciences and ecology as well as in the social sciences, with respect to sustainability and it also examines their genesis. Many of these issues are further developed in subsequent chapters of this volume, as outlined in the next section.

The environment-development discourse of the 1970s was concerned mainly with the ecological limits to economic growth, and focused on the probable exhaustion of non-renewable natural resources. This debate was partly stimulated by oil price rises and the perceived scarcity of fossil fuel during the early 1970s, and also by the publication of the well-known study by Meadows *et al.* (1972) entitled *The Limits to Growth*. Meadows *et al.* developed a neo-Malthusian model which assumed that population and industrial capital would grow exponentially, leading to a similar growth in the demand for food and non-renewable resources which were assumed to be absolutely finite. Such growth in demand would inevitably lead to systemic breakdown, the model predicted. The debate which ensued involved a range of critiques from both the economic and the ecological perspectives (see Ekins, 1993, for a review) and also resulted in a number of international meetings, commissions and other fora.

During the late 1970s and 1980s the discourse shifted from one primarily concerned with limits to growth, where the environment was regarded mainly as a source of materials, to concerns of pollution and global environmental change, where the biosphere is primarily a sink (Brown *et al.*, 1993). The environment is therefore seen as something which is impacted upon by the process of development, rather than simply as a source of the raw materials necessary to fuel economic growth. The relationship between development and the environment, seen as in conflict by the *Limits to Growth* view, is seen as interdependent and complementary by the Brandt and Brundtland Commissions. Brundtland stresses the need for global environmental management and puts faith in scientific solutions to perceived environmental and ecological crises, and the UNCED in 1992 developed the global institutions thought necessary to implement this agenda (Brown *et al.*, 1993).

Post-UNCED, a range of different views is being articulated which challenges the assumptions of global environmental management as a key to sustainable development. On the one hand these views criticize the process of globalization of the environment (Sachs, 1993), whilst on the other a 'new ecology' is emerging which questions some of the fundamental assumptions about how ecosystems operate and the models and rules which govern their predictive powers and therefore the policy relevance of the discipline as a whole (Howarth, 1995; Zimmerer, 1995). These paradigm shifts have important implications for the faith put in environmental management. The new thinking highlights the problems in understanding and modelling complex, dynamic non-equilibrium systems, and stresses the role of uncertainty (Hilborn and Ludwig, 1993; Ludwig *et al.*, 1993). Conventional approaches to sustainable harvest and maximum sustainable yield prescribed by population biologists and natural resource economists alike are seriously challenged. Under this new paradigm, sustainability has become a fiercely debated topic, as has the role of biological sciences in informing natural resource management.

Links between ecological concepts such as diversity, stability, conservation and carrying capacity and resource management and economic growth are increasingly being analysed under inter-disciplinary banners such as ecological economics (for example, Constanza, 1991). Concepts such as resilience, sustainability and carrying capacity are being approached as both ecological and socio-economic phenomena (for example, wa-Githinji and Perrings, 1993; Arrow *et al.*, 1995) and ecological and economic systems are characterized as being dynamic, non-equilibria.

Increasingly, the complementarity of the approaches of the social sciences and a range of non-economic perspectives stress issues such as property rights, institutions, livelihoods, and cultural diversity. For example, wa-Githinji and Perrings (1993, p. 110) use the term social sustainability 'to capture a feature of human societies which is very closely related to the resilience of ecological systems; i.e. the ability of the institutions of human societies to continue functioning in the face of stress and shocks'.

A number of scholars from broadly defined development studies perspectives concentrate on sustainable livelihoods, an approach which gives a specific poverty focus to the analysis of sustainable development (Conway, 1985; Chambers, 1992). This work has also highlighted the role of different institutions in supporting sustainable development, ranging from small, informal community groups to more formalized and politicized NGOs. Another focus is on property rights and the relationship between access to resources, natural resource management, equity and sustainable development. The literature on common property resources and on collective action, especially applied to the management of natural resources, is particularly strong and is developing links between community and communal initiatives and sustainable development (e.g. Berkes, 1989). Much of this work grew from the marriage of institutions and natural resource economics and political science (Ostrom, 1990; Bromley, 1991). Norgaard (1994) develops these ideas and conceptualizes the 'co-evolution' of ecological systems and institutions.

A range of disciplines and scholars has criticized conventional growth-oriented paradigms of development as part of a modernist project which promotes the institutions and culture of the North whilst denigrating the science and knowledge and needs of the South (e.g. Redclift and Sage, 1994). These views link a number of different views on sustainable development, including institutional economics approaches (Jacobs, 1994), anthropology (Croll and Parkin, 1992; Hobart, 1993) and sociology and political science (Redclift and Benton, 1994; Redclift and Sage, 1994). These critiques highlight knowledge, culture and values as overlooked aspects of sustainability. For example, Redclift and Sage (1994) argue that the way people value nature in other cultures materially affects the ability of any culture to manage the environment in sustainable ways and that development cannot be sustainable unless it works with rather than against other cultural traditions. This involves understanding how people view nature in other cultures, as well as the view they take of future generations. Thus, the establishment of environmental 'value' within informal livelihood-based economies may have more to do with cultural mores, and traditional community practices, than the apparatus of centralized policy-making. These views expose another contradiction of sustainable development whereby, according to Redclift (1994, p. 17), 'Married to the idea of "development" sustainability represents the high-water mark of the Modernist tradition. At the same time, the emphasis on cultural diversity, which some writers view as the underpinning of sustainability, is a clear expression of Postmodern-ism.'

Participation and empowerment are major themes of the current discourse, being the mechanisms by which sustainable development can be achieved at a local level, and the means by which development can benefit the poor in developing countries. Customary and communal systems of land tenure are stressed by writers, as is the strengthening of indigenous and traditional institutions (e.g. Berkes, 1989; Ghai, 1994) and also systems of knowledge and science (Croll and Parkin, 1992; Hobart, 1993). According to Redclift and Sage (1994) successful environmental management depends on local empowerment, and it is only when this is achieved that anything resembling sustainable development or anything approaching sustainability will be brought about.

## An Overview of the Book

The book is sub-divided into three main sections (Sections II to IV). Section II deals with approaches to sustainable development and comprises four chapters. The orthodox economist's view is presented by Kirk Hamilton in Chapter 2 which surveys progress towards incorporating sustainability at the macro-economic level into the national accounting framework. He does so with specific reference to 'fund' or non-renewable resources such as minerals, drawing on examples from sub-Saharan Africa. In Chapter 3, James Winpenny evaluates the application of the orthodox approach at the micro-economic level to the management of renewable or flow resources. He does so with reference to the formidable technical problems associated with the incorporation of environmental costs into the utilization of water resources in developing countries.

John Cameron adopts a more questioning tone towards the application of the economic approach to sustainability by drawing attention to the broad range of economic activities from which the poor derive their income. His chapter (4) deals with the labour force and rural livelihoods in low-income Bangladesh. He notes the complexity which is introduced by a consideration of the income strategies of rural groups which are often based on numerous diverse sources rather than, say, fishing or farming alone. Cameron provides a timely note of caution against the tendency of individual disciplines to over-simplify the solutions to sustainability problems. Katrina Brown addresses some of the social and ecological dimensions of sustainability in the concluding chapter to Section II of the book. Her chapter (5) asks the question: 'Is sustainable utilization a grand illusion?' Katrina Brown adopts an inter-disciplinary approach to examine the problems which arise from making sustainable development operational. She draws attention to the increasing concern within the development literature to the need for 'bottom-up' solutions to environmental problems, but she also notes the very practical problems which it involves.

Sections III and IV are concerned with the application of sustainability criteria to rural problems and industrial/urban problems, respectively. Tim Dyson examines population and food trends in South Asia up to the year 2020 in Chapter 6. He queries the relevance of sustainability concepts when the immediate priority is to prevent famine in an area which is already densely settled and where population continues to rise.

Pastoralism is the subject of Chapter 7 in which Oriel Kenny re-assesses the response of pastoralists to mounting population pressure in the Marsabit District of Kenya. She argues that herders' strategies are often rational 'opportunist' responses to change and that efforts to settle nomadic herders are therefore likely to be misguided. The next chapter, Chapter 8 by Sara Parker, evaluates the Annapurna Conservation Area Project (ACAP) in Nepal. She develops the 'bottom-up' approach to sustainable development further with reference to the ACAP which is widely regarded as an innovative approach to securing the participation of local people in sustainable development. Philip O'Brien takes up this same theme in Chapter 9 in Latin America. He examines Colombia's ambitious participatory environmental programme which seeks to engage the government, business, NGOs and local communities in the resolution of environmental issues.

Industrialization provides the focus of Section IV of the book. In Chapter 10, Richard Auty applies the theoretical concepts discussed earlier by Hamilton to explore the progress which is being made towards sustainable mineral-driven development in two contrasting countries, Jamaica and Chile. Whereas densely-settled Jamaica has long had to mediate between the conflicting interests of farmers and mining companies, Chile's mining regions, one of sparse population (the Atacama Desert) and one of medium population density (the Central Valley), have moved more slowly in the absence of an effective environmental policy. The chapter notes the varying capacity of each region to absorb mine pollutants and discusses the practical problems of assigning monetary values to natural capital depletion.

In Chapter 11, Richard Auty and Michael Tribe examine pollution patterns in the industrialization process. They review evidence to date concerning the evolving relationship between the scale and composition of pollution at different levels of per capita income. They find that, as countries pass through the industrial transition, underlying regularities in the scale and composition of pollution can emerge which provide pointers towards practical policies for reducing the future 'pollution-intensity' of GDP. Such hopeful trends may be especially difficult to replicate, however, in the so-called 'transition' economies which are in the process of moving from a planned economy to a market economy. The transition economies form the subject of Chapter 12, by Tim Forsyth, which deals with sustainable industrialization in Vietnam. Forsyth assesses the practical difficulties of achieving environmental improvements which arise in a situation where local people lack a democratic means of expressing their opinions. He notes that long-standing frictions between the different tiers of government are compounded by suspicions concerning the alliances between foreign investors and the central government.

Chapter 13 by Andrew Jordan and Katrina Brown discusses the international dimensions of sustainable development by examining how the agreements signed at UNCED have fared in the five years since the Rio conference. It also looks at the international institutions which deal with environment and development issues within the UN system. The tensions which were identified at the time of the Rio conference − especially those along North–South lines − have continued to dog post-Rio progress on implementation of sustainable development. Finally, in Chapter 14 the editors synthesize the insights provided by the authors' very diverse approaches to sustainability issues and take stock of our understanding of the theoretical and operational dimensions of sustainable development.

# References

Arrow, K., Bolin, B., Constanza, R., Dasgupta, P., Folke, C., Hilling, C.S., Jansson, B.O., Levin, S., Maler, K-G., Perrings, C. and Pimental, D. (1995) Economic growth, carrying capacity and the environment. *Science*, **268**, 520–1.

Berkes, F. (ed.) (1989) *Common Property Resources: Ecology and Community-based Sustainable Development*. London: Belhaven Press.

Bromley, D. (1991) *Environment and Economy: Property Rights and Public Policy*. Oxford: Blackwell.

Brown, K., Adger, W.N. and Turner, R.K. (1993) Global environmental change and mechanisms for north–south transfer. *Journal of International Development*, **5**(6), 571–89.

Chambers, R. (1992) Sustainable livelihoods: the poor's reconciliation of environment and development. In P. Ekins and M. Max-Neef (eds), *Real-Life Economics: Understanding Wealth Creation*. London: Routledge, pp. 214–29.

Cline, W.R. (1992) *The Economics of Global Warming*. Washington, DC: Institute for International Economics.

Constanza, R. (1991) *Ecological Economics: The Science and Management of Sustainability*. New York: Columbia University Press.

Conway, G. (1985) Agroecosystem analysis. *Agricultural Administration*, **20**, 31–55.

Croll, E. and Parkin, D. (1992) *Bush Base: Forest Farm, Culture, Environment and Development*. London: Routledge.

Daly. H.E. (1977) *Steady State Economics*. London: Earthscan.

Daly, H.E. and Cobb, J.B. (1989) *For the Common Good*. Boston: Beacon Press.

Dasgupta, P. (1995) Optimal development and the idea of net national product. In I. Goldin and L. A. Winters (eds), *The Economics of Sustainable Development*. Cambridge: Cambridge University Press, pp. 111–43.

Ekins, P. (1993) 'Limits to growth' and 'sustainable development': grappling with ecological realities. *Ecological Economics*, **8**, 269–88.

Ghai, D. (ed.) (1994) *Development and Environment: Sustaining People and Nature*. Oxford: Blackwell.

Hartwick, J. and Hageman, A. (1993) Economic depreciation of mineral stocks and the contribution of El Serafy. In E. Lutz (ed.), *Toward Improved Accounting for the Environment*. Washington, DC: World Bank, pp. 211–35.

Hilborn, R. and Ludwig, D. (1993) The limits of applied ecological research. *Ecological Applications*, **3**(4), 550–2.

Hirsch, F. (1977) *Social Limits to Growth*. London: Routledge and Kegan Paul.

Hobart, M. (ed.) (1993) *An Anthropological Critique of Development*. London: Routledge.

Holling, C.S. (1973) Resilience and stability of economic systems. *Annual Review of Ecology and Systematics*, **4**, 1–23.

Howarth, J. (1995) Ecology: modern hero or post modern villain? From scientific trees to phenomenological wood. *Biodiversity and Conservation*, **4**, 786–97.

Jacobs, M. (1994) The limits to neo-classicism: towards an institutional environmental economics. In M. Redclift and T. Benton (eds), *Social Theory and the Global Environment*. London: Routledge, pp. 67–90.

Lovins, A.B. (1977) *Soft Energy Paths*. Harmondsworth: Penguin.

Ludwig, D., Hilborn, R. and Walters, C. (1993) Uncertainty, resource exploitation and conservation: lessons from history. *Ecological Applications*, **3**(4), 547–9.

Mankiw, N.G. (1995) The growth of nations. *Brookings Papers on Economic Activity*, **1**, 275–310.

Meadows, D.H., Meadows, D.L., Randers, J. and Behrens, W. (1972) *The Limits to Growth*. New York: Universe Books.

Mikesell, R.F. (1992) *Economic Development and the Environment*. London: Mansell.

Mikesell, R.F. (1994) Issues in environmental and resource accounting (ERA). Working Paper for EDF Meeting, Oregon.

Nordhaus, W.D. (1992) Is growth sustainable? reflections on the concept of sustainable growth. Mimeo. Paper prepared for the International Economic Association, Varenna.

Norgaard, R. (1994) *Development Betrayed: The End of Progress and a Co-evolutionary Revisioning of the Future*. London: Routledge.

O'Riordan, T. (1988) The politics of sustainability. In R.K. Turner (ed.), *Sustainable Environmental Management: Principles and Practice*. London: Belhaven Press, pp. 29–50.

Ostrom, E. (1990) *Governing the Commons: The Evolution of Institutions for Collective Action*. Cambridge: Cambridge University Press.

Owens, S. (1994) Lands, limits and sustainability: a conceptual framework and some dilemmas for the planning system. *Transactions of the Institute of British Geographers*, **19**, 439–56.

Peskin, H.M. (1993) Sustainable resource accounting. In RMNO (ed.), *Sustainable Resource Management and Resource Use: Policy Questions and Research Needs*. The Hague: Advisory Council for Research on Nature and Environment, pp. 89–96.

Redclift, M. (1994) Sustainable development: economics and the environment. In M. Redclift and C. Sage (eds), *Strategies for Sustainable Development: Local Agendas for the Southern Hemisphere*. Chichester: John Wiley, pp. 17–34.

Redclift, M. and Benton, T. (eds) (1994) *Social Theory and the Global Environment*. London: Routledge.

Redclift, M. and Sage, C. (eds) (1994) *Strategies for Sustainable Development: Local Agendas for the Southern Hemisphere*. Chichester: John Wiley.

Sachs, W. (ed.) (1993) *Global Ecology: A New Arena of Political Conflict*. London: Zed Books.

Summers, L.H. (1992) Summers on sustainability. *The Economist*, 30 May, p. 91.

Turner, B.L., Clark, W.C., Kates, R.W., Runords, J.F., Mathews, J.T. and Meyer, W.B. (1990) *The Earth as Transformed by Human Action*. Cambridge: Cambridge University Press.

Turner, R.K., Pearce, D. and Bateman, I. (1994) *Environmental Economics*. London: Harvester Wheatsheaf.

wa-Githinji, M. and Perrings, C. (1993) Social and ecological sustainability in the use of biotic resources in sub-Saharan Africa. *Ambio*, **22**(2–3), 110–16.

World Bank (1992) *World Development Report 1992*. Washington, DC: World Bank.

World Commission on Environment and Development (1987) *Our Common Future*. Oxford: Oxford University Press.

Wynne, B. (1992) Uncertainty and environmental learning: reconceiving science in the preventative paradigm. *Global Environmental Change*, **2**, 111–27.

Wynne, B. and Meyer, S. (1993) How science fails the environment. *New Scientist*, **138**, 5 June, 33–5.

Zimmerer, K.S. (1995) Human geography and the 'new ecology': the prospect and promise of integration. *Annals of the Association of American Geographers*, **84**(1), 108–25.

# II
# Approaches to Sustainable Development

# 2

# Accounting for Sustainability

## Kirk Hamilton

Governments have committed themselves to achieving sustainable development, both as a result of the United Nations Conference on Environment and Development in 1992 and in response to the report of the World Commission on Environment and Development (the Brundtland Commission). Sustainable development as a concept does not lack definitions, in fact, Pezzey (1989) lists several dozen possible definitions. Until quantifiable measures of progress towards sustainable development are available, however, there is room for considerable doubt about governments' ability to follow through on the commitments they have made.

Concerns such as this have been one of the prime motivations for the development of 'green national accounts'. Because sustainable development is an all-encompassing concept, it is felt by analysts including Repetto *et al.* (1989) that only comprehensive indicators of the state of the economy, such as provided by the System of National Accounts (SNA), can provide suitable sustainability indicators.

Beyond the immediate problems of macro-economic stabilization, inflation and unemployment (to which the traditional national accounts speak effectively), the policy priorities of governments concerned about the longer term should be the creation and maintenance of wealth. This is at the core of 'sustainable development', however defined. The process will have a different flavour for developed and developing countries, where produced assets make up the majority of the wealth of the former and natural assets the major part of the latter. But it is clear that our accounting systems must begin to deal more directly with the measurement of total wealth (natural and produced), and that the relevant short-term indicators of wealth creation, or destruction, will be greener measures of net savings.

This chapter will give a brief presentation of a formal model of green national accounts, then examine the empirical evidence for progress towards sustainable development in sub-Saharan Africa using this model. Some implications for policy will be drawn in the final section.

## The Formal Green Accounting Model

Formal approaches to national accounting can be dated from the seminal paper by Weitzman (1976), with Hartwick (1990), Mäler (1991) and Hamilton (1996) providing the extension of this work to the greening of the national accounts.

We assume a simple closed economy with a single resource producing a composite good that may be consumed, invested or used to abate pollution, so that $F(K,R) = C + K + a$, where $R$ is resource use and $a$ is pollution abatement expenditures. Pollution emissions are a function of production and abatement, $e = e(F,a)$, and pollutants accumulate in a stock $M$ such that $\dot{M} = e - d(M)$, where $d$ is the quantity of natural dissipation of the pollution stock. The flow of environmental services $B$ is negatively related to the size of the pollution stock, so that $B = B_0 - \alpha M$. Resource stocks $S$ grow by an amount $g$ and are depleted by extraction $R$, so that $\dot{S} = -R + g(S)$, and resources are assumed to be costless to produce. The utility of consumers is assumed to be a function of consumption and environmental services, $U = U(C,B)$.

If we assume that there is a social planner who wishes to maximize the present value of utility over an infinite time horizon, for some fixed pure rate of time preference $r$, then there is a close relationship between the Hamiltonian function for the optimal control problem and the measure of current welfare for the society. The problem is expressed as:

$$\max \int_0^\infty U(C,B)e^{-rt}dt \text{ subject to:}$$
$$\dot{K} = F - C - a$$
$$\dot{M} = e - d$$
$$\dot{S} = -R + g$$

The Hamiltonian is given by:

$$H = U + \gamma_K \dot{K} + \gamma_M \dot{M} + \gamma_S \dot{S},$$

where $\gamma_K$ is the shadow price of capital, in utils, $\gamma_M$ the shadow price of pollution, and $\gamma_S$ is the shadow price of the resource.

While the presentation of the problem is rather abstract, a straightforward economic interpretation can be given. The social planner wishes to maximize the present value of utility. The policy (or 'control') variables available are $C$, $a$ and $R$, with the levels of the other variables characterizing the system (the 'state' variables) being determined in consequence. The Hamiltonian function is an extended utility function combining both current utility $U$ and the determinants of future utility, investment $\dot{K}$, the increment or decrement to pollution stocks $\dot{M}$, and the change in resource stocks $\dot{S}$, with the latter variables being shadow priced in units of utility. In general these elements of the Hamiltonian will be in conflict, in the sense that more investment will decrease current consumption and therefore current utility, while more consumption will increase pollution stocks and decrease resource stocks. The optimal choice of the policy variables, the choice that maximizes the present value of utility, will maximize the Hamiltonian function at each point in time.

The first order conditions for maximizing the Hamiltonian, setting the partial derivatives with respect to the control variables $C$, $a$, and $R$ to 0, yield the following:

$$H = U + U_C \dot{K} - U_C b(e-d) - U_C(1-be_F)F_R(R-g).$$

Here $b \equiv -1/e_a$ is the marginal cost of abating a unit of pollution, while $F_R$ is the unit resource rental rate, and $be_F$ is the effective emissions tax rate on production. The measure of economic welfare ($MEW$) is derived by valuing each flow at its shadow price in utils, then converting to consumption units by dividing through by $U_C$ (and so preserving relative prices), yielding:

$$MEW = C + \dot{K} - b(e-d) - (1-be_F)F_R(R-g) + \frac{U_B}{U_C} B.$$

It can be shown, e.g. in Hamilton (1996), that the marginal cost of abatement is equal to the marginal social cost of pollution emissions, which is in turn equal to the level of the optimal Pigovian tax required to maximize welfare. Note that $p_B \equiv U_B/U_C$ is the price that a utility-maximizing consumer would be willing to pay for a unit of environmental service, and that resources are priced at their marginal product less the value of the emissions tax on production. Therefore this expression for welfare, although derived from optimal control, corresponds to what would be attained in a competitive equilibrium with a Pigovian pollution tax.

The level of *genuine* saving ($S_g$) in this model, to use the terminology of Hamilton (1994a), is the level of net savings less the value of resource depletion and environmental degradation,

$$S_g = \dot{K} - b(e-d) - n(R-g),$$

where $n \equiv (1-be_F)F_R$ is the net rental rate on natural resources. These savings are genuine in the sense that they are in excess of what is needed to maintain at a constant level the total real value of assets (produced capital and natural resources) and liabilities (stocks of pollution).

As shown in Hamilton and Atkinson (1996), if genuine savings are persistently negative then eventually welfare must decline. Genuine saving is therefore the key indicator of sustainable development that will be used in what follows.

The expression for economic welfare generalizes in obvious ways. Dropping the final welfare term yields sustainable national income, since consuming more than this implies negative genuine savings. A purely cumulative pollutant is represented by dropping the term in dissipation $d$. For a non-living resource the term in growth $g$ would be dropped.

The measure of genuine saving used in the empirical section that follows is:

$$S_g = GNP - C - D - \sigma(e-d) - n(R-g),$$

where $D$ is the depreciation of produced assets and $\sigma$ is the marginal social cost of pollution emissions. This measure therefore includes depreciation and foreign savings (exports minus imports), effects that were ignored in the formal model presented above.

## Measuring Genuine Savings

Pearce and Atkinson (1993) presented some of the first empirical measures of genuine savings in 20 countries. New evidence for developing countries is presented below.

Notions of genuine saving would have little impact if all countries were prudent managers of their portfolio of economic assets. There is abundant evidence, however, that many countries are not on a sustainable path. Using data from World Bank (1995), Figure 2.1 plots genuine savings on a regional basis for a range of developing countries.

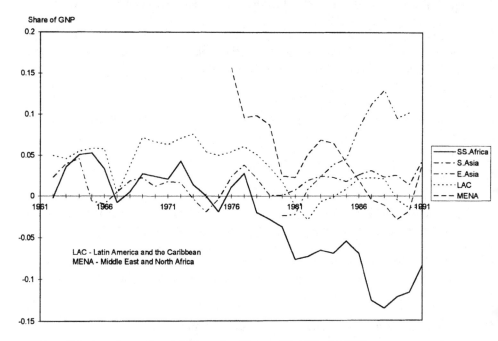

**Figure 2.1** Genuine savings rate by region (*Source*: World Bank, 1995)

The savings rates in Figure 2.1 account for the depletion of oil, major minerals and net deforestation. The calculations of resources rents are crude, assumed to be equal to 50 per cent of the market value of resource extraction and harvest, but sufficiently accurate (see Hamilton, 1994b) to serve as a useful indicator. Carbon dioxide emissions are the only pollutants considered in these calculations, with the global social costs of each tonne of carbon valued at US$20 in 1990 (Fankhauser, 1994). Depletion of fish stocks and degradation of soils, with the latter being particularly important in many developing countries, are not included in these figures.

The inter-regional comparison of savings behaviour over this 30-year period turns up some interesting trends, although a number of caveats are required. Both South Asia (SA) and Latin America and the Caribbean (LAC) had genuine savings rates that were moderately positive on average over this period, with savings briefly going negative at the time of the oil crisis in SA and at the time of the debt crisis (roughly speaking) in LAC. The short-time series for the Middle East and North Africa shows a substantial decline in genuine saving, but the data coverage for these figures should encourage caution in their interpretation; in addition, the 'net price' method of calculating rents may not be particularly appropriate for countries having many decades of reserves of oil (i.e., a discount factor should be factored into the depletion calculation, as in El Serafy, 1989).

The two trends that stand out in Figure 2.1 are for East Asia, where the rise of the 'tigers' was associated with very strong saving performance (and where primary resource activities are a declining proportion of GNP), and sub-Saharan Africa[1] (SSA), which started dissaving roughly at the time of the oil crisis and has continued on this unsustainable path into the 1990s.

Figure 2.2 shows the results of a more refined calculation of genuine savings (based on Hamilton, 1994b) for a sample country in sub-Saharan Africa, Malawi.

One striking aspect of this figure is that traditional net saving in Malawi was negative in 1981 and 1984–87. By standard national accounting measures, therefore, Malawi was marginally sustainable during the 1980s. When the extra 5 to 7 per cent of GNP for resource depletion and $CO_2$ emissions is included, Malawi was clearly unsustainable during this decade, and this excludes the value of soil erosion in this highly agricultural country.

There is ample evidence, therefore, that many countries have been on an unsustainable development path, at least since the mid-1970s. Sub-Saharan Africa (SSA) is noteworthy in this regard, and it is to this region that we now turn our attention.

## Genuine Savings and the Sub-Saharan African Experience

In a paper reviewing the literature on long-term development and growth in SSA, Ndulu and Elbadawi (1994) cite a number of broad conclusions:

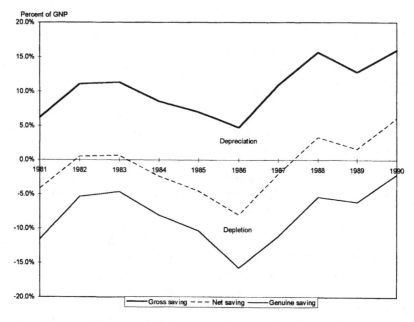

**Figure 2.2**   Malawi: genuine savings rate 1981–90 (*Source*: Hamilton, 1994b)

- SSA has grown more slowly than other developing countries since the mid-1970s;
- lower savings rates and levels of human capital have helped prevent it from catching up with other developing countries;
- the policy climate in SSA has not been conducive to sustained growth, characterized as it has been by disincentives to save, over-valued and variable exchange rates, high public consumption, and under-developed financial systems;
- the economies of SSA have been subject to elevated levels of external shocks, both economic and physical (in the form of drought and other severe weather patterns), and political instability.

Table 2.1 presents the rates of genuine saving for selected countries in sub-Saharan Africa in the mid to late 1980s. The rather eclectic selection of countries reflects limitations in data availability. The pattern presented in the table appears to be 'the curse of the mineral-rich' (cf. Gelb, 1988). Countries such as Kenya, Rwanda, Burundi and Niger, with relatively few exports of oil and minerals, have the most promising saving performance. On the other hand, mineral-rich South Africa and Zimbabwe both exhibited positive genuine savings. As noted earlier, the figures for Nigeria are probably skewed owing to the substantial size of the deposits of crude oil. Zaire is the other anomalously large dissaver – while these effects may again be

**Table 2.1** Genuine saving in sub-Saharan Africa

| | Percent of GNP | | | | |
|---|---|---|---|---|---|
| | *1986* | *1987* | *1988* | *1989* | *1990* |
| Burundi | 1 | −2 | 3 | −1 | 5 |
| Côte d'Ivoire | −6 | −10 | −14 | −13 | −17 |
| Cameroon | −1 | −3 | 0 | −4 | −9 |
| Congo | −40 | −69 | −36 | −51 | −42 |
| Ghana | −7 | −4 | −3 | −2 | −2 |
| Kenya | 7 | 7 | 4 | 6 | 3 |
| Mali | −13 | −5 | 1 | 1 | 2 |
| Mauritania | −12 | −18 | −10 | −3 | −8 |
| Malawi | −10 | −16 | −11 | −5 | −6 |
| Niger | 1 | 5 | −5 | 6 | −4 |
| Nigeria | −15 | −24 | −31 | −38 | −41 |
| Rwanda | 9 | 8 | 5 | 5 | 4 |
| Senegal | −14 | −7 | −3 | 0 | −2 |
| Sierra Leone | −2 | −7 | −11 | −8 | −9 |
| Chad | −26 | −22 | −17 | −10 | −17 |
| Uganda | −12 | −7 | −6 | −15 | −15 |
| South Africa | 5 | 7 | 11 | 10 | 9 |
| Zaire | −18 | −21 | −28 | −30 | −32 |
| Zimbabwe | 2 | 4 | 4 | 10 | 6 |

*Source*: derived from Hamilton (1994b).

overstated for technical reasons having to do with the valuation of resource depletion, it is also true that the economic policy climate has been particularly unfavourable in Zaire for many years.

## Policy Implications

There appears to be ample evidence for negative rates of genuine savings in a range of developing countries. The key question, therefore, is what policy implications follow from the measurement of negative genuine savings. The first and most direct implication was derived in the presentation of the formal model: persistent negative genuine savings must lead, eventually, to declining welfare.

A basic determinant of genuine savings rates for developing countries is the value of resource depletion. However, it would be wrong to conclude that the policy response regarding savings and natural resources is to boost genuine savings by restricting resource exploitation. One of the key lessons from growth theory, alluded to in Weitzman (1976), is that the discovery of a natural resource, properly managed, leads to a permanent increase in the sustainable stream of income for a country. The question with regard to natural resources is therefore one of what constitutes 'proper management'.

Clearly, an important policy concern is the achievement of efficient levels of resource exploitation. The policy considerations are therefore:

- Do tenurial regimes encourage sustainable exploitation?
- Are royalties set correctly to capture resource rents while leaving the exploiting firms with adequate rates of return?

Another element of proper management of the resource endowment is to ensure that royalties on natural resource exploitation are invested in other productive assets — it is this rather simple concept of 'preserving capital' that is captured by genuine savings measures. A basic question for countries with natural resources is:

- Are the royalties from natural resources invested or consumed?

The export of natural resources necessarily involves the liquidation of some amount of the natural resource base. From the perspective of genuine savings an important question is therefore:

- Do policies to promote natural resource exports also embody plans for the investment of the resource royalties?

Although the social costs of pollution emissions did not figure in any major way in the empirical part of this analysis, which was limited to the value of carbon dioxide emissions, it is clear that in many developing countries rapid urbanization and industrialization is leading to major problems of environmental quality — this is particularly so in Asia and Latin America. The policy questions this poses are:

- Do policies with respect to pollution emissions aim for the economic optimum, where total social benefits and total abatement costs are equated at the margin?
- Even if the optimum is achieved, are sufficient savings being made to offset any increments to pollution stocks that this may entail?

Finally, it should be obvious that the gross savings rate is a basic determinant of the genuine savings rate. This leads to consideration of the whole range of micro- and macro-economic policies that affect savings behaviour by individuals and institutions, including:

- Is the level of government current expenditure appropriate and sustainable?
- Does the tax system penalize or encourage saving?
- Does monetary policy set positive real interest rates?
- Do government policies support a viable financial sector?

There are some important caveats that need to be added to this discussion. First, not all saving is the same, in the sense that savings sitting in foreign bank accounts belonging to a small segment within a society may not lead to development. There are distributional issues to be considered, in other words. Second, not all investment is the same, in the sense that there are both productive and wasteful investments. A key concern that follows from the consideration of genuine savings, therefore, is the quality of investment. Investments in human capital, especially in primary education in developing countries, are likely to be important in this regard.

## Conclusions

This chapter has presented a theoretical approach to green national accounting and argued that the measurement of genuine saving, net saving less the value of resource depletion and environmental deterioration, can serve as an indicator of sustainable development.

While growth theory indicates what the long-run steady state rate of saving should be in a simplified model of aggregate production with no technological change,[2] this provides relatively little guidance for policies with respect to saving and investment in the real world. Similarly, the analysis of genuine saving does not answer the question 'How much should a country save?'

The measurement of genuine savings, however, does answer another fundamental question: Are countries being provident?

The empirical evidence on genuine savings suggests that many countries, particularly in sub-Saharan Africa, have been on an unsustainable path. The difficulties these countries have experienced have been obvious for many years from the basic economic data. What is now clear is that the situation with regard to future well-being is worse than the standard national accounts suggest: wealth is being dissipated.

It may be granted that for a subsistence economy consuming natural wealth may be a rational policy, if starvation is the alternative. What green national accounting can achieve is to highlight the extent to which this is happening and to call attention to the fact that 'poverty traps' involve not just produced assets but natural assets as well. Broadening the asset base in our models to include natural resources and environmental amenities should lead to a broader conception of the process of development.

Including human capital in the asset base should lead to a still broader conception. Green national accounting then becomes fundamentally wealth accounting. And the management of development then becomes a process of portfolio management to meet development objectives.

## Notes

1  The African figures are influenced by the performance of the oil states, especially Nigeria and Gabon – the earlier caveat about discount factors applies here as well.

2  For a recent exposition see Barro and Sala-i-Martin (1995).

# References

Barro, R. and Sala-i-Martin, X. (1995) *Economic Growth*. New York: McGraw-Hill.

El Serafy, S. (1989) The proper calculation of income from depletable natural resources. In Y.J. Ahmad, S. El Serafy and E. Lutz (eds), *Environmental Accounting for Sustainable Development*. Washington, DC: The World Bank.

Fankhauser, S. (1994) Evaluating the social costs of greenhouse gas emissions. *The Energy Journal*, 15(2), 157–84.

Gelb, A. (1988) *Oil Windfalls: Blessing or Curse?* New York: Oxford University Press.

Hamilton, K. (1994a) Green adjustments to GDP. *Resources Policy*, 20(3), 155–68.

Hamilton, K. (1994b) Estimated rental rates for minerals and crude oil. Mimeo. Environment Department, World Bank, Washington, DC.

Hamilton, K. (1996) Pollution and pollution abatement in the national accounts. *Review of Income and Wealth*, 42(1), 13–33.

Hamilton, K. and Atkinson, G. (1996) Air pollution and green accounts. *Energy Policy*, 24(7).

Hartwick, J.M. (1990) Natural resources, national accounting and economic depreciation. *Journal of Public Economics*, 43, 291–304.

Mäler, K.-G. (1991), National accounts and environmental resources. *Environmental and Resource Economics*, 1, 1–15.

Ndulu, B. and Elbadawi, I. (1994) Long-term development and sustainable growth in sub-Saharan Africa, presented to the Colloquium on New Directions in Development Economics – Growth, Equity and Sustainable Development, March 9–11. SAREC, Stockholm.

Pearce, D.W. and Atkinson, G. (1993) Capital theory and the measurement of sustainable development: an indicator of weak sustainability. *Ecological Economics*, 8, 103–8.

Pezzey, J. (1989) Economic analysis of sustainable growth and sustainable development. Environment Department Working Paper no. 15, The World Bank, Washington, DC.

Repetto, R., Magrath, W., Wells, M., Beer, C. and Rossini, F. (1989) *Wasting Assets: Natural Resources in the National Accounts*. Washington, DC: World Resources Institute.

Weitzman, M.L. (1976) On the welfare significance of national product in a dynamic economy. *Quarterly Journal of Economics*, 90.

World Bank (1995) *Monitoring Environmental Progress*. Washington, DC: Environment Department, The World Bank.

# 3

# Sustainable Management of Water Resources: An Economic View

## James T. Winpenny

## Introduction

The central purpose of this chapter is to examine how far economists can contribute to the cause of sustainability in the water sector. Is there a definition of sustainability in this context that is sufficiently precise for operational purposes? Is the application of marginal cost pricing a sufficient, as well as a necessary, condition for sustainable water use? Is the opportunity cost of water of any practical relevance? What is the point of estimating the value of water in different uses, and how can that information be used?

The approach taken is to regard the usual definitions of sustainability as being insufficiently useful for operational and management purposes. Marginal cost pricing, expanded to include environmental and user (depletion) costs, is a necessary condition for sustainable use, but its many practical problems, and the failure to adopt it universally, mean that pricing alone will not achieve sustainability. Hence the importance of developing other data useful to planners, notably the value of water in different uses. This can assist the development and allocation of water resources, the appraisal of specific supply or conservation options, inform pricing decisions, and furnish information relevant to the development of water markets and other transfers.

## The Sustainability Rule

The neatest definition of SD in the water sector is 'the use of water resources which imposes no cost on future generations, such as might arise through depletion of the resource or through a reduction in its quality' (from Dubourg, 1994b).

More precisely, the sustainability rule for water has been formulated as:

- abstraction should be met out of net runoff only;
- water quality should not decline over time (Dubourg, 1994a).

First, we examine the robustness of these concepts under the headings of renewable yield and quality.

### Renewable Yield

Water is largely a renewable resource. Certain deep-lying deposits are more akin to mineral reserves (e.g. those under southern Libya now being tapped by the Great Man-Made River pipeline). Many underground aquifers are being exploited well in excess of their rate of natural replenishment, so that they too are in practice a depletable resource. However, in the absence of storage, the water in rivers, streams and other surface flows cannot be 'depleted' taking one year with the next, and taking a broad picture at the level of the watershed, natural catchment or river basin. (Certain parts of a river basin can be more or less permanently depleted of water if surface flows are diverted upstream, and if there is heavy consumptive use, or the diversion of drainage elsewhere.)

The possibility of storing water in reservoirs, natural lakes, tanks or through the artificial recharge of groundwater introduces the complication of inter-temporal transfers. The whole point of storage is to even out annual fluctuations in precipitation and yield. However, if the amount of water drawn down from storage exceeds the additions to it in the long term, then this is clearly another facet of unsustainable use.

Another complication is the geographical dimension to sustainable use. It would be ludicrous to apply the principle for every village, farm or square mile of occupied land. Most habitations, many regions and some countries permanently 'import' water to offset the deficit between consumption and renewable water yield. This implies that one needs to take an appropriate view of the total geographical area within which sustainability is to be judged. There are economic and political factors to be taken into account. Egypt has been importing 'virtual water' for years through free or cheap grain (Allan, 1992). South Africa has no qualms about importing water from Lesotho, but in the Middle East several countries do have political problems in excessive reliance on their neighbours for water.

### Quality

The first complication is the definition of 'quality' in this context. Water acquires many chemical and organic ingredients in its passage through the atmosphere (cf. acid rain), through its contact with soil, vegetation and river beds, and even more so in percolating through soil and rock into groundwater bodies. 'Quality' is the product of all these additions, net of what is removed during treatment (and in the course of use and disposal, water quality is modified in other, more radical ways). 'Purity' is not an original, unsullied state, but a concept determined by personal, social, economic or even political attitudes. In some cases, 'purity' is quite an arbitrary concept, in others it is the weighted product of a large number of variables. In a recent report, the UK's Drinking Water Inspectorate identified over 50 different water quality attributes that are routinely tested.

A few illustrations will suffice. European Union directives on drinking water standards imply that generations of Britons have been drinking fluid of an unacceptable quality. In the UK, treated tap water, which in the Thames Valley has typically been recycled several times, appears on some tests to be of 'better' quality than water drawn from natural springs, bottled, and sold at a very high cost per unit! Does the addition of fluoride to public water, carried out to improve the public's dental health, raise or lower water quality? Spa water, highly prized by some, is undrinkable to many more. The effect of certain mineral trace elements in water on human health, positive and negative, is often unclear, or the subject of controversy.

In short, it is difficult or impossible to track water 'quality' over time with any precision:

- the concept itself is elusive and subjective;
- the impact of changes in water ingredients and other characteristics on human health, aesthetics, or the environment is subject to debate and uncertainty;
- where different measures of quality move in opposite directions it is difficult to describe an overall trend unless weights are applied to the different measures. Such weighting could easily be subjective and arbitrary.

A further complication arises from the fact that certain declines in water quality can be reversed – at some financial and economic cost – while others are effectively irreversible. In a number of old industrial regions of the USA and Western Europe, rivers, canals and lakes which were grossly polluted, even written off as 'dead' by environmentalists, have been cleaned and revived. The appearance of salmon in the lower parts of the Thames is a well-known symbol of the progress that can be made in reducing pollution in 'post-industrial' societies.

One characterization of historical trends in pollution is the Environmental Kuznets Curve, which holds that, in the early stages of industrial development, pollution will increase, but that at a certain mature point pollution will decline as attitudes to the environment change, the industrial structure alters, and public funding for environmental purposes increases.

If we took the canon of sustainability set out in the first paragraph literally, this course of action would be outlawed. However, it might be a rational choice for an industrializing society, provided the decision was explicit, the population was well-informed, the costs of pollution were known, and no irreversible process were involved. After all, the economic concept of Optimal Pollution implies a rational choice between the costs and benefits of pollution control. Its corollary is that water pollution *should* be allowed to increase if the costs of pollution control exceed the benefits from it. Thus there is an apparent discrepancy between sustainability criteria and orthodox environmental economic principles. In short, changes in water quality over time may quite reasonably be seen as a subject for rational social choice. Societies can rationally choose the kind of water they want at any one time in the light of what they are willing and able to pay for it at that time.

Where irreversible processes are entailed, different considerations apply. Depletion of an aquifer close to the sea, or a fresh-water 'lens' in a small island, causes a risk of saline intrusion which would ruin the groundwater as a source of potable supply. The same might happen if groundwater were polluted, e.g. by toxic waste from industry, mines or solid waste disposal sites. In such cases, where the resource is important, the Precautionary Principle has much to commend it: society should avoid irreversible developments to the maximum extent permitted by its social, economic and political circumstances.

## Salvaging the Sustainability Principle

The above discussion has strongly qualified the opening sustainability principle: its absolute propositions have been rendered into relative terms. The net runoff/sustainable yield principle has been shown to depend on the relevant geographical area, which itself is largely within national choice according to economic, social, technical and political factors. The water quality principle also turns out to be less objective than it might appear, and the choice of quality standard over time is quite reasonably a matter for social choice — again in the light of social, economic, technical and political factors.

However, this critique can go too far. Abstraction and/or pollution may become unsustainable in the sense that they impose costs which come to be seen as 'excessive' by society. Although 'excessive' may be a relative social and economic construct, it has substance nonetheless. This is even more true where irreversible processes are set in motion, such as long-term contamination, destruction of attractive landscapes, loss of aquifers from depletion, saline intrusion, and pollution, etc.

## Pricing for Sustainability

Since the sustainability rule gives equivocal answers to water planners and policy-makers, economists fall back on resource pricing as the key to sustainability. If the full costs of using a resource can be captured in its price (including the costs of eventually replacing a non-renewable source) then consumption based on this price can be regarded as 'sustainable'.

The traditional concept of marginal cost pricing has been modified to produce the following rule: the price of a unit of the resource (water) should equal its marginal social opportunity cost, comprising its marginal cost of production, its marginal environmental cost, and its marginal user cost. These concepts will be explained briefly below.

The net benefits of an economic activity are maximized when prices are equal to the marginal cost of production. This is because prices measure consumers' marginal willingness to pay, and, therefore, the value, of a commodity or service. The marginal cost is the quantity of resources which must be diverted from some other valuable use to produce a single extra unit of the commodity. When price equals marginal cost, it indicates that the cost of the marginal unit of production is just equal to, and, therefore, justified by, the value of the extra consumption.

If the marginal cost is higher than the marginal benefit (or price), then too much production is taking place, and welfare could be increased by cutting production. Conversely, if price is greater than marginal cost, resources used elsewhere would be better utilized in this sector, and production should be increased.

In simple terms, when a consumer is presented with the marginal cost price of water, he/she is being asked: this is the real cost of providing you with this extra unit of water — are you willing to pay it? If you are, this indicates that society is better off by you consuming the water. If not, society would be better off leaving the water where it is.

Certain qualifications need to be made to the above pricing rule:

- The 'cost of production' should be interpreted more widely to include the impact on the *environment*. The true social costs of production are all those costs which result in a loss of welfare elsewhere. The production of commodity 'A' reduces welfare elsewhere by diverting resources away from other potentially valuable uses. Similarly, damage to the environment can lower welfare directly (e.g. through reduced amenity), or indirectly, through the need to spend more on water treatment.
- The marginal pricing rule works best when inputs are perfectly divisible, i.e. inputs to production can be combined in infinitely small quantities. But in practice, sectors like water supply are often characterized by significant indivisibilities in production. Investments often have to be made in large lumps of capital. Distribution networks are often cited as an example of this; dams and reservoirs might be others.

Such indivisibilities can lead to economies of scale, in which average costs of supply fall as output is increased, because the large fixed investment is used more fully. In this case, pricing at marginal cost causes a problem. Within the relevant range of production (i.e. until the full capacity of the fixed investment is reached) marginal cost would lie below average cost. If the firm or agency applied marginal cost pricing principles, this would result in financial losses. Then we might expect a private firm to go out of business, or a public agency to require funding out of general or other taxation. In either case, we cannot expect economic efficiency without some form of intervention.

---

**Box 1: Aquifer depletion in northern China**

This is a case study of the Hangu Region in Tianjin Municipality, in north-east China. It is situated at the eastern end of the North China Plain near the mouth of the Huange He (Yellow River). Hangu is a coastal city where the rapid growth of its population, agriculture and industry have led to rapid groundwater withdrawal and a depletion of its aquifer. The city's authorities are exercised by the cost of future water supplies for a growing population and economy, the approaching exhaustion of the aquifer, and the growing costs of pumping and of land subsidence.

Hangu has a large industrial base, including metallurgical, textile and chemical factories. Groundwater is the main source of water, supplemented with river water for irrigation and industrial cooling. Depletion of the aquifer has led to land subsidence which in certain areas had amounted to 2 m over the last 20 years. Current rates of subsidence in the vicinity of the chemical factory are over 80 mm p.a.

The costs of over-exploitation of the aquifer are several. There are the direct costs of extra investment and pumping involved in extracting water from greater depths. There are the depletion (user) costs from the need to replace groundwater sources in future. There are, thirdly, the various environmental costs of subsidence, such as structural damage, extra flood damage, the risk of saline intrusion, etc.

The study estimated the current marginal cost of water, including the three elements above, to be Yuan 0.63 per cu.m. Around 70 per cent of this was the direct cost of extra pumping, and a further 20 per cent was due to the investment cost of new wells and pipelines. The environmental costs of land subsidence were relatively minor. No data were available on depletion costs. The above cost can be compared with the prices currently charged industrial users (Y 0.09/cu.m) and householders (Y 0.35/cu.m).

*Source*: British Geological Survey (1994).

- When the resource is non-renewable any current use must reduce the amount of water available for use in future periods. This would apply to any store of water, such as an aquifer or lake, which is being used in excess of its recharge rate. The continued exploitation of the aquifer, lake or reservoir must at some time lead to exhaustion. Hence, current use of the resource has an opportunity cost which is the cost of use forgone in the future. This cost is known as the user cost, or as a depletion premium. It is exactly the same concept as the depletion premium used in costing natural gas and petroleum. Box 1 illustrates how user cost and the various other costs of aquifer depletion were estimated in a recent study in Northern China.

The size of the user cost depends on a number of factors:

- the size of the stock;
- how quickly it is exploited;
- the cost and availability of substitutes in the future;
- the rate at which future consumption is discounted.

Substitution can be achieved by switching to another, 'backstop' technology (e.g. desalination, or treatment of wastewater), or by switching to alternative stocks of the resource (e.g. a different aquifer). The user cost is the present value of the cost of replacing the depleted asset at some future date. It is the extra cost of the replacement resource, as compared with the current one.

The user cost will be smaller, the greater the stock, the lower the rate of exploitation, and the lower the current exploitation cost. These variables are quite likely to be positively correlated. Suffice it to say, when reserves of a resource are abundant, then the marginal user cost is likely to be small. It might only be large enough to be important for resources which are near to exhaustion.

In practice, most sources of water, and the 'sink' function of water bodies, are renewable. Aquifers recharge when water is pumped from them, and water quality improves over time as wastes are assimilated. However, these resources could clearly be exhausted if, for instance, an aquifer is depleted faster than it can recharge, or if wastes are discharged faster than they can be assimilated. Moreover, in certain cases, the rate at which a resource is renewed might be so low as to render the resource non-renewable for all practical purposes.

The above qualifications lead us to restate the marginal cost pricing principle as follows (Warford, 1994):

$$MOC = MPC + MUC + MEC$$

where:

MOC is the marginal opportunity cost,
MPC is the marginal cost of production (or extraction),
MUC is the marginal user cost,
MEC is the marginal environmental (or external) cost.

## Applying Marginal Cost Pricing in the Water Sector

Various formulae exist on which marginal cost pricing policies can be based, and which take into account the indivisibilities which are a feature of water sector investment. All tend to emphasize the importance of signalling the *future* costs of water supply in *current* prices, and some also attempt to give signals about the appropriate timing of investments. In most countries, the water sector faces increasing marginal costs as supply increases. Providing indications of future supply costs also signals the increasing *economic scarcity* of freshwater in the future.

A serious objection to the literal use of the marginal cost principle is that it implies very unstable prices. Where the demand for water is pressing on the capacity of the system, the marginal cost of meeting an extra unit of demand is very high, which argues for setting a high price. However, once investment in additional capacity has taken place, the marginal cost of meeting increases in demand becomes very low again. To maintain high prices in this situation would discourage consumption of a resource which has become very cheap to supply. Hence the new situation would call for low prices. The implied fluctuation of prices would be confusing to water users, and inconvenient and impractical for water authorities to implement. In the above situation, the use of 'textbook' marginal cost pricing would also make it difficult for the water authority to recover its investment costs and service its debt.

One compromise is to use average incremental cost (AIC) to approximate long-term marginal cost. AIC measures the total discounted cost per unit of the next investment programme undertaken to satisfy the expected growth in demand. This formula produces a smoother price path, but one which still reflects the general trend in supply costs. In most situations we would expect the AIC price path to be upward-sloping over time, as increases in water supply tend to be increasingly costly. In practice, a pricing regime based on AIC will tend to be an iterative process. This is because the actual timing of water investment projects will depend on the interaction between investment costs and the price elasticity of demand. When price is set at AIC, there will generally be a (negative) demand response which will slow the rate at which new projects are required. This implies a different AIC estimate, a different demand response, and hence another different investment plan. In an extreme case, raising prices to the AIC level may cause demand to fall back to the point where the investment is unnecessary!

**Practical Aspects**

Although the AIC concept is a compromise on pure marginal cost principles it has certain practical advantages:

- It signals future water costs to both current consumers and those who are about to place additional demands on the system.
- It provides stable prices, to the benefit of consumers and users planning water-intensive investments.
- In most situations, it would ensure financial profitability to the water provider, thus guaranteeing the resources necessary for efficient operation, maintenance and expansion.

How exactly the AIC concept can be translated into tariffs is an important practical matter that will not be discussed here. However, one key issue is whether prices should vary geographically and according to time and season.

Because the artificial transport of water is expensive the economic cost of water varies in different parts of a country, and within a locality, depending on the circumstances of its supply. Political and social factors may favour uniform national or regional prices. Economic factors would suggest otherwise: the price of water charged to users in different locations should vary to reflect the respective costs of supply and disposal. There is usually scope for introducing regional variations in the water tariff. Within localities, the cost of servicing remote or awkwardly sited consumers can also be reflected in premia and surcharges. Unless water prices take some account of the real differences in costs of supply in different areas, large water users will continue to locate in the 'wrong' areas, implying a waste of national resources.

## Conclusion on Marginal Social Opportunity Cost Pricing

Is the use of economic pricing for water sufficient to ensure its sustainable use in the long term? Economists would argue that it is certainly a necessary condition for sustainability. Whether it is a sufficient condition is more debatable.

The concept has a number of problems:

- Estimating and quantifying environmental and user costs is imperfect and incomplete. Placing economic values on all the main categories of environmental costs (and benefits, where applicable) is difficult, often arbitrary, partial, and controversial. Estimating user costs entails taking a view of replacement technologies and costs decades into the future.
- The estimation of marginal costs depends fundamentally on the choice of the discount rate at which future cost streams are reduced to their present value. The same point applies to the estimation of user costs, which are derived from discounting differential cost streams beginning some time

ahead. The appropriate size of the discount rate for environmental appraisal is a matter of some controversy.

- Even if the terms in the pricing equation could be accurately estimated, there are considerable practical difficulties in translating them into a feasible water tariff or pollution charge. Different countries and even different communities have followed their own routes to marginal cost pricing. Every tariff is a crude compromise on the theoretical ideal.
- In practice, the application of marginal cost pricing has been very uneven, and has made most headway in urban and industrial supply. In arid and semi-arid countries, this normally makes up a minor part of use. There are serious problems in pricing agricultural water in this way, not the least of which is the difficulty of measuring farm water consumption.

Such factors as these imply that reliance on pricing alone is unlikely to ensure sustainable water use.

## Opportunity Costs

If all water consumption were subject to marginal cost pricing in its expanded sense, and if irreversible environmental effects were avoided, then water consumption would be sustainable. Only those water sources that consumers were willing to pay for would be drawn upon. Consumption in excess of renewable yields (e.g. groundwater) would fully cover the cost of its future replacement.

If all consumers faced the same marginal costs (e.g. a small country or community drawing water from the same source) then the use of marginal cost pricing would ensure that everyone's marginal water productivity was the same. This would satisfy the Pareto criterion for optimality, namely that it is impossible to improve aggregate welfare by redistribution. The *average* value or productivity of water would of course differ among different consumers: it is just the value of the last unit of consumption in each case that is equalized. This allocation of water would also result in the maximum aggregate value from its use.

In real life, marginal costs vary, and water is supplied from many different systems, which are not properly inter-connected. Irrigators drawing water from run-of-the-river schemes face a different cost curve from industrial firms with their own groundwater supplies or hotels using desalination units. Even if it were feasible to charge all users their (different) marginal cost prices, this would not necessarily result in an overall optimal allocation of water (it would mean that utilization of each individual system, considered in isolation, was optimal). If it were possible to redistribute water from low-cost sources to users with relatively high marginal values, aggregate welfare and productivity would increase. This is an argument for the creation of a 'national grid' in water, and for the amalgamation of different water systems and networks to the maximum extent that is feasible in hydrological and economic terms. Great differences in the costs and values of water can only persist where there are barriers between different users. These barriers may be geographical and hydrological (e.g. distance, altitude), economic (e.g. the cost of transporting water, or of constructing conveyances), or social/political (e.g. certain groups' privileged access to free or cheap water).

Where it is feasible to transfer water from one supply/consumption system to another, the marginal cost pricing principle should be supplemented by the opportunity cost criterion: in principle, the price of water for each user should not be less than the opportunity cost of the water in that situation. If irrigated farmers exist cheek-by-jowl with residential domestic users, the price they pay for their marginal water supplies should in theory equal the marginal values of household consumption. If it were less, overall welfare (= consumers' surplus) would be increased by transferring water from farmers to households. The opportunity cost principle implies knowledge of the values of water in different uses, to which we now turn.

## Values of Water

The economic approach to the allocation of resources uses prices and markets to ensure that the resource is applied to its most valuable uses. Where the supply of water is not unlimited, and marginal units of supply have a positive cost, the value of water consumption is maximized when net marginal benefits are equal in all uses. In that case, it is impossible to raise total net value by reallocating water from one user to another. This is a theoretical ideal. But it conveys the important practical lesson that the allocation of limited water supplies should take into account what the water is worth to different kinds of users. If one group of users, sector A, is applying it to valuable purposes, while another, sector B, is using it for low-value applications, by reallocating it from B to A the total consumption value of water may be increased. Although A has a higher *average* value of water use, increasing applications would normally cause diminishing *marginal* values, while the same process would happen in reverse with B. If the process continued to the limit, *marginal* values of water would be the same in both sectors, and there would be no point in making any further reallocations. It should be noted that in the above situation, the *average* value of water use would continue to be higher in A than in B, even though *marginal* units have the same value. Average values are of considerable interest for the purpose of reallocating water, and many empirical studies are concerned with average values. However, it is the equality of *marginal* values that is the aim.

For large users, such as farmers, the average value of water under a particular crop tells us very little about what marginal amounts of water would be worth to them — they might be willing to pay only very small sums for a little extra: conversely, taking marginal amounts away from them to supply some other user might deprive them of very little. But it is also true that the first units of water supplied to farmers are likely to be relatively valuable, even if the average value is low. This explains why water values observed in trades and auctions are often very much higher than what we would expect average values to be.

This section starts by reviewing the *methods* by which water values are estimated in different sectors, and then assesses some of the results that have been obtained.

### Methodology of Water Valuation

The methods of valuing water are highly eclectic, depending on the sector or type of use (Gibbons, 1986). In the case of household, or municipal, use, users' willingness-to-pay is the common criterion. Willingness-to-pay can be obtained either from direct survey, or by inference from changes in consumption following a tariff change.

For irrigation, one approach is to obtain estimates of the marginal productivity of water from crop-water trials, and apply economic values to the changes in yield. A more common method is to derive water values as a residual from farm budget data, after all other costs have been allowed for (the net back method).

Industrial water valuation poses more of a problem. Water is normally a tiny part of total costs, and it would be misleading to attribute the whole residual value to this factor. Much industrial water is also self-supplied, either from wells, direct abstraction from rivers, or from recycling. One device is to regard the cost of recycling (treatment and reuse) as the upper limit on industrial willingness-to-pay − since for values higher than this the firm would rationally use its own supplies rather than buy in (Gibbons, 1986).

A cruder short-cut to industrial water values is to compute ratios of gross output or value added to the volume of water involved in the process (British Geological Survey, 1994). Although these measures indicate the water-intensity of different industrial sub-sectors, and the upper limit of willingness-to-pay for water, these ratios do not indicate the real productivity of water, nor do they give a realistic pointer to willingness-to-pay.

The value of in-stream water for waste assimilation can be estimated by comparing the cost of natural assimilation with the reduction of pollution by other means (e.g., reduction at source). Likewise, the value of water for navigation can be regarded as the cost advantage of waterborne transport over the next cheapest mode (e.g., railway). This can be a negative item when waterborne transport is unprofitable, before subsidy.

Hydropower water is normally valued according to the cost advantage of hydro over other, thermal, alternatives. In this, as in other cases, values differ according to whether a short- or a long-term viewpoint is taken (which affects whether capital costs enter the computation). The value of water for recreation and tourism can be inferred from the travel costs of visitors, and the pure existence value of watery sites can be illustrated using contingent valuation methods (opinion surveys).

This does not exhaust the different uses of water. In some river basins, maintaining in-stream water flow is essential for flushing sediment out of river beds and channels. Its value for this purpose (rather than for other uses involving abstraction and consumptive use) is again measured in relation to the extra cost of alternatives such as dredging (Dixon *et al.*, 1994).

## Comparative Water Values: International Evidence

There are wide variations in the economic value of water used by different sectors. Although there are many estimates of water values in individual sectors, such as irrigated farming and rural households, there are few comprehensive studies of such values across the different sectors. This section reviews two notable exercises, both using US data.

In the early 1970s the US National Water Commission carried out a systematic and comprehensive review of the economic value of water in all the main user sectors and environmental functions – agriculture, industry, domestic (municipal), hydroelectric generation, waste assimilation, navigation, recreation, and fisheries and wildlife habitat (Young and Gray, 1972). The results of this study are summarized in Table 3.1. The original estimates, in 1972 dollar prices, have been updated to 1991 values using the index of consumer prices reported to the IFS (International Financial Statistics, 1993), and the original unit of measurement – the acre-foot – has been converted to cubic metres.

For *agriculture*, the higher values tend to apply to major, non-marginal, schemes such as new irrigation projects, replacement of groundwater with surface sources, and the diversion of water from farms to other users. Marginal changes, such as supplementary supplies to an existing water system, or the withdrawal of marginal water, have very little economic value. One factor adduced in explanation for these very low values is the likelihood of 'substantial' excess capacity in the irrigation sector.

Within *industry*, 80 per cent of consumptive use was for cooling, especially in steam-electric generation, and quality was not an issue. Cooling water values are very low. For industrial process use, values are higher. Estimates in the range quoted in Table 3.1 were for the value of additional supplies to an established plant – much higher values apply to water in the context of a new development.

Water for *domestic* use has several purposes, only a fraction of which is for essential life support: 'so small is the daily requirement for survival that water is no longer invaluable after a quart or two have been made available' (Young and Gray, 1972). Only 6 per cent of national consumptive use of water was for domestic purposes, and a fraction of this was for drinking, cooking and

**Table 3.1**  Economic value of water

| Sector/use | Value/acre-foot, 1972 prices (US$) | Value/acre-foot, 1991 prices (US$) | Value/cu.m, 1991 prices (US cents) |
|---|---|---|---|
| *Agriculture* | | | |
| Major new supply schemes | 5–25 | 16–81 | 1–6 |
| Supplementary, marginal changes | 0–1 | 0–3 | 0 |
| *Industry* | | | |
| Cooling process | 3 | 10 | <1 |
| Existing plant | 3–27 | 10–120 | 1–10 |
| New project | 100–300 | 325–975 | 26–79 |
| *Municipal (domestic)* | | | |
| In-house | 101 | 328 | 26 |
| Outdoor use | | | |
| West | 66 | 214 | 17 |
| East | 16 | 52 | 4 |
| *Waste assimilation* | 1–7 | 3–23 | 0–2 |
| *Navigation* | 0–1 | 0–3 | 0 |
| *Recreation* | | | |
| Remote areas | <1 | <3 | 0 |
| Near developed areas | 150 | 488 | 40 |
| *Fisheries and wildlife habitat* | 1–13 | 3–42 | 0–3 |
| *Hydropower* | 0.4–4 | 1–13 | 0–1 |

*Source*: After Young and Gray (1972), converted to 1991 prices by the present author.

washing. Garden watering is the largest component of use in the western states, and its price elasticity of demand is not negligible.

*Waste assimilation* was found to be of low value, though likely to increase as pollution loads grow. *Navigation* was also a low-value use, partly because much waterway transportation had become unprofitable and uneconomic. *Recreational* values were observed to be rising rapidly, and were especially high in the vicinity of urban areas. The values quoted exclude fishing, and non-contact activities such as sightseeing and picnicking, which gives them a conservative bias. Values for *fisheries and wildlife habitat* tend to be low. So, surprisingly, are those for *hydropower generation*. The latter only seems to be justified so long as water can be regarded as a free good. As soon as competition for the water arises, that is, when it starts to become scarce, hydropower becomes a low-value claimant – except for existing schemes where the costs of generation and storage are sunk.

The second study reviewed here was published some fifteen years later, in 1986, again drawing almost entirely on US data (Gibbons, 1986). Its results are summarized in Table 3.2. Part of the evidence it reviewed was that used by Young and Gray. To avoid duplication, the latter is omitted in the following discussion.

**Table 3.2** Economic value of water

| Sector | Value/acre-foot, original prices (US$) | Value/acre-foot, 1991 prices (US$) | Values/cu.m, 1991 prices (US cents) |
|---|---|---|---|
| *Residential* | | | |
| Winter | 25.00–105.00 | 41.25–173.25 | 3.35–14.17 |
| Summer | 17.00–28.00 | 28.05–46.20 | 2.27–3.78 |
| Water market | 300.00 | 495.00 | 40.15 |
| *Irrigation* | | | |
| South-west (1979) | 3.00–20.00 | 4.95–33.00 | 0.40–2.70 |
| Rocky Mountains (1983) | 10.00–20.00 | 16.50–33.00 | 1.34–2.70 |
| *Industry* | | | |
| Cooling | | | |
|    Electricity | 5.00 | 8.25 | 0.67 |
|    Oil refining | 11.00 | 18.15 | 1.47 |
| Process | | | |
|    Food industry | 327.00–456.00 | 539.55–752.40 | 43.76–61.52 |
|    Textiles | 133.00 | 219.45 | 17.80 |
| *Waste assimilation* (Salinity dilution) | 9.00 | 14.85 | 1.20 |
| *Recreation* | 6.00–75.00 | 9.90–123.75 | 0.80–10.12 |
| *Fishing* | 16.00–40.00 | 26.40–66.00 | 2.14–5.40 |
| *Navigation* | 1.00–275.00 | 1.65–453.75 | 0.13–37.10 |
| *Hydropower* | 1.00–32.00 | 1.65–52.80 | 0.13–4.32 |
| Short-term value | 1.00–32.00 | 1.65–52.80 | 0.13–4.32 |
| Peak | 18.00–80.00 | 29.70–132.00 | 2.41–10.79 |

*Source:* After Gibbons (1986), converted to 1991 prices by the author.

Estimates for *residential* values are based on data from Tucson, Raleigh (NC), Toronto and the Colorado water market. Values for the first three are shown here as single point estimates for ease of presentation, representing the value of a 10 per cent reduction from present consumption. Values differ widely, depending on which point on the demand schedule is taken, and whether summer or winter demand is used. Thus, the highest values – $358 per acre-foot – were observed for a 200 cu.ft. reduction from average monthly winter consumption in Raleigh. In contrast, the value of a 50 cu.ft. drop in summer use in the same city was only $6.

There are many estimates of the value of water in *irrigation*. The range of values depends on the method of calculation, whether the short or long run period is used, the type of crop, the region of the USA, the season of the year, whether marginal or non-marginal amounts of water are involved, the efficiency of irrigation, etc. For example, alfalfa is one of the lowest value water uses, cereals are also clustered in the lowest range of values, cotton, rice, soybeans and sugar beet occupy the middle range of values, while vegetables, salads and fruits exhibit the highest returns to water. It also depends on the level of crop prices at the time of the study, which makes the date of the estimate important.

These observations should, however, be tempered by noting the great variations in individual estimates for the same crop, the result of factors noted above. The crops offering the higher value water uses, such as vegetables, would be well able to compete for scarce water with municipal, industrial and recreational demand. But such crops account for relatively little agricultural water use; in 1974 only 9 per cent of irrigated land in the western states was devoted to high-value fruit and vegetables. Any expansion of the area under their production would soon encounter market limits.

Values for *industry* show the expected gulf between the low estimates for cooling and the very much higher ones for process uses. Because of the method used to value industrial water (based on the cost of recycling) values are increasing as a result of pollution control regulations encouraging a higher level of recirculation. However, as an offsetting trend, advances in recycling technology would reduce water values. The same is true of the trend in the values of water for *waste assimilation*, which are already low.

*Recreation* values vary greatly, depending on the visitation rate, the location of the site relative to visitor concentrations, the quality and rarity of the site, the quality of water, etc. The exercise also presupposes that it is meaningful to calibrate this use of water by a standard denominator such as acre-feet. The values quoted in Table 3.2 are quite modest, partly because some of them refer to sites in less populous regions, partly because non-user values (e.g. option and existence values) are not considered, and partly because *fishing* – an important activity – is estimated separately in the table.

Values for *navigation* fall into two main types. The use of water for navigation on free-flowing rivers is generally a low-value use, and in the increasingly frequent event of conflicting claims, navigation loses out to irrigation, flood control, water supply and occasionally hydropower. But the relatively small amount of water necessary to fill locks for the movement of barges and craft on slack-water rivers can have a high value, compared to others uses such as hydropower. Within the range quoted in Table 3.2, the typical navigation value will be very low.

Finally, the values for *hydropower* are somewhat larger than those estimated in the earlier study. Much depends on the choice of period – short run values, when fixed costs are sunk, can be high. If, as is increasingly common in the USA, hydropower is used for peak-load purposes, this also boosts its value. Another basic influence on value is the 'head' of the river, which affects its power-generating potential. Since the earlier study was done, it is likely that the real value of water in *existing* hydro schemes has increased in view of the increased relative attractiveness of power from hydro rather than thermal sources. This would not necessarily apply to the attractiveness of *new* hydro projects.

## Conclusions on Differential Water Values

The two studies reviewed here produce a similar ranking of water values between different sectors and absolute values that are broadly consistent. The lowest value uses include low-value farm crops, industrial cooling, waste assimilation, navigation and hydro-electric generation. The highest values – a multiple of the former – are found in speciality crop production, industrial process use, in-house domestic consumption and some recreational sites.

Almost all categories show a wide range of values, for sector-specific reasons. In every case, the chosen valuation method vitally affects the result. For these reasons, it is important to examine the fine print attached to each valuation exercise before using the values as representative of a sector, or in transferring the result for analytical purposes elsewhere.

---

**Box 2: Water modelling in the Yellow River Basin, China**

The Yellow River in northern China is almost 5500 km in length, and its average annual flow is virtually the same as Egypt's share of the Nile. However, the Yellow River sustains a population of around 120 million, twice that of Egypt's, and irrigates an area twice that of the Nile. It has the highest sediment concentration of any major river in the world. It also has extreme seasonal and year-to-year variability, making flood control the main preoccupation of the river basin managers.

The river is of vital importance to irrigated agriculture, which supplies food to the basin's large population. There is also a sizeable municipal and industrial demand for water. Planned and anticipated growth in population, irrigated area, industry and cities are expected to exceed available water supplies in the near future, unless drastic changes are made to the pattern of use.

Quite apart from the magnitude of water demands from the different sectors, managers of the Yellow River's water (e.g. the various hydroelectric schemes and the three large multipurpose reservoirs) are confronted with awkward trade-offs. The main concerns – flood prevention, sediment control, irrigation, power – are often in conflict, which is made worse by the fragmented institutional arrangements in the basin. For instance, using the limited reservoir storage for flood control constrains the supply of irrigation water at the optimum time, nor does it coincide with maximizing power generation. On the other hand using the reservoirs for flood control and power generation may worsen sedimentation. An important concern is to maintain sufficient in-stream flows in the lower reaches to flush out sediment – but this water has a high opportunity cost in irrigation benefits foregone.

Water flows in the basin were simulated on a nonlinear programming model, using a constrained optimization approach. The objective function to be maximized was the value added from Yellow River water, subject to a variety of hydrological, physical and agronomic constraints. In the course of constructing the model, the authors estimated marginal and average values for water in its main uses. The value of municipal and industrial water was not estimated on the grounds that these uses received priority.

The average value of water used in irrigation was found to be *c.* Y 0.24/cu.m. while its marginal value, at critical times and in the most productive regions, was *c.* Y 0.80/cu.m. (farmers seldom pay more than Y 0.02–0.08). The marginal value of water for power production is estimated to be *c.* Y 0.15/cu.m.

Although hampered by a shortage of suitable data, the model enabled certain preliminary conclusions to be drawn. The future overall water balance depends overwhelmingly on the amount of water needed for flushing sediment (i.e. this use of water has a very high opportunity cost). Given the high marginal values of water in irrigation, improvement of the present inefficient methods of distributing and applying the water should have priority. Plans for expanding the irrigated area will be foiled by a shortage of water and/or competition from other uses. The opportunity cost of water for power generation has been overlooked by planners.

The authors note that the implied redistribution of water will be prevented in some cases by the absence of the necessary physical infrastructure. A further reservation to be made is that several million poor farmers would stand to lose if water were reallocated to other uses.

The model helps to justify proposed public investment in the Xiaolangdi Dam. By trapping large amounts of sediment the Dam would provide an efficient way of downstream sediment control, releasing large amounts of water currently needed for flushing. As noted, this water has a high opportunity cost.

*Source*: Kutcher *et al.* (1992).

## The Wider Use of Water Value Data

The estimation of water values has several purposes:

- indicating the productivity or benefits arising from water in its different uses. This information is useful in planning and allocating water in a region or basin, where supplies are becoming scarce or where future provision is likely to be costly. Box 2 illustrates the use of water value data for modelling purposes;

- providing information useful for considering the feasibility of encouraging water markets and transfers;
- enabling the benefits (and opportunity costs) of water supply and conservation schemes to be determined more accurately;
- providing evidence on likely willingness-to-pay and elasticity of demand, in the context of setting charges for household, industrial, agricultural, and other water supplies.

## Final Observations

This discussion of sustainability in the water sector has illustrated some of the difficulties in applying categorical principles such as the sustainability rule. It has argued that the use of the (expanded) marginal cost pricing principle is a necessary step towards ensuring sustainable water use, though it is unlikely to be a sufficient one, given the typical structure of the water industry in most countries. The presence of numerous water sub-systems, and of various kinds of barriers between suppliers and consumers, favours an approach incorporating opportunity costs and differential water values. These values are useful for a variety of purposes.

What started as a discussion of sustainability has ended as one about optimality. But in the long run no use pattern is sustainable which does not makes best use of its limiting resource.

## References

Allan, T. (1992) Fortunately there are substitutes for water: otherwise our hydropolitical futures would be impossible. Paper for ODA Conference on Priorities for Water Resources Allocation and Management, Southampton.

British Geological Survey (1994) *Aquifer Overexploitation in the Hangu Region of Tianjin, People's Republic of China.* Nottingham: BGS.

Dixon, J.A., Scura, L.F., Carpenter, R. and Sherman, P.B. (1994) *Economic Analysis of Environmental Impacts.* London: Earthscan.

Dubourg, W.R. (1994a) *Pricing for Sustainable Water Abstraction in England and Wales: A Comparison of Theory and Practice.* London: Centre for Social and Economic Research on the Global Environment (CSERGE).

Dubourg, R. (1994b) The sustainable development of water resources. In D. Pearce *et al.*, *Blueprint 3.* London: Earthscan.

Gibbons, D.C. (1986) *The Economic Value of Water.* Washington, DC: Resources for the Future.

International Financial Statistics (1993) Washington, DC: IMF.

Kutcher, G., McGurk, S. and Gunaratnam, D.J. (1992) China: Yellow River Basin. Water investment planning study. Paper presented to a World Bank Irrigation and Drainage Seminar.

Warford, J. (1994) *Marginal Opportunity Cost Pricing for Municipal Water Supply.* Singapore: Economy and Environment Program for Southeast Asia.

Young, R.A. and Gray, S.L. (1972) *Economic Value of Water: Concepts and Empirical Estimates. Final Report to the National Water Commission.* Fort Collins, CO: Department of Economics, Colorado State University.

# 4

# Labour Force Analysis as a Means to Understand the Livelihood Dimension of Sustainability

## John Cameron

## An Analytical Framework

A major study from the United Nations Research Institute for Social Development (UNRISD) on the linkages between population, environment and development (UNRISD, 1993) arrived at the finding that government policy was failing the studied rural communities. The conclusion suggested that, without improvement or at least stabilization in livelihood status, the communities studied would erode their ecological base and their human populations would tend to grow. In that sense, the security of livelihoods is prioritized for policy purposes. Similarly, a World Bank study on poverty and the environment stresses poverty alleviation (and migration) as virtual prerequisites for environmental conservation (Jagannathan, 1989).

For sustainability to be established as a core concept, there is a need to achieve an analytical balance between ecological, human demographic, and economic livelihoods dimensions of sustainability. In principle, there is no reason why any of the following stylized combinations might not occur in any bounded territory and its resident human population:

| Ecological change | Population growth | Economic livelihoods |
|---|---|---|
| Adaptation | Rapid | Loss |
| Degradation | Rapid | Loss |
| Adaptation | Rapid | Gain |
| Degradation | Rapid | Gain |
| Adaptation | Stable | Loss |
| Degradation | Stable | Loss |
| Adaptation | Stable | Gain |
| Degradation | Stable | Gain |

It is possible to identify prima facie past or present examples of each of these hypothetical combinations. This might suggest that the three dimensions are causally independent and can be analysed separately, and western scientistic method tends to encourage such an approach. But it is more plausible that the primary determinant of the different combinations is the immense variability of local ecologies. These variations permit all the combinations to exist as local phenomena – even if the global tendency is to environmental degradation, rapid population growth and livelihood gain. Thus the ecological dimension seems a promising starting point to understand how local patterns of human livelihoods can vary with differing potential for sustainability.

The technological optimism of the 1950s and 1960s was challenged by threats of famine in South Asia and computer simulations of global limits to growth. Discussions in the 1960s and 1970s tended to be conducted in neo-Malthusian/neo-Boserupian terms concerned with the ecology/population frontier (e.g. Barnett, 1977). While this debate has become more sophisticated in the 1980s and 1990s, the fundamental terrain has remained recognisable with neo-Malthusians shading the advantage (e.g. Bilsborrow, 1987; Shaw, 1989) as 'green revolution' optimism was overtaken by 'greenhouse effect' pessimism.

The interaction between ecological and demographic dimensions of sustainability is complicated by human migration as a key factor in evaluating local sustainability. Migration from an ecologically homogeneous locality pushes analysis towards the wider economy and consideration of more diverse ecologies (e.g. Ghimire, 1992), including urban ecologies. Similarly, while the economic livelihoods/demography frontier has long been dominated by the concept of national demographic transition, international migration is a complicating factor (Skeldon, 1992). The impact of migration on livelihoods (let alone quality of life) in rural and urban areas is theoretically ambiguous and empirically very difficult to isolate (Vijverberg, 1989). Understanding human migration and evaluating its sustainability impact is a significant part of the analysis here.

On the ecology/economic livelihood frontier, economic responses to the petroleum products' price rise in the 1970s tended to reduce the rate of growth of their consumption suggesting that market forces work to ration scarce 'natural resources' and the relationship between ecological and economic processes had a benign, or at least mitigating, nature. This observation fitted with the neo-liberal, neo-classical economics assertion that market forces work both to ration non-renewable resources and to induce ecologically appropriate technological change. But this optimism was challenged by widespread observations of ecological degradation in areas where resources were largely allocated by open market forces.

In the 1990s following the 1992 Rio de Janeiro conference, developmental economists are attempting to bridge the gap between ecological conservation and conventional economics measurement by suggesting adaptations to national accounts and project/programme appraisal techniques, though with limited impact in practice to date (Tisdell, 1988). Such modifications of economic analysis have been an insignificant factor compared to the impact of grass-roots political struggles on the local frontiers where ecological degradation meets economic livelihood losses (e.g. Grzybowski, 1989; Guha, 1989). Improving the conceptual and empirical framework for understanding the interaction between ecological and economic livelihood dimensions of sustainability is the focus of the analysis here.

This overview leads to three propositions on the sustainability of patterns of interactions between ecology, demography, and economic livelihoods:

1. Theory rules out nothing a priori, therefore, careful observation and measurement is essential for understanding greater sustainability as an outcome of interaction between ecological, demographic, and economic factors.
2. Economic livelihood considerations are crucial to analysis and policy on sustainability.
3. The widespread phenomenon of human migration forces economic livelihood measurement on to a larger territorial scale than often appropriate for sensitive ecological evaluation.

The implication of these propositions is that it is vital to be able to measure livelihood patterns, demands and potential on a scale which includes origins and destinations of significant migration flows. This is especially important for territories where both livelihoods and ecologies are currently strongly challenged and the human population is estimated to more than double in the next 30 years. Bangladesh is such a case and the following discussion is intended both to analyse the situation in Bangladesh and to set a model for analysis of similar cases in other parts of the world.

## The Weaknesses of Existing Aggregate Statistics in Understanding Livelihood Generation

The most direct route to livelihood analysis on a large scale is through labour force statistics. Estimation of the total size of the labour force being used and available for use are complicated by differences in definitions used in the two major sources – population censuses and labour force surveys – and changes in definitions within those sources across time. Three basic formal causes of differences can be identified:

1. Activities designated as constituting economic activity.
2. The reference period in which the activities have to have taken place.
3. The minimum length of time for which designated activities have to be undertaken in the reference period for a person to be counted as in the labour force.

In practice, these causes of differences are not independent. The wider the range of designated activities or the shorter the minimum acceptable time period then the tighter the reference period required to achieve an acceptable time of interview and level of accuracy. Population censuses have tended to be more restrictive in defining activities and time and operated with a longer reference period; labour force surveys have operated less restrictive definitions and used shorter reference periods, with interviews being staggered over 12 months in order to control for seasonality. In a situation such as Bangladesh, where people frequently move between part-time activities (e.g. Muqtada and Alam, 1986), there is much to be said for the formal approach used in the labour force surveys, though it must be emphasized that these are sample surveys subject to both statistical sampling error and stratification aggregating error, unlike the population censuses.

Less formally, there is an important question of how far enumerators have actively sought to identify women and young people who are in the labour force in terms of availability and willingness to undertake economic activity but unemployed in the reference period. Differing presuppositions of enumerators about women being 'housewives' and young people being 'idle' may produce significant differences in rates of labour force participation, given that unemployed people available and willing to undertake economic activity conventionally are counted as part of the labour force.

In Bangladesh, changes in definitions and enumerator practices were associated with a predictable significant increase in the labour force participation rate from previous labour force surveys in 1983–84, 1984–85 and 1985–86. All these labour force surveys produced labour force participation rates much higher than the 1981 population census, probably primarily due to definitional differences. These differences have caused much confusion in subsequent writing on the size of the labour force in Bangladesh as in the contributions to the Workshop on Dissemination of Current Statistics (Bangladesh Household Survey Capability Programme, 1991) and the Human Development in Bangladesh report (UNDP, 1993).

The range of designated activities in the 1989 Labour Force Survey was wider than previously and the minimum length of time required in the reference period of one week was shortened to one hour for activities, including those with no direct monetary reward (Rahman, 1993). There is also reason to believe that enumerators were trained to probe more deeply into women's economic activity – though this may have stopped short of identifying all the fully unemployed. Thus in terms of breadth of coverage, the 1989 Labour Force Survey represents a 'best practice' data set for any livelihood and ecologically challenged society and presents an excellent opportunity to examine how much surveys can be used for livelihood analysis. It is desirable that this practice be adopted on a global scale and further developed to more fully and accurately record patterns of time and energy use of women and men in gaining livelihoods.

## Improving the Measurement of Livelihoods

To reduce the general confusion surrounding labour force data, a clear vision of the purposes of the labour force data is required; a vision which does not exist at this time. For instance, it is noteworthy that labour force data have not been specifically directed at policy issues in Bangladesh other than efforts to reconcile supply and demand for professional and technical skills in the early 1980s (ILO-ARTEP, 1981).

A major policy challenge for labour force information in the 1990s is to evaluate whether broadly defined 'sustainability' is threatened by people seeking local natural resource intensive economic activity. It is an aspect of sustainability that people find sufficient work with high enough rates of earnings to justify concluding that the quality of life is improving for the vast majority of the population. In vulnerable, natural resource constrained environments, such as high mountains or low-lying river deltas, it is to be expected that the direct and indirect natural resource demands of the human populations for economic livelihoods will shift towards the wider global environment.

Labour force data, as collected in well-designed and well-executed labour force surveys, are an invaluable starting-point for such an evaluation and a tool for any necessary policy redesign. But to be used as an efficient indicator of livelihood pressures on sustainability, the following two ambiguities need to be recognized in data sets.

First, rates of economic activity among young people aged 10 to 15 are not useful statistics in livelihood analysis as:

- any increase in wage-paid activity in this age group cannot be regarded as positive in the manner that increased wage-paid activity among groups over the age of 15 is treated. To aggregate statistics that we would expect to fall with development with those we would expect to rise can only create confusion; for instance, a significant proportion of those recorded as fully employed are aged 10 to 14, leading to a possible conclusion that social welfare would be improved with more child labour;
- micro-evidence from Bangladesh suggests much economic activity in the 10 to 15 age group is for relatively short hours in the family situation. The judgement about what level of such participation in day-to-day family life is desirable or undesirable again will confuse the interpretation of labour force statistics.
- inclusion of labour force participation rates for this age group may confuse international comparisons of labour force statistics. Internationally, it is more usual to measure the labour force from about age 15 rather than 10 as is current practice in Bangladesh.

Second, increasing economic activity in terms of numbers of people in the labour force is not necessarily an indicator of quality of life gains if the same amount or even less time in total economic activity is merely being shared among more people with no productivity gains. In societies with very limited 'safety nets' labour force supply and labour force demand are closely interrelated. Lack of rights to minimal subsistence forces people to compete for, or more benignly agree to share, very low productivity work opportunities which could result in more and more people sharing the same amount of work time and incomes. Registering an increase in the occupied labour force in terms of numbers of people in such a process of competitive impoverishment would not indicate livelihoods gain.

Thus, for the purposes of demonstrating here the general principles of livelihood analysis applied to Bangladesh, young people aged 10 to 14 will be excluded and, as far as feasible, the labour force will be measured in terms of millions of person hours per annum rather than number of persons economically active irrespective of hours active.

It is worth emphasizing that the first change from current practice does not mean that the lives of young people aged under 15 are of no interest for evaluating quality of human life. The overall responsibility for measuring the quality of life of people under 15 years of age and acting on such findings, whether or not the young people are actually in school should lie with those authorities responsible for education. Specific responsibilities for identifying and stopping abuse of young people at work should lie with workplace inspectorates, NGOs, trades unions, and researchers (e.g. Ahmad and Quasem, 1991). Information on the economic activity of all young people under the age of 15 could continue to be collected in labour force surveys and population censuses, but this information should be analysed and reported separately from the actual labour force data for those aged 15 and over.

The second change (which is consistent with approaches in distributionally sensitive social accounting matrices such as that developed by the Bangladesh Planning Commission) that the labour force be measured in terms of total time rather than in terms of numbers of people will still leave two limitations:

1. Differential and changing real rates of reward to labour are not included in the indictor. The variability entailed in this omission will be less significant if it is assumed that a floor to rates of reward for labour are set, and will continue to be set by the food-for-work rates paid on public works schemes. If this is accepted then it can be deduced that additional person-days in economic activity will be rewarded at least at that rate and be at least that productive at the margin;
2. A measure of total time available for economic activity but not utilized is required in theory but difficult in practice given the subjective element involved in terms of type of work, rate of reward, household time reorganization, and location of work which would be acceptable. Labour force statistics in the mid-1980s failed to identify a large pool of women willing and able to work long hours in the garments industry. It appears that a large pool of labour time with internationally tradable productive potential utilizing natural resources from the wider global ecology was missed. Labour force surveys need to be extended to measure all forms of underemployment and estimate total potential livelihood demands.

From the perspective of sustainability as a process, it is vital that the snapshots of labour force surveys and population censuses give insights into aspirations and motivations which will operate in conjunction with changing patterns of opportunity to modify pressures on the local natural resource base. Improved questionnaire design can help achieve this.

The following analysis attempts to show how the aggregate labour force statistics, especially the 'best global current practice' 1989 Labour Force Survey, can be combined with insights from more local information to understand the pressures on economic livelihoods and the implications for wider processes threatening sustainability. It is hoped that the methods described here will be applicable to any society where a vulnerable, degrading ecology is combined with significant demographic growth in the resident human population and great pressure on economic livelihoods. The broad conclusions from the analysis may also be applicable in such situations.

## Adjusting the 1989 Bangladesh Labour Force Survey Results

The 1989 Labour Force Survey identified a labour force of 50.7 million of whom 4.2 million were aged 10 to 14. Thus the labour force of 15 or more

**Table 4.1** Economically active population/labour force (millions) in 1989 by age and gender with Labour Force Participation Rates (LFPR)

| Age group | Male | Female | LFPR (Male) % | LFPR (Female) % |
|-----------|------|--------|---------------|-----------------|
| 15–19 | 3.5 | 2.3 | 71 | 55 |
| 20–59 | 21.3 | 16.1 | 95 | 72 |
| 60+ | 2.5 | 0.9 | 77 | 45 |
| Total | 27.3 | 19.3 | 89 | 68 |

*Source*: Calculated from 1989 Labour Force Survey.

years of age was estimated at 46.5 million. Table 4.1 shows the breakdown of this labour force by age and gender and refined labour force participation rates calculated for each age group. As to be expected the labour force is overwhelmingly aged 20 to 60 though the labour force participation rates for those aged 15 to 19 and 60 or more are highly significant, suggesting poverty-pressure to work outside prime working years rather than be in education or retirement.

To put these figures in terms of time available requires an element of approximation as figures for hours of work in the labour force survey were not broken down by age, a special problem given the desirability of extracting 10- to 14-year-olds from the statistics. However, mean hours of work measured by employment status appear to best approximate individual hours of work available. The average hours per male of 10 years and more per week derived from employment status statistics was 29 hours per week. The figure per female was 13 hours per week. These are likely to be underestimates for those aged 15 or more. This underestimate can be partially allowed for by assuming those aged 10 to 14 worked the hours associated with their pattern of economic status as shown in Table 4.2. The estimate for males aged 10 to 14 years is 22 hours and females 14 hours. Applying this result to give an estimated figure for those of 15 years or more would increase the male estimate from 29 hours to 30 hours while the female would remain at 13 hours.

These figures apply to those economically active but not unemployed. Therefore, a further calculation is required to take account of the unemployed in the labour force survey. Finally, a figure for underemployment, though this involves a very restricted definition, as recorded in the 1989 Labour Force Survey can be added. This calculation is shown in Table 4.3. The number of economically active hours being worked or offered in the year 1989 according to our calculations on the 1989 Labour Force Survey were 43,524 million male hours and 13,640 million female hours – a total labour force in terms of time of 57,164 million hours in 1989.

The education and skill composition of the employed labour force in 1989 is shown in Table 4.4. The table is dominated by those in agriculture, forestry and fisheries with no formal education. Flexibility in the labour force is

**Table 4.2** Estimate of hours per week worked by economically active people of 15 years of age or more

| Employment status | Percentage of those aged 10–14 | | Average hours worked by aged 10+ | |
|---|---|---|---|---|
| | M | F | M | F |
| Employer | 0 | 0 | 36 | 15 |
| Employee | 10 | 8 | 50 | 49 |
| Self-employed | 8 | 3 | 30 | 20 |
| Unpaid family helper | 64 | 85 | 17 | 10 |
| Irregular/casual/ day worker | 18 | 3 | 23 | 30 |

Therefore average estimated hours per week for those aged 10 to 14 recorded as economically active in 1989 Labour Force Survey:

| | |
|---|---|
| Male: | 22 hours |
| Female: | 14 hours |

*Source*: Calculated from 1989 Labour Force Survey.

**Table 4.3** Estimate of hours worked and involuntarily idle by the labour force, economically active people of 15 years of age or more, 1989

| Type of person | Number in group (million) | | Hours per week per person | | Total hours in year (millions) | |
|---|---|---|---|---|---|---|
| | M | F | M | F | M | F |
| Employed | 26.9 | 19.1 | 30 | 13 | 41964 | 12912 |
| Unemployed | 0.3 | 0.2 | 40* | 40* | 624 | 416 |
| Underemployed | 0.9 | 0.3 | 20* | 20* | 936 | 312 |
| Total | n/c | n/c | n/c | n/c | 43524 | 13640 |

*Notes:*
*: author's estimate
n/c: column not summable

*Source*: Calculated from 1989 Labour Force Survey.

indicated by the considerable proportion of professional and technical positions occupied by those without a school-leaving certificate.

Though this may suggest a shortage of more educated workers, no specific shortage of skills is identified other than in the fields working with computers. Despite such flexibility and absence of skills shortage, the widespread lack of basic education must lead to the conclusion that the Bangladesh labour force is educationally ill-prepared for significant structural change in the 1990s.

Even if this structural change was towards more intensive agriculture there is reason to be concerned that in so far as the change requires basic literacy, many farmers will not be adequately equipped. Outside agriculture, the depth and breadth of skill acquisition through work experience also appears

**Table 4.4**  Education and skill composition of the employed population, 1989

| Occupations | | Education | | | |
|---|---|---|---|---|---|
| | Total (millions) | No education (%) | Classes 1–10 (%) | SSC (%) | Above SSC (%) |
| Professional/technical | 1.4 | 23 | 18 . | 30 | 22 |
| Admin./managerial/ clerical | 1.1 | 10 | 34 | 35 | 21 |
| Sales | 3.7 | 40 | 46 | 11 | 3 |
| Service/production/ transport/labourers | 6.8 | 64 | 31 | 5 | 0 |
| Agriculture/forestry/ fisheries | 37.0 | 68 | 27 | 3 | 0 |
| Total (millions) | 50.1 | 32.3 | 14.3 | 2.5 | 0.8 |

*Note*: Not all percentage rows sum to 100 and first column and bottom row do not sum to totals as small unclassified groups have been omitted.
*Source*: Calculated from 1989 Labour Force Survey.

unpromising, though micro-studies suggest that artisan and trading skills are widespread among the many people who shift seasonally from agricultural to non-agricultural occupations.

The pattern of education and skills of the unemployed and temporary migrants may indicate the extent of a pool of more qualified and skilled people potentially available to the Bangladesh economy if there is a structural shift towards occupations demanding such people. An indicative summary of the situation in 1989 is attempted in Table 4.5. The figures do suggest there was a significant stock of educated and, therefore, potentially skilled/professional workers among the unemployed – experience with the development, and subsequent overdevelopment, of dental technician skills shows the possibility of rapidly filling small, specific gaps in skills and the problems of meeting a problem of labour 'stock' deficiency through provision for continuing increased 'flows'! Given the gender composition of the educated unemployed, training programmes would have to be designed to be attractive to women as well as men.

The stock of professionals and technicians on temporary work contracts outside Bangladesh was small in terms of proportion of those actually working in Bangladesh, though there was undoubtedly a depth and breadth of valuable 'non-professional' skills in the wider migrant workforce of approximately a quarter of a million on temporary contracts in 1989. But overall, the Bangladesh labour force in 1989, in terms of education and skills, shows no reason for optimism in being able to sustain any radical shift towards new occupations with higher productivity.

The education and skill composition of the large Bangladesh labour force in 1989 was not compatible with a significant capacity to adopt and indigenize high technology, even taking into account the pools of more

**Table 4.5** Comparison of employed labour force skills with education/skill profiles of unemployed and Bangladeshi temporary migrant workers in 1989 (in thousands)

| Occupations/ education | Employed (a) | | Employed (b) | | Unemployed (b) | | Migrants (c) | |
|---|---|---|---|---|---|---|---|---|
| | No. | % | No. | % | No. | % | No. | % |
| Professionals/ post-SSC | 1433 | 3 | 3222 | 6 | 121 | 28 | 14 | 4 |

*Notes:*
(a) Includes professional/technical only.
(b) Includes all those with SSC or higher.
(c) As classified in migration statistics, gross outward flows are summed from 1986 to 1989 to indicate stock of Bangladeshis in professional occupations on temporary contracts outside Bangladesh.
*Sources*: 1989 Labour Force Survey and 1991 *Statistical Yearbook of Bangladesh.*

educated unemployed and temporary economic migrants. Analysing the labour force in this manner reveals more about the livelihoods bottom line than the raw Labour Force Survey data. The situation of mass ill-preparedness for a radical shift in livelihoods in the future is also probably true for much of South Asia, sub-Saharan Africa and large pockets of China and Latin America.

## Discerning Trends in the 1980s

The next section intends to combine aggregate statistics with micro-level studies to give insights into the processes at work in the 1980s. Sustainability is a dynamic concept operating at all territorial levels. The methodological challenge of combining macro- and micro-levels, survey and ethnographic techniques, is especially relevant for sustainability challenged societies due to the more complex patterns of livelihoods, frequently involving movements across space and sectors; plus the greater likelihood of gaps in data coverage, across time and space, due to resource constraints in the national information system.

The basic differences in measures of economic activity between the population census and the labour force surveys in Bangladesh make meaningful comparison impossible between the 1981 Population Census and the labour force surveys of the 1980s. Comparisons between labour force surveys can be made to discern trends, though these are also hazardous. The 1989 Labour Force Survey sets a new higher standard for labour force analysis but, in order to make comparisons, compromises have to be made with previous lower standards of labour force surveys. The 1989 Labour Force Survey itself includes such a compromise reporting some highly aggregated figures in terms of comparing numbers of types of people who would have been considered economically active under previous labour force survey definitions. These comparisons suggest an annual growth rate of total labour force of 3 per cent per annum between 1985–86 and 1989, with the female rate rising at closer to 4 per cent.

An age-specific comparison was made at the Workshop on Dissemination of Current Statistics in 1991 (Hossain *et al.*, 1991). The comparison removed the types of activities added in 1989 and graphically compared the residual female Labour Force Participation Rate with those of 1985–86. The results suggested no significant shift in the graph on the most restrictive assumptions but a significant increase of 2 to 5 percentage points in most age groups (from 15 to 59) over the period of two and a half years on slightly less restrictive assumptions. These results would bracket the rise in Labour Force Participation Rate implied in the aggregate comparative results reported for females in the 1989 Labour Force Survey. It therefore seems plausible to conclude that there is underlying buoyancy in female Labour Force Participation Rates compared to that of males.

A further comparison can be made by taking the narrowest definition from the 1989 Labour Force Survey as reported in Hossain *et al.* (1991) and comparing that to the projections from the 1983–84 Labour Force Survey for 1990. This comparison is summarized in Table 4.6. The table suggests that the male labour force was growing at a rate of between 2.5 and 3 per cent per annum in the late 1980s, with the pressure shifting slightly away from the extremes of the age range. The base for female participation is growing but not as fast as the 8.5 per cent per annum in the projection, though in the case of women there seems to be slightly greater participation at the extremes of the age range than warranted in the 1983–84 Labour Force Survey.

An insight into changing qualifications in the workforce can be best gauged through comparing the education profile of economically active males in the 1983–84 Labour Force Survey with that of the 1989 Labour Force Survey. This comparison is made in Table 4.7. There is some evidence of educational gain between 1983–84 and 1989 with more people available with Secondary School Certificate–Higher School Certificate (SSC–HSC) education or better, following a rapid growth in the numbers of professionally and technically qualified people in the period 1972 to 1985 from a very low base (Taskforces on Bangladesh Development Strategies, 1991, p. 175). However, the major proportional and numerical gain has been in a shift from no schooling to basic schooling. But challenges remained in increasing the numbers of children completing basic education, to keep more 15- to 19-year-olds in education, and to ensure that education is meaningful in terms of educational and skill profiles appropriate to the next century.

In summary, the labour force in terms of a simple head-count grew slightly faster than the population in the second half of the 1980s. Allowing for the changes in definitions there does appear to be a significant underlying growth in female labour force participation rates. There are also signs that the education profile of the population improved providing a better potential for skill development, but a realistic assessment would recognize that the

**Table 4.6**  Comparison of narrowly defined Labour Force Participation Rates derived from the 1989 Labour Force Survey with the 1990 projections from the 1983–84 Labour Force Survey

| Age | Female | | Male | |
|---|---|---|---|---|
| | 1989 | 1990[a] | 1989 | 1990[a] |
| 15–19 | 10.1 | 10.0 | 67.1 | 67.6 |
| 20–59 | 10.2 | 11.9 | 92.5 | 94.8 |
| 60 + | 8.2 | 6.9 | 73.3 | 78.1 |

*Note:*
(a) starts from the base of the 1983–84 Labour Force Survey and assumes male labour force grows at 2.9% per annum and female labour force at 8.4% per annum.
*Sources*: Hossain *et al.* (1991) and calculations from the 1983–84 Labour Force Survey.

**Table 4.7**  Comparison of educational profile of the whole population in the 1983–84 and 1989 Labour Force Surveys

| Level of education | 1983–84 | | 1989 | |
|---|---|---|---|---|
| | Number (000s) | % | Number (000s) | % |
| No education | 47555 | 60 | 48263 | 54 |
| Class 1 to 10 | 27657 | 35 | 35553 | 39 |
| SSC-HSC and above | 4153 | 5 | 5544 | 6 |
| Other | 150 | – | 745 | 1 |
| Total | 79515 | 100 | 90105 | 100 |

*Sources*: Labour Force Surveys 1983–84 and 1989.

improvement is from a very low base and gives no reason to conclude that the Bangladesh labour force could face the global economy of the 1990s with confidence.

As in the measurement of the labour force, it would be highly desirable to measure labour use in terms of time rather than number of people, given the fact that any individual might have been engaged in a particular activity for as little as one hour or for more than 70 hours in the reference week. It would also be desirable to exclude people aged 10 to 14, as it was for labour force measurement.

Unfortunately, the published tables are not generally in a form to permit these adjustments. All but one of the tables giving hours of work appear to be presented in terms of hours of work in an occupation or a sector of the economy only for the reference weeks in which the activity was undertaken, not the average over the year. Thus occupations with any degree of seasonality, of which Bangladesh has many (see Muqtada and Alam, 1986; Rahman and Islam, 1988), show high numbers of hours (often over 50 for men) in the reference week, but this gives a totally misleading indicator for the year. For instance, the 1989 Labour Force Survey figure of 51.12 hours a week for harvesting and collection for males may describe the average number of hours spent by men in a week of the harvesting season, but says nothing about the average over the year unless we know how many weeks are spent on harvesting and collection in the whole year. The labour force survey time-use tables are generally not presented in a form to permit the separation of people aged 10 to 14. In effect, much of the time-use data is uninterpretable as it is currently presented.

Where the tables deal with individuals' use of time, rather than times in occupations and sectors, a picture of weekly labour use in terms of time averaged over a year can be obtained. Thus a table can be constructed for weekly hours in varying economic statuses as in Tables 4.2 and 4.3, and the parameters from these tables can be applied to occupations and sectors in proportion to the prevalence of the various economic statuses. A table showing economic status information also exists for people aged 10 to 14 thus allowing an estimate of their participation to be subtracted from the labour use data in terms of economic status.

Using this approach, tables can be constructed making a distinction between the broad sectors used for macro-economic monitoring and planning purposes in terms of their economic status profiles. However, another warning is appropriate here. The distinction between agriculture and non-agriculture, with probable differing demands on the local natural resource base, is very sensitive to the weighting given to urban and rural responses in the labour force surveys. The sampling frame for the surveys stratifies between rural and urban enumeration areas and the aggregation into national figures is sensitive to the relative weights used. If the degree of urbanization has been underestimated then the numbers of people in non-agricultural sectors, and notably in the more formal parts of those sectors, will also be underestimated – this appears to be the case in Bangladesh in the 1980s.

Labour use times for the sectors in 1989 are estimated in Tables 4.8 and 4.9. The tables suggest that the services sector was highly significant in utilizing labour time in Bangladesh, with large numbers of regular employees, about 40 per cent, estimated to have been in the public sector. Agriculture's dominance of labour use was still present but not as pre-eminent as when the calculations are done in terms of individuals rather than labour time. Nevertheless, taking the figures at face value suggests that, in 1989, the split between agriculture and non-agriculture in labour use for those aged 15 or over was still in favour of agriculture, with over 50 per cent of labour time being devoted to agriculture, close to the proportion of agriculture in GDP. Agricultural activity was still central to the use of labour time in Bangladesh at the start of the 1990s.

Any trend in agricultural employment is difficult to discern because of that sector's sensitivity to activity definitional changes. A crude comparison can be made by taking the most compatible definitions between the 1983–84 and 1989 Labour Force Surveys as was done in the previous section. In 1989, 48 per cent of all males over the age of 10 were in agriculture as a primary

**Table 4.8**   Economic status profiles of the major sectors in 1989 for those aged 15 or more

| Sector | Employment status (%) | | | | |
| --- | --- | --- | --- | --- | --- |
| | Employer | Self-employed | UFW | Employee | Day labourer |
| Agriculture/forest/fisheries | 1 | 27 | 53 | 0 | 18 |
| Manufacturing | 2 | 17 | 60 | 13 | 8 |
| Construction/transport | 2 | 48 | 0 | 21 | 29 |
| Trade | 3 | 72 | 10 | 12 | 4 |
| Community/personal services | 1 | 23 | 0 | 70 | 5 |
| Other | 1 | 36 | 5 | 26 | 31 |
| Average hours per week | 35 | 30 | 12 | 50 | 24 |

Source: Calculated from 1989 Labour Force Survey.

**Table 4.9**   Estimate of labour time used by sector in 1989 for those aged 15 or more

| Sector | Estimated average, hours per week | Number of workers (000s) | Total hours per year (millions) |
| --- | --- | --- | --- |
| Agriculture/forest/fisheries | 19 | 29530 | 29375 |
| Manufacturing | 26 | 6528 | 8826 |
| Construction/transport | 33 | 1892 | 3203 |
| Trade | 31 | 3908 | 6261 |
| Community/personal services | 43 | 3151 | 7119 |
| Other | 32 | 1057 | 1769 |
| Total | 23 | 46067 | 56553 |

Note: Rows and columns do not sum precisely due to rounding.
Source: Calculated from 1989 Labour Force Survey.

economic activity and 7 per cent of females. The comparable figures in 1983–84 were 49 per cent for males and remained at 7 per cent for females. These figures suggest no underlying change in the proportions of people depending upon agriculture for their primary livelihood.

This stability does not necessarily mean that the proportion of labour time devoted to agriculture and closely related activities in Bangladesh has been constant in the 1980s. In situations of widespread self-cultivation and self-provisioning, there are possibilities of work-sharing which could give the illusion of growing economic activity in terms of numbers of economically active people. However, in the context of Bangladesh, as in other societies with irrigable land, such work-sharing may involve some positive marginal productivity gain associated with variations in cultivation techniques.

Even households with small farms do have technical options for changing agricultural practices. But micro-evidence suggests that such changes are labour-demanding, especially at peak times. In addition, the complexity and variability of social and technical relations in Bangladesh agriculture are well documented at the micro-level for the 1980s, showing the problems of making general statements about removing constraints on technical innovation (see Muqtada and Alam, 1986; Rahman, 1986; Rahman and Islam, 1988, and the associated comment by Chowdhury, 1990; Mott MacDonald, 1992).

Agriculture was changing in the 1980s and was probably changing towards greater labour use in peak periods, especially associated with irrigation provision of a wide variety of types. In the market for agricultural labour, this tendency to peak shortages of labour may have been responsible for some buoyancy in agricultural real wage rates in normal monsoon years in the 1980s. Judging by evidence from micro-studies, sectoral and locational mobility were significant features of the Bangladesh labour market in the 1980s which makes generalization on trends very difficult.

This flexibility and fluidity of labour use reaches into the non-agricultural sectors. Agricultural and non-agricultural appeared often to be complementary rather than competitive in terms of their demands on labour time in the 1980s. A wide range of non-agricultural activities appeared to be undertaken in agricultural slack periods when the opportunity cost of labour time may have been set by food-for-work rates in public works.

It is to the credit of people in Bangladesh that they have maintained low levels of formal unemployment by showing a capacity for creating income opportunities with little or no non-human resource investment. It might be expected that trade and personal services would provide such opportunities, followed by micro-scale construction and transportation. But it is also notable that the employment status structure of manufacturing in 1989, as shown in Table 4.8, has over three-quarters of people in manufacturing appearing to be the self-employed or their unpaid family helpers (the dynamism and mobility of people in the broadly defined 'informal' sector in both rural and urban areas is brought out in several contributions to Islam and Muqtada (1986), though the important handloom sector, employing almost one million people in 1990, showed little gain in employment from 1978 judging by the findings in the Bangladesh Bureau of Statistics 1991 Report on Bangladesh Handloom Census).

But this predominance of small-scale household labour use has been taken by commentators on the 1980s as highlighting the weakness of the larger scale, wage employing sub-sector of manufacturing. Full-time employees are a group who should be accurately recorded in labour force surveys, indeed such workers are the central concern of conventional surveys. Therefore, the findings in labour force surveys in the latter half of the 1980s that numbers of 'regular' employees in manufacturing were falling should be a matter of real concern.

However, two qualifications can be made to these findings. First, any underweighting of urban enumeration areas in the 1989 Survey would have a significant impact on the national aggregate figure for such a strongly urbanized group. Second, the total number of wage workers, regular plus casual, in manufacturing has not fallen dramatically. A process of

**Table 4.10**   Changes in employment in major industries, 1983–90

| Industry | 1983 | 1990 | Percentage change |
|---|---|---|---|
| Cotton mills | 84969 | 72500 | −15 |
| Jute mills | 303995 | 176730 | −42 |
| Sugar mills | 24477 | 21300 | −13 |
| Cement, lime and potteries | 2221 | 5608 | 152 |
| Glass | 4770 | 2271 | −52 |
| Matches | 11850 | 5801 | −51 |
| Papermills | 8027 | 8160 | 2 |
| Engineering | 53703 | 29900 | −44 |
| Total | 494012 | 322270 | −35 |

Source: Chief Inspector of Factories and Establishments published in 1991 *Statistical Yearbook of Bangladesh*, Bangladesh Bureau of Statistics.

'casualization' or 'contractualization' may well have been taking place in Bangladesh in the 1980s, as in other parts of south Asia, with employers reviewing their employment policies in the context of liberalization.

Nevertheless, much micro-level information does suggest a lack of consistent growth in employment among larger scale enterprises in the 1980s (see Table 4.10), though the overall average annual growth figure in employment was respectable over the particular time period shown. Some major industries suffered net job losses in the 1980s associated with continuing financial losses and lack of investment but there has been some compensating growth in smaller enterprises in newer sectors, notably garment-making.

Censuses of Manufacturing Industry recorded employment in establishments employing 50 or more workers, but the coverage of the 'census' leaves much room for doubt. The total employment recorded for such establishments in the Census for 1987–88 was only just over half a million workers. Bangladesh large-scale industry was not a consistent source of new opportunities for labour use in the 1980s, though reports of its death were premature (Bakht, 1993)!

Closely associated with the uncertainties of large scale industry in the 1980s was the selling of public sector enterprises to the private sector and a general policy thrust to reduce and simplify public sector activity in Bangladesh society. No monitoring and evaluatory procedures have been instituted to collect data and analyse the impact, if any, of these initiatives on labour use.

There is some evidence that a significant proportion of units which were privatized in the mid-1980s have disappeared as enterprises after privatization (Farid, 1993), but whether the machinery and associated jobs have moved elsewhere in the Bangladesh economy or been lost is unclear. Given the state of under-capacity working in the textile sector in Bangladesh and the failure of linkages to be constructed up-stream from the growing garments industry, there are grounds to believe that jobs have been lost in

**Table 4.11** Public and private sector employment in formal manufacturing

| Year | Public manufacturing enterprises employment (000s) | Percentage change in CMI total employment in manufacturing |
|---|---|---|
| 1980–81 | 326 | +5.0 |
| 1981–82 | 329 | +4.2 |
| 1982–83 | 246 | −1.6 |
| 1983–84 | 224 | +0.8 |
| 1984–85 | 230 | +3.6 |
| 1985–86 | 236 | −0.4 |
| 1986–87 | 239 | +2.6 |
| Change p. a. | −4.1 | +3.3 |

*Sources*: Censuses of Manufacturing Industry (CMI) and Ministry of Finance SABRE Reports.

the privatized parts of the textile sector. Overall, however, the Census of Manufacturing Industry statistics suggest a shift from the public sector to the private sector in the 1980s to equality in employment terms with neither a dramatic loss nor gain in jobs (see Table 4.11).

Statistics of total permanent employment in the civil public service are not kept systematically, but figures for 1991 from the Ministry of Establishment identify just over 1 million sanctioned posts in Classes I to IV with just over 100,000 posts vacant. This estimate of the size of the civil service excludes contracted project workers, but the total figure is probably about 40 per cent of the total number of employees recorded in the 1989 Labour Force Survey. It is probable that the civil public service was growing in the 1980s at a rate at least equivalent to the rate of growth of the total labour force. No formal programme for controlling the size of the civil public service was brought into existence in the 1980s. The significance of the civil public service as an absorber of labour time was understated by the simple number of employees, as these employees were working 'full-time', at least nationally.

International migration on temporary work contracts tended to increase in the 1980s, though with annual fluctuations as shown in Table 4.12. The costs and benefits of this movement are well covered (Mahmud, 1989). But, from a labour use perspective, the numbers involved are small. Gross emigration in 1989 was just over 100,000 people, compared to about 1.5 million people entering the labour force in that year. Even allowing for the long hours generally worked by emigrant workers in the Gulf, migration was not a significant issue in terms of the quantity of employment for the people of Bangladesh in the 1980s, especially if returnees, on whom there is no information, are netted out of the gross figures.

In terms of the qualitative impact of emigration, the people officially recorded as emigrating for employment were disproportionally profession-ally and technically qualified compared with the proportions in the Bangladesh labour force as a whole (see Table 4.5), where the estimate of the stock of professionals on temporary work contracts outside Bangladesh

**Table 4.12**   Annual migration on official temporary employment contracts (000s)

| Year | Skill levels | | | | |
|------|------|------|------|------|------|
| | Professional | Skilled | Semi-skilled | Unskilled | Total |
| 1980 | 0.6 | 1.8 | 0.5 | 3.2 | 6.1 |
| 1981 | 3.9 | 22.4 | 2.4 | 27.0 | 55.8 |
| 1982 | 3.9 | 20.6 | 3.2 | 35.0 | 62.8 |
| 1983 | 1.8 | 18.9 | 5.1 | 33.4 | 59.2 |
| 1984 | 2.6 | 17.2 | 5.5 | 31.4 | 56.8 |
| 1985 | 2.6 | 28.2 | 7.8 | 39.1 | 77.7 |
| 1986 | 2.2 | 26.3 | 9.3 | 30.9 | 68.7 |
| 1987 | 2.2 | 23.8 | 9.6 | 38.3 | 74.0 |
| 1988 | 2.7 | 25.3 | 10.8 | 29.4 | 68.1 |
| 1989 | 5.3 | 38.8 | 17.7 | 39.9 | 101.7 |
| 1990 | 6.0 | 35.6 | 20.8 | 41.3 | 103.8 |
| 1991 | 9.0 | 46.9 | 32.6 | 58.6 | 147.1 |
| 1992 | 11.4 | 50.7 | 31.0 | 95.1 | 188.1 |

Source: Unpublished information from records of the Manpower, Employment and Training Bureau provided to the author by the Bureau.

amounted to 1 per cent of the total number of professionals working in Bangladesh.

The large-scale manufacturing sector appears to have spent the 1980s treading water, if not actually sinking, in profitability terms, although the implications for employment are not clear given data limitations. The movement of enterprises from the public to the private sector and wider liberalization appear to be neutral to negative as far as labour use is concerned, but objective monitoring is needed. The large civil public service was waiting for a staffing strategy at the end of the 1980s. Growing temporary work contracts and international migration, though undoubtedly important at household level and possibly in terms of pressure on the market for salaried employment, was not significant in terms of overall labour use.

The pattern showed the continuing importance of agriculture in Bangladesh and revealed the significance of the service sector, notably the formal service sector in time employment terms. Micro-studies in the 1980s brought out the complex dynamics of agriculture that have maintained it as the dominant sector. Much activity in the non-agricultural sector is self-created and, while this says much for the initiative of people in Bangladesh, the productivity implications are unclear. Stake-holding in agricultural activities as a local natural resource-intensive, livelihood source is still widespread, suggesting that shocks, such as those associated with 'liberal-ization', will produce increased pressure on the local natural resource base threatening to reduce sustainability.

There are great empirical challenges in using conventional labour force statistics, even from relatively strong labour force surveys, to derive trends in livelihood patterns. Such statistics need to be augmented by other surveys and micro-level studies. With such augmented analysis it can be concluded that underlying processes of human resource development and use for societies like Bangladesh in the 1980s were not compatible with relieving demands on the local natural resource base and shifting towards greater use of wider global natural resources through shifts to different sectoral and skill patterns in labour force time use and international migration.

## Unemployment and Underemployment and Livelihood Sustainability

Likely future shocks, such as ocean level rise as one consequence of global warming and the possibility of increased cyclone activity, will only add to any existing deficiencies in livelihood provision. The question must be asked: what is the extent of those deficiencies and what are the mechanisms that prevent those deficiencies appearing as demands on the local natural resource base?

As in most societies with low levels of per capita income and little in the way of official social security, Bangladesh's unemployment rate in terms of numbers of people wholly unemployed tends to be below 2 per cent of the labour force. The Labour Force Surveys of the 1980s measured unemployment at between 1.0 and 1.8 per cent of the labour force measured from age 10 – 165,000 of the 596,000 people recorded as fully unemployed in the 1989 Labour Force Survey were under 15.

In the 1989 Labour Force Survey, those people found to be wholly unemployed were disproportionately young, urban, and unemployed for more than 25 weeks. The rates of unemployment tended to increase with level of education with dramatically high rates for women with degrees. Eighty per cent of the unemployed expressed specific interest in full-time work. Such unemployment is consistent with a job search pattern in which young people, with their consumption desires met by their families, are willing and able to tolerate a significant period of unemployment before finding employment of the type originally desired or accepting employment below original aspirations.

Over 60 per cent of the unemployed expressed interest in any kind of work for earnings. If it is assumed that these people would be willing to be geographically mobile as well as occupationally mobile, then there appeared to be a pool of about 400,000 people in Bangladesh in 1989 immediately willing and available to meet any emerging bottlenecks on the demand side of the labour market providing there was sufficient flexibility among employers in providing training and adopting non-discriminatory recruitment procedures. Generally, the aspirations of these unemployed people mean they are unlikely to move aggressively into local natural resource intensive activities.

On the fringes of this relatively clear central pool of open unemployment, there are more opaque areas from which labour time could be made available for additional economic activity with varying degrees of flexibility under changed institutional arrangements. The labour force surveys are virtually silent on the dimensions of this availability. The 1989 Survey defined underemployment in terms only of working less than 40 hours in the reference week and not surprisingly found the vast majority of respondents citing household work and education as reasons for not working more hours. Under 200,000 people were estimated as underemployed due to seasonal factors or full-time work not being available.

These findings need to be reconciled with local-level studies in rural areas, which suggest significant seasonal lack of local employment opportunities even if there does appear to be heavy employment in agricultural peak periods (see Rahman, 1986; Rahman and Islam, 1988). The 1989 Labour Force Survey data on hours of work in reference week by occupation are consistent with full employment in agricultural peak seasons, suggesting men worked around 50 hours a week and women around 45 hours a week in the major cropping activities at peak times. The hours of work for most other agricultural and non-agricultural activities also suggest peaks in which men and women are temporarily fully employed.

The high proportions of men to women in the metropolitan centres recorded in the 1991 Population Census (with gender ratios of 111:132, female to male) and micro-study observation of rural–rural and rural–urban movements (Muqtada and Alam, 1986; Quasem, 1992) do indicate that households frequently divide and men migrate to take advantage of peaks in activity patterns, weakening any segmentation between urban and rural labour markets.

Local level evidence suggests significant flexibility with many people changing sectors, occupations and locations in response to changing opportunities, both seasonally and structurally. Such flexibility suggests the labour market is not generally segmented (though Rahman, 1986, makes a case for segmentation working against rural women) and that labour shortages at peak periods are not due to barriers to entry or high entry costs but due to physical/technical conditions. If this is the case, then having available time without economic activity could be an outcome compatible with competitive forces in the labour market operating within constraints set by inflexibilities in the production system.

In terms of aggregate labour time, a synthetic estimate of unutilized labour time in 1989 can be made on the following basis:

- assume the 27.2 million men aged over 15 years in the labour force would be fully employed at an average economically active week of 40 hours – a total of 56,576 million hours in 1989;
- assume the 19.3 million women aged over 15 years in the labour force would be fully employed at an average economically active week of 20 hours (as women on average spend 20 hours a week more than men in

'domestic' work according to the 1989 Labour Force Survey) – a total of 20,072 million hours in the year 1989, giving a combined total of 76,648 million hours;
- 26.9 million of these economically active men were estimated to being actually economically active on average for 30 hours a week and 19.1 million of the women for 13 hours a week — a combined total of 54,876 million hours for 1989.

On this basis, 21,772 million hours were available for economic activity but not utilized in Bangladesh in 1989 (a time unemployment rate of 28.4 per cent). Of this total, only 1080 million hours can be accounted for by wholly unemployed men and women willing to work to a full 40 hours a week permanently in the Labour Force Survey. The remainder seems to be largely accounted for through a highly complex pattern of gaps between periods of intense activities, despite the efforts of people to keep these spaces to a minimum.

Micro-studies on underemployment estimated underemployment at 30 per cent to 40 per cent in the 1970s (Rahman, 1993) and studies in the 1980s found rates (estimated on days of work) of 19 per cent (Hossain, 1988), 25 per cent (Rahman and Islam, 1988) and 16 per cent to 23 per cent (Rahman, 1993). Estimates of work only being available for between 185 days (115 in crop production, 70 in allied activities) and 200 days (handlooms) a year are made in a World Bank report on rural employment (World Bank, 1983) in arriving at the conclusion that, while underemployment in Bangladesh cannot be tackled as if it were open unemployment, quantitatively, it could be considered to be equivalent to roughly one-third of the agricultural labour force being unemployed. The calculation here in terms of hours rather than days of work and using an imposed standard in terms of number of hours constituting full employment over 50 weeks of the year may involve an upward bias but represents a step towards reconciling Labour Force Survey data with micro-studies data.

It is reasonable to conclude there is extensive time underemployment of people in Bangladesh, but it is important to recognize that tapping into this resource requires a subtle understanding of how people already move between activities in order to generate income. It would certainly be inaccurate to assume that large numbers of people are idle or available for casual work on an insecure basis if that threatens overall survival strategies dependent on being available for specific labour peaks.

The issue of underemployment in terms of rates of earnings failing to meet the aspirations of a person in terms of consumption opportunities and/or job satisfaction is even more complex. The previously mentioned micro-studies of movements between self- and wage-employment in agriculture and between non-agricultural, informal sector activities and food-for-work public works do suggest active choices between being made on the basis of relatively small differences in rates of reward. People move towards higher rates of earnings and in that sense there is a healthy dissatisfaction with the generally low rates prevailing in Bangladesh.

On the other hand, it is widely asserted in Bangladesh, as in wider south Asia, that there is a preference towards non-manual, clerical occupations which leaves places on broadly defined artisan training programmes vacant if the entrance requirement is set at ten years' schooling. This suggests less healthy aspirations in the sense of restricting the pool of educated people willing to acquire technical skills.

A leading group of candidates for time, productivity and aspirations underemployment are those employed as 'unpaid family workers', especially outside agriculture. The labour force surveys suggest that unpaid family workers are time underemployed on average with men working average weeks of about 16 hours and women about 10 hours. But more sensitive investigation is needed to assess how far these people are underemployed, not only in terms of time, but also in terms of productivity and aspirations – and the degree to which those aspirations are realistic in the Bangladesh context.

In summary, it is possible to argue that there was a time unemployment rate of 28.4 per cent in Bangladesh in 1989. But that resource is not easily accessible as much of this time can be seen as holes of varying sizes in tightly woven survival strategies, which cannot be rationally discarded without guarantees of alternative, secure incomes.

Beyond time unemployment lie the more complex underemployment issues of income and aspirations to which unpaid family workers may be especially subject. The socio-economic complexity of patterns of under-employment and the fragility of livelihood 'portfolios' may be preventing radical shifts in local natural resource use either for or against sustainability. In societies like Bangladesh, the livelihood poor (despite diversified activity 'portfolios' and time unemployment rates of over 20 per cent) cannot afford the risk of radical shifts in processes of surviving and coping – though these processes themselves may be continuously degrading the ecology and/or making it more vulnerable to external shocks.

## Using Labour Force Statistics for Livelihood Projections and the Growing Challenge to Sustainability

Changes in labour use, and hence livelihoods, can be seen as depending on two basic factors. The rate of economic growth in value terms and the sensitivity or elasticity of physical labour with respect to that economic growth. Measurement of elasticity is often controversial and very sensitive to choice of time period. For instance, elasticities can be calculated from aggregate statistics for the whole Bangladesh economy of 1.24 for the period 1980–81 to 1985–86 and 3.28 for the period 1985–86 to 1989–90 (Rashid,

1993). Both figures are unbelievably high by international standards as well as wildly different, mainly reflecting differences in overall definitions of economic activity in the Labour Force Surveys.

Disaggregating into sectors can improve the accuracy of elasticity estimation. The Fourth Five Year Plan (Planning Commission, 1990) had both sectoral growth and employment growth estimates but they were not explicitly combined into employment elasticities. The implied elasticities can be calculated from the two tables in the Plan document. These elasticities were as follows:

| | |
|---|---|
| Agriculture | 0.48 |
| Industry | 0.76 |
| Power, gas | 0.88 |
| Construction | 1.72 |
| Transport and communication | 1.00 |
| Trade | 1.28 |
| Public sector activity | 0.73 |

Again these elasticities are difficult to accept in terms of international experience. At present, there is no clear guide to the fundamental nature of employment responses to either aggregate or sectoral economic growth. In the absence of acceptable aggregate elasticities, micro-studies can give some guide to the order of magnitude of the four major sector's elasticities, though their representativeness must be in question and therefore the chosen ranges must be robustly wide.

Studies of agriculture suggest that the dominant force for change is the adoption of HYV rice associated with the extension of irrigation on to previously rain-fed land. While there is agreement that this change significantly increases labour use, the predominant view is that the elasticity of increased labour use, relative to increased quantity or value of output, is well below one. The estimates vary from a third to a half the rate of growth of output (World Bank, 1983) to about 0.5 (Taskforces on Bangladesh Development Strategies for the 1990s, 1991, hereafter Taskforces) to 0.6 (Muqtada and Alam, 1986, who also report labour use per hectare increases of 30 per cent with the adoption of HYVs).

A recent study associated with the national Deep Tubewell Project (Mott MacDonald, 1992) shows the potential and problems of employment elasticities associated with improved irrigation. The results for six different sites are summarized in Table 4.13. The results all show employment gains and possible high employment elasticities but with great variability (a phenomenon also found by Rahman and Islam, 1988, and emphasized by Chowdhury, 1990, in his comment on their paper).

**Table 4.13**  The impact of irrigation provision on employment

| Change % | | Small farms | Medium farms | | Large farms | |
|---|---|---|---|---|---|---|
| Gross margin | | 27.8–62.7 | 14.9–57.2 | | −6.9–70.6 | |
| Labour use | | 23.3 | 31.9 | | 24.3 | |
| | | | Six agro-ecological zones | | | |
| | a | b | c | d | e | f |
| Gross margin | 100.7–197.4 | 10.7–85.5 | 2.7–57.5 | 1.3–10.5 | 45.3–61.7 | 2.5–9.5 |
| Labour use | 57.8 | 28.1 | 24.9 | 10.2 | 23.6 | 16.3 |

Source: Mott MacDonald (1992).

Beyond food-grain cultivation, the Taskforces analysis considers elasticities are likely to be considerably higher with changes towards crop diversification and livestock rearing. More widely, agriculture offers many households with small farms an opportunity to create some additional productive activity for themselves at the margin as owner-cultivators or tenants, which will tend to raise the overall employment elasticity (Muqtada, 1986; Taslim, 1990). For the agricultural sector as a whole, in the agronomic and social context of Bangladesh, a range for employment elasticities of 0.6 to 0.9 will be used here.

Estimating a range of elasticity values for the manufacturing sector also has to acknowledge the diversity of the sector. The whole sector is generally more capital-intensive than agriculture (Rahman and Ahamed, 1989), which tends to set a lower ceiling on the whole sector's employment elasticity, especially in Bangladesh where most capital goods are imported. In the 1990s, the tendency towards 'rationalization' of larger scale enterprises could produce negative elasticities for some sub-sectors with rising output being associated with falling employment. Across the whole sector, exposure to global competition will tend to encourage increasing productivity rather than increasing employment. Therefore, a range below that of agriculture is appropriate and 0.4 to 0.6 is used here.

The services sector is again very diversified with a strong regular employee section alongside self-employed and unpaid family workers. As in large-scale manufacturing, there will be pressure on the public civil service element of the services sector to increase productivity while shedding jobs. On the other hand, the sector will continue to be a centre of job self-creation. It is considered that this mixture could lead to elasticities as low as 0.5 and as high as 0.7.

The 'other activities' sector is dominated by construction and transport, both of which have labour-intensive sub-sectors. While parts of the sector, such as the railways, are under pressure to 'rationalize' and reduce staffing (Farid, 1993), the construction sector has a history of being relatively labour-intensive (Rahman and Ahamed, 1989) and the ubiquitous bicycle rickshaw is also a feature of this sector. Therefore, a high value of 0.9 is used here with a low value of 0.5.

The labour force in terms of numbers of people will continue to grow at between 2 and 3 per cent per annum in the 1990s. With sectoral elasticities clustered around a value a little over 0.5, a GDP growth rate of between 4 and 6 per cent per annum is needed merely to absorb the numbers of people coming into the labour force. And even this absorption, if achieved, would not guarantee the number of hours of work or sufficient rate of earnings to prevent increasing numbers of households falling into absolute poverty.

Although the Bangladesh economy has not even been growing at 4 per cent per annum on average in the 1980s, the World Bank (World Bank, 1993) and the Taskforces have made projections of the Bangladesh economy growing at a rate of around an average of 5 per cent per annum between 1990 and 2000. The World Bank envisages this increased growth as an 'acceleration' induced by increased international private investment as a result of a greater commitment to liberalization. The Taskforces advocate greater government intervention and infrastructure construction for rural development, but also see a place for labour-intensive exporting. But regardless of the mix of private and public, national and international sourcing for investment, the growth rates and aggregated sectoral patterns of growth appear similar in both projections.

The World Bank sectoral economic growth paths are used here as high estimates. But it is important to note that the World Bank has significant influence on the development strategy of Bangladesh, and all countries in similar substainability stressed situations, and the use of such optimistic growth scenarios tends to encourage complacency about the possibility of moving the stress towards global natural resources.

## Simulating Labour Use and Livelihoods Looking Towards 2000

Table 4.14 summarizes the elasticity and growth assumptions used to generate the low and high estimates of labour use shown in Table 4.15. The simulation results are reported for 1995 and 2000. The 1995 situations are relatively close as the 'accelerated' path is coming from a lower growth base than the 'normal' path. By 2000, the 'accelerated' simulation involves considerably greater labour use. In both cases, the relatively slow growth rate and short hours in agriculture mean the sector moves significantly below 50 per cent of total labour use.

The simulation results are compared with the Taskforces employment projections for 1999–2000 in Table 4.16, which were derived from more detailed, if somewhat non-systematic, considerations of physical and demand-side factors in each major sector. The simulation results are similar to those of the Taskforces for agriculture, but labour use in the industrial

**Table 4.14**  Sectoral output growth rates (% per annum) and sectoral output growth elasticities of employment

| Years | Sector | | | |
|---|---|---|---|---|
| | *Agriculture* % | *Manufacturing* % | *Services* % | *Other* % |
| 1989–92 | 1.9–2.3 | 6.0–4.0 | 5.2–3.5 | 3.9–7.8 |
| 1992–96 | 1.9–2.6 | 6.0–6.6 | 5.2–5.0 | 3.9–8.0 |
| 1996–2000 | 1.9–3.0 | 6.0–10.2 | 5.3–7.3 | 3.9–8.0 |
| Elasticities | 0.6–0.9 | 0.4–0.6 | 0.5–0.7 | 0.5–0.9 |

*Note*: 'Normal' growth rates refer to mean growth rates 1985–91. 'Accelerated' growth rates are from World Bank (1993).
*Sources*: World Bank (1993), Mott MacDonald (1992), Khan and Chowdhury (1986), World Bank (1983), Rahman and Islam (1988) and Report of the Task Forces on Bangladesh Development Strategies for the 1990s (1991).

**Table 4.15**  Labour use estimates in millions of person hours per year, 1989–2000

| Year | Sector | | | | |
|---|---|---|---|---|---|
| | *Agriculture* | *Manufacturing* | *Services* | *Other* | *Total* |
| Low employment elasticities and 'normal' economic growth | | | | | |
| 1989 | 29375 | 8826 | 13380 | 4972 | 56553 |
| 1995 | 31482 | 10304 | 15758 | 5613 | 63157 |
| 2000 | 33429 | 11997 | 18374 | 6272 | 70072 |
| High employment elasticities and 'accelerated' economic growth | | | | | |
| 1989 | 29375 | 8826 | 13380 | 4972 | 56553 |
| 1995 | 33482 | 9852 | 15952 | 7508 | 66794 |
| 2000 | 38216 | 12989 | 20153 | 10629 | 81987 |

*Sources*: Calculated using data from 1989 Labour Force Survey, World Bank (1993), and Report of the Task Forces on Bangladesh Development Strategies for the 1990s (1991).

and manufacturing sector is larger in the Taskforces model, and the services sector is smaller. The higher figure for manufacturing depends upon seeing strong manufacturing employment growth in the labour force surveys of the mid-1980s as replicable over the whole of the 1990s, with 15 per cent per annum employment growth in new leading export sectors, such as garments. There appears to be no consideration of the impact of retrenchment, in addition to continuing stagnation in the large-scale manufacturing sector. The services sector result is less intelligible as the Taskforces see the sector as the sector of last resort but still allow unemployment to increase substantially in the 'business as usual', relatively low growth, case.

The results of bringing the labour force and labour use simulations together suggest a possible balance in the combination of low labour force and high labour use. Time unemployment only increases slightly in 1995 on the 1989 proportion and the economy moves into significant labour shortage

**Table 4.16** Comparison of high labour use and low labour use simulation results with Taskforces' two scenarios results (in millions of person years, by the year 2000)

| | | Taskforces | | |
|---|---|---|---|---|
| | Low labour use | 'Business as usual' | 'Optimistic' | High labour use |
| Agriculture | 16.99 | 17.48 | 19.80 | 19.11 |
| Industry/manufacturing | 5.73 | 6.51 | 7.02 | 6.49 |
| Services | 8.87 | 7.30 | 8.42 | 10.08 |
| Transport/construction/other | 3.07 | 3.62 | 4.26 | 5.31 |
| Total | 34.66 | 34.91 | 39.50 | 40.99 |

*Source*: Taskforces on Bangladesh Development Strategies for the 1990s (1991).

in 2000. But the nature of this 'balance' needs examination. The low labour force figure is an outcome of accepting relatively low hours of work as normal and dampening the entry of women into the labour force. The positive side is that more young people are in full-time education but they will emerge from education into a society with the low productivity associated with high employment elasticities.

The worst case is one in which time unemployment grows to 40 per cent of the full-time employment equivalent. Given the low employment elasticities in this scenario, there may be productivity gains for those whose labour time is actually utilized. If people's needs for livelihoods are growing to this level and yet being frustrated with growing affluence among profit receivers, given increasing competition for work will place a ceiling on real wage rates, then the outcome moves beyond economic forecasting and enters the field of politics.

The mean position can be categorized as another turn of a screw already familiar to many people in Bangladesh. The change from 17 per cent time unemployment to 24 per cent over a decade will exert a further squeeze on many very poor people, but probably without causing widespread famine in the absence of extreme weather events. But not all will be squeezed, as there is room within this mean position for some sub-sectors to grow and raise productivity by operating on lower employment elasticities. Inequality in terms of consumption opportunities may increase.

There is a general limited ability to forecast labour use and livelihood patterns, except within wide ranges which run from almost acceptable additional strain to political incomprehensibility. But a general tendency towards increasing pressure on livelihoods in Bangladesh is likely to be echoed on a much wider scale in Asia, Africa and Latin America. Governments under structural adjustment pressures are in no position to improve these forecasts or take imaginative steps if they understood more, especially if World Bank advice is based on extremely optimistic elasticities and growth rates. The implications of the Bangladesh forecasts for local ecological sustainability in Bangladesh and all similar situations cannot be positive, but the degree of threat will depend upon the aggregation of local human responses to growing pressures.

## People's Responses to Growing Imbalance

While there is a small 'window of opportunity' for the employment situation in Bangladesh in terms of proportion of unemployed time to improve slightly in the 1990s, there are strong forces pushing towards deterioration. This 'window' depends upon the population growth trend suggested by the 1981 and 1991 Population Censuses being accurate (though the impact of unexpectedly low population growth will not really be felt until after 2000), economic growth accelerating towards 7 per cent per annum, children aged 10 to 14 being out of the labour market, and a great increase in people aged 15 to 19 in education. If these events occur then the employment situation could be at its worst in the mid-1990s and slightly improving by the year 2000.

Outside this 'window', people will continue to endeavour to improve their chances of survival (Herbon, 1992) producing feedbacks in the labour market which will operate to moderate the impact of an increase in proportion of unemployed time, but generally merely serving to produce pressure elsewhere. These responses can be categorized under five headings:

1. *Work-sharing*　The high prevalence of unpaid family labour gives opportunities for work-sharing which gives exchange entitlements to some consumption. This will not reduce the amount of time unemployment but will mitigate its impact, pushing the problem towards income underemployment and chronic poverty, though providing exchange entitlements against starvation − an ecological sustainability neutral response.
2. *Involution*　Associated with work sharing may come small improvements in labour techniques (which can be characterized as involutionary or Boserupian developments) which actually use significantly more labour for small gains in overall production pushing the problem towards productivity underemployment. There is a considerable literature on choice of technology and institution building which utilizes this willingness to innovate and shows how this willingness can be frustrated or encouraged (World Bank, 1983; ILO-ARTEP, 1985; Scott and Carr, 1985). A sustainability complex response though tending to ecological degradation.
3. *Discouraged withdrawal*　Some people will declare themselves unavailable for economic activity in the face of widespread time unemployment pushing the problem towards underemployment in terms of aspirations. In the circumstances of Bangladesh, as in much of the world, discouraged

withdrawal is likely to fall heavily on women. Chaudhuri (1991) brings out the importance of labour demand in terms of women participating in the labour force and in a joint publication discusses a development approach emphasizing women's participation (Chaudhuri and Islam, 1991) – an ecological sustainability neutral response.

4. *Asset selling*  Some people may be able to raise resources by selling assets and thus afford to withdraw from the deteriorating labour market but this is likely only to postpone declarations of time underemployment, especially in the case of distress sales, and produce further concentration in wealth holding. Probably an ecological sustainability undermining response, if profitability increasingly becomes the driving motivation in resource use.

5. *Migration*  An optimistic estimate could envisage two billion working hours being transferred to the Gulf and other labour migration-friendly economies out of the 24 billion unutilized in Bangladesh on the mean assumptions in the year 2000. But there is a view among those close to the Gulf migration flows that the effective rates of earnings for skilled people were equalizing between the Gulf and Bangladesh and real wage rates for the less skilled were falling. The international competition for work in the Gulf, especially between people from south Asian countries may be lowering real rates of reward for labour in the Gulf towards an international equilibrium. People from Bangladesh who have the basic language and other skills required in the global temporary labour market may not choose to migrate when relative rewards for migration are falling, squeezing out those for whom international migration is not an option. This would leave much of the pressure of the livelihood search being expressed through the 'normal' channels of internal migration and attempted movement towards neighbouring economies. An ecological sustainability complex response, especially if impact on Bangladesh urban ecologies is considered.

Overall, there are no responses moving towards environmental improvement. Those responses which are neutral are associated with a decline in numbers or levels of economic livelihoods, with uncertain political implications. The pressure on livelihoods is unlikely to encourage a demographic transition and will become pressure on vulnerable rural and urban ecologies in Bangladesh. The present global order provides little room for manoeuvre to shift pressure for livelihoods on to the wider global economy in terms of external 'natural' resources for livelihoods in Bangladesh or people of Bangladesh moving to external 'natural' resources. This situation is likely to be similar for many other societies.

## Implications for the Wider Debate on Sustainability

There are many situations that are ecologically, demographically and economic livelihood challenged. Society-wide livelihood improvements are crucial to relieving ecological pressure and encouraging lower population growth. Yet, the data on livelihoods is very weak in conceptualization and collection practice. Reform of international conventions on labour force surveys and related sets of statistics is long overdue and special consideration in such a reform needs to be given to relevance to the wider sustainability debate in situations like Bangladesh.

However, manipulation of aggregate data and combination with micro-studies can help improve understanding of pressures on economic livelihoods. Such insights from Bangladesh suggest continuing, though complex, pressure on sustainability through the search for livelihoods at bare subsistence levels in an unpromising policy environment. The pressure on local natural resource bases by people seeking subsistence will not decrease and significant numbers of people have a sufficient stake in agriculture as the locally most natural resource intensive sector could increase significantly as pressures on livelihoods grow.

International migration, as much as international investment, is a major sustainability issue if pressures on local ecologies in ecologically, demographically and livelihood stressed societies are to be dispersed to more resilient areas of the wider global ecology.

# References

Ahmad, A. and Quasem, M.A. (1991) *Child Labour in Bangladesh*. Discussion Paper, Bangladesh Institute of Development Studies.

Ahmad, M. (1993) Public enterprise reforms, employment and productivity. Paper presented to the National Tripartite Workshop on Social Dimensions of Economic Reforms in Bangladesh, sponsored by ILO-ARTEP.

Ahmed, M.U. and Mondal, A.H. (1993) Structural Adjustment, labour market reforms, industrial relations and productivity in Bangladesh. Paper presented to the National Tripartite Workshop on Social Dimensions of Economic Reforms in Bangladesh, sponsored by ILO-ARTEP.

Bakht, Z. (1993) Economic reforms, industrial strategy and employment growth in Bangladesh. Paper presented to the National Tripartite Workshop on Social Dimensions of Economic Reforms in Bangladesh, sponsored by ILO-ARTEP.

Bangladesh Bureau of Statistics (1986) *Final Report on Labour Force Survey 1983–84*. Government of Bangladesh.

Bangladesh Bureau of Statistics (1988) *Census of Non-Farm Economic Activities and Disabled Persons 1986*. Government of Bangladesh.

Bangladesh Bureau of Statistics (1991) *Report of Bangladesh Handloom Census 1990*. Government of Bangladesh.

Bangladesh Bureau of Statistics (1991) *Preliminary Report: Population Census 1991*. Government of Bangladesh.

Bangladesh Bureau of Statistics (1991) *Report on Bangladesh Census of Manufacturing Industries 1987–88*. Government of Bangladesh.

Bangladesh Bureau of Statistics (1992) *Report on Labour Force Survey 1989*. Government of Bangladesh.

Bangladesh Bureau of Statistics (1992) *Report on Integrated Annual Survey of Non-Farm Economic Activities 1989–90*. Government of Bangladesh.

Bangladesh Household Survey Capability Programme (1991) *Proceedings of the Workshop on Dissemination of Current Statistics*. Bangladesh Bureau of Statistics.

Barnett, A.S. (1977) A note on the man–land relationship in Papua New Guinea. *Oceania*, 48(2), 141–5.

Bilsborrow, R.E. (1987) Population pressures and agricultural development in developing countries: a conceptual framework and recent evidence. *World Development*, 15(2), 183–203.

Cameron, J. and Irfan, M. (1991) *Enabling People to Help Themselves*. ILO-ARTEP.

Chaudhuri, S. (1991) Participation of rural women in the labour force: levels and determinants. *Bangladesh Development Studies*, 19(4).

Chaudhuri, S. and Islam, L. (1991) *Towards Integrating Women in MSFSCIP, GOB-IFAZ-GTZ Marginal and Small Farm Systems Crop Intensification Project*.

Chowdhury, N. (1990) Labour use in rural Bangladesh – an empirical analysis: a comment. *Bangladesh Development Studies*, 18(2).

Farid, S.M. (1993) Economic reforms, poverty and social safety nets. Paper presented to the National Tripartite Workshop on Social Dimensions of Economic Reforms in Bangladesh, sponsored by ILO-ARTEP.

Farooq, C.M. and Ofosu, Y. (1991) *Population, Labour Force and Employment: Concepts, Trends and Policy Issues*. ILO World Employment Programme Paper No. 9.

Ghimire, K. (1992) *Forest or Farm: The Politics of Poverty and Land Hunger in Nepal*. Delhi: Oxford University Press.

Grzybowski, C. (ed.) (1989) *Fight for Forest: Chico Mendes in His Own Words*. London: Latin American Bureau.

Guha, R. (1989) *The Unquiet Woods: Ecological Change and Peasant Resistance in the Himalayas*. Delhi: Oxford University Press.

Herbon, D. (ed.) (1992) *Agrarian Reproduction in Bangladesh*. Germany: University of Gottingen.

Hossain, M. (1988) *Nature and Impact of Green Revolution in Bangladesh*. Research Report 67, IFPRI-BIDS.

Hossain, M.S., Rahman, M.H. and Islam, M.N. (1991) Women in labour force: a new dimension. In *Proceedings of the Workshop on Dissemination of Current Statistics*. Bangladesh Bureau of Statistics.

Hunting Technical Services Limited (1992) *Project Impact Evaluation of Chalan Beel Polder–D. Bangladesh Flood Action Plan FAP 12, FCD/1 Agricultural Study*. Government of Bangladesh.

ILO-ARTEP (1981) *Manpower Planning in Bangladesh: Projections, Policies and Planning with Special Reference to the Second Five Year Plan*. Bangladesh Planning Commission.

ILO-ARTEP (1985) *Employment Expansion through Rural Industrialization in Bangladesh: Potentials, Problems and Policy Issues*. Report to the Bangladesh Planning Commission.

ILO-ARTEP (1987) *Planning, Monitoring and Implementation of an Employment Strategy in Bangladesh*. Bangladesh Planning Commission.

Islam, R. and Muqtada, M. (ed.) (1986) *Bangladesh: Selected Issues in Employment and Development*. Delhi: ILO-ARTEP.

Jagannathan, N.V. (1989) Poverty, public policies and the environment. World Bank Environment Working Paper No. 24.

Khan, A.R. (1984) Real wages of agricultural workers in Bangladesh. In A.R. Khan and E. Lee (eds), *Poverty in Rural Asia*. ILO-ARTEP.

Khan, M. and Chowdhury, N. (1986) Trade, industrialization and employment. In R. Islam and M. Muqtada (eds), *Bangladesh: Selected Issues in Employment and Development*. ILO-ARTEP.

Mahmud, W. (1989) The impact of overseas labour migration on the Bangladesh economy: a macro-economic perspective. In R. Amjad (ed.), *To the Gulf and Back*. ILO-ARTEP.

Ministry of Establishment (1991) *Statistics of Civil Officers and Staff of the Government of the People's Republic of Bangladesh 1991*. Government of Bangladesh.

Mott MacDonald (1992) *Annual Monitoring Survey 1991, Deep Tubewell II Project*. Government of Bangladesh.

Muqtada, M. and Alam, M.M. (1986) Hired labour and rural labour market in Bangladesh. In S. Hirashima and M. Muqtada (eds), *Hired Labour and Rural Labour Markets in Asia*. Delhi: ILO-ARTEP.

Planning Commission (1990) *The Fourth Five Year Plan 1990–95*. Government of Bangladesh.

Quasem, M.A. (1992) Non-traded inputs and share-cropping. *Bangladesh Development Studies*, 20(2), 15–30.

Rahman, A. and Islam. R. (1988) Labour use in rural Bangladesh – an empirical analysis. *Bangladesh Development Studies*, 16(4), 33–46.

Rahman, R.I. (1986) *The Wage Employment Market for Rural Women in Bangladesh*. Dhaka: Bangladesh Institute of Development Studies.

Rahman, R.I. (1993) Employment, unemployment and poverty in the Bangladesh economy. Paper presented to National Workshop on Challenges of Rural Poverty by the Year 2010 organized by Rural Social Science Network/Winrock International/ Bangladesh Agricultural Research Council.

Rahman, R.I. and Ahamed, C.S. (1989) *A Study on the Impact of Public Investment on Output and Employment in Bangladesh, A Report to the Bangladesh Planning Commission*.

Rashid, M.A. (1993) Bangladesh: output and employment effects of macroeconomic reforms in the 1980s. Paper presented to the National Tripartite Workshop on Social Dimensions of Economic Reforms in Bangladesh, sponsored By ILO-ARTEP.

Scott, G.L. and Carr, M. (1985) The impact of technology choice on rural women in Bangladesh: problems and opportunities. World Bank Staff Working Papers No. 731.

Shaw, R.P. (1989) Rapid population growth and environmental degradation: ultimate versus proximate factors. *Environmental Conservation*, 16(3), 11–17.

Skeldon, R. (1992) The relationship between migration and development in the ESCAP region. Selected paper for pre-conference seminar, Fourth Asian and Pacific Population Conference, ESCAP, Bangkok.

*Statistical Yearbook of Bangladesh* (1991), Bangladesh Bureau of Statistics.

Taskforces on Bangladesh Development Strategies for the 1990s (1991) *Policies for Development: Volume One*. Dhaka: University Press.

Taslim, M.A. (1990) The explanations of the inverse size-productivity relation in agriculture: a critical review. *Bangladesh Development Studies*, 18(2).

Tisdell, C. (1988) Sustainable development: differing perspectives of ecologists and economists and relevance to LDCs. *World Development*, 16(3), 373–84.

UNDP (1993) *Human Development in Bangladesh*. Dhaka: UNDP.

UNRISD (1993) *Linkages between Population, Environment and Development: Case Studies from Costa Rica, Pakistan and Uganda*. Geneva: UNRISD.

Vijverberg, W.P.M. (1989) Labour market performance as a determinant of migration. Living Standards Measurement Study Working Paper No. 59. Washington, DC: World Bank.

World Bank (1983) *Bangladesh: Selected Issues in Rural Employment*. Washington, DC: World Bank.

World Bank (1993) *Bangladesh: Implementing Structural Reform*. Washington, DC: World Bank.

# 5

# Sustainable Utilization: A Grand Illusion?

## Katrina Brown

## Introduction

This chapter examines the sustainable utilization of biological resources. These resources have two important characteristics in this context: they are renewable, indeed they are self-renewing, and they are diverse in nature. This second facet, that of biological diversity, adds a dimension to resource use which is little understood but which is hypothesized to be central to human interaction with the natural environment. Sustainable utilization of natural resources is one of the fundamental requirements of sustainable development, yet the concept is a rather 'slippery' one. This chapter demonstrates this complexity through addressing some ecological and socio-economic aspects of renewable natural resource use in protected areas in Nepal. A number of different issues are explored concerning the difficulties in defining a level of sustainable extraction from the perspectives of natural and social sciences. Ecological aspects include the uncertainty in scientific understanding of complex habitat dynamics, particularly the role of disturbance and perturbations; the lack of an historic perspective on past land use; and the impacts of human intervention. From the socio-economic perspective, issues of equity in access to resources and the distribution of their benefits fundamentally determine sustainability. These factors, which contribute to the intangibility of sustainable utilization, have significant implications for development and conservation policy.

The Royal Bardia National Park in Nepal is used to illustrate these issues. Here extraction of grass and reeds takes place annually under a licensing system, but other uses of park resources by local communities are outlawed, and the protected area effectively functions as a restrictive extractive reserve.

The current management strategy has evolved in part to ameliorate relations between local villagers, who depend on grass products for many subsistence needs, and park authorities, and partly because regular cutting and burning of grasses is conventionally viewed as 'good' conservation practice. Is sustainable utilization a useful operating principle or merely a grand illusion? And how does it inform management policy? Definitions of sustainable utilization and its relation to sustainability and sustainable development are first discussed. Problems with sustainable utilization are assessed from the ecological and socio-economic perspectives with reference to management of the protected area, and some conclusions about the utility of sustainable utilization are presented.

## Between Rhetoric and Reality – Definitions of Sustainability and Sustainable Utilization

This chapter illustrates some of the problems of operationalizing the concepts of sustainability and sustainable use with regard to habitat conservation in one of the poorest countries in the world, Nepal. It may be simplistically assumed that there are direct trade-offs between development, in terms of improving human welfare and prosperity, and conserving biological diversity. Alternatively, it might be conceived that sustainable development depends on the sustainable use of natural resources, of which biodiversity is an especially valuable and ecologically critical component. Within the sustainable development paradigm this second approach must guide policy while acknowledging that trade-offs, especially in the short term and perhaps at a local level, may be necessary for the long-term, global good.

It is necessary first to define the terms used and particularly to distinguish and clarify the relationship between sustainable utilization, sustainability and sustainable development. These have been discussed, in Chapter 1, but their use needs to be delineated within this study. That earlier discussion highlighted, among other things, the multi-disciplinary nature of the sustainable development concept, and the importance of both *inter-generational* issues, conventionally regarded as the main focus of environmentalist views, and *intra-generational* equity, often considered as the concern of development specialists (characterized as economists by Jaeger, 1995). It also distinguished between *weak* and *strong* sustainability, and it is worth considering the implications of these different approaches in terms of the conservation of biodiversity.

*Strong sustainability* is characterized by the recognition of critical natural capital that should be preserved at all costs. Such a view would translate, in biodiversity terms, to advocating the preservation of certain species, and at its extreme, the conservation of every species, as we cannot, with any certainty, identify redundant species. This would imply the need to protect large areas of natural and semi-natural habitat, in order to conserve not just the species currently known to science but those (the majority) as yet unidentified. A strict preservationist approach would, therefore, be advocated, with no trade-offs in terms of loss of habitats and species, and taken to its logical extreme, even a decline in populations of current species, which would result in decline in genetic diversity, might be unacceptable.

A *weak sustainability* view on the other hand, would regard technological advances in genetic engineering and biotechnology as powerful tools in protecting options for development, and could enable genetic material to be conserved *ex-situ* while allowing conversion of habitats for more conventionally 'productive' uses. Current conservation policy lies some way between these two extremes, with most countries using both *in-situ* and *ex-situ* approaches. This is reflected in the various global and international institutions governing habitat, species and genetic conservation, and in global scientific assessments of the issue (Heywood and Watson, 1995). For example, the Convention on Biological Diversity advocates *in-situ* backed up by *ex-situ* measures. The current international conservation and development discourse stresses an approach which recognizes an essentially utilitarian rationale − especially in poorer developing countries − for conservation, and a popular slogan is 'use it or lose it'. A premise underlying this approach is that utilization will take place in a sustainable way. However, this concept has a range of different meanings, as our subsequent inquiry will reveal.

The interpretation of sustainable utilization, or sustainable use, which is used here corresponds to that of the Convention on Biological Diversity (United Nations, 1992) which states as its objectives 'the *conservation* of biological diversity, the *sustainable use* of its components and the *fair and equitable sharing of the benefits* arising out of the utilization of genetic resources' (Article 1: emphasis added). Sustainable use is defined by the Convention as 'the use of the components of biological diversity in a way and at a rate that does not lead to the long-term decline of biological diversity, thereby maintaining its potential to meet the needs and aspirations of present and future generations' (Article 2). This definition is clearly different from the concept of sustainable harvesting or sustainable production, and puts sustainable use clearly within the sustainable development paradigm, in borrowing the final phrase almost directly from the Brundtland definition of sustainable development (WCED, 1987). Sustainable harvest or sustainable production are expressions commonly associated with the utilization of wild populations, for example, for some years the concept of maximum sustained yield guided fisheries management, and sustainable yield has been the mainstay of timber harvesting. However, experience shows that these concepts have often been misguided in their application, and the elimination of fishing stocks and destruction of forests world-wide are testament to these practices (Ludwig *et al.*, 1993). The key distinguishing feature of the approach taken in this study to sustainable utilization is that we examine the impact of use not only on that particular species or population, but on other aspects of biodiversity. So, for example, research detailed in this chapter investigates how the harvesting of one product, grass, impacts on sward composition, the habitat and its associated flora and fauna. This extends the definition from the conventionally more narrow interpretation of sustainable harvest or sustained yield.

An underlying assumption of the sustainable development discourse is that for most natural resources, a level of sustainable utilization exists and that it is able to be objectively measured and identified. This perhaps has its roots in the conventional use of the sustainable harvest/yield concept in population biology approaches. The premise is that natural science can define the level, or scale, of sustainable use, and social science can identify the policy tools to enforce it. This assumption has profound implications for the way in which questions of resource management and biodiversity conservation are addressed from both the policy and the research perspectives. Importantly, it negates the socio-economic and political dimensions of sustainability, and puts undue emphasis on natural science to define sustainable use where, in reality, uncertainty of complex processes and dynamics may preclude such definition. The next section of this chapter describes attempts to define sustainable use of grassland products from habitats inside protected areas in southern Nepal, and then goes on to discuss some of the issues highlighted above in that context.

## Use of Biomass Resources in Royal Bardia National Park, Nepal – An Inquiry into Sustainable Utilization

Royal Bardia National Park (RBNP) covers an area of 968 sq km in Bardia and Benke District in Southern Terai in the mid-western region of Nepal. The protected area consists of sal (*Shorea robusta*) forest and areas of grassland, and harbours a number of internationally endangered wildlife species, including the Bengal tiger (*Panthera tigris*), Asian one-horned rhinoceros (*Rhinoceros unicornis*), Hispid hare (*Caprophagus hispidus*) and Bengal florican (*Houbaropis bengalensis*). As a result of its designation as a National Park only very limited exploitation of natural resources is allowed, and no human habitation inside the Park is permitted. This has not always been the case, and in fact part of the area was inhabited and cultivated up until as recently as 1984 when the National Park was extended (see Brown, 1997).

Changing conservation policies and shifts in designation and property rights have meant a gradual extension in the size of the protected area and a decline in rights of access to and use of various resources. Until the 1950s, the forests were protected as property of the Rana rulers, and were then nationalized in 1956. In 1976 the area was declared a Royal Hunting Reserve, although local people had free access to the forest and to graze their livestock. An area of 386 sq km was officially gazetted as the Royal Karnali Wildlife Reserve in 1976, renamed the Royal Bardia Wildlife Reserve in 1982.

In 1984 this area was extended, and it was upgraded to a national park in 1988. Figure 5.1 shows the present extent of the protected area and its location.

### The Ecology and Human Ecology of Royal Bardia National Park (RBNP)

Unlike the mountainous terrain of the more renowned parts of the Kingdom (and as described in Chapter 8) the RBNP covers an area of flat floodplain and low hills, an extension of the Ganges plain. The landscape of the National Park is dominated by the wide, braided Karnali river which forms the western boundary of the Park. Seven major vegetation types have been identified inside the RBNP (Pokharel, 1993); four types of forest, and three different grassland habitats. The *sal (Shorea robusta)* forest covers approximately 70 per cent of the park area, dominating the alluvial floodplain, and is also found on parts of the south-facing slopes of the Churiya Hills to the north. Three types of grassland have been identified: wooded grassland, open areas of grassland known as *phanta*, and floodplain grassland. The first two types consist of tussock forming perennials such as *Imperata cylindrica, Saccharum spontaneum, Erianthus ravennae* and *Vetivera zizanoides*. The wooded grassland is savannah type, often dotted with *simal (Bombax ceiba)*, or silk cotton trees. The *phantas* consist of open areas; the most significant of these are shown in Figure 5.1. These habitats are thought to represent previously disturbed and cultivated sites. The third grassland habitat is found in the floodplain and along the banks of the Geruwa, Babai and Aurai rivers in areas commonly inundated during the monsoon. These areas are characterized by tall grasses including *Saccharum spontaneum, Saccharum bengalense* and *Phragmites karka*. The combination of these different habitats; the patches of forest, grassland and floodplain, provide the cover for the special range of floral and faunal species which has defined the area as being of supreme importance for biodiversity conservation. They also mean that in a country of high human population, where much of the land consists of the steep slopes and thin soils of the mountains and hills, areas such as the RBNP are among the most highly productive in the Kingdom.

Relatively little documentary evidence exists detailing the human use of the area prior to its designation as a National Park. A range of different ethnic and caste groups now inhabit the Terai and this has changed considerably over time. The oldest ethnic group are the Tharu, believed to have lived in the Terai for more than 600 years (Cox, 1990) and considered to be the indigenous people of the region. Migration and land colonization occurred to a minor extent from the second half of the nineteenth century, but since 1960 land shortages in the uplands and a malaria-eradication programme led to a rapid expansion in the human population of the area. By 1990 more than 50 per cent of Nepal's population resided in the Terai. Land use and cultivation has intensified, and in some cases pressures on the natural

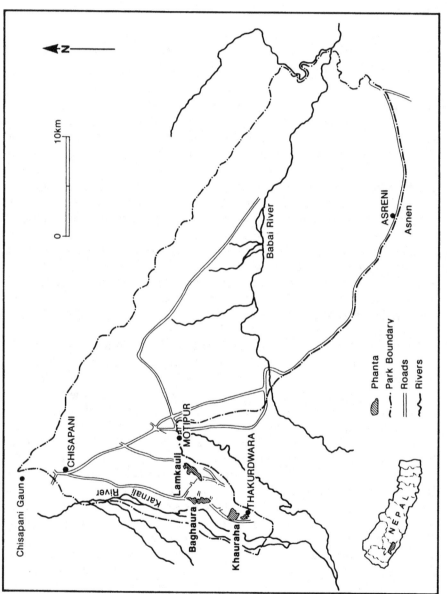

**Figure 5.1** Royal Bardia National Park

resources of protected areas and the conflicts between land uses for conservation and production have increased. A number of studies highlight so-called Park–People conflicts in RBNP, as well as in the other protected areas of the Terai, such as the Royal Chitwan National Park and Kosi Tappu National Reserve (examples include Mishra, 1984; Sharma, 1990; Heinen 1993; Nepal and Weber, 1993).

Most of the discussion presented here focuses on the grassland habitats and the use of grass from the *phantas*. Pokharel (1993) describes the history of the *phantas* as being quite obscure. Dinerstein (1979) reported that Baghaura and Lamkauli *phantas* were under cultivation prior to 1975. Pokharel states that a number of people used to cultivate the *phantas* and are still residing outside the park, though very close to it. One of these informants is recorded by Pokharel (1993, p. 13):

> According to Gopi, in 1965 when he was one year old, his father and friends came down from Surkhet in search of cultivable land. Obtaining land at that time was no problem. They found Baghaura a very suitable open place to live and cultivate. Later they settled there with 15 different families from Surkhet. They were the first inhabitants of Baghaura. Cultivation of Lamkauli could have taken place much later than Baghaura, according to Gopi. He did not know if Khauraha was cultivated before. Baghaura could have been a small open and flat grassland in 1965, which was expanded according to the need of new inhabitants by peripheral deforestation in the jungle.

Thus, such simple trade-offs as human utilization or preserved biodiversity may in fact be irrelevant. In the case study area the preservation of what is considered to be an endangered habitat may only have been possible through past human habitation. As discussed below, for the case study area, the present conservation of the habitat may be dependent on active human intervention and management.

## Utilization of Grasses and Habitat Management

Grass cutting has been a regular activity in Bardia, but it is difficult to trace when this began. In RBNP the *phantas* were cultivated and grazed between 1965 and 1975. Records from the RBNP show authorized grass cutting since 1983, six years before the National Park was created. Livestock grazing in the *phantas* and other areas prior to 1975 was apparently very common. After 1976 the area was fenced and livestock grazing prohibited. Fire has also been used as a management tool, and in the past, uncontrolled burning in the park was described. Fire is generally set at the end of the dry season when grass cutting is completed; in RBNP this is mainly carried out by park authorities. To what extent maintenance of the sward requires cutting and burning and, therefore, the necessity of human intervention to maintain the patchwork of habitats is relatively unknown. It can be hypothesized that grazing by domestic and wild animals, and especially the destructive browsing of elephants, was instrumental in maintaining grassland in the past when large herds were prevalent. The extent to which annual cutting and human-set fires recreate or mimic these natural processes can only be postulated, and whether the resulting grassland communities resemble those present in the past is uncertain (see Peet, 1994).

A number of different grass species are utilized by people from the RBNP. The three major products extracted are thatch grass, building materials and rope. Table 5.1 shows the most important grass species harvested from RBNP, and their main uses. *Khar* is collected primarily from the wooded savanna areas and the *phantas, kharai* from the floodplains, and *buncas* from the foothills. Much of the analysis presented in this chapter concerns the collection and use of thatch or *khar*.

In response to the perceived tensions caused by designation of the protected area, and by way of compensation for loss of rights to various resources inside the protected area, a system which allowed the collection of particular biomass resources by people living in local villages has developed. Such a system is in evidence in each of the protected areas in the Terai. Authorized grass cutting by local villagers began in the RBNP in 1983. Initially the permit system was such that park authorities sold individual licences to cut grass for one rupee per season, a sum which went some way to cover administrative costs and effectively acted as a means of keeping track of the numbers of people entering the park. Each permit allows one person to enter the protected area daily and cut and carry as much grass as possible. Until 1994–95 the cutting period was 15 days, but it was then reduced to 10 days. This period occurs towards the end of the dry season in late December

**Table 5.1**   Grasses collected from Royal Bardia National Park

| Grass species | Local name | Uses and names |
|---|---|---|
| Narenga porphorycoma | Khadai or kharai | Cane, if burned, used for building etc. (*sakhata*)<br>Cane, not burned, whole used for grain silo (*phank*)<br>Cane, top part only (*silicili*) |
| Saccharum bengalense | narkat | Cane for walls and ceiling (*chatati*)<br>Cane for baskets (*kenari*) |
| Phragmites kharka | | Cane for lamp-stand for Diwali festival |
| Tifa augustifolia/ Tifa elephantina | pat or pater | Mats, fans, mattresses, howdahs |
| Imperata cylindrica | khar | Thatch, brooms; flowerhead used for ceremonial lamp (*kuwar bati*) |
| Eulaliopsis binata | buncas, sabai, babiyo | Rope, used for beds, chairs, bullock carts, tying thatch; paper |
| Saccharum spontaneum | khans | Reeds and canes for walls, bed, thatch<br>Fodder |

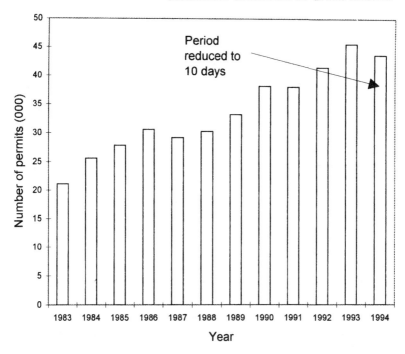

**Figure 5.2** Grass-cutting permits sold in Royal Bardia National Park (*Source:* Royal Bardia National Park)

or early January. Figure 5.2 shows RBNP records of the number of permits sold annually since 1983. This shows a steady increase in numbers, from 21,000 to 45,500, more than doubling in numbers, and faster than the population increase. 1994 shows the first drop in numbers, when 43,000 permits were sold. The price of one permit has risen to 12 rupees (£1 = 75NR in 1994), which is about one quarter of the official daily agricultural wage (40NR).

There are a number of different dimensions to sustainable utilization when the use of these resources is examined. One aspect of the sustainability of these practices, depends on how the demand for the grass by local communities compares with the supply of biomass inside the RBNP. There is an assumption by conservationists that over-exploitation, caused by increased numbers of cutters entering the park, is leading to changes in the composition of the grassland, and there is some anecdotal evidence of a decline in the quality of the thatch grass, perhaps caused by a change in the species mix. The change in quality may be a result of changes in the species mix, in the growth habit or quality of the plants themselves, or because cutters are utilizing more marginal areas of grassland. However, cutting and/ or burning is required to discourage the colonization by taller grass species, shrubs and small trees, and possibly, therefore, slow the succession to *sal*

**Table 5.2**   Estimates of biomass production in five southern *phantas* in RBNP

|  | Area (ha) | Production (t/h)* | Yield (t/ha) | No. of bundles available |
|---|---|---|---|---|
| Upper Baghaura | 41.6 | 13.98 | 8.5 | 140673 |
| Lower Baghaura | 58.7 | 8.06 | 4.9 | 114442 |
| Upper Khauraha | 94.7 | 11 | 6.7 | 251973 |
| Lower Khauraha | 34.5 | 8.57 | 5.2 | 71517 |
| Lamkauli | 111.3 | 9.74 | 5.9 | 262220 |
| Total bundles |  |  |  | 840825 |

*Note:* *Production is net primary production.

forest. There are also likely to be other ecological impacts of the regular removal of such large quantities of biomass which will depend in part on local environmental conditions, including for example the removal of nutrients.

Using the observations and measurements from a survey carried out during December 1994 and January 1995, and data from Pokharel's study (1993) on the area of the *phantas*, the total amount of thatch grass available from the five southern *phantas* (Upper and Lower Baghaura, Upper and Lower Khauraha, and Lamkauli) is estimated and shown in Table 5.2. These calculations indicate that a total of 841,000 bundles of *khar* were available from the five southern *phantas* in RBNP in January 1995. Observations of the grass collection, based on a sample of cutters entering and leaving the Park at Thakadwara Gate in the south-west, indicate that the possible total harvest of *khar* may be in the region of 1,050,000 bundles, or approximately 2650 tonnes. This figure is larger than the estimates for the *phantas* alone, as small patches of grassland occur throughout the RBNP and will be utilized by local people.

How do these estimates of harvest relate to the predicted demand? According to village surveys, many households have at least one thatched roof, and in response to household interviews, a typical roof might require 250 bundles of *khar* for thatching every 2 to 3 years. Given the estimates of the yield, this implies that only 56 bundles are available per household in the Buffer Zone surrounding the National Park each year, or enough to thatch one roof per household every 4 to 5 years. These figures indicate a shortfall in thatch available, which is confirmed to a certain extent by the interviews and information obtained from key informants. It may also go some way to explain the drop in the number of permits sold. A perception of scarcity of the grass means that people are not willing to invest the permit fee when they are not sure of collecting enough grass for their needs.

## Socio-economic Aspects of Grass Utilization

As has been highlighted by other contributions to this volume, sustainable development is a multi-disciplinary phenomenon, requiring not only an understanding of the ecological aspects of resource use, but also the socio-economic and political dimensions. Social and economic sustainability are of critical importance if sustainable development is to be achieved, especially if a strong sustainability approach is adopted, and if the inter- and intra-generational criteria of sustainability are to be met. The Convention on Biological Diversity states in Article 1 that its objectives are not only the conservation and sustainable use of biodiversity, but also the 'fair and equitable sharing of the benefits arising from the utilization of genetic resources' (United Nations, 1992). Hand in hand with attempts to understand the ecological parameters of sustainable utilization then, comes the need to consider social, economic and political aspects of the use of biological resources.

Some of the distributional aspects of utilization of grass products from inside the protected area were investigated in selected villages surrounding the RBNP. A fuller account of this study can be found in Brown (1997). The findings highlight the different rates of dependency of households on collecting these resources from the RBNP. This differentiation is such that poorer households, and those from indigenous Tharu groups, are more dependent on grassland products for a wide range of different uses, a very small number of which are shown in Table 5.1. These uses include building and furniture construction, as well as significant ceremonial uses.

Traditionally constructed Tharu longhouses are made entirely from grassland products, including reed poles for external walls, small reeds for grain silos which form the internal dividing walls, and thatch for roofing. The most widespread use of grass is for roofing. Although materials for making tiles, the alternative to thatch for roofing, are available locally, this method is not adopted by all families. The relative scarcity of tile-making skills and the capital outlay for re-roofing using tiles means that the tiles option is well beyond the means of poorer families. It can, therefore, be concluded that poorer households are more dependent on grassland products collected from the RBNP and that any changes in access to the resources of RBNP are likely to adversely impact on them. This observation is confirmed by a study in Royal Chitwan National Park reported by Lehmkuhl *et al.* (1988). However, more information is required on the distribution of benefits between households and particularly on the reciprocal arrangements and trade between households.

## Sustainability and Grass Utilization

The grassland habitats inside the protected areas of the Terai are an important resource for both wildlife and local villagers. Grasses are utilized by local people, particularly the Tharu groups, for a wide range of uses; they are important subsistence products which make significant contributions to the welfare of local villagers, as outlined above. Without access to the grassland products, traditional methods of house building could no longer be maintained and there are virtually no sources of thatch and cane outside the protected areas. In addition to the biomass utilization detailed above, grassland products play an important role in livelihood strategies through reciprocal arrangements within communities allowing spread of labour demands across the slack season. Ethnobotanical investigations show that grassland products are themselves diverse, often with medicinal or ceremonial properties and uses (Brown, 1997).

The ecological impacts and sustainability of biomass extraction are currently uncertain, although on-going ecological experiments intend to shed light on any changes occurring in the grasslands. On the one hand, biologists argue that the disturbance associated with cutting and burning will have detrimental impacts on small animals, insects and birds, while on the other, the flush of short grass resulting from burning may encourage certain grazing species. These in turn attract large predators such as tigers, which are most highly prized by tourists. There is, therefore, much uncertainty, further clouded by the vested interests of the parties concerned, over the relative benefits and costs of current management regimes (see Brown, 1996). It may well be that certain types of cutting and burning at particular times of the year produce the mosaic of habitats which optimize multiple uses by both animals and humans. The diversity of the grasslands, where a patchwork of diverse habitats is provided by micro-scale differences of site, means that management of the protected area needs to take localized features into account, rather than attempting to implement one regime across all the Terai protected areas.

In summary, the rich biological diversity of the Terai protected areas is maintained in part by human intervention; and current cutting practices bring benefits to both local communities and to wildlife. Whether the practices are sustainable, and in what way they can be made so, is open to question, but the current focus of conservation and development policy is to relieve perceived pressure on resources inside the protected areas by encouraging the more intensive use of those in the designated Buffer Zone surrounding the National Park (HMG, 1993; HMG/UNDP, 1994). This chapter now returns to some of the more general issues concerning the ecological and socio-economic understanding of sustainable utilization and sustainability.

## Problems with Sustainable Utilization

The grassland study highlights some of the problems associated with defining and implementing sustainable utilization of natural resources as part of a move towards more sustainable modes of development in poorer countries. These problems arise in both the natural science and social science dimensions of sustainability.

## Ecological Aspects of Sustainability

The research into the impacts of different management and utilization strategies for tall grassland habitats in Nepal has identified a number of issues where conventional ecological approaches are deficient in helping to understand and to formulate policy for sustainable utilization. These problems are primarily associated with scale and with the dynamics of change.

The first area concerns a lack of understanding of complex habitat dynamics and the diversity between and within habitats and patches. It is the patchiness, the mosaic of different habitats which contributes towards the richness of biological diversity of the ecosystem, but makes it difficult to set policy prescriptions, for example, on cutting and burning of grass, for the protected area as a whole. The second aspect where an understanding of dynamics and scale is lacking is in terms of knowledge of historical patterns of land use; we have little historic perspective of the use and management of these areas decades ago, let alone centuries ago. A third related area concerns the role of disturbance and human intervention in these systems. Evidence from tropical forests, savannahs and forest fringe ecosystems point to similar issues of temporal scale and disturbance (see for example, Gomez Pompa and Kaus, 1992; Fairhead and Leach, 1995; Lugo, 1995). Systems which were previously assumed to be 'pristine' or 'natural' are now thought to have been subject to human intervention to greater or lesser degrees over time. Human intervention has had both positive and negative impacts on habitats and their biodiversity. These views meet with varying degrees of resistance from conventional conservationists, who often see human intervention in natural systems as by definition a 'bad thing' and that human-induced changes in habitats are detrimental to biodiversity.

The observations of ecologists that both disturbed and undisturbed natural systems are in dynamic states rather than equilibrium systems reaching a climax state are part of a movement towards a 'new ecology'. These concerns represent a significant shift in the dominant paradigms of the 1960s and 1970s, with an emphasis on stable systems, towards a focus on disequilibria, instability and chaotic fluctuations in biophysical environments. This new ecology has profound implications for interpretations of sustainability, especially in terms of our understanding of issues such as environmental change, human impacts on ecosystems, models of ecological 'carrying capacity' and specifically for biodiversity, area–biodiversity relationships and biodiversity–stability relationships (Zimmerer, 1994). The new ecology likewise recognizes the importance of history, spatial scale, and subjectivity (see for example, Symanski, 1994). The underlying conception of the biological system therefore fundamentally determines the translation of information into resource management and policy.

### Socio-economic Equity and Sustainability

Some of the issues highlighted above in terms of new ecology thinking are mirrored by shifting paradigms in the social sciences, and these impact on our understanding of socio-economic and political aspects of sustainability. Political ecology approaches (see Brown, 1996) highlight the differentiated experiences of different sets of actors and the different perceptions of interest groups involved in biodiversity conservation and development. Resource management and regulation based on the concept of sustained yield maximizing net economic benefits both simplify the ecological system and ignore the social dynamics of sustainability. There is a need to grasp the different meanings and realities constructed by these different groups within society in order to understand better the multi-dimensional character of sustainability and to explain why past and present resource use have been unsustainable, as evidenced in the biological sphere through species decline, for example.

Equity, both within and between generations, is a central tenet of sustainable development and a number of different aspects of equity are highlighted by the Nepalese example, again as issues which further complicate the definition of sustainable utilization. These include property rights and institutions governing use and access to different resources, the distribution of resources and benefits, and the role of alternative resources. In the Bardia case, this has resulted in loss of traditional rights to resources and the impoverishment of indigenous people who are more dependent on grassland resources. This is where a concern for sustainable utilization is shown to be explicitly part of the harsh realities of the political economy at a number of different scales, local, national and global.

## Conclusions

Sustainability is regarded almost universally, by both development and conservation discourses alike, as a good thing (notable dissenters include Wilfred Beckerman, as discussed in Chapter 1). Sustainable utilization is conceived of as one aspect of sustainable development which is able to be defined and measured in scientific terms. However, our evidence has shown that sustainable utilization consists of part conventional wisdom, and part wishful thinking. The premises underlying the concept are now being challenged in both the natural and social sciences, sustainability being described by Duffus (1993, p. 442), for example, as a 'scientifically threadbare' myth.

Sustainability will continue to be the goal of natural resource management for the foreseeable future. Current approaches to ecology and social science will fail to deliver however. According to a Foucauldian analysis, the status of ecology depends on its predictive powers which are geared to revealing 'surfaces of power' where intervention in natural systems can be effected (Howarth, 1995). However, uncertainty about the dynamics of complex ecosystems undermines this ability to manage habitats in a sustainable way, as has been shown by this study. Hilborn and Ludwig (1993) explain the limits to ecological research as a primary tool guiding policy. First, the rate of learning about ecological systems is slow enough that waiting for better scientific knowledge to provide iron-clad answers is futile; second, the decisions have to be made now, given current knowledge; and third, in many resource systems the only way to learn about their sustainability is to exploit them.

The problems emerging in defining sustainable utilization and operationalizing it include, among others, competing knowledges and interests from the often conflicting perspectives of conservation and development; between different resource users; between local and global needs (see Dovers, 1995) and other scale issues (Brown, 1996). All too often, the expectation is that the level of sustainable use is defined by natural science, where the policy instruments required to enforce it are identified by social science research. The challenge for sustainable development – for sustainability in its widest sense – requires information gathered in many different dimensions, necessitating methods which transcend traditional disciplinary boundaries and the need to devise policy under uncertainty in our knowledge of complex ecological, social and economic systems.

## Acknowledgements

Fieldwork was conducted under the auspices of the UEA Tall Grasslands Research Project which is funded by the UK Department of Environment Darwin Initiative for Survival of Species, in collaboration with the Department of National Parks and Wildlife Conservation in Nepal. The author would like to thank the following people for their assistance and advice: Dr Uday Sharma, Dr Bijaya Kattel, Mr Karki, and Mr B. Pathak at DNPWC; Mr T. Khatri at the King Mahendra Trust for Nature Conservation; Mr Gopal Sharma, Ram Din Mahato, Nic Peet and Neil Adger. Views expressed here are the author's alone, and any omissions or errors remain sole responsibility of the author. An earlier version of this chapter was presented at the Development Studies Association Conference in Dublin, September 1995.

## References

Brown, K. (1996) Conservation or development in the Terai? The political ecology of natural resources in Nepal. In R. Auty and J. Toye (eds), *Challenging the Orthodoxies*. London: Macmillan, pp. 205–27.
Brown, K. (1997) Plain tales from the grasslands: extraction, value and utilisation of

biomass in Royal Bardia National Park, Nepal. *Biodiversity and Conservation*, forthcoming.

Cox, T. (1990) Land rights and ethnic conflict in Nepal. *Economic and Political Weekly*, June 13–23, 1318–20.

Dinerstein, E. (1979) An ecological survey of the Royal Karnali-Bardia Wildlife Reserve, Nepal. Part 1: Vegetation, modifying factors and successional relationships. *Biological Conservation*, 15, 127–50.

Dovers, S.R. (1995) A framework for scaling and framing policy problems in sustainability. *Ecological Economics*, 12, 93–106.

Duffus, D. (1993) Tsitika to Baram: the myth of sustainability. *Conservation Biology*, 7(2), 440–2.

Fairhead, J. and Leach, M. (1995) Local agro-ecological management and forest–savanna transitions: the case of Kissidougou, Guinea. In T. Binns (ed.), *People and Environment in Africa*. Chichester: John Wiley, pp. 163–70.

Gomez Pompa, A. and Kaus, A. (1992) Taming the wilderness myth. *BioScience*, 42(4), 271–9.

Heinen, J.T. (1993) Park–people relations in Kosi Tappu Wildlife Reserve, Nepal: a socio-economic analysis. *Environmental Conservation*, 20(1), 25–34.

Heywood, V.H. and Watson, R.T. (eds) (1995) *Global Biodiversity Assessment*. Cambridge: Cambridge University Press.

Hilborn, R. and Ludwig, D. (1993) The limits of applied ecological research. *Ecological Applications*, 3(4), 550–2.

HMG (1993) *Nepal Environmental Policy and Action Plan: Integration Environment and Development*. Kathmandu: Environment Protection Council.

HMG/UNDP (1994) *Parks and People Project Document*. Kathmandu: DNPWC.

Howarth, J. (1995) Ecology: modern hero or post modern villain? From scientific trees to phenomenological wood. *Biodiversity and Conservation*, 4, 786–97.

Jaeger, W.K. (1995) Is sustainability optimal? Examining the differences between economists and environmentalists. *Ecological Economics*, 15, 43–57.

Lehmkuhl, J.F., Upretti, R.K. and Sharma, U.R. (1988) National parks and local development: grasses and people in Royal Chitwan National Park, Nepal. *Environmental Conservation*, 15(2), 143–8.

Ludwig, D., Hilborn, R. and Walters, C. (1993) Uncertainty, resource exploitation and conservation: lessons from history. *Ecological Applications*, 3(4), 547–9.

Lugo, A. (1995) Management of tropical biodiversity. *Ecological Applications*, 5(4), 956–61.

Mishra, H.R. (1984) A delicate balance: tigers, rhinoceros, tourists and park management vs. the needs of local people in Royal Chitwan National Park, Nepal. In J. McNeely and K.R. Miller (eds), *National Parks, Conservation and Development: Role of Protected Areas in Sustaining Society*. Washington, DC: Smithsonian Institution, pp. 197–205.

Nepal, S.K. and Weber, K.E. (1993) *Struggle for Existence: Park–People Conflict in the Royal Chitwan National Park, Nepal*. Bangkok: Division of Human Settlements Development, Asian Institute of Technology.

Peet, N. (1994) *Fire and Biodiversity Conservation in the Tall Grasslands of Nepal and North India*. Mimeo. School of Biological Sciences, University of East Anglia.

Pokharel, S.K. (1993) Floristic composition, biomass production and biomass harvest in the grassland of the Royal Bardia National Park, Nepal. MSc Thesis, Agricultural University of Norway, As, Norway.

Sharma, U.R. (1990) An overview of park–people interactions in Royal Chitwan National Park, Nepal. *Landscape and Urban Planning*, 19, 133–44.

Symanski, R. (1994) Contested realities: feral horses in outback Australia. *Annals of the Association of American Geographers*, 84(2), 251–69.

United Nations (1992) *Convention on Biological Diversity*. New York: United Nations.
WCED (1987) *Our Common Future*. Oxford: Oxford University Press.
Zimmerer, K.S. (1994) Human geography and the 'new ecology': the prospect and promise of integration. *Annals of the Association of American Geographers*, **84**(1), 108–25.

# III

## Rural Applications of Sustainability

# 6

# Population and Food in South Asia: Recent Trends and Prospects

## Tim Dyson

## Introduction

The relationship between population growth and food supply in South Asia has often been regarded from a neo-Malthusian perspective. Indeed, the influence of Malthus on how this subject has been viewed is fairly direct. During the period 1805–34 Malthus worked at the East India College at Haileybury, where he taught company servants before they were posted to the Indian subcontinent. The writings of these and subsequent officials throughout the nineteenth and early twentieth centuries frequently show the clear imprint of Malthus' basic perspective: the subcontinent is portrayed as overpopulated, beyond its food resource-base, and consequently subject to famine. Broadly similar sentiments characterized some official Government of India pronouncements in the years immediately after 1947. And, from the 1960s to the present day, many external commentators have viewed South Asia's prospects for feeding its population from essentially a Malthusian perspective.[1]

Of course, there has been *no* great Malthusian crisis. But, nevertheless, population growth in the Indian subcontinent has posed – and continues to pose – a major challenge for the region's systems of agricultural production. Accordingly this chapter attempts to provide an overview of the relationship between population and food supply in South Asia. We consider trends since the early 1950s, and we also try to tentatively explore the evolution of *future* conditions of food demand and supply for the next 30 years. Our main focus will be on India which constitutes about 75 per cent of the region's population and produces a similar fraction of its agricultural output. Valuable insights can be gained from the experience of neighbouring countries; therefore, Afghanistan, Pakistan, Nepal, Bangladesh and Sri Lanka also receive some consideration.

Finally, by way of introduction, a word must be said about *data*. In order to ensure some degree of international comparability the main sources of statistics used here are (i) United Nations' Food and Agriculture Organization (FAO) publications dealing with food production, consumption and agricultural resources and (ii) UN population estimates from the 1992 world population revision.[2] The data provided by these two statistical sources are often derived from official figures provided by national governments. But as we shall see, they sometimes depart from the official figures – or extend them – in significant ways.

## Past Trends and the Current Situation

Table 6.1 presents relevant demographic background data. As mentioned before, in 1990 India constituted about three-quarters of South Asia's population. Pakistan and Bangladesh each comprised a further 10 per cent, and the remaining three countries constituted under 5 per cent of the region's total population (see Table 6.1).

Estimates of recent levels of per capita calorie supply and composition are given in Table 6.2. These figures are mainly derived from national data on both the production and trade (including donations) of food. The most striking feature is the very low level of daily per capita calorie supply shown for all countries in the region. Indeed, the regional total (2214) is actually slightly lower than the corresponding figure for sub-Saharan Africa (2250).[3] Also noteworthy are the very low levels and proportions of daily calorie availability derived from animal products – although here Pakistan is something of an exception. However, pulses are a particularly important source of protein in the South Asian diet.[4] Table 6.2 suggests that the situation of Bangladesh is especially extreme with very low levels of daily calorie supply, virtually all of which is estimated to derive from vegetable products. This said, note the indication that overall levels of per capita daily calorie supply have improved in all countries since the early 1960s; gains seem to have been greatest in India, Nepal and Pakistan, but only negligible in Bangladesh (see Table 6.2).

The regional population total in Table 6.1 (1131 million) is so large, and the estimated regional per capita daily calorie availability figure in Table 6.2 is so low (2214) that – if we accept conventional FAO/WHO standards of recommended calorie intake – it is probably true to say that almost half of all the world's chronically undernourished people live in South Asia.[5] Of course, the validity of applying such standards in the Indian context has been questioned, most notably by P.V. Sukhatme. But irrespective of one's views

**Table 6.1** Summary demographic measures and projections, principal countries of South Asia, 1950–2020

| Country | Population (millions) | | Per cent urban | | Average annual rate of population growth % | | |
|---|---|---|---|---|---|---|---|
| | 1990 | 2020 | 1990 | 2020 | 1950–90 | 1980–90 | 1990–2020 |
| Afghanistan | 16.6 | 41.6 | 18.2 | 35.9 | 1.54 | 0.30 | 3.06 |
| Bangladesh | 113.7 | 209.2 | 16.4 | 38.2 | 2.50 | 2.54 | 2.03 |
| India | 846.2 | 1328.6 | 27.0 | 47.3 | 2.15 | 2.06 | 1.50 |
| Nepal | 19.6 | 37.3 | 9.6 | 26.8 | 2.18 | 2.76 | 2.14 |
| Pakistan | 118.1 | 240.9 | 32.0 | 53.1 | 2.74 | 3.26 | 2.38 |
| Sri Lanka | 17.2 | 23.8 | 21.4 | 38.6 | 2.02 | 1.50 | 1.08 |
| Total | 1131.4 | 1881.4 | 25.9 | 46.3 | 2.23 | 2.20 | 1.70 |

Notes: The totals given above and in subsequent tables relate only to the countries listed. As noted in the text the United Nations figures given above sometimes diverge slightly from recent official figures; but such divergences are of little consequence for present purposes.
Sources: United Nations (1991, 1992).

**Table 6.2** FAO estimates of average per capita daily calorie supply and its composition, principal countries of South Asia, 1988–90

| Country | Calories per person per day, 1988–90 | % change since 1961–63 | Calories in 1988–90 derived from | | Percentage derived from animal products |
|---|---|---|---|---|---|
| | | | Vegetable products | Animal products | |
| Afghanistan | [2196] | n.a. | n.a. | n.a. | n.a. |
| Bangladesh | 2037 | +3 | 1983 | 54 | 3 |
| India | 2229 | +12 | 2075 | 154 | 7 |
| Nepal | 2205 | +15 | 2062 | 143 | 7 |
| Pakistan | 2280 | +27 | 1994 | 286 | 14 |
| Sri Lanka | 2246 | +6 | 2136 | 110 | 5 |
| Total | 2214 | +11 | 2058 | 156 | 8 |

Notes: The estimate of per capita daily calorie supply given for Afghanistan in fact relates to 1983–85 – the most recent year for which we have been able to find a figure. The regional total per capita calorie supply estimate for 1988–90 includes the figure shown for Afghanistan. But the other totals exclude Afghanistan. Here and subsequently n.a. denotes not available.
Sources: FAO (1992); World Bank (1992).

about the existence of homeostatic mechanisms which may (or may not) adjust for low energy intake, the figures in Table 6.2 are surely indicative of a huge and continuing problem of human undernutrition in South Asia.[6]

In examining past trends in the relationship between population and food we will concentrate mainly on *cereal* production. Rice, wheat and coarse grains such as jowar (sorghum), bajra (pearl millet) and maize account for at least two-thirds of total calorie intake in South Asia. Moreover, changes in cereal production can be conveniently decomposed into changes in gross harvested *area* and changes in *yield*.

Figure 6.1 shows trends in per capita cereal production for the region as a whole since 1951. It is clear that the overall trend has been upward, although there has been considerable fluctuation from year to year – reflecting the crucial role played by the monsoon rains. Nevertheless, cereal production has evidently increased significantly faster than population growth. The moving average indicates that South Asia's per capita cereal output has risen from about 185 kg to about 215 kg between the mid-1950s and the late 1980s. Figure 6.1 also shows the marks of previous major food crises – most notably in the mid-1960s and early 1970s. This said, the general impression is one of considerable steady improvement in more recent times, perhaps particularly since the mid-1970s. But because of the dominance of India in Figure 6.1 it is probably best to consider country-specific trends.

Figure 6.2 shows the progress of per capita cereal production in each country since 1951. And Table 6.3 decomposes these trends for 1951–91 and 1982–91 into changes in per capita area harvested and changes in yield. It is immediately clear that the principal countries of South Asia have experienced very different per capita cereal production trends over the long-run since 1951. While for the region as a whole per capita output increased at 0.50 per cent per year, in three countries the long-run trend has actually been *negative* (see Table 6.3).

In the case of Afghanistan – where in most years levels of per capita cereal production tended to be relatively high – output per person declined slowly throughout the 1960s and 1970s. But per capita cereal production then collapsed in the 1980s due to the civil war. Large areas of cropland fell out of cultivation and yields also declined (see Table 6.3). Refugee migration from Afghanistan to Pakistan helps explain the extremely low population growth rate during the 1980s in the former country and the unexpectedly high population growth rate in Pakistan (see Table 6.1).[7] In Bangladesh too the long-run trend in per capita cereal output was negative, with increases in yield failing to keep up with declines in per capita area harvested (see Table 6.3). Again, in 1971–72 we glimpse briefly signs of how political instabilities can adversely affect levels of per capita cereal production (see Figure 6.2). However, the late 1980s seem to have witnessed a significant improvement in the overall position in Bangladesh. Finally, Nepal has also experienced faster growth of population than of cereal production over the long run.

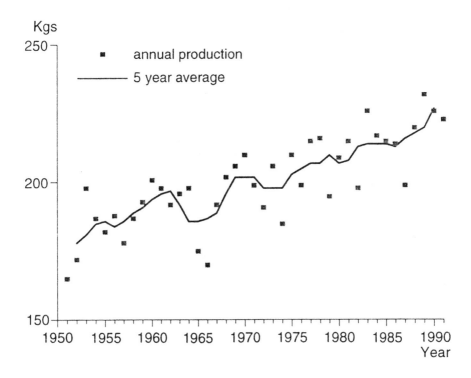

**Figure 6.1** South Asia's per capita cereal production, 1951–91 (*Sources*: FAO, 1987; United Nations, 1992)

Levels of per capita cereal production fell quite dramatically from the 1950s. But, as in Bangladesh, there are signs of some moderate recovery in the situation during the 1980s (see Figure 6.2 and Table 6.3).

Turning to those countries which have experienced *increases* in per capita cereal production, perhaps the most interesting picture is provided by Pakistan. In no other country in the developing world was the 'green revolution' in agriculture so truly revolutionary as it was in Pakistan. Figure 6.2 shows the really great effect on per capita cereal production levels that the sudden introduction of Mexican high-yielding varieties (HYVs) of wheat had in the late 1960s. The results were so very dramatic partly because Pakistan's cereal production was predominantly of wheat, and partly because a large fraction of the country's cropland was already irrigated and hence could benefit from HYVs.[8] However, since the 'revolution' of the late 1960s Pakistan's performance has been indifferent, with per capita cereal production declining during the 1980s (see Table 6.3).

Sri Lanka's rate of per capita cereal increase over the period 1951 to 1991 has actually exceeded that of Pakistan. The country's levels of per capita

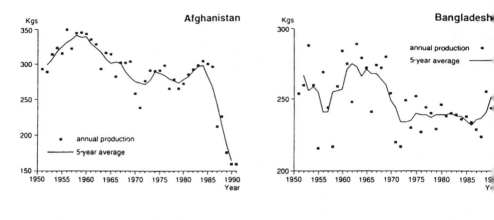

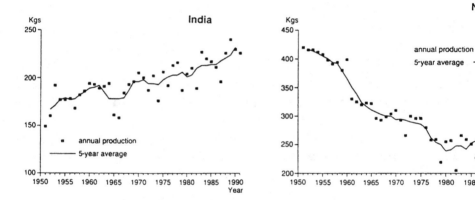

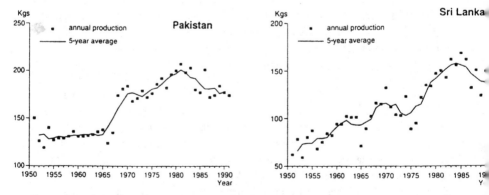

**Figure 6.2**   Country measures of per capita cereal production, 1951–91 (*Sources*: FAO, 1987; United Nations, 1992)

**Table 6.3** Summary measures of cereal production, area harvested and yield, in the principal countries of South Asia, 1951–91

| Country | Average annual rates of change 1951–91 | | | Average annual rates of change 1982–91 | | |
|---|---|---|---|---|---|---|
| | Per capita cereal production | Per capita area harvested | Yield | Per capita cereal production | Per capita area harvested | Yield |
| Afghanistan | −0.83 | −1.65 | 0.80 | −9.33 | −8.09 | −1.35 |
| Bangladesh | −0.51 | −1.83 | 1.38 | 0.32 | −3.09 | 3.41 |
| India | 0.67 | −1.57 | 2.30 | 0.99 | −2.41 | 3.40 |
| Nepal | −1.47 | −1.29 | −0.24 | 3.52 | 0.72 | 2.84 |
| Pakistan | 1.41 | −1.37 | 2.80 | −1.70 | −2.57 | 0.86 |
| Sri Lanka | 1.98 | 0.32 | 1.71 | −2.59 | −2.65 | 0.07 |
| Total | 0.50 | −1.58 | 2.13 | 0.52 | −2.56 | 3.08 |

*Notes:* The average annual rates of per capita cereal production change are approximately equal to the sum of the rates of change of per capita area harvested and yield (discrepancies being due to interaction effects). Harvested area refers to *gross* harvested area. Rates of change were calculated from group averages.
*Sources:* FAO (1987); United Nations (1992).

cereal output are comparatively low, partly because it continues to depend upon imports to a significant degree (see below). But Sri Lanka's high long-run growth rate in per capita cereal production has also been achieved in a relatively distinct way, because it is the only country in South Asia that has experienced an *increase* in harvested area per person (see Table 6.3). Of course, a major reason for this increase was that malaria eradication programmes in the late 1940s opened up large areas of the country's dry zone for agricultural resettlement. Irrigation projects such as those in the Mahaweli Scheme have specifically been viewed by the government as a way of relieving rural population pressures in parts of the wet zone, creating employment, and increasing the production of food. However, during the 1980s per capita cereal output in Sri Lanka has generally declined (see Figure 6.2 and Table 6.3). This partly reflects poor performance by some of the agricultural programmes. But in all probability the civil war is also a major reason for the decline.

Finally we come to India. A simple comparison of Figures 6.1 and 6.2 underlines the country's dominance in determining South Asia's cereal production trends. Over the period 1951–91 India has actually achieved quite a respectable growth rate in per capita cereal production – with yield increases more than offsetting declines in area harvested per person (see Table 6.3). This said, by no means all of these per capita cereal *production* increases have been translated through into increases in per capita *consumption*. This is partly because since the 1950s the country has reduced its dependence on imports[9] – hence the much-heralded claim that it is now 'marginally self-sufficient' in cereals – and partly because the government has accumulated sizeable cereal stocks. Government of India estimates of per capita cereal consumption levels, from both the Ministry of Agriculture and the National Sample Survey, suggest that there has been virtually no change in per capita cereal consumption since the 1950s. However, serious doubts have been raised about the validity of both these sets of official cereal consumption estimates.[10] And, faced with Figure 6.2, and other developments like reduced losses due to improved storage and probable reductions in the allowances which need to be made for seed, it is difficult to believe that there has been no increase in average levels of per capita consumption (even if some groups have not benefited commensurately).

Figure 6.2 can certainly be used to illustrate one way in which the long-run upward trend in per capita cereal production *has* benefited India's population. Thus the crash in production levels in 1965–66 triggered widespread conditions of near-famine, most notably in Bihar. Also, the deterioration in per capita cereal production in the early 1970s corresponded to the food crisis in Maharashtra and neighbouring states (note that this difficult agricultural period of the early 1970s was shared to some extent by most countries in the region). There is little doubt that the Maharashtra crisis caused a sizeable number of excess deaths.[11] In contrast, the avoidance of widespread famine conditions and mortality in 1987, despite severe drought, was certainly partly due to the overall improvement in domestic cereal production and, relatedly, the existence of considerable reserve cereal stocks.

The moving average in Figure 6.2 certainly gives some hope that conditions of widespread near-famine – such as occurred in the mid-1960s and early 1970s – have been assigned to India's past. Moreover, given doubts which have been expressed about the momentum of green revolution developments in the country, it is important to note that India has actually experienced an *acceleration* of per capita cereal production during the 1980s (see Table 6.3). In a country as agroclimatically diverse as India, it is perhaps not surprising that the green revolution of the late 1960s does not reveal itself in the time series in such a dramatic way as it does for Pakistan (see Figure 6.2). On the other hand, the very diversity which prevents the occurrence of a sudden transforming national 'miracle' also provides a multiplicity of circumstances in which progress can be made – albeit more spread out in time and space. Thus in India the 'green revolution' has been a much more diffuse *process*. Initially northern areas, notably Punjab, experienced similar dramatic per capita wheat production increases to those of Pakistan.[12] Subsequently the momentum has shifted to HYVs of rice, and to other areas like western Uttar Pradesh. In the late 1980s there have also been significant increases in harvested areas of HYVs of both jowar and bajra.[13]

Returning to the comparative international context, several further observations regarding the interaction of food production and population factors must be made – especially in relation to the statistics in Table 6.3.

First, comparing the long-run (1951–91) experience of the principal countries in South Asia, there are no indications from the simple cross-sectional relationship that countries with higher rates of population growth have experienced lower rates of growth of per capita cereal output. This should not really surprise us, since both variables are affected by many additional factors. Thus Afghanistan has experienced the lowest rates of change of both population and per capita cereal production – due largely to warfare. On the other hand, because of its particular suitability to wheat HYVs, Pakistan has benefited from the region's second fastest rise in per capita cereal production while also experiencing the fastest rate of population growth (see Tables 6.1 and 6.3).

Second, and perhaps a little more surprisingly, there is no evidence that countries with higher rates of demographic growth have experienced greater declines in per capita area harvested of cereals. Again this is due to confounding factors. For example, warfare has massively reduced the total harvested area in Afghanistan, while in Sri Lanka malaria eradication enabled a considerable expansion of the area under cereals. This latter process has operated quite widely in other parts of South Asia too – most notably in the Terai which has attracted land-clearing migrants both from the hill regions of Nepal and from proximate, comparatively densely-populated parts of Bihar and Uttar Pradesh. Of course, there are still other factors influencing the area harvested of cereals, such as the extent of multiple cropping (itself often conditioned by possibilities for irrigation) and the transfer of land out of cereals into better-paying crops.

Third, and despite the considerations of the previous paragraphs, there is absolutely no doubt that demographic growth *is* rapidly changing the basis of South Asia's agricultural production. Table 6.3 shows that although the regional growth rate in per capita cereal production during 1982–91 was only slightly higher than the long-run 1951–91 growth rate, in the more recent period per capita output gains have become much more dependent upon increases in *yield*. Relatedly, because the scope for increasing the cropland area is becoming increasingly constrained, the rate of change in per capita area harvested is becoming ever more negative (see Table 6.3). This basic theme is echoed across most of the subcontinent and can be illustrated in various ways. For example, in Bangladesh over the period 1951–91 approximately 27 per cent of total cereal output increase came from increases in area harvested and 73 per cent came from rises in yield. But *all* of the cereal production increase in Bangladesh during 1982–91 came from increases in yield. Again, in India over the 15 years from 1970–71 to 1985–86 the proportion of operational holdings of less than one hectare rose from 51.0 to 57.8 per cent and the average size of holdings fell from 2.3 to 1.7 ha. Agrawal and his colleagues observe that '[p]erhaps the most dominant and somewhat intractable problem of agriculture [in India] is the stupendous marginalization of holdings under the pressure of population'.[14] The urbanization and workforce data from the 1991 census provide evidence of structural change in the Indian economy away from agriculture.[15] Nevertheless, the signs are that what Ashish Bose has termed the 'long anticipated great "shaking loose" of the rural peasantry from the villages' is going to be a difficult affair.[16]

To summarize and conclude this discussion of past trends in South Asia's evolving balance between population and food, Table 6.4 summarizes trends in FAO's index of per capita food production since the early 1950s. This index uses price data to weight estimates of production quantities of all the main foodstuffs, excluding those that are used as seed or fed to animals. Clearly, such a complex measure, based on diverse data sources, should be interpreted with care. Also note that the index is expressed with reference to the level of food output in a given period, rather than as an absolute quantity. Nevertheless, the overall impression is of significant progress in India (especially during the 1980s) and also Pakistan. But elsewhere in South Asia for most periods the record has generally been rather dismal (see Table 6.4).

**Table 6.4** FAO indices of food production per capita, principal countries of South Asia, 1952–91

| Country | Period | | | |
|---|---|---|---|---|
| | *1959–61*<br>*(1952–56 = 100)* | *1969–71*<br>*(1961–65 = 100)* | *1979–81*<br>*(1969–71 = 100)* | *1989–91*<br>*(1979–81 = 100)* |
| Afghanistan | 107.0 | 93.3 | 98.7 | n.a. |
| Bangladesh | n.a. | 92.0 | 93.3 | 96.6 |
| India | 106.7 | 103.0 | 102.3 | 120.3 |
| Nepal | n.a. | 96.3 | 85.7 | 123.9 |
| Pakistan | 100.7 | 113.7 | 104.7 | 105.2 |
| Sri Lanka | 101.0 | 97.3 | 146.3 | 90.5 |
| Total | 105.5 | 102.7 | 102.1 | 115.9 |

*Notes*: The indices are computed by the Laspeyres method and are related to production quantities and prices during the specified base periods. Because of changes in data sources, concepts, coverage, weights, etc. over time, the indices should be regarded as broadly indicative rather than exact. Moreover the scale of change indicated for any decade can be heavily influenced by the particular agricultural conditions prevailing during the base and subsequent three-year periods used. The estimate for Pakistan in 1959–61 is inclusive of Bangladesh. The regional total indices for 1959–61 and 1989–91 respectively exclude Nepal and Afghanistan.
*Sources*: FAO (various years).

## Patterns of Trade and Food Aid

Before we consider future prospects for food demand and supply in the context of demographic trends, some brief consideration of the recent trading position is desirable. In this context Table 6.5 implies that India, Nepal and Pakistan are now *not* dependent upon cereal imports. But during the late 1980s Afghanistan, Bangladesh and Sri Lanka depended upon imports for a significant proportion of their total cereal consumption. In the case of Afghanistan this need was clearly conditioned by the civil war; note that the volume of cereal food aid was equivalent to about 74 per cent of imports – much of it World Food Program purchases. The situation of Bangladesh is also of concern. Its cereal imports constitute about 9 per cent of its domestic production. And the country receives cereal food aid equivalent to nearly 60 per cent of imports. Most food aid is from US and EU sources. In volume terms Bangladesh is the world's second largest receiver of cereal aid.[17] Lastly, the situation of Sri Lanka, which is a major exporter of tea, is relatively distinct. For many decades the country has quite deliberately relied upon imports to meet a significant fraction of its cereal requirements, and in this context the exceptionally low prices of cereals on world markets during the 1980s and early 1990s have certainly worked to its advantage. Sri Lanka does receive cereal food aid – overwhelmingly donations from the US. But statistics on food aid have to be interpreted with particular care because they often say more about conditions and priorities in the donor countries than in the receiving countries. It is certainly a very reasonable supposition that Sri Lanka is less dependent upon food aid than is, for example, Bangladesh.

**Table 6.5** Cereal production, trade and aid, by volume, principal countries of South Asia, 1987–90

| Country | Average cereal production 1988–90 (000 MTs) | Average annual net trade in cereals, 1987–89 (000 MTs) | Average annual cereal donations or receipt of cereal food aid, 1987–89 | Net trade as % of production | Cereal aid as % of cereal imports |
|---|---|---|---|---|---|
| Afghanistan | 3463 | 256 | 190 | 7 | 74 |
| Bangladesh | 27382 | 2328 | 1382 | 9 | 59 |
| India | 193601 | 875 | 221 | 0 | 25 |
| Nepal | 5451 | 40 | 17 | 1 | 43 |
| Pakistan | 20387 | −62 | 515 | 0 | - |
| Sri Lanka | 2289 | 883 | 307 | 13 | 35 |
| Total | 252573 | 4320 | 2632 | 1 | 61 |

*Notes*: The numbers in this table should be regarded as broadly indicative rather than exact. The ultimate source of most of the above data is the Food and Agriculture Organization. The negative number shown for Pakistan under net trade indicates net export. Here and subsequently MTs denotes metric tons. Although we have expressed cereal aid as a percentage of net cereal trade, it should be stressed that the data on net trade are *exclusive of cereal donations and cereal aid*.
*Source*: World Resources Institute (1992).

# Future Prospects for Population and Food

We now assess future prospects for population and food supply in South Asia over the period to 2020. For convenience, and because of their importance, we again concentrate upon cereals. First we consider the main factors affecting their *demand* and then those factors which will affect their *supply*. Finally, some broad illustrative calculations enable us to relate demand and supply and elucidate the magnitude of the task which lies ahead. The obviously speculative nature of this exercise should require no further emphasis here.

## Factors Affecting Demand

The two main factors which together will determine the future evolution of the region's 'demand' for cereals are: (i) growth in population and (ii) growth in income. Of these, population growth will certainly be the most important factor. Moreover, although population projections inevitably carry a significant margin of uncertainty, there is little doubt that we can assess much more confidently future prospects for population growth than we can prospects for growth in per capita income.

In this context Table 6.1 summarizes the 'medium variant' United Nations demographic projections. South Asia's population is projected to rise by 66 per cent to 1881 million by the year 2020. Of the total increment of 750 million an increase of 482 million is projected to occur in India. Although we will work with this medium variant figure of 1881 million, it should be noted that the corresponding 'low' and 'high' variant projection totals for the region are 1783 and 1980 million. Of course, these alternative totals reflect differences in assumptions regarding the speed of fertility decline. Excluding the happening of truly extraordinary events there is no reason to believe that mortality variation – including, for example, the extremely unlikely occurrence of huge famines – will have a major influence on South Asia's demographic growth to the year 2020.[18] Note that Table 6.1 indicates what is generally agreed, namely that rates of population growth will decline in virtually all countries during the next few decades. Thus the projected regional average growth rate over the period 1990–2020 is 1.7 per cent per year. During the 1980s total cereal production in South Asia has increased on average at about 2.7 per cent per year. So, provided there is no decline in the growth rate of total cereal output, there would inevitably be an increase in *per capita* production levels over the period 1990–2020. However, this rather simple calculation ignores the fact that to some extent past growth in total output has been driven by demographic growth; more importantly, the calculation takes no account of possible production *constraints* (see below).

Table 6.6 shows that if we assume (i) that the medium variant population projections apply and (ii) that per capita cereal consumption stays constant at

1990 levels, then total cereal demand for South Asia will also rise by 66 per cent to reach 427,186,000 metric tons in 2020. However, it is much more difficult to assess by how much this increase in demand will be further augmented by income growth. To do this requires both an assessment of the likely long-run growth prospects for incomes in the region and an estimate of the overall income elasticity of cereal demand. In fact short-run forecasts for South Asia's economy are quite promising. For example, the World Bank projects per capita GDP to increase at 3.4 per cent per year over 1992–2002. The Indian economy, especially, is seen as benefiting from adjustment reforms, and attracting inflows of equity investment as stock markets are opened up. These inflows could become large if there is regulatory reform. However even the Bank admits that there are serious 'downside risks' that this scenario may not materialize.[19] And it is even more difficult to assess the individual prospects for other countries in the region, which are likely to be quite different particularly over the longer run. Accordingly here we have adopted a more straightforward approach to allow for income effects on food demand. Specifically, we have assumed that one-third of total future demand increase will be due to income growth and two-thirds due to population growth. This broad assumption can be justified with reference to studies for India, other countries in Asia, and indeed the developing world in general.[20] Table 6.6 shows that on this basis South Asia's volume of cereal demand in 2020 will be about 512,330,000 metric tons, almost exactly *double* current levels of consumption.

Before we consider whether this volume of demand is likely to be met

**Table 6.6**   Projected demand for cereals, principal countries of South Asia, 2020

| Country | Cereal consumption around 1990 | | Projected demand in 2020 (000 MTs) based on | |
|---|---|---|---|---|
| | Total (000 MTs) | Per capita (kgs) | Population increase only | Population plus income increase |
| Afghanistan | 3719 | 224 | 9320 | 12121 |
| Bangladesh | 29710 | 261 | 54664 | 67141 |
| India | 194476 | 230 | 305342 | 360775 |
| Nepal | 5491 | 280 | 10450 | 12930 |
| Pakistan | 20325 | 172 | 41459 | 52026 |
| Sri Lanka | 3172 | 184 | 4389 | 4998 |
| Total | 256893 | 227 | 427186 | 512333 |

*Notes*: Total national cereal consumption figures around 1990 are based on the production and net trade data shown in Table 6.5. The estimates of per capita cereal consumption around 1990 are based on the population figures shown in Table 6.1. The projected demand figures based on population increase only have been derived using the population statistics in Table 6.1. Thus for the total region 427,186 = 256,893 × (1881.4/1131.4). To roughly estimate projected demand on the basis of population *plus* income growth, an inflation factor of 1.5 was used to further raise the projected regional increase (see text). Thus 512,333 = 256,893 + 1.5 (427,186 − 256,893). All figures should be regarded as approximate. Totals do not always add, due to rounding etc.

from within South Asia's own agricultural resources, several interconnected comments are in order. First, it is quite possible that some countries in the region will experience very much smaller – if any – increase in demand from per capita income growth. Second, the distribution of any income increase will have an important influence on the volume of demand which is generated. This is because income elasticities of cereal demand in South Asia may be close to zero for the rich and close to unity for the poor. So poverty alleviation, if successful, could have a very powerful positive effect on cereal demand.[21] Third, differential patterns of urbanization will probably also have a significant influence on the evolution of demand (see Table 6.1). For example, in India town dwellers are probably more likely to consume wheat and rice compared with traditional cereals. Finally, at the moment virtually no cereals are used to feed livestock in South Asia. Thus in India in 1990 only about 2 per cent of total grain consumed was fed to animals. But as incomes rise this situation may change significantly as demand for livestock products increases.[22]

## Factors Affecting Supply

Table 6.7 presents estimates of the supply of *potential* arable land and of the areas already used for crops. While the figures are rough, it is undoubtedly the case that most arable land is already in use. Only Nepal, Pakistan and Sri Lanka have any reserves of consequence, and these are dwindling due to population growth and in-migration. For example, around 1983 64 per cent of Nepal's potential arable land was used as cropland,[23] but by 1989 this had risen to 68 per cent (see Table 6.7). Unlike some other world regions South Asia has no significant reserves of potential arable land. The data on per capita cropland in use underline the particular pressure on land in Bangladesh.

Nearly one-third of South Asia's cropland is irrigated (see Table 6.7). Indeed, India's irrigated area ranks second in the world (after China) and Pakistan's irrigated area ranks fifth. Irrigation has been essential to the spread of HYVs with their increased yields. Most of the region's increase in cereal production has occurred in the irrigated area, in fact, production gains have been very limited in the dry farming sector. So it is not surprising that emphasis has always been given to the expansion of irrigation. Nevertheless, the possibilities for expansion are diminishing fast, and the costs of development are increasing. For example, some analysts suggest that India will develop most of its remaining irrigation potential well within the time frame under consideration here.[24] And in both India and Pakistan current capital costs for new irrigation canal capacity are estimated to be between US$1500 and 4000 per ha.[25]

We cannot address problems of irrigation in detail here (let alone important related issues, such as falling water tables due to overpumping, or competition for water posed by fast expanding urban areas like Delhi,

Table 6.7 Factors affecting the supply of food, principal countries of South Asia, c. 1990

| | Arable land | | | Cropland in use per capita (ha) | Percentage of cropland irrigated, 1987–89 | Average annual fertilizer use (kg/ha of cropland), 1987–89 | Average cereal yields (kg/ha), 1988–90 |
| | Potential (million ha) | In use as cropland (million ha) | In use as % of potential | | | | |
|---|---|---|---|---|---|---|---|
| Afghanistan | 8.2 | 8.1 | 99 | 0.49 | 33 | 8 | 1338 |
| Bangladesh | 9.4 | 9.3 | 99 | 0.08 | 26 | 86 | 2483 |
| India | 169.0 | 169.0 | 100 | 0.20 | 25 | 62 | 1861 |
| Nepal | 3.8 | 2.6 | 68 | 0.14 | 34 | 23 | 1832 |
| Pakistan | 23.1 | 20.7 | 90 | 0.17 | 78 | 85 | 1745 |
| Sri Lanka | 2.7 | 1.9 | 70 | 0.11 | 29 | 107 | 2892 |
| Total | 216.2 | 211.6 | 98 | 0.19 | 31 | 63 | 1901 |

Note: ha = hectares.
Sources: Alexandratos (1988); World Resources Institute (1992).

Bangalore and Karachi). But two facts are very clear: first, the main contribution of irrigation in the future will come from improved *efficiency*; second, there is considerable scope for such efficiency gains.[26] Clearly, throughout much of South Asia there is huge potential for improvements in irrigation management and greater cost-recovery from farmers' fees. To a considerable degree the spread of tubewells in canal command areas has occurred as a direct response to ineffective irrigation management. And studies in diverse locations throughout South Asia indicate that irrigators with groundwater wells can double the cereal yields attained by neighbouring farmers who have to rely solely upon canal water.[27] Furthermore, the potential for expanding the gross harvested area through multicropping lies almost entirely within the irrigated sector.

Lastly in this brief review of factors affecting food production we come to a consideration of fertilizers and yields. Two points immediately arise from the estimates of chemical fertilizer use in Table 6.7. First, although there has been an approximate doubling of the regional use of fertilizers per hectare during the last decade, the overall level of application in South Asia (63 kg per ha) is low by international standards. For example, this figure is only about 25 per cent of current use levels in China.[28] Second, within South Asia there is a strong positive relationship between levels of fertilizer application and yields, with Afghanistan and Sri Lanka representing each of the extremes (see Table 6.7). Indeed, the low levels of fertilizer use in South Asia do much to explain why average yields in the region are also quite low by international standards (see below).

Focusing for a moment on India, the growth in use of chemical fertilizers has been very concentrated in 'green revolution' areas such as Punjab, Haryana and western Uttar Pradesh. Partly as a consequence of this concentration, there are signs that marginal returns to increased fertilizer use in India may be declining. The challenge, therefore, is to profitably expand fertilizer applications elsewhere, for example in eastern India, where there is also scope for increased use of HYVs and the development of minor forms of irrigation. Some analysts believe that this expansion will be facilitated if greater emphasis is given, where appropriate, to phosphate, potash and indeed organic manures.[29] Given India's relatively good supplies of coal and natural gas it should be feasible to expand indigenous fertilizer capacity broadly in line with requirements. Even generally pessimistic neo-Malthusian observers — such as Lester R. Brown of the Worldwatch Institute in Washington, DC — concede that in India there is large potential for profitably boosting fertilizer use and hence increasing yields.[30]

Of course, the foregoing statements about the possibilities for improving irrigation efficiency and raising fertilizer use rather conveniently side-step several major problems — such as the costs involved, and even more importantly, the demographic and institutional contexts in which improvements must be brought about. Such problems frequently relate to issues of land distribution, small operational holdings, and the particular difficulties of the dry farm sector. We will briefly touch on some of these issues in the chapter's final section. But before we do so, it is worth considering some simple calculations which attempt to relate the foregoing cereal demand scenarios (summarized in Table 6.6) to the possible expansion of supply.

## Reconciling Future Demand and Supply

In assessing how the future production of cereals in the principal countries of South Asia might compare with the projected growth in demand, we make two broad simplifying assumptions. First, we assume that the long-run 1951–91 average annual growth rates in yield will continue to hold for the period to 2020. Note from Table 6.3 that yields in the region as a whole increased at 3.08 per cent per year in the 1980s compared with 2.13 per cent per year over the long-run. So working on the basis of the latter figure could be regarded as a conservative assumption.[31] Second, we assume that the total area harvested of cereals in the year 2020 will be the same in each country as it was around 1988–90, i.e. the gross harvested area is assumed to remain constant. This too could be regarded as a conservative assumption; after all, we have seen that especially in Nepal, areas of new cropland are still being brought into use, and elsewhere there are certainly possibilities for increased multiple cropping. However, against this it should be noted that during the 1980s there has actually been a slight decline in the total area harvested of cereals in South Asia – partly due to the transference of land to other crops like oilseeds as relative prices have changed.

Table 6.8 shows the results obtained with these assumptions and allows comparison of the projected quantities of cereal demand and supply. First we will consider the region's three demographic giants.

On these assumptions cereal yields in Bangladesh would rise from 2.483 to 3.756 metric tons per ha. Total cereal production in 2020 would be 41.4 million tons, which falls far short of the output needed just to meet demand arising from population growth (i.e. 54.7 million tons). Moreover, if Bangladesh experiences any per capita income growth then it will probably be even more dependent on cereal imports in 2020 (see Table 6.8). It might be objected that during the 1980s Bangladesh achieved a growth rate in yields well above its long-run growth rate (see Table 6.3). But unfortunately we can be virtually certain that the country cannot sustain its recent yield annual growth rate (3.41 per cent) for the next 30 years, because this would result in cereal yields higher than those prevailing in any country in the world today. Even if Bangladesh were to achieve the very high yields of contemporary Egypt (5.254 tons per ha), which is extremely unlikely, it would still only just produce enough cereals to meet the projected increase in demand generated by population growth alone. The conclusion seems clear

**Table 6.8** Comparison of projected cereal demand and supply calculations for 2020, principal countries of South Asia

| Country | Projected range of cereal demand in 2020 (million MTs) | Average cereal yields (MTs/ha) | | Area harvested of cereals (million ha), 1988–90 | Projected cereal production (million MTs), 2020 | Net cereal deficit range in 2020 (million MTs) |
|---|---|---|---|---|---|---|
| | | 1988–90 | 2020 | | | |
| Afghanistan | 9.3–12.1 | 1.338 | 1.701 | 2.588 | 4.4 | 4.9–7.7 |
| Bangladesh | 54.7–67.1 | 2.483 | 3.756 | 11.028 | 41.4 | 13.3–25.7 |
| India | 305.3–360.8 | 1.861 | 3.710 | 104.030 | 385.9 | (80.6)–(25.1) |
| Nepal | 10.5–12.9 | 1.832 | 1.705 | 2.975 | 5.1 | 5.4–7.8 |
| Pakistan | 41.5–52.0 | 1.745 | 4.042 | 11.683 | 47.2 | (5.7)–4.8 |
| Sri Lanka | 4.4–5.0 | 2.892 | 4.830 | 0.791 | 3.8 | 0.6–1.2 |

*Notes:* The purely illustrative purpose of these calculations should be stressed. Net cereal deficits given in brackets represent positive (i.e. surplus) quantities. Projected ranges of cereal demand are taken from Table 6.6; cereal yields in 1988–90 are taken from Table 6.7; projected yields for 2020 are based on the 1951–91 yield growth rates in Table 6.3 (e.g. for Afghanistan $1.701 = 1.338 \times e^{30 \times 0.0080}$); areas harvested of cereals are based on 1988–90 yields and corresponding production estimates in Table 6.5 (e.g. $2.588 = 3.463/1.338$); lastly, projected cereal production figures in 2020 are the products of 1988–90 areas harvested and projected yields (e.g. $4.4 = 1.701 \times 2.588$).

that Bangladesh will have to greatly increase its volume of net cereal imports (including donations) in the years ahead.

In sharp contrast, the calculations in Table 6.8 suggest a very much better situation for India. Both current and projected (i.e. 2020) yields for the country are below those for Bangladesh. Nevertheless, India's projected cereal production of 385.9 million tons is well above the volume of demand generated by the combined effects of both population and income growth. Indeed, it is the only country in South Asia projected to be in such a position. Furthermore, it is probably reasonable to think that India can attain cereal yields of 3.710 tons per ha by the year 2020. For one thing, such a yield level is broadly comparable to yields currently achieved by countries like Chile and Indonesia. Moreover, even relatively productive regions of India – such as Punjab, Haryana and western Uttar Pradesh – have current cereal yields of only about 3 tons per ha; yet both yield levels attained by many individual farmers in these regions, and international comparisons, indicate considerable scope for further improvement.

The calculations in Table 6.8 suggest an intermediate outcome for Pakistan. Its projected cereal production in 2020 falls in the middle of the projected range for cereal demand. The country's situation seems to be much better than that of Bangladesh, but not nearly as tractable as that of India. Furthermore, Pakistan did not manage to increase its growth rate in yields during the 1980s (see Table 6.3). The greater problems likely to be faced by Pakistan, compared with India, stem directly from its much higher rate of population growth projected for the period 1990–2020 (see Table 6.1). So while Pakistan has largely been self-sufficient in food since 1947, projections which suggest that it may soon become a net importer appear to be entirely plausible on the basis of the present analysis.[32]

Finally, Table 6.8 suggests that all three of the region's smaller countries will be unable to meet their growth in cereal demand from their own production. In the case of Sri Lanka, a traditional importer, the projected shortfall is modest. Moreover, per capita incomes in Sri Lanka are comparatively high. But for Afghanistan and Nepal the projected net cereal deficits are very large, even if they are assessed solely on the basis of future population growth. It might be objected that the projected yields for these two countries of around 1.7 metric tons per hectare, based upon 1951–91 rates of change, are unduly pessimistic. This may well be true. But even if we assume 2020 yields in both countries of 3 tons per hectare neither country could avoid running large net cereal deficits.

In summary, for South Asia as a whole projected cereal production by 2020 seems capable of meeting the volume of demand likely to be generated by population growth alone. But this is largely because of India's seemingly relatively good prospects. And in all probability Afghanistan, Bangladesh, Nepal and Sri Lanka (but not Pakistan) would all be sizeable net importers. If, however, we make an additional allowance for demand generated by income growth then the present calculations suggest that only India would be able to meet such demand from its own agricultural resources. Even so, South Asia as a whole would require net imports of around 5 per cent of its projected production, compared with a figure of about 1 per cent today (see Table 6.5). Moreover this projected figure of 5 per cent rather unrealistically assumes that Bangladesh's net deficit of 25.7 million tons would be annulled by India's similarly-sized surplus of 25.1 million tons (see Table 6.8). Yet, of course, there is no reason to believe that any such net transfer within the region would necessarily take place. Indeed, some analysts doubt whether even India will be able to remain self-sufficient in foodgrains during the 1990s if it simultaneously achieves success in economic growth and poverty reduction.[33]

Of course, 'demand' as it has been used here is not an immutable, concrete entity. It is quite conceivable that much of the projected volume of demand – especially that component deriving from income growth – simply remains unmet. In some countries levels of per capita cereal consumption could possibly decline. Alternatively, economic success may facilitate the purchase of imports. However, a reasonably firm conclusion which can be drawn from Table 6.8 is that South Asia is going to experience a large increase in cereal imports in the coming years. By far the greatest volume of these imports will go to Bangladesh. But Afghanistan, Nepal and perhaps to a lesser extent Pakistan, may also have to import sizeable quantities.

## Conclusions and Discussion

It is obvious that a simple Malthusian paradigm – in which population expands faster than food production, leading to recurrent famines – has not applied in the Indian subcontinent during modern times. Instead, as we have seen, cereal production and food output in general have both increased faster than population. Relatedly, levels of per capita calorie availability have risen modestly in most countries.

Furthermore, famine has become a much rarer and more circumscribed event. We now know with fair accuracy that about 2 million excess deaths occurred during the Bengal famine of 1943–44;[34] and, almost certainly, there has been sizeable famine mortality from several subsequent food crises in South Asia, such as those in both India and Bangladesh in the early 1970s. However, this subsequent famine mortality has generally been on a much smaller scale, and India's performance in coping with the severe drought of 1987 is eloquent testimony to the reduced risk of a severe famine occurring in the region now. Of course, many factors, related to policies, politics and improvements in disease control, have contributed to this general record of success against famine. But in our view it would be a major mistake if we failed to acknowledge the important role played by increased levels of per capita food production. This has not only raised average daily calorie availabilities per person, but in India at least it has also permitted the accumulation of sizeable reserve stocks of grain.

Yet despite these achievements South Asia's population is arguably the worst fed in the world. High levels of poverty – food poverty in particular – and unequal income distribution mean that the region is particularly susceptible to sudden and unpredictable shocks. Looking to the future, climate change – especially apropos the behaviour of the monsoon – could be one such possible perturbation. However, the likelihood of such change, and its possible consequences for the region's agriculture, are both very difficult to assess. Unfortunately, what seems a much more likely hazard, from the modern history which we have reviewed in this paper, is that violent socio-political upheavals could disrupt both agricultural production and food distribution, and possibly provoke famine and major migration flows. Afghanistan, Sri Lanka and Bangladesh all provide fairly recent examples of this danger. South Asia is by no means the only world region to face this risk – witness Somalia or Bosnia. But its great demographic size and chronic food poverty combine to make it particularly vulnerable. So, for example, when we state that the significant improvement in levels of per capita cereal production shown in Figure 6.2 for India holds out promise that famine may now be firmly assigned to the country's past, it is with the crucial proviso that conditions of socio-political stability are maintained.

But if a simple Malthusian model does not apply to South Asia, few can deny that population growth has posed, and continues to pose, a major challenge to the region's ability to produce adequate supplies of food. More people have to be fed. And rural demographic growth, in particular, reduces the average size of landholdings, fragments farms, and contributes to the rise in landlessness. Some scholars suggest the adoption of co-operative forms of farming to help limit the consequences of such adverse trends.[35] With virtually no new supplies of land, the future of South Asia's agricultural production must come from increases in yield. From our brief examination of the possibilities for increased irrigation (including efficiency gains), more multiple cropping, and perhaps most importantly, greater fertilizer application, there certainly seems to be considerable scope for increases in yield – although often involving significant investment costs. We can probably be most confident of seeing such developments in the case of India – if for no other reason than that it is administratively and scientifically the most sophisticated country in the region. But even in India the government may have difficulties in making the necessary investments in the rural infrastructure, particularly apropos water.

So far as future demand for food is concerned, we have seen that population growth will overwhelmingly be the determining factor. Most of the region's countries will benefit from lower rates of population growth in the next three decades. But of the larger countries, India will clearly be the main beneficiary from slower population growth.

We emphasize again that the projections presented here which compare the demand and supply of cereals to the year 2020 are inevitably speculative. For example, as we noted, some countries may experience no rise in food demand from economic growth because per capita incomes simply may not increase. On the supply side, it may be overly conservative to assume no change in the area harvested of cereals, when clearly there is scope for expansion (through multicropping); but on the other hand, it may be optimistic to assume that future yields will increase at a compound (as opposed to a linear) rate.[36] To reiterate, the calculations are for illustrative purposes only.

This said, we think it both significant and revealing that the results are relatively favourable for India, intermediate for Pakistan, and rather unfavourable for Bangladesh. As previously noted, some analysts consider that even India could soon resume its role as a sizeable net importer of food. Against this, we would merely point out that the country's performance during the 1980s does not show any sign of deterioration in per capita cereal production (see Table 6.3). But in the case of Bangladesh, already seriously dependent upon large quantities of cereal aid (see Table 6.5), the present exercise must raise the question as to whether the country will ever become self-sufficient in food in the foreseeable future, even should it enjoy significant manufacturing and other export success.

A dominant concern raised by this chapter is that we can probably expect increasing inequality in per capita food availability between the countries of South Asia in the decades immediately ahead. Differential rates of population growth will contribute to this increasing inequality, though as in the past confounding factors will also come into play. At one extreme India's aggregate prospects seem comparatively good; while at the other extreme Bangladesh's prospects seem very poor. Of the other countries, the circumstances of Pakistan and Sri Lanka seem better than those of Afghanistan and Nepal. But more specific assessments as to outcomes are beyond our scope here.

If increasing inequality seems a probable scenario between the countries of South Asia, similar processes may well operate within these countries too. This may be especially true in an era of so-called economic 'liberalization'. For example, in India there will be continued progress in the already agriculturally advanced regions, and in such locations the development of diffuse urbanization may promote further fertility decline and demographic transition. But attempts to spread 'green revolution' approaches to the eastern region (which is currently often viewed with such promise) will confront a gamut of problems from poor infrastructure to exploitative tenancy systems. What will be required will be fundamental changes in agrarian structures, and these will be much more difficult to bring about. We know too that further productivity gains from dry farming regions, for example much of the Deccan, will probably be rather limited. Therefore in the future the already existent urban–rural and regional inequalities within the country may further expand. In part, migration will probably act as an important redistributive mechanism. After all, the figures in Table 6.1 imply that over 80 per cent of India's total population increase between 1990 and 2020 will occur in urban areas. But even so, it will be vital both to invest in rural infrastructure (e.g. roads, irrigation, inputs, etc.) and to protect the interests of the rural and urban poor if India's past progress in feeding its population is to continue in the coming years. It is in these two areas of policy that the future challenge really lies.

## Acknowledgement

Research for the present paper was conducted under a Research Fellowship from the Global Environmental Change Programme of the UK Economic and Social Research Council.

## Notes

1    Examples are Paddock and Paddock (1968) and Myers (1991).
2    See in particular FAO (1987) and United Nations (1992). For very recent years food statistics have also been taken from various editions of the FAO *Production Yearbook*.
3    See Dyson (1994) on how these figures were calculated.
4    According to Tyagi (1990, p. 57) India is the largest producer of pulses in the world, with about one-fifth of its area under foodgrains devoted to pulses.
5    For more on this, see FAO (1992) and Dyson (1994).
6    A good review of these issues is provided by Kumar and Stewart (1992). The present writer is uncomfortable with setting lower calorie requirements for South Asian populations. However, remote sensing and other data suggest that actual levels of food output may be significantly understated by the official production data (Pravin Visaria, personal communication).
7    According to the United Nations (1992) the rate of natural increase in Pakistan during the 1980s was about 3.14 per cent per year. This compares with a population growth rate (inclusive of migration) of 3.26 per cent per year (see Table 6.1).
8    Pakistan promoted the spread of HYVs partly by maintaining high cereal prices relative to fertilizer costs.
9    According to the data provided by Tyagi (1990, p. 50) in 1951 India's net foodgrain imports were equal to 12 per cent of net production.
10   See, for example, Sarma and Gandhi (1990, p. 88). Also see the estimated changes in calorie availability given in Table 6.2. The long reference period of one month used by the NSS to capture food intake may well be too long – leading to an understatement of food consumption in India.
11   See Dyson and Maharatna (1992).
12   And, of course, both the Indian and the Pakistani Punjab have attracted migrants due to their relative agricultural success.
13   See Agrawal *et al.* (1993, p. 122) for detailed statistics. Of course, the absolute yield increment from HYVs of these last two grains will be relatively small.
14   See Agrawal *et al.* (1993, p. 117).

15   See Mohan (1992).
16   The quotation by Bose appeared in the *International Herald Tribune* of 22 February 1982, and is cited in Skeldon (1984, p. 28). Increased rural electrification and opportunities for commuting may help to slow the pace of urbanization in the region.
17   In 1987–89 Egypt was the largest recipient of cereal aid with 1,683,000 metric tons; see World Resources Institute (1992, p. 278).
18   On the comparatively small impact that mortality variation is likely to have on India's population growth, and a demonstration that even major famines would have only a relatively modest effect, see Cassen and Dyson (1976).
19   See World Bank (1993, p. 68).
20   See respectively Sarma and Gandhi (1990, p. 86); Iio *et al.* (1979, pp. 33–4) and IFPRI (1993).
21   This issue is explored extensively in Sarma and Gandhi (1990).
22   The statistic on grain fed to livestock in India is taken from World Resources Institute (1992, p. 277). In the Indian context milk is probably the most important livestock product. But in the future better animal breeds and reduced possibilities for forage may both raise the demand for grain to feed to livestock.
23   See Alexandratos (1988, p. 319).
24   See Crosson and Anderson (1992, p. 46).
25   See Postel (1989, p. 9).
26   Postel (1989, p. 30) cites work by Robert Chambers which suggests that irrigation management improvements in India could enable an additional 8 million ha to be irrigated. This would represent an almost 20 per cent increase in the country's irrigation capacity without developing any new water sources.
27   See Shirahatti (1989) and Postel (1989).
28   The greater proportion of land under irrigation in China only explains a modest part of the overall differential.
29   See Sarma and Gandhi (1990, p. 39).
30   See Brown (1991, p. 13).
31   On the other hand, it could be considered that assuming a linear change in yields with time might be more appropriate. However, in the present context, and given the existence of other offsetting considerations mentioned in the text, here we have worked with compound rates. Certainly, the results obtained are reasonably plausible. But for a linear-based analysis with broadly similar regional results to those obtained here see Dyson (1996).
32   For mention of such projections see Myers (1991).
33   See Sarma and Gandhi (1990). It should also be noted that self-sufficiency in production may not be a rational strategy in all market conditions.
34   See Dyson and Maharatna (1991) for new estimates derived from important and freshly discovered data.
35   See for example Shirahatti (1989, p. 93).
36   See note 31 above.

# References

Agrawal, A.N., Varma, H.O. and Gupta, R.C. (1993) *India: Economic Information Year Book 1992–93*. New Delhi: National Publishing House.
Alexandratos, N. (ed.) (1988) *World Agriculture: Toward 2000, an FAO Study*. London: Belhaven Press.
Brown, L.R. (1991) The new world order. In L.R. Brown (ed.), *State of the World 1991*. London: Earthscan.

Cassen, R.H. and Dyson, T. (1976) New population projections for India. *Population and Development Review*, **2**(1), 101–36.

Crosson, P. and Anderson, J.R. (1992) *Resources and Global Food Prospects, Supply and Demand for Cereals to 2030*. Washington, DC: World Bank.

Dyson, T. (1994) World population growth and food supplies. *International Social Science Journal*, **141**, August, 361–85.

Dyson, T. (1996) *Population and Food: Global Trends and Future Prospects*. London: Routledge.

Dyson, T. and Maharatna, A. (1991). Excess mortality during the Bengal famine: a re-evaluation. *Indian Economic and Social History Review*, **28**, 281–97.

Dyson, T. and Maharatna, A. (1992) Bihar famine, 1966-67 and Maharashtra drought, 1970–73: the demographic consequences. *Economic and Political Weekly*, **27**(26), 1325–32.

FAO (1987) *World Crop and Livestock Statistics 1948–1985*. Rome: Food and Agriculture Organization of the United Nations.

FAO (1992) *World Food Supplies and Prevalence of Chronic Undernutrition in Developing Regions as Assessed in 1992*. Rome: Economic and Social Policy Department of the Food and Agriculture Organization of the United Nations.

IFPRI (1993) *Population and Food Security Nexus*. Washington, DC: International Food Policy Research Institute.

Iio, K., Hirooka, T. and Kato, S. (1979) *Population Growth and Food Problems in Selected Asian Countries*. New York: United Nations Fund for Population Activities.

Kumar, G. and Stewart, F. (1992). Tackling malnutrition: what can targeted nutritional interventions achieve? In B. Harriss, S. Guhan and R.H. Cassen (eds), *Poverty in India*. Bombay: Oxford University Press.

Mohan, N.C. (1992) The movement away from agriculture. *Economic Times*, 3 January.

Myers, N. (1991) *Population, Resources and the Environment: The Critical Challenges*. New York: UNFPA.

Paddock, W. and Paddock, P. (1968). *Famine 1975*. London: Weidenfeld and Nicolson.

Postel, S. (1989) *Water for Agriculture: Facing the Limits*. Washington, DC: Worldwatch Institute.

Sarma, J.S. and Gandhi, V.P. (1990) *Production and Consumption of Foodgrains in India: Implications of Accelerated Economic Growth and Poverty Alleviation*. Washington, DC: International Food Policy Research Institute.

Shirahatti, P.P. (1989). Agriculture – long term prospects. In N. Bhaskara Rao (ed.), *India 2021*. Baroda: Operations Research Group.

Skeldon, R. (1984) *Migration in South Asia: An Overview*. Bangkok: Economic and Social Commission for Asia and the Pacific.

Tyagi, D.S. (1990) *Managing India's Food Economy*. New Delhi: Sage Publications.

United Nations (1991) *World Urbanization Prospects 1990*. New York: United Nations.

United Nations (1992) *World Population Prospects: The 1992 Revision*. New York: United Nations.

World Bank (1992) *World Development Report 1992*. New York: Oxford University Press.

World Bank (1993) *Global Economic Prospects and the Developing Countries, 1993*. Washington, DC: The World Bank.

World Resources Institute (1992) *World Resources 1992–93*. New York: Oxford University Press.

# 7

# Land, Livestock and Livelihoods: Towards Sustainable Pastoral Development in Marsabit District, Kenya

## Oriel Kenny

## Introduction

This chapter examines some of the key issues for pastoral development in Marsabit District, Kenya today.[1] Pastoralism in Kenya is found mostly in arid and semi-arid lands (ASALs), which account for over 80 per cent of the land area and support half of Kenya's livestock and approximately 20 per cent of the population. Over the last decade, land has become an increasingly political issue in Kenya, arising from perceived land hunger and the ensuing urge to claim land title. The underlying assumption is that individual ownership is the way forward even though such tenure arrangements are largely unsuitable for pastoral areas. The land problem also points to a future where more people in Kenya will derive their livelihoods from sources other than land.

Pastoralism is unpopular with most African governments as it is considered to be environmentally destructive and even economically irrational (Hogg, 1992). Pastoralism is also maligned by the assumption that it represents a primitive, pre-agricultural stage of economic development and hence that it is backward and needs to be eradicated. Aligned to this has been an agenda to transform pastoralists into farmers on the wetter margins of the range, although it is not clear whether agriculture can be sustainable in these areas. The intention is that agriculture, by more intensive and productive land use, would be able to support more people. In practice, evidence of successful pastoral development projects is difficult to find (Baxter and Hogg, 1990). The droughts of the 1970s and 1980s led to an acceleration in the process of sedentarization which has given pastoralists greater access to services and increased security. However, the existence of towns at sites which were previously livestock water sources has irrevocably affected the pastoral system.

During the same period there has been a shift in thinking about range ecology, acknowledging the differences between equilibrium and non-equilibrium environments, the latter referring to arid and semi-arid zones with high rainfall variability. Here the production potential of both grassland and livestock is so dominated by rainfall and periodic drought that carrying capacity and degradation are no longer regarded as key concepts (Scoones, 1995). The variability of rangeland productivity in both time and space, therefore, dictates that mobility is essential to achieve optimal use. Thus development professionals are learning what nomadic pastoralists have known all along: that pastoralism is probably the most sustainable use of the rangelands.

## Background

Marsabit is the largest district in Kenya, covering 78,000 sq km,[2] and is also one of the most arid and least populated (Figure 7.1). It is mainly inhabited by nomadic pastoralists, predominantly Boran, Gabra, Rendille and Somali, though the towns have attracted settlers from other parts of the country. During the colonial period it was underdeveloped and treated as a restricted area with controlled access, and even today there are regular police barriers to control movement both inward and outward. Most of the district is covered by typical arid land vegetation with various mosaics and associations, annual grassland and acacia woodland. On the mountains wooded permanent grassland dominates with closed mist forest (KARI, 1988). The area is subject to periodic droughts: traditionally a severe drought was expected to occur every seven years but now the interval may be as frequent as every four years. Pastoralists have adapted to these conditions and there is an acceptance of peaks and crashes in the livestock populations upon which they depend.

In the 1980s (and previously) development agencies working in Marsabit were of the opinion that nomadic pastoralists needed to settle in order to develop. At the same time the rangeland would be divided into grazing blocks/ranches to achieve better rangeland management through a sense of ownership. This implies a very different pattern of land use, as well as a shift in attitudes, since traditionally land is not owned but held in common for periodic use. However, for some of these agencies this was not a policy as

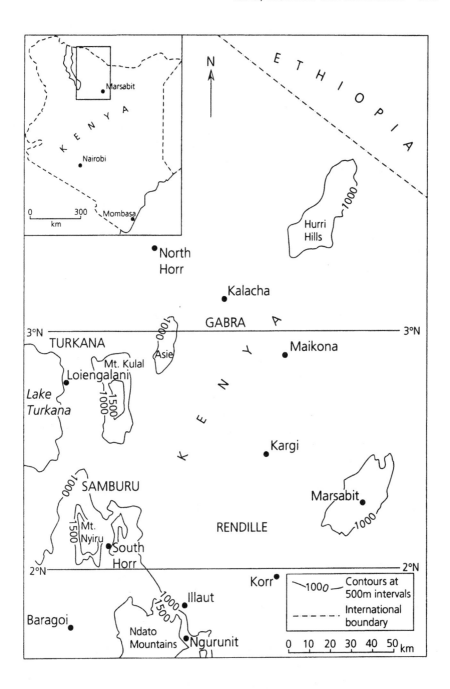

**Figure 7.1**   Map of Kenya and Marsabit area

such but arose from their attempts to assist pastoralists made destitute by the 1970s droughts for whom, at that time and having no stock, there seemed to be no option in the short term. Thus in the late 1970s several 'schemes' were established on Marsabit Mountain for these groups. The tragedy is perhaps that what was a temporary solution to an acute crisis has become a permanent fact despite many efforts to the contrary such as restocking schemes to enable re-entry to pastoralism. Settlement, or at least appropriation of dry-season grazing for agriculture, has continued and accelerated in all dry-season grazing areas, especially Marsabit Mountain but also in areas such as Hurri Hills, even though there is little water available there. This contradicts the pastoralists' wisdom that each part of the pastoralists' domain is essential but that no single area can sustain the system throughout the year.

In the years 1976–85 UNESCO ran an Integrated Project in Arid Lands (IPAL) project in Marsabit. It had been initiated at the 1976 UN Conference on Desertification in Nairobi, which concluded that degradation of arid lands was due to mismanagement and overstocking; hence IPAL focused mainly on ecological research and improved livestock marketing and veterinary care because of the view that the pastoralists had too many animals. IPAL was subsequently replaced by the Kenyan Agricultural Research Institute (KARI) National Arid Land Research Centre.

Over the last ten years, several new agencies have begun working in Marsabit District, notably the Marsabit Development Project, a joint venture between the ministries of Livestock Development and Agriculture with GTZ. There are also more NGOs such as Interaid, and Food for the Hungry has expanded its operations. However, since there is increasing recognition that pastoralism is the best and most efficient/effective use of arid lands, development efforts are now being directed more towards improving pastoralism in Marsabit at the margins, for example improving animal health and range management, rather than any attempt at transformation. However, most development initiatives continue to be in agriculture and concentrated in settled areas.

## Property Regimes

Marsabit District would seem to fulfil the criteria that make a common property regime the best option for range management, having low incomes, minimal economic surplus and climatic unpredictability in time and space (Runge, 1992). However, since pastoralism in Marsabit has, in common with other situations, generally been regarded as environmentally destructive and unsustainable, various grazing regimes and systems of tenure have been advocated and sometimes instituted to transform pastoralism. None have existed long term but they have continued to influence pastoralists' survival prospects. Perhaps the most significant influence cumulatively has been the alienation of land from the pastoral system mostly due to poor security and dry-season grazing lost to agriculture but also to forest conservation and urban encroachment (which is increasing).

Historically the district has been subjected to a range of external agents and their policies: formal tenure over natural resources has been vested in the state since colonial times. During the colonial period, the pastoral areas of Kenya, including the Northern Frontier District, were designated 'special areas' with movement in and out restricted. For example, from 1922 cattle exports from Isiolo were prohibited to protect European ranchers from competition in the meat market and from disease (Spencer, 1973; Hogg, 1986). The incursion of settlers to the highlands also disrupted linkages between herders north and south of the Rift Valley (Campbell, 1984, cited in Kenny, 1987) which had been important for trade and improvement of livestock.

Colonial range management was based on the division of the land into grazing territories on tribal lines. The artificial boundaries thus imposed sometimes divided traditional grazing territories and at various times caused hardship, stock loss and sociological problems (Oba, 1992), although some divisions such as the Boran–Somali line were beneficial in that they afforded protection from raids. Overall, colonial policy encouraged the continuation of. nomadic pastoralism and allotted exclusive grazing rights to each group with temporary adjustments permitted in drought conditions (Hogg, 1984). However, enforced exclusion from the market economy (although partly intended as a protection for the pastoralists and their way of life) made integration more difficult even when restrictions were lifted after independence and in many ways the effects are still felt today.

At independence the new government wanted to remove tribal distinctions, and tribal grazing areas were abolished, thereby inaugurating a period of 'open access'. However, this was quickly curtailed with the onset of the Shifta War 1963–67 when livestock movement was restricted. In the case of Isiolo District, livestock were restricted to within a 5-mile radius of three trading centres with a consequent livestock population crash (Hogg, 1984). In the early years of independence, settlement and cultivation were actively encouraged and from the late 1960s irrigation schemes were established along the Ewaso Nyiro river at the southern border of Marsabit District. Although irrigation schemes can be deemed a form of common property these were seen very much as government/agency projects by the participants, mainly because they were not included in decision-making. Therefore, the participants looked to the government to address problems such as maintenance and by 1983 most of the irrigation schemes had collapsed.

More recent government policy has been to restrict movement with the institution of grazing blocks which would confer the responsibility of a form of ownership and allow division/allocation of land on the basis of kinship and tribe. This was also advocated by IPAL as a means of managing grazing as well as enhancing security and the delivery of services to people and animals. However, block grazing is unenforceable – even were there support for it from the local people – because of the large area covered and inaccessibility. Anecdotal evidence suggests that people are grazing across boundaries as necessary. Even groups relatively advantaged by being allocated more favourable land, notably dry-season grazing, find that it cannot withstand year-round use and so find it beneficial to exchange use-rights upon traditional lines.

There is a fundamental issue regarding whether natural resource mismanagement is caused by common property arrangements or by external pressures/influences upon them. While the former view has been widely held, privatization of natural resources has been strongly advocated (with its connotations of secure ownership leading to responsibility and investment) but has often proved to be unsustainable in practice. The latter view would support customary systems of resource management and encourage flexible and highly mobile use of the remaining rangeland. It would seem that customary tenure is a good basis from which to develop locally manageable systems of range management for the future (Swift, 1991).

## Climate Versus Grazing Effects and the Agriculture Debate

Little experimental work has been done to attempt to distinguish grazing and climate effects on range degradation. Marsabit's vegetation is the result of sporadic and low rainfall associated with an arid ecosystem. The predominance of *Acacia tortillis* tree species and large shrubs suggests an original acacia woodland that has been degraded until only a few remnant trees remain (KARI, 1988). This is not to distinguish cause and effect. Range problems have traditionally been ascribed to pastoralists over-grazing, particularly during the 'boom' phase of the boom–bust cycle of pastoral livestock population. However, in Marsabit, arguably more destruction has been caused by clearing indigenous tree, bush and plant species for cultivation, which is at best risky and often temporary and unable to guarantee a sustainable alternative livelihood. If cultivation is subsequently abandoned the damage has often been done as, although the range has high potential for recovery, fragile native species may have been lost. As cultivation usually implies individual ownership, even if the land later reverts to grassland, it has been lost from common use.

Rainfall in Marsabit District is unreliable and sporadic with a bimodal distribution, occurring mainly in April/May (the long rains) and October/November (short rains). In the years 1989–91 the annual rainfall for Marsabit Mountain was 757.6, 877.2 and 404.6 mm respectively while Kargi received about half those amounts (KARI, 1991). Recent work on climate (Ellis and Galvin, 1994) has illustrated why the East African rangelands are less suitable for agriculture than areas of West Africa with similar levels of rainfall because of its biomodal distribution (as well as high interannual variability). West Africa receives almost all its rainfall in one rainy (i.e. growing) season so that 600 mm over a period of 90 to 120 days (i.e. 5–6.6 mm per day) is sufficient for short maturation crops. Conversely, in East Africa a similar amount of rain is spread throughout the year with peaks so that approximately 300 mm falls during the long rains, or 3 mm per day, which is enough to support only minimal crop production. Thus, the amount and variability of rainfall in Marsabit cannot really sustain agriculture over time but this is at variance with the widespread enthusiasm in Kenya for the subdivision of land into individual holdings.

There are continuing attempts to make agriculture viable on former dry-season grazing despite its poor prospects under a biomodal rainfall regime. Even where families are partly settled and cultivation is important, the rainfall is so unreliable that household security cannot be based upon grain alone. The only farms which are realistically viable on Marsabit are on the margins of the forest, for example, Leyai and Lpus on the north-west of the mountain, although these settlements are also the most remote, involving a walk of more than 10 km to market. There is more rain here and many of the shambas also have gravity-piped water. The only promising new crop I found in production in 1995 was *miraa* (a natural amphetamine) which benefits from the irrigation mentioned above while the town lacks a regular water supply. In strictly agronomic terms, it is an ideal small-holder crop in the same way as coca is in South America, being a small bushy perennial which needs little attention, can be harvested almost continually and commands a very good price. Marsabit *miraa* apparently compares very favourably with that from the previous source, Meru, which suffered from spending two days in transit. No new conventional crops seem to have been adopted to any significant extent in the last ten years, although more drought-resistant crops such as millet and sorghum are being tried in demonstration plots, for example, in the Food for the Hungry (FH) shambas at Ulanula. Lablab beans, which are drought-loving, may also be promising as forage crops. Previously, the IPAL project had achieved good (experimental) results with marama beans from the Kalahari and tepary beans. These 'new' crops have not been adopted by the local people, even those who live adjacent to the FH shamba and have spent a period working there. The reason given is the probability of elephant damage although that is also a risk for the maize and beans which they continue to plant. Several villages now have electric fences to ward off the elephants (and take the problem elsewhere) but most have fallen into disrepair and are no longer effective.

Over the last ten years many shambas in the settlement schemes have been left fallow. Since the crop fails so frequently or cannot be stored or sold, the people see no return for their effort and outlay. In a good year, when there is the prospect of a good harvest, animals are also more productive and so there is less necessity to cultivate. Agriculture only seems preferable during drought because grain could have been stored while animals die. However, once land is owned individually, even if it remains fallow, it has been removed from the stock of grazing land. Perhaps the only advantage of the move to individual land ownership among pastoralists is that it prevents outsiders obtaining it – which was a significant problem when the rangelands were first gazetted[2] in the 1980s.

## Marketing

There is evidence that livestock numbers are declining relative to people among East African pastoralists and this tends to negate the tragedy of commons argument, which assumes that herders will continually increase their numbers of animals on the range as the 'cost' in terms of degradation is shared between all users of the common rangeland. Also, the view that pastoralists are reluctant to sell their stock is changing (Sandford, 1983) but what they are willing to sell are bulls and steers, i.e. not productive cows which represent long-term security. However, it must also be noted that pastoralists are buyers as well as sellers so marketing of stock will not necessarily achieve increased offtake. Increasing dependence upon grain for diet, as well as other financial commitments such as school fees, has made pastoralists more willing to sell animals. This is particularly the case for families which do not have enough stock to subsist as true pastoralists (on milk, meat and blood) or where the settled part of the family does not have regular access to milk and blood because the main herd is far away in the *foora*. It has been calculated (McCabe *et al.*, 1992) that an offtake of 7 per cent of the ideal herd (7.5 livestock equivalents per reference adult) in sales is necessary to meet family grain requirements alone. Where families do not have sufficient stock for pure pastoralism, the offtake necessary is a much higher percentage of their herd and makes the search for livelihood alternatives more pressing. Ultimately these are the only solution apart from food aid when reciprocal arrangements become stressed or exhausted.

Several calculations have been made of the number of stock of all types a pastoral family needs to survive. This is usually expressed in terms of protein intake and sustainable offtake but fails to recognize (explicitly) that animals have many other purposes for pastoralists beyond food – ceremonies, bride wealth, reciprocal assistance. If that is not acknowledged their need to accumulate animals is not understood, and hence is put down to ignorance or the tragedy of the commons. Pastoralists are used to a boom–bust cycle of livestock populations in line with periodic droughts and know that large herds lose proportionately much less in a crisis and are an effective hedge against the possibility of destitution.

There are limits to the advantage of increased marketing for pastoralists: they do not need much money except to buy more animals; it may be several days' journey to a bank to retrieve the money whereas livestock could be sold *in situ* for instant cash. There are also many other negative aspects: poor prices, restrictions on livestock movement, poor infrastructure – especially roads but also telecommunications, vehicle hire, poor access to credit and lack of insurance.

## Sedentarization

Sedentarization has been widely assumed to be the solution to the pastoral 'problem'. By settling, a marginal and insufficiently integrated group will be transformed into good citizens by modernization and education. Indeed, it has to be said that settlement does allow access to these services (O'Leary, 1984) and a measure of security but, whether intentional or not, the expansion of structures such as schools, hospitals, communications and famine relief outlets/provision has encouraged settlement. It is interesting that settlement is often advocated because of pastoralists' poor range management and yet ecological problems and range degradation are much more evident around settlements, due to reduced mobility and hence uneven use of the range. As one approaches Korr and Kargi in the west of Marsabit District, the land becomes increasingly denuded until the town is reached. Nomadic use allowed for rest and recovery between grazing periods but in settled areas continuous trampling and grazing have caused a change in plant composition and a reduction in palatable species (KARI, 1991). The damage is most acute when a settlement is also a major water source for livestock (O'Leary, 1984). IPAL's Kargi fenced plot demonstrated the high potential for natural recovery of degraded rangeland if it can be left ungrazed. Once denuded, soil erosion prevents recovery of the original forage plants and so livestock are put at a nutritional disadvantage with consequent reduced growth rates, lower milk yields and greater susceptibility in time of drought.

Once established, new urban centres expand and attract further settlement. What may have been envisaged as a temporary solution to drought crises has become permanent. In the last ten years Marsabit town has grown and there is increasing competition for town plots, with structures appearing literally overnight followed by protracted disputes about planning permission. Similarly, the cost of agricultural land has increased dramatically – if it can be bought. Many attempts at encouraging pastoralists to move again by restocking have failed and since they stay around trading centres with their new herds, range degradation accelerates in the vicinity.

As a response to the drought of the 1970s several settlement schemes were established on Marsabit Mountain for herders whose animals had died. This involved the Kenya Government, the Catholic mission and CARE. The new villages were usually established 5 to 20 km from the town on land often previously used for dry-season grazing. Typically each household was given a *mabati* (corrugated aluminium) house and 3 acres to cultivate. Extension advice was offered but the transition from pastoralism to farming is not an easy one, involving also dietary changes and often the division of households between the mountain and remaining livestock camps. In some cases the land was farmed collectively, as at Gabra Scheme, but now most plots have been subdivided. Only the villages on the margins of the forest, with higher rainfall and often gravity-fed water supplies, have been able to provide a sustainable livelihood based on agriculture. Further away, for example in Manyatta Jillo, many plots have been left uncultivated since the 1992 drought by families who have sufficient stock and other sources of income.

With settlement, the process of pastoralists' integration into the market economy has accelerated through their evolving consumption practices and the requirements of clothes, education, health care and permanent shelter. However, there are not many possibilities for income-generating activities and much competition. Fatuma, for example, has been sewing clothes in the town for 15 years. Even when she lost lucrative school uniform contracts with the departure of child sponsorship agencies, there was still enough work for herself and three other tailors. Now that there are several more tailors in the market, as well as new tailoring shops, this source of income has become increasingly precarious and she often sits in the market all day but receives only two or three customers. The competition has also kept remuneration low; for sewing a dress she can charge 30sh, which can buy six bananas or five bunches of *sukuma wiki* (spring greens). A women's group that was running one of the two bakeries in Marsabit town had to break up when they calculated that the income was too little when shared between 12 women. Now five women run the bakery and seven are dealing in grain.

A KARI survey (KARI, 1991) found that only 10 per cent of pastoral households in Marsabit district have a source of income supplementary to livestock (usually wage work or petty trade) but in the town the figure was 70 per cent, of which over 42 per cent have a permanent commercial activity (KARI, 1991). Hence there is an incentive to move into town even from adjacent villages. The shift to town has also caused wider socio-economic changes. Whereas previously poorer households would survive by herding for richer households in return for the loan of milk animals for their families, they are now more likely to move to town to seek wage work even though there are few job prospects for those with little education. Since education does not guarantee a job there is evidence, for example among the Gabra, that they are sending fewer children, particularly girls, to school (Venturino, personal communication).

Sedentarization can also be seen as another strategy for survival by the possibility of diversification into (urban) economic activities. The herd may also be divided between urban centres (with easier access to water) and the traditional livestock camps. For poorer herders, settlement is dictated by their circumstances, such as loss of stock in times of drought. Richer pastoralists, on the other hand, may choose to settle to exploit opportunities in other sectors (while at the same time having an easier life). Hence it is the richest and the poorest who settle, and for the latter group it is becoming the only alternative. A third group of settlers who will become increasingly significant are the educated children of nomadic pastoralists, who have taken on something of the outsiders' view of pastoralism as backward (as well as hard work!) as a by-product of their schooling. Their reluctance to follow the lifestyle of their parents will be crucial to discussion of the future of pastoralism.

Although settlement is often intended to be a temporary strategy, in practice few herders succeed in moving again. Gabra scheme was established on Marsabit Mountain in 1978 when 50 houses were constructed. With marriages over the years there were 75 houses by 1994 and only eight of the original families have returned to nomadic herding exclusively. This is interpreted by young educated people as a manifestation of their elders' lack of education. In a certain way this is true, as without formal education older people have not taken on the outsiders' view of pastoralism as backward.

## Drought Response and Food Aid

The curtailment of pastoralists' traditional nomadic livelihoods has led to increased food insecurity and poverty (Bush, 1995). This is exacerbated by insecurity, which renders large tracts of the range unusable, and the appropriation of dry-season grazing areas for cultivation. These factors then affect the pastoralists' ability to cope with periodic droughts. However, if it is accepted that pastoralism – despite current problems – is still the only economically and environmentally sustainable use for arid and semi-arid areas, then every effort must be made to avoid pastoralists becoming destitute. This would imply the necessity of early intervention, as few who drop out of pastoralism ever manage to return. In Marsabit almost all of the families who settled after the 1970s and 1980s droughts have remained and for them food insecurity and food aid have become permanent rather than temporary issues.

In the absence of a coherent service infrastructure, the Christian missions – notably the Catholic Church and the African Inland Mission (AIC) – have been very significant in the provision of education and healthcare. They were a convenient conduit for the distribution of famine relief during the droughts of the 1970s and 1980s and pastoralists flocked to the trading centres to receive food aid. During the 1985 famine, the population of Korr and Kargi reached 9000, 45 per cent of all Rendille (O'Leary, 1984; Fratkin, 1992). By 1990 the town population had stabilized to around 2500 mainly poor pastoralists who did not have enough stock to move again.

Food aid can be both a cause and a consequence of the breakdown of traditional reciprocal social networks. Whichever has been the case, the result is the onset of a culture of dependency which is extremely hard to change. The real problem with food aid is knowing when to stop: by the time people are feeding it to their animals or brewing it into local beer it has already gone on too long. By then it has also created a vision of aid agencies and a dependency in the local people that are very hard to change.

The churches administering food aid were not able to foresee the long-term consequences, understandably in that they had trained as priests rather than development workers. One priest told me: 'We got it wrong. We came here and built so many structures without explaining to people or consulting them. As the Gabra saw it, Europeans did no work – since work means herding animals – but seemed to have a lot of money.'

Although most agencies in the district now talk of self-help, participation and community management in various ways, it has become very difficult to convince the settled population of the benefits of this new way of working when they have become accustomed to seemingly unlimited assistance.

## Conclusion

In the last ten years life has not improved much for the people of Marsabit and for many it has become more difficult. Most people are preoccupied with the issues of water and security. Young, educated people with salaries feel that life is easier – despite deterioration in the supply of water and electricity to the town – but in the surrounding villages life is harder, particularly for families with young children. The relationship between poverty and the stage of the family life cycle was very evident when comparing 1985 and 1995. Families with young children who had been struggling in 1985 were now better off, with remittances from working children and women being free to work away from home. In contrast, a recently formed family in 1985 was by 1995 struggling, with four children under ten for whom school fees were a drain on resources as well as the fact that childcare responsibilities restricted the mother's economic activities. Also water and firewood both involve much longer journeys for most of the year and leave little time for other activities. In several villages women's groups which were previously active now exist mainly as revolving loan groups, as there is no time to meet. The co-operation evident in the early years of settlement is no longer possible as people spend most of their time away from the village, either trying to earn some money in town or, having abandoned cultivation, going back to the *foora* when children are old enough to be left.

The history of livestock development in Africa has been dominated by attempts to impose equilibrium solutions on non-equilibrium environments (Scoones, 1995). The pastoral system is economically and environmentally rational (Kenny, 1987) and over time, pastoralists' livelihood strategies have proved to be more successful and sustainable than many 'modern' solutions such as group ranches and irrigation schemes. The indications are that pastoralism is still the most appropriate use of the rangelands but that its sustainability is being undermined by outside factors, particularly the alienation of land from the pastoral system. However, in Marsabit it is in some ways too late to reverse the policy and practical effects which have ensued from the concentration on agriculture, that is, changes in ecology and loss of dry-season grazing and increased sedentarization.

It is questionable whether pastoralists can survive better by combining cultivation and herding and whether surplus production should be kept as stored grain or reinvested in the herd (Mace, 1994). Cultivation is becoming increasingly necessary for survival alongside herding, but it cannot replace livestock entirely. The best strategy now seems to be to combine livestock and cultivation in order to spread risk. Households able to perform transitions between livestock and agriculture regularly have the best survival prospects (Mace, 1994). Permanent cultivation removes the better land from the pastoral system and makes people more unwilling to move, even when it would be the best strategy to cope with drought. Further consequences are at least partial sedentarization and the need to establish ownership or use rights over farmland as non-mobile individual property.

Even if nomadic pastoralism can be shown to be the only possible use of the rangelands, a coming problem is the rising generation of pastoralists' children who do not want to be pastoralists and yet for whom no viable alternatives are yet available. Pastoralists have been told for so long that their way of life is backward – through contact with outsiders and particularly through education – that they have begun to believe it and increasing numbers want to leave pastoralism and settle. There is thus a pressing need to create new job opportunities, some of which could involve provision of health, veterinary and marketing services to pastoralists. In the rangeland areas, gum arabic and commipher trees have some potential for augmenting incomes, particularly as production is highest in dry periods when animal production is low. This points to a need for more research in the area of alternative livelihood strategies within the pastoral area. As land alienation continues and pastoralists are increasingly linked into the wider economy, the question of what happens to people who leave pastoralism will become more pressing.

Opportunistic tracking strategies have been advocated to achieve optimal use of non-equilibrium grazing systems by maximizing resource use in good years and minimizing costs in bad years (Toulmin, 1995). This clearly approximates to what pastoralists themselves intend to do but implies the necessity of supportive government policy, including a mechanism for timely destocking in response to drought warnings, with an assurance of having access to livestock for purchase after the drought. The questions of restocking also needs to be revisited: some promising programmes in North Eastern Province are based on traditional systems of stock redistribution within the community and are directed by the people themselves. However, restocking needs to be seen in a broader context than meeting the immediate needs of individual households in the aftermath of drought. For pastoralism to be sustainable in the future, it seems most promising to link post-drought restocking with pre-drought destocking.

On a wider scale, water development policy needs to be addressed both to even out grazing pressure on the range and to ensure supplies for human consumption. Some water sources, particularly wells and boreholes, are effectively managed collectively (Swift, 1991) but they and adjacent pasture are often subject to intense pressure. Also, the issue of security has become more prominent – even in settled areas – and needs to be tackled to ensure mobility of herding populations and that settled populations are able to cultivate.

## Notes

1   This chapter arises from my reflections of working in development extension and training in Marsabit District, Kenya, in 1981–85 and a return visit in 1995.
2   At the time of writing the creation of the new Moyale District has just been announced.
3   After land registration, allocations were published in the government gazette to enable a limited period for others to claim title to the land.

## References

Baxter, P.T.W. and Hogg, R. (1990) *Property, Poverty and People: Changing Rights in Property and Problems of Pastoral Development.* Manchester: University of Manchester.
Bush, J. (1995) The role of food aid in drought and recovery: Oxfam's North Turkana (Kenya) drought relief programme 1992–94. *Disasters,* **19**(3), 247–59.
Campbell, D.J. (1984) Response to drought among farmers and herders in southern Kajiado District, Kenya. *Journal of Human Ecology,* **12**, 35–64.
Ellis, J. and Galvin, K.A. (1994) Climate patterns and land-use practices in the dry zones of Africa. *Bioscience,* **44**(5), 340–9.
Fratkin, E. (1992) Drought and development in Marsabit District, Kenya. *Disasters,* **16**(2), 119–30.
Hogg, R. (1984) The politics of drought: the pauperization of Isiolo Boran. Discussion Papers in Development Studies No. 8502, University of Manchester, Manchester.
Hogg, R. (1986) The new pastoralism: poverty and dependency in Northern Kenya. *Africa,* **56**(3).
Hogg, R. (1992) Should pastoralism continue as a way of life? *Disasters,* **16**(2), 131–7.
KARI/National Arid Land Research Centre (1988) *Annual Report.*
KARI/National Arid Land Research Centre (1991) *Annual Report.*
Kenny, O.E.F. (1987) Pastoralists' rationality and strategies for drought. MSc Dissertation, University of East Anglia.
McCabe, J.T., Perkins, S. and Schofield, C. (1992) Can conservation and development be coupled among pastoral people? *Human Organisation,* **51**(4), 353–66.
Mace, R. (1994) Transitions between cultivation and pastoralism in sub-Saharan Africa. *Current Anthropology,* **34**(4) 363–82.
Oba, G. (1992) Ecological factors in land use conflicts, land administration and food insecurity in Turkana, Kenya. Pastoral Development Network Paper 33a, ODI, London.

O'Leary, M. (1984) Ecological villains or economic victims: the case of the Rendille of Northern Kenya. *Desertification Control Bulletin*, **11**, 17–21.

Runge (1992) Common property and collective action. In D.W. Bromley (ed.), *Making the Commons Work*. San Francisco: ICS Press.

Sandford, S. (1983) *Management of Pastoral Development in the Third World*. London: ODI.

Scoones, I. (ed.) (1995) *Living with Uncertainty: New Directions in Pastoral Development in Africa*. London: IIED/ITDG.

Spencer, Paul (1973) *Nomads in Alliance: Symbiosis and Growth among the Rendille and Samburu of Kenya*. Nairobi: Oxford University Press.

Swift, J. (1991) Local customary institutions as the basis for natural resource management among Boran pastoralists in North Kenya. *IDS Bulletin*, **22**(4), 34–7.

Toulmin, C. (1995) Tracking through drought: options for destocking and restocking. In I. Scoones (ed.), *Living with Uncertainty: New Directions in Pastoral Development in Africa*. London: IIED/ITDG, pp. 95–115.

# 8

# Annapurna Conservation Area Project: In Pursuit of Sustainable Development?

## Sara Parker

## Introduction

Nepal is a landlocked nation covering 141,000 km$^2$, with a population of over 19 million. It is ranked as the fifth poorest nation by the World Bank with a GNP per capita of US$170 (World Bank, 1994). The majority of the population live in rural areas and depend upon subsistence agriculture for a livelihood. Over 90 per cent of Nepal's energy requirements are met by forests, and the environmental problems in Nepal are well-documented (Blaike *et al.*, 1980; Seddon, 1987; Metz, 1991). According to the *World Development Report 1994*, agriculture accounts for 67 per cent of GDP. Tourism has become the country's leading foreign exchange earner, with international arrivals increasing from 6000 in 1962 to almost 260,000 by 1988 (Wells, 1993). According to Wells (1993), the importance of 'nature' tourism, and hence protected areas, in attracting these visitors must not be underestimated. The Annapurna Conservation Area (ACA) is one of these protected areas and is located in the Western Himalayas (see Figure 8.1). Before looking in detail at the ACA, a brief outline of conservation policies in Nepal will be given and the role of protected areas examined.

## Commitment to Conservation

The government of Nepal has long since recognized the need to conserve the biological diversity within both the lowlands and Himalayan ranges. Nepal is considered a leader among developing nations in the promotion of

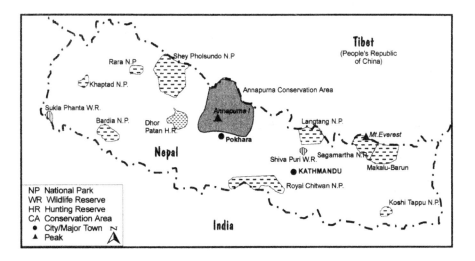

**Figure 8.1** Nepal's protected areas

enlightened conservation legislation and practices' (Heinen and Yonzon, 1994, p. 61). Since 1973, 14 National Parks and protected areas have been formed in Nepal (see Figure 8.1 and Table 8.1 below). These protected areas play an important role in attracting tourists to Nepal (Wells, 1993).

Over 10 per cent of the land in Nepal is currently under designated status; hence Nepal meets the recommendations made at the IVth Congress on National Parks and Protected Area held in 1992 (Pimbert and Pretty, 1995a). However, the limitations of designating protected-area status are becoming increasingly evident on a global scale, as evidence of people–park conflicts are reported (see Heinen and Kattel, 1992; IIED/ODA, 1994; Pimbert and Pretty, 1995a, b).

Pimbert and Pretty (1995a) examine the limitations of current professional thinking and practice with respect to the designation of protected areas. They outline the main limitations as being:

- the neglect of local people
- social costs and conflict
- high cost of preservation and
- the bias of the tradition of 'normal science'.

The proposed alternative calls for a change in perspective and emphasizes participation by local inhabitants; 'it will therefore be essential for conservation to focus on the appropriate process for participation if

**Table 8.1** The national parks and reserves of Nepal

| Name | Location | Size (km²) | Date of establishment |
|------|----------|-----------|----------------------|
| Royal Chitwan NP | C. Terai | 932 | 1973 |
| Rara NP | Mid-W. Himalaya | 106 | 1976 |
| Sukla Phanta WR | Far-W. Terai | 155 | 1976 |
| Koshi Tappu WR | E. Terai | 175 | 1976 |
| Royal Bardia NP | Mid-W. Terai | 968 | 1976 |
| Sagamartha NP | E. Himalaya | 1148 | 1976 |
| Lantang NP | C. Himalaya | 1710 | 1976 |
| Parsa WR | C. Terai | 500 | 1984 |
| Dhor Patan HR | Mid-W. Himalaya | 1325 | 1984 |
| Shey Pholsundo NP | Mid-W. Himalaya | 3555 | 1984 |
| Shivapuri WR | Kathmandu Valley | 114 | 1985 |
| Khaptad NP | Far West Hills | 225 | 1985 |
| Annapurna CA | W. Himalaya | 3400 | 1988 |
| Makalu-Barun | E. Himalaya | 2330 | 1991 |
| | Total Area | 16643 | |

*Notes*:
WR = wildlife reserve   NP = national park   HR = hunting reserve   CA = conservation area
*Source*: Heinen and Kattel (1992), p. 51.

sustainability and biodiversity goals are to be met' (Pimbert and Pretty, 1995a, p. 11).

With reference to Nepal, Heinen and Kattel (1992) provide a comprehensive account of the approach taken to conservation with descriptions of each of the designated protected areas and the problems they face. These problems include:

- illegal grazing and resource use in protected areas;
- poor relations between local residents and the reserves;
- the use of army guards to protect the resources;
- a lack of benefits for local people from tourism in the protected areas.

In addition to these problems Wells (1993) reports a growing consensus that Nepal's protected areas are becoming increasingly degraded. Due to the existence of important unique habitats, Heinen and Yonzon (1994) feel that further extension of nature reserves is needed. However, they also recognize the potential difficulty of increasing the amount of land for complete protection and propose that integrated conservation schemes (such as the Annapurna Conservation Area Project) may need to be considered. Before examining the alternative that ACAP represents, a brief outline of political change and the changing role of non-governmental organizations in Nepal is needed.

# Political Change and Non-government Organizations

Since the late 1980s and early 1990s, Nepal has been undergoing a political transition from the partyless panchayat system to a multi-party democracy. May 1991 saw the re-introduction of a multi-party democracy with the election of the Nepali Congress Party into government with 110 seats (followed by the United Marxist Leninist Party with 69 seats) (Hutt, 1994). Since then, further elections were held in December 1994 which saw the United Marxist Leninist Party being elected into government. Following the elections in 1991, the National Planning Commission provided guidelines for the next five-year plan (1992–97) in which it defined development as 'a social and political process of mobilizing and organizing people to the desired goals' and stated that 'this will be possible only when the people themselves are associated in the decision making process ... more importantly in benefit sharing' (Hutt, 1994). Thus grassroots activity was highlighted as a means of devolving power away from the central government to the people. The mechanisms for achieving this decentralization are the Village Development Committees and District Development Committees. Due to the political change in Nepal there has been widespread recognition of the potential role Non-Governmental Organizations can play in this process (Rademacher and Tamang, 1993; Seddon, 1994).

## NGO Increase

NGOs do not have a long history in Nepal though it is recognized that establishment of community groups has traditionally played an important role in village-level development initiatives. Since the mid-1970s NGOs have been on the increase, giving rise to the formation of the Social Service National Co-ordination Council (SSNCC) in 1975 to co-ordinate their activities (SSNCC was replaced by the Social Welfare Council (SWC) in 1992). The number of NGOs registered has risen from 220 in May 1990 to over 1200 in July 1993 (Rademacher and Tamang, 1993). 'The right to organize established by the new government of April 1990 has led to a proliferation of NGOs' (Shreshtra, 1993, p. 201).

The King Mahendra Trust for Nature Conservation is one of the largest NGOs in Nepal and is the organization that pioneered the Annapurna Conservation Area Project.

## King Mahendra Trust for Nature Conservation (KMTNC)

The King Mahendra Trust for Nature Conservation is an autonomous non-government and non-profit-making organization. It was established by the special King Mahendra Trust for Nature Conservation Act in 1982 and became functional in 1984 (KMTNC, 1994). The KMTNC represents a change in the overall approach to conservation. Through the Annapurna Conservation Area Project it offers an alternative to the designation of National Park status in the attempt to achieve conservation for development. The two main projects of the KMTNC are the ACAP and Nepal Conservation Research and Training Center based in Chitwan. The KMTNC regards itself as a 'catalyst' to achieving sustainable development.

## Annapurna Conservation Area

The Annapurna Conservation Area is located in the Western Himalayas (see Figure 8.1) and covers an area of over 7600 km$^2$ (Figure 8.2). The Annapurna Conservation Area (ACA) is the catchment for three major rivers, having the deepest river valley (Kali Ghandaki) and two of the highest mountains in the world (Annapurna 1 and Dhaualgiri). It is bordered by a major trekking route, the Annapurna Circuit. The geographical features of the terrain provide many micro-climates ranging from sub-tropical conditions in the south to alpine steppe and arid conditions in the north. The biological diversity is illustrated by a recent study that identified over 1200 species of plants, 101 mammals, 474 species of birds, 39 species of reptiles and 22 species of amphibians (KMTNC, 1994). Among these are the endangered snow leopard, blue sheep, musk deer and over 100 varieties of orchid. The biological diversity is matched by cultural diversity, with more than nine ethnic groups living in the ACA. The majority of the population live at subsistence level with a high level of dependence upon the natural resources. Over 90 per cent of local energy needs are met by the forests (Gurung and De Coursey, 1994).

Due to the spectacular landscape and diversity of the region, the ACA has attracted an increasing number of tourists over the past two decades from just over 14,000 in 1980 to over 43,000 in 1994 (Lama and Lipp, 1994). The ACA attracts over 55 per cent of all trekkers visiting Nepal with three times as many people visiting the ACA compared to the next most popular destination, Mount Everest (Gurung and De Coursey, 1994). Due to the additional staff employed by trekkers, such as porters and guides, the total number of trekkers entering the ACA each year is greater than the local population (approximately 60,000 people). Trekkers are concentrated both in peak seasons and limited localities within the ACA leading to impacts in the area such as increased use of forest resources. The environmental impact of tourism upon resource use has been well documented and the economic gains recognized (ACAP, 1989; Eber, 1992; Gurung and De Coursey, 1994; Shackley, 1994). For the ACA to continue to benefit from tourism it is recognized that strategies that promote 'sustainable' tourism need to be employed. Due to environmental pressures, in the mid-1980s it was recognized that the ACA required protected status in order to prevent excessive environmental degradation in the area. Rather than create a National Park and focus upon flora and fauna conservation, a government

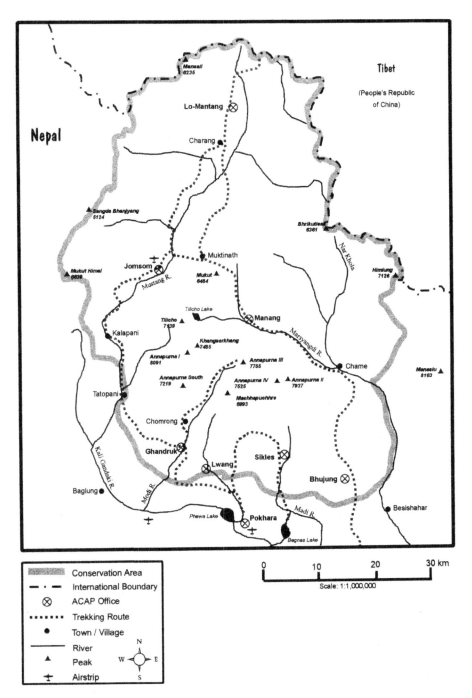

**Figure 8.2** The Annapurna conservation area (*Source*: ACAP/KMTNC, 1995)

Act was passed in 1986 that designated the Annapurna Conservation Area as a protected area. The ACA is one of the latest designated protected areas in Nepal (see Table 8.1). Prior to 1988 there was no protected area status in the Annapurna Region. In conjunction with this designation the King Mahendra Trust formed the Annapurna Conservation Area Project to facilitate the management of the area.

## The Annapurna Conservation Area Project

Following a pilot study in 1985, the KMTNC established the Annapurna Conservation Area Project in 1986. At the inception of the project it was recognized that for sustainable development to be achieved in the area, a range of skills and expertise would need to be drawn upon. Furthermore, local participation would be crucial to the entire process. Hence the ACAP recognizes itself as *lami*, or matchmaker, in the process towards realizing sustainable development.

The long-term objectives of the ACAP (KMTNC, 1990) are stated as:

- to conserve the natural resources of the ACA for the benefit of present and future generations;
- to bring sustainable social and economic development to the local people;
- to develop tourism in such a way that it will have a minimum negative environmental impact.

In order to achieve these objectives and due to the large size of the designated area, the ACAP took a phased approach. The initial phase was to form a pilot area with headquarters in Ghandruk. This area was chosen due to the environmental impacts that were being noted along one of the major trekking routes up to the Annapurna Sanctuary. Based on the experience in Ghandruk, Conservation Development Committees became the focal institutions that the ACAP promoted with other organizations forming through local level initiatives, depending upon specific local needs. In Ghandruk for example Lodge Management Committees play an important role in policy formation due to the economic important of tourism within the area.

Phase I saw an expansion into two more areas, Lwang and Sikles, each with its own focus reflecting the diversity within the ACA (see Figures 8.2 and 8.3). Phase II of ACAP started in July 1993 and resulted in the area of operation expanding from 1500 km$^2$ to 7600 km$^2$ with the opening of four new regional offices (see Figure 8.1). Each of these regions have their own specific objectives based upon assessment surveys, carried out by ACAP staff working with local villagers (Lama and Lipp, 1994). The increase in size of the project area has potential implications for the ACAP which shall be discussed later. Implications of NGOs 'scaling up' are discussed within the literature, with concern expressed over the organizations maintaining their

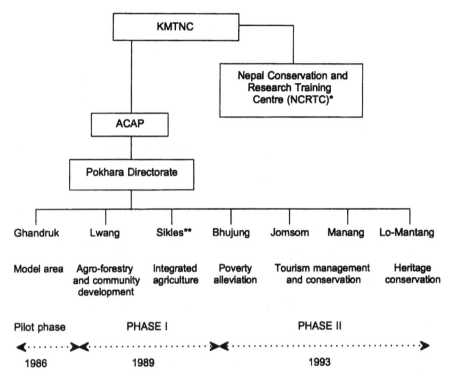

**Figure 8.3**  Phased approach and zoning in ACA

comparative advantage over government agencies (Annis, 1987; Fowler, 1988; Edwards and Hulme, 1992). Before examining the approach of the ACAP, the factors which make it unique in Nepal need to be outlined.

## What Makes ACAP Different in Nepal?

As noted earlier there has been a rise in the number of NGOs in Nepal and KMTNC is one of the largest. The following section will explore some of the factors that makes the ACAP a pioneering example within Nepal.

● The designation of the ACA represents the first time management of a protected area has been handed over to a NGO in Nepal. The main impetus behind this change in policy was the recognition that the people—

park conflict is still unresolved in Nepal and that past attempts to encourage participation of local communities in resource management have had limited impact. As environmental problems are multifaceted within ACA, a holistic approach is required that addresses the needs of the local people while at the same time promoting nature conservation and tourism management (Gurung and De Coursey, 1994).

- Environmental degradation due to tourism pressure, as well as from increasing local population, has resulted in the ACAP focusing on promoting sustainable tourism. The ACAP pilot study found that on average a tourist spends US$3 a day, and on average, less than twenty cents of this remains within the local community (ACAP, 1989). To increase the sustainability of tourism the ACAP has introduced a trekking fee to all tourists which will eventually form the main source of funding for projects in the area. This both increases the revenue gained from the tourism industry and promotes financial sustainability of the ACAP.

- Unlike the Department of National Parks and Wildlife, the ACAP has been granted the right to collect revenue directly from tourism entry fees rather than through government agencies. By charging a trekking fee to all tourists entering the ACA, the project aims to create an endowment fund to allow long-term self-sufficiency and sustainability. The ACAP is operating with relative autonomy with the revenue from tourist trekking permits being crucial to the long-term financial sustainability of the project. In order to increase revenues from tourists the trekking permit fee was raised from Rps 200 to Rps 650 in 1992. Due to this increase and the growth in tourist numbers visiting the region, ACAP aims to be self-supporting by the year 2000 (KMTNC, 1994). The entry fee collected by KMTNC has quadrupled from 7,282,000 Rps in 1989/90 to 28,165,000 in 1993/94. (KMTNC, 1994).

- The ACAP initiative pioneers the involvement of local people in a protected area from its inception rather than attempting to include local people in the planning process at a later date. The main impetus behind the project was to avoid excluding people from their environment in the pursuit of sustainable development thus avoiding the need for buffer-zone policies and special access rights. To achieve sustainable development it was recognized that local people's needs must be considered and stewardship over the environment handed over to them. Through the formation of Conservation Development Committees and a policy of requiring local people to contribute at least 50 per cent towards the support of local projects (either finance or labour), local people are included in the planning and decision-making process as well as in the implementation of conservation and development programmes (Gurung, 1993).

**ACAP**

Conservation Development Committees      Conservation Education and Extension
(CDCs)*      Programme (CEEP)

*Programmes*
Forest conservation
Alternative energy
Literacy
Health and sanitation
Community development projects
Income-generating projects
Tourist awareness schemes

*Note:*
*Along with CDCs, depending upon the local circumstance, other committees such as Lodge Management Committees, Forestry Management Committees and Alternative Energy Committees have been formed. Following the recognition of the role women play in conservation and in the use of the environment 'Ama Toli' groups were formed in 1990.

**Figure 8.4** The components of the ACAP approach

# Approach

To facilitate the process of conservation for development, the ACAP chose to re-introduce management practices that reflected the traditional resource management systems that were in place pre-1950s. These indigenous management systems vary within the ACA, but are essentially based on community consensus and common property type regimes. By encouraging communities to form Conservation Development Committees (CDCs) and through a Conservation Education and Extension Programme (CEEP), the ACAP aims to promote sustainable development.

The ACAP operates a number of programmes to provide the necessary support (both technical and financial) required for CEEP knowledge to be put into action through the CDCs. These programmes, such as alternative energy schemes and plantation programmes, are integrated into the whole approach rather than seen as independent programmes (see Figure 8.4). Brown and Wyckoff Baird (1992, p. 51), in their account of Integrated Conservation and Development Projects, describe the ACAP as potentially 'one of the more advanced and ambitious Integrated Conservation and Development Projects'. It is important to note that CDCs and the CEEP have been placed at the centre of the ACAP approach since its inception in 1986.

## Participation and the role of Conservation Development Committees

In the past decade there has been increased recognition of the benefits of participatory development (Cohen and Uphoff, 1980; Chambers, 1983; Oakley and Marsden, 1984; Midgley, 1986; Korten, 1987; Burkey, 1993; Rahman, 1993; Stiefel and Wolfe, 1994). Paralleling this literature has been a focus on the role NGOs can potentially play in promoting participatory development (Midgley, 1986; Fowler, 1988; Clark, 1991; Edwards and Hulme, 1992).

Participation is both an ambiguous and a contested concept. Participation ranges from local people being involved in implementing development or conservation programmes to being actively involved in all stages of the development process including the decision-making process. The literature acknowledges the complexity of defining participation with definitions including 'extreme participation' (Cohen and Uphoff, 1980), 'authentic participation' (Goulet, 1989) and 'self reliant participation' (Burkey, 1993), which ranges between participation through the involvement of labour to the empowerment of people through the political process.

Some NGOs become involved in the 'conscientization' approach pioneered by Freire while others aim to empower the 'community' rather than focusing on individuals or the 'oppressed'. Agenda 21 emphasized the role of participation in attempts to promote sustainable development and states that 'environmental issues are best handled with the participation of all concerned citizens at the relevant level' (Quarrie, 1992, p. 11). A common definition of participation cited in the literature is that of the United Nations Research Institute for Social Development, which states that participation is 'the organized efforts to increase control over the resources and regulative institutions in given social situations, on part of groups and movements hitherto excluded from such control' (Stiefel and Wolfe, 1994, p. 5). This definition highlights the importance of organization in participation and the role of community empowerment.

Recently there has been a focus of attention on the potential role NGOs can play in promoting participatory development. Fowler (1988) illustrates that many NGOs have the potential comparative advantage when pursing participatory development due to their close relationship with beneficiaries and their organizational form. Not all NGOs realize this potential especially if they operate on a 'top-down' basis as opposed to taking a 'bottom-up' approach. ACAP is attempting to pursue a 'bottom-up' approach by incorporating people into institutions to manage the resource base for the benefit of the local residents through the formation of Conservation Development Committees.

## Historical Context and the Aim of CDCs

In 1957 the Private Nationalization Act transferred the management of resources away from the people to government. This has led to an acceleration in the exploitation of resources as communal management systems were replaced with a government-controlled one (Furer-Haimendorf, 1964; Seddon, 1987; Bista, 1993; Gilmour and Fisher, 1992; Shreshtra, 1993). For instance, Farrington and Shreshtra (1993) note that nationalization and hence state control of Nepal's forests in 1957 merely resulted in over-exploitation of forest resources.

Seddon (1987) attests that some form of communal control over resources is needed in order to promote both communal and self-interest in the conservation and regeneration of the land. He goes on to argue that regeneration requires both ownership of the forests by villages and that the management of this resource should be handed over to the panchayat, co-operatives or other appropriate local institutions. The Panchayat Act in 1961 and Panchayat Forest Rules of 1978 attempted to promote wider participation in resource management. There is little evidence, however, to suggest that any genuine popular involvement in the political process under the panchayat system was achieved. Furthermore, the panchayat system enhanced inequalities of power and influence at the village level reinforcing the position of those who were already in positions of power within the village and outside of the villages (Seddon, 1987). According to Farrington and Shreshtra (1993) the panchayat often proved too large a unit to mobilize general interest.

The ACAP pilot study found that the panchayat system had weakened traditional resource management systems. Gilmour and Fisher (1992) document a number of indigenous management systems in Nepal that determine the use of environmental resources at the village level in Nepal. Pignéde (1966) gives a brief account of the indigenous organization, based upon a village headman and council, within the Gurung population (see Harrison and Macfarlane, 1993).

ACAP aims to re-introduce and support indigenous forest and community development management systems in order to empower the local people through organizational development. In the main, ACAP aims to create new local level institutions that become the guardians of the environment while at the same time promoting village development. By creating CDCs, the project is attempting to redress the problems associated with the panchayat system and return the ownership of the land to the people.

The ACAP aims to facilitate a process by which the control of resources is returned to the local custodians. To facilitate this process the ACAP is involved in capacity-building through aiding institutions to re-evolve to manage the resources within the local community. In addition to this, by acting as *lami* (matchmaker) the ACAP is assisting the transfer of funding from donors and tourist revenue to locally identified community develop-ment projects. CDCs are the main institutions responsible for policy and programme formulation related to natural resource management and community-identified programmes (Lama and Lipp, 1994).

## CDC Formation

The ACAP comes into contact with villages through the extension activities run under the Conservation Education and Extension Programme (CEEP). They explain the philosophy of ACAP and inform villagers of the conservation area status and ACAP's approach to promoting conservation for development. CDCs are formed by local communities within the ACA and comprise 15 elected members.[1] The formation of a CDC is kept within the indigenous framework. CDCs stimulate the formation of other management committees as the need arises, such as Lodge Management Committees, Electricity Management Committees, Health Post Management Committees and Kerosene Management Committees. Since 1990, ACAP has actively promoted the involvement of women through the formation of mothers' groups (Ama Toli groups).

The Annapurna Conservation project has established 24 CDCs (supported by sub-CDCs) with 360 members in the project areas since 1986. It is interesting to note the high number of mothers' groups that have formed with over 120 in the area forming since 1990 (see Table 8.2 below). 'Traditional mothers' groups were more focused on religious activities while now they are the key groups in initiating community activities such as clean-up campaigns, trail and bridge repair and community plantations' (Lama and Lipp, 1994, p. 7).

CDCs and sub-CDCs are given legal empowerment by ACAP to make decisions regarding sustainable use of resources. Guidelines and rules are established through consultation with CDCs and local people. CDCs are theoretically politically neutral in that they are not associated with any one political party.[2] Training given through support programmes is aimed at increasing the capacity of people to manage their own resources. The long-term aim is to enable committees to function in the absence of the ACAP, thus promoting sustainable development and complete autonomy.

It is not just the formation of CDCs that leads to conservation and

**Table 8.2**   Institutions formed in ACA

| Sector | CDC | Sub CDC | Mothers' groups | Other |
|--------|-----|---------|-----------------|-------|
| Ghandruk | 4 | 18 | 40 | 14 |
| Lwang | 3 | 15 | 30 | 4 |
| Sikles | 3 | 6 | 25 | 8 |
| Bhujung | 6 | 2 | 18 | 7 |
| Manang | 4 | 0 | 0 | 2 |
| Jomsom | 3 | 5 | 0 | 6 |
| Lo-Mantang | 1 | 8 | 11 | 12 |
| Total | 24 | 54 | 124 | 53 |
| Members | 360 | 540 | 1488 | 557 |

*Source*: Lama and Lipp (1994, p. 7)

development but ultimately it is the decisions and policies which these institutions make and their ability to enforce these rules that will determine their success. Decisions made by CDCs range from designating forest user zones (with fines attached for non-compliance), identification of community projects such as investment in alternative energy sources or school infrastructure. Other decisions include a ban on hunting and associated fines. Often reaching such decisions and enforcing them causes conflict within villages due to the opposing interests of villagers. The chairman of the CDC in Sikles feels that:

> Sikles faces many many problems convincing the people about the aims of conservation and development schemes, and often there are hot talks with the villagers and *even* with the committee members. It has been happening because of the ignorance of the people and to some extent the selfishness of the people. My own work is difficult because so many people do not understand. (personal communication, emphasis in original)

Raising the awareness of villagers of the need to conserve the biodiversity is recognized by the ACAP and is reflected in the equal importance it gives to the Conservation Education and Extension Programme (CEEP). CDC formation and functioning are strongly related to the Conservation Education and Extension Programme (CEEP).

## Conservation Education and Extension Programme (CEEP)

Since the approval of the National Conservation Strategy (NCS) for Nepal in 1988 'the need for incorporating environmental concerns into all forms of education has been recognized, and this is reflected in the fact that all major policy documents published within the past four years have stressed the need for environmental education' (NCS, 1994). The eighth Five Year Plan (1992–97) stresses the importance of environmental education in raising environmental awareness in Nepal and makes provisions for environmental education at all levels (NCS, 1993). The National Conservation Strategy for Nepal sets out an agenda for conservation action within Nepal covering both formal and non-formal sectors (NPC/IUCN, 1991). The ultimate aim of environmental education is to promote action to conserve the environment. The Conservation Education and Extension Programme pursued by the ACAP has been in place since the inception of the ACAP. 'Conservation education is considered the backbone for the success and sustenance of the project' (Gurung, 1993). Initially funded by the ACAP budget (mainly from trekking permit revenue), since 1993 the CEEP has received additional funding under the Overseas Development Administrations Joint Funding Scheme. The aim of the CEEP (ACAP, 1995) is:

- to disseminate information of the ethos of the ACAP;
- to facilitate community consensus building;

- and to encourage community mobilization towards conservation for development.

CEEP aims to raise awareness and thereby foster direct action towards projects being planned, implemented and monitored by local institutions (CDCs). In particular it hopes to encourage action that is aimed at protecting the environment and ensure that local resources are used and managed in a sustainable manner. The CEEP has both formal and non-formal components to its programme. The non-formal element comprises extension activities such as mobile awareness camps, study tours, audio-visual events and theatre performances. These events are used to achieve a number of objectives but aim mainly to increase awareness and mobilize communities into conservation activities (such as clean-up campaigns or sanitation programmes). Extension activities are also demanded by CDCs which aim to increase awareness among the community regarding specific environmental problems.

Many of the programmes such as plantation schemes and alternative energy schemes are actively involved in extension activities that form part of CEEP. Extension activities relate to all ACAP's programmes and form a central pillar of the ACAP's approach. The adult literacy project designed by the ACAP, aimed mainly at women within the Annapurna Conservation Area, can also be categorized as a CEEP activity. Through increasing the literacy levels of women in the ACA, the formation of mothers' groups (Ama Toli groups) is stimulated, as women gain the skills required to record decisions and hold meetings about activities they will undertake. The education package used to teach literacy skills includes a book of stories written by local women through a learner-generated material approach, which addresses the problem of a lack of relevant material for the course to be run. The stories written by the women are centred around environmental issues in the communities.

## Formal Education

The formal education component of the CEEP is a curriculum which is implemented in local schools from grades six to eight. One problem noted by the Conservation Education Assistants of the ACAP was that students, though they enjoy the conservation classes, do not take them as seriously as their other subjects as they do not contribute towards their school-leaving certificate grade and have little recognized academic value. From a workshop held in May 1995 (with the aim of gathering information for CEEP Progress Report of ODA's JFS requirements) a number of issues were raised with regards to success of the formal conservation classes. The curriculum is currently under review as teachers are demanding more specific curriculum guidance and additional resources for teaching.

The CDC and CEEP form the pillars of the ACAP. Due to the size of the region, the ACAP has taken a phased approach focusing on different issues in each of its operational regions (see Figure 8.2 and Figure 8.4). However, in each area both CDC and CEEP remain core features of the ACAP approach and are significantly linked to its success. It is important to note that project staff concerned with the individual programmes offered by ACAP are all involved in some form of educational activity and feel the CEEP is crucial to the successful design and implementation of the conservation and development programmes.

## Programmes

By an effective Conservation Education and Extension Programme that raises the awareness of local residents to the necessity for conservation schemes, it is hoped that CDCs will identify local conservation and development needs. The ACAP supports CDCs by offering a number of schemes. This enables the ACAP to act as 'matchmaker' whereby it brings in the external expertise and funding for use in the ACA. The programmes identified and implemented through CDCs reflect local needs and, as can be seen from Figure 8.3, each area has its own focus reflecting the diversity of needs within the ACA.

If ACAP is to truly represent an innovative approach to achieving conservation for development it is essential that it can evaluate both its programmes and its approach. As with all initiatives that are 'process'-orientated, such evaluation procedures are complex and require in-depth, on-going assessment. In order to validate the claim that a participatory approach is being adopted it is essential that the 'beneficiaries' are included in this evaluation process.

## Success versus sustainability

The literature reviewed reflects a general acceptance that the ACAP is an example of a successful project aimed at promoting conservation for development (Hough and Sherpa, 1989; Brown and Wyckoff Baird, 1992; Eber, 1992; Heinen and Kattel, 1992; Wells and Brandon, 1992; Gurung, 1993; Wells, 1993; Gurung and De Coursey, 1994; Pye-Smith and Feyerbrand, 1994). Internationally, ACAP has received a number of awards in recognition of its achievements (including Global 500 Roll of Honor (1994), John Paul Getty Wildlife Conservation Award (1992) and Tourism for Tomorrow Award (1991)). The awards have been achieved mainly by the model area and headquarters of the ACAP, Ghandruk. ACAP has been operational in Ghandruk for nearly ten years which has enabled its impact to be assessed. However, the local context of Ghandruk may not represent a typical village within the ACA due to the fact that it is located on two of the busiest trekking routes (the Annapurna Circuit and the Annapurna Base Camp Trek). Evaluation of other villages is required to assess how typical the

'Ghandruk Experience' really is (see Bell, 1994). 'Ghandruk is always cited as a success story but ACAP is more than Ghandruk and people don't realize this!' (S. Thakali, personal communication, May 1995). This reflects the tendency of research to have a 'project bias' where research generates more research (Chambers, 1983).

## General Considerations and Context

Reflecting on the wider context in which the ACAP is operating, Wells and Brandon (1992) outline four key advantages the ACAP has:

1. personal interest of the monarchy
2. specific supporting legislation
3. the autonomy of the KMTNC
4. field surveys and extensive discussion in the field which *preceded* the establishment of the conservation area status.

Wells further emphasizes the autonomy of the KMTNC, and hence the ACAP, to bypass 'many of the inefficiencies associated with government agencies' (1993, p. 461). In addition to these findings Heinen and Kattel (1992) discuss the important role of the high level of training the project staff have undergone (with many undertaking university degrees overseas) as well as the importance of capacity-building at the 'grassroots' through training programmes.

## CDC – Reports of Success

ACAP's success is often based on its ability to involve people in the decision-making process through the high numbers of CDCs formed (see p. 156). The programmes run by the ACAP are evaluated by quantitative indicators such as the number of trees planted, clean-up campaigns conducted or toilets constructed in different villages. However, to date there has been a lack of on-going, in-depth evaluation of the project and in particular a lack of research at the grassroots. Though it is recognized that the evaluation of 'process'-orientated projects is often both complex and time consuming it is vital that such evaluation is undertaken.

Participatory Rural Appraisal is recognized widely as a tool used to achieve qualitative evaluation (Chambers, 1983: Oakley and Marsden, 1984; Brown and Wyckoff Baird, 1992; Messerschmidt, 1995). The ACAP itself recognizes the value of such approaches to evaluation, especially in light of recent donor demands for evidence of its success in order to secure on-going funds for its projects. While recognizing the fact that local people are incorporated into the decision-making process, to date little has been done to involve the local people in the evaluation procedures. For ACAP to leave behind sustainable institutions this issue needs to be addressed. ACAP staff at the directorate in Pokhara have recently undergone a short PRA training session provided by the Institute of Forestry in Pokhara in order to pilot some PRA techniques in the field and incorporate local opinions into evaluation procedures.

Further examination of the decisions made on programmes implemented needs to be undertaken. The CDCs within the ACA have an impressive record of initiating projects such as plantation programmes, toilet building campaigns and the formulation of rules and regulations. Through the ACAP the CDCs have been designated the right to formulate policies regarding the use of environmental resources. By developing the capacity of local inhabitants to manage their surrounding environment both access to natural resources and a legitimate management system have been created. Many attempts to enable community management of wildlife resources often fail to successfully include local people in the decision-making process (IIED/ODA, 1994). Decisions made within the ACA by CDCs include enforcing restricted zoning of forest use and the introduction of a ban on hunting (with fines based upon the type of animal hunted). It now remains for the local people to become involved in the evaluation process if self-reliant participatory development is to be achieved. This re-emphasizes the need for PRA tools to be utilized.

## CEEP – Success Stories

The Conservation Education and Extension Programme is particularly difficult to assess due to the ambiguous nature between the cause and effect relationship between education and subsequent actions. The Conservation Education Assistants employed by the ACAP feel that CEEP is crucial to both the successful implementation of projects as well as the functioning of the CDCs. To satisfy the ODA's Joint Funding Scheme evaluation requirements, in-depth reports are needed reflecting qualitative as well as quantitative evaluation. Evaluating the impact of education programmes is particularly complex due to the diversity of impacts education programmes can have. Baseline data are needed on a number of variables, such as general awareness over environmental issues.

It is interesting to note that different areas within the ACA report of different components of the CEEP being more successful than others in attracting participants, altering attitudes and stimulating action (such as plantation sites and clean-up campaigns). The problems and issues raised by the Conservation Education Assistants (CEAs) at the workshop held in May 1995 illustrated the different achievements and problems the CEEP has experienced within the ACA. The information in Table 8.3 is a summary of issues raised at the workshop held in May 1995 (attended by the author).

A marked difference was noted between the enthusiasm of newly incorporated villages and the constructive criticism of villages that have been

**Table 8.3** Achievements and problems of the CEEP as perceived by the Conservation Education Assistants

| Sector | Achievements | Problems |
|---|---|---|
| Ghandruk | Extension programme and study tours motivate villagers, particularly in clean-up campaigns, and create a high level of awareness towards the approach of ACAP. | Conservation education teachers are demanding improvements be made to the curriculum and resources available. |
| Lwang | Conservation education classes have started in a number of schools. Workshop led by ACAP led to CDCs organizing and running their own workshop with ACAP staff invited to participate. | Conservation teachers – similar comments to those in Ghandruk. |
| Sikles | Conservation classes spreading to a number of schools throughout the sector. Audio-visual is particulary successful method of disseminating conservation information. | Clean-up campaigns and sanitation are a problem due to the steep terrain and lack of space for constructing toilets. |
| Bhujung | Home visits and ward visits more effective than large meetings needed to motivate people. Study tour dispelled many misconceptions and fears about ACAP. | Adult literacy is a problem due to the heavy workload of villagers. |
| Manang | Study tour particularly successful and mobile camps are often followed by conservation activities, e.g. clean-up campaigns. | Clean-up campaign and sanitation programme not very successful despite extension programmes.[3] |
| Jomsom | Audio-visual most successful method as it overcomes the local language barrier. | No CEA and language problems – staff spend disproportionate time on educational activities. |
| Lo-Mantang | Study tour and workshops proved effective at dispelling confusion over the role of ACAP. | Same as Jomsom: high level of confusion due to other agencies activities in the area. |

in contact with the ACAP for a number of years. An example of constructive criticism comes from teachers who have been 'testing out' the ACAP conservation curriculum in local schools. Teachers have expressed the need for a more in-depth and class specific curriculum (in both Nepali as well as English language) and for such a curriculum to be supported by improved resources.

Staff of the ACAP noted a number of changes resulting from extension programmes, run under the CEEP, such as greater motivation towards forming mothers' groups and conducting clean-up campaigns. The study tours to Chitwan National Park (mainly for new members of CDCs and mothers' groups) were seen as having a significant impact on the attitude of local people towards the ACAP as villagers on their return would share the information they had gained. Study tours are seen as playing an important role in gaining villagers' trust and motivation.

One issue raised was that extension programmes reach a large number of people on an irregular basis and the formal programme reaches a large number of schoolchildren within the ACA. However, this leaves the children not attending school with little contact with conservation education. This is recognized by the ACAP staff as causing problems, since it is precisely these children who have a high level of contact with the use of environmental resources. It remains to be seen how this problem is tackled.

The success of the Conservation Education and Extension Programme (CEEP) pursued by the ACAP lies not in the separate course it offers or in the methods of disseminating information. Rather, it lies with the approach taken. In particular the large number of programmes and alternatives available to the ACAP staff enables a flexible approach to be pursued. If one extension activity fails others can be tried. If looking to replicate the success of the ACAP in other areas, it needs to be the approach that is adopted rather than the components of any of the programmes offered.

## Programme Success

The successful design and implementation of programmes such as plantation schemes, micro-hydro projects, adult literacy classes or income-generating projects is highly dependent upon an effective CEEP and formation of CDCs. Natural resource conservation has been promoted in a number of ways in the ACA. Since it has been established ACAP has facilitated the following (Lama and Lipp, 1994):

- more than 18 nurseries have been established with over 11,600 seedlings;
- over 24.7 hectares of community plantations have been created;
- over 39,370 seedlings have been planted in the community and over 83,400 seedlings in private plantations;
- 2 micro-hydro projects have been completed (one more under construction);
- 6 kerosene depots have been established and back boilers and slow cookers introduced into many villages;
- over 20 school improvement projects have been supported.

It is important to note that the success of ACAP should not be based on the number of projects completed as the decision-making process through the CDCs should ensure that viable, non-sustainable projects are not initiated. CDCs' ability to make decisions and implement projects that can be sustained in the long term needs to be assessed. Again this requires that local people are included in the evaluation of the ACAP at facilitating CDCs in their role of promoting conservation for development. Qualitative participatory research is one way of including the voices of the local people in the evaluation procedure.

## Funding and Donor Considerations – ACAP the 'Matchmaker'

The programmes that have been initiated in the ACA often require external sources of funds in order to be financially viable. Wherever possible, the ACAP applies the policy that local contributions should make up 50 per cent of the financial input (though in some cases input in the form of labour is accepted as sufficient commitment to the projects). The long-term aim of the ACAP is that the revenue gained from tourist entrance fees will allow the project to be financially sustainable and provide the money needed for CDCs to implement community and conservation projects (see p. 152). In the medium term, however, and possibly longer term, funding from donors is required. With the increase in size of the ACAP operational area and reports of the Project's success there has been an increase in the amount and sources of funds the project has access to. For the ACAP to pursue an approach of promoting sustainable development external funds are required to enable the decisions made by local people to be translated into actions and programmes that promote conservation within the ACA.

In order to attract such funding the ACAP and KMTNC feel the need to promote 'stories of success'. However, there is also concern that once donor agencies feel that ACAP is achieving its goals, without realizing the crucial role external funds play, the funding will be withdrawn. 'With all our stories of success we are giving the wrong information' (S. Thakali, personal communication, 1995). It is essential that the ACAP and KMTNC adapt to their changing role within the ACA if they are to continue to promote sustainable development initiatives. Development literature reports of the problems many NGOs face when they attempt to 'scale up' their activities (Annis, 1987; Fowler, 1988; Edwards and Hulme, 1992). ACAP needs to be aware of these challenges and respond to them accordingly.

## Donor Evaluation Requirements

The expansion in the area under the remit of the ACAP and increase in sources of external funding mean that the project needs to satisfy an increasing number of donor conditions and requirements. Donor organizations' evaluation requirements of the ACAP range from technical reports to more in-depth evaluatory assessment that requires the beneficiaries' reflections to be included. ACAP needs to adapt to its new role as a large NGO that is accountable not only to the local beneficiaries but increasingly to external donors. The requirement of external donors for detailed evaluation reports can promote the process of initiating participatory, qualitative evaluation. However, questions are raised over who the ACAP is ultimately accountable to; is it the donors, the KMTNC or the local residents of the ACA?

At the same time the goals and philosophy of what Brown and Wyckoff Baird (1992) class as projects pursuing Integrated Conservation and Development Programmes (Icdps) need to be taken into consideration by external funders. According to Brown and Wyckoff Baird when organizations are pursuing process-orientated sustainable development 'donors need to recognize that, in most cases, more time and funding than they are accustomed to providing will be required to demonstrate the value of Icdps' (1992, p. 58). This point reinforces the role of training of project staff either nationally or internationally in meeting donor requirements and adapting to the different stages of being involved in Icdps.

## Conclusion – the ACAP a Successful or Sustainable Project?

As noted earlier the ACAP staff have found working with the community and building trust to be a timely process. This raises questions over when the project should be evaluated. Evaluation should be an on-going process that serves to inform decision making at both village and central level. The effectiveness of the ACAP in the long term may be dependent upon the ability of the project to critically evaluate its success and to build upon the capacity within communities for local level institutions to carry out this evaluation.

The ultimate aim of the ACAP is to withdraw from the area leaving behind a network of institutions through which local people can take control over the management of local resources and have access to funding from outside the community. The definitive measure will be the continuity of the CDCs to function after the project has withdrawn from the area. Brown and Wyckoff Baird note that at present 'there is insufficient evidence to be confident that the forest management committees (within ACA) would continue to function in the absence of the project' (1992, p. 56). However, they also point out that internalizing the values of conservation that ACAP promotes is a long-term process. As S. Thakali points out 'you cannot measure our *true* success until we have gone!' (personal communication, May 1995).

In-depth, systematic evaluation is lacking both by researchers and academics as well as internally by the staff of the ACAP. While recognizing the complexities of evaluating projects that are process-orientated rather than target-orientated, such evaluation is needed in order to draw conclusions from the Annapurna Conservation Area Project experience, not only to address questions of transferability of approach but also for the financial sustainability of the organization.

## Acknowledgement

I would like to thank Shailendra Thakali (Senior Programme Officer at KMTNC), S. Bajracharya, Dibya Gurung, Nilam Gurung and ACAP staff in

Sikles for their time and effort whilst in the field. The views expressed in the article are those of the author.

## Notes

1　The Chairman of the Village Development Committee automatically becomes an ex-officio member. Each village has nine wards and from each ward one person is elected. Chairman and vice-chairman then elect one more person totalling 12. An additional three members are nominated by ACAP in an attempt to encourage participation and representation of women and socially disadvantaged classes.
2　The national election in November 1994 and subsequent change of government has created some conflict within local CDCs within the ACA. In Dhampus political factions due to strong affiliations of opposing leaders had led to the CDC no longer functioning (ACAP/KMTNC, 1995).
3　In one particular village the CDC Chairman was reported as saying 'even if you pay me 10,000 rupees (over £1000) I will not move that rubbish' due to the feeling that moving rubbish was 'below' the status held by Managi people.

## References

ACAP (1989) *Annapurna Conservation Area Project*. Brochure.
ACAP (1995) *Conservation Education and Extension Programme, Progress Report April 1994–March 1995*. Submitted to ODA–UK and KMTNC (UK).
ACAP/KMTNC (1995) Information displayed at the ACAP Regional Headquarters in Ghandruk.
Annis, S. (1987) Can small scale development be large scale policy? *World Development*, **15** (Supplement), 129–37.
Bell, J. (1994) *Cook Electric: The Ghandruk Experience*. London: Intermediate Technology.
Bista (1992) *Fatalism and Development: Nepal's Struggle for Modernization*. Orient Longman.
Blaike, P., Cameron, J. and Seddon, D. (1980) *Nepal in Crisis: Growth and Stagnation in the Periphery*. Milton Keynes: Open University Press.
Brown, K. (1994) Conservation or development in Nepal's Terai? Resolving land use conflicts in Asia's last land frontier. CSERGE Working Paper.
Brown, M. and Wyckoff Baird, B. (1992) *Biodiversity Support Programme: Designing Integrated Conservation and Development Projects*. Washington, DC: World Wildlife Fund/The Nature Conservancy.
Burkey, S. (1993) *People First: A Guide to Self-reliant Participatory Rural Development*, 2nd edn. London: Brooks.
Cater, E. and Lowman, G. (eds) (1994) *Ecotourism: A Sustainable Option?* Chichester: John Wiley & Sons in association with the Royal Geographic Society.
Chambers, R. (1983) *Putting the Last First*. London: Longman Scientific & Technical.
Clark, J. (1991) *Democratizing Development: The Role of Voluntary Organizations*. London: Earthscan.
Cohen and Uphoff (1980) Participation's place in rural development: seeking clarity through specificity. *World Development*, **8**, 213–35.
Eber, S. (1992) Beyond the green horizon. A discussion paper on Principles for Sustainable Tourism. Tourism Concern and WWF-UK.
Edwards, M. and Hulme, D. (1992) *Making a Difference: NGO's and Development in a Changing World*. London: Earthscan.

Farrington, J. and Lewis, D.J. (eds) (1993) *Non Government Organizations and the State in Asia: Rethinking Roles in Sustainable Agricultural Development.* London: Routledge.

Farrington, J. and Shreshtra, N.K. (1993) Non-government interaction in Nepal. In J. Farrington and D.J. Lewis (eds), *Non Government Organizations and the State in Asia: Rethinking Roles in Sustainable Agricultural Development.* London: Routledge, pp. 189–223.

Fowler, A. (1988) NGO's in Africa achieving comparative advantage in relief and micro development. Institute of Development Discussion Paper 249, University of Sussex.

Freire, P. (1972) *The Pedagogy of the Oppressed.* Harmondsworth: Penguin.

Furer-Haimendorf, C. von (1964) *The Sherpas of Nepal's Buddhist Highlands.* Berkeley, CA: University of California Press.

Gilmour, D.A. and Fisher, R.J. (1992) *Villagers, Forests and Foresters: The Philosophy, Process and Practice of Community Forestry in Nepal.* Nepal: Sahayogi Press.

Goulet, D. (1989) Participation in development: new avenues. *World Development,* **17**(2), 165–78.

Gurung, C.P. (1993) People's participation in conservation: Annapurna Conservation Area Project. In King Mahendra Trust for Nature Conservation German Committee (ed.), *Appropriate Technologies and Environmental Education as Possibilities for Intercultural Perception in the Himalayan Area* (proceedings of an international conference, Kathmandu).

Gurung, C.P. and De Coursey, M. (1994) The Annapurna Conservation Area Project: a pioneering example of sustainable tourism? In E. Cater and G. Lowman (eds), *Ecotourism: A Sustainable Option?* Chichester: John Wiley, pp. 179–94.

Harrison, S. and Macfarlane, A. (1993) English edition of Pignéde (1966) *The Gurungs: The Himalayan Population of Nepal.* Nepal: Ratna Pustak Bandar.

Heinen, J.T. and Kattel, B. (1992) Parks, people and conservation: a review of management issues in Nepal's protected areas. *Population and Environment,* **14**(10), 49–84.

Heinen, J.T. and Yonzon (1994) A review of conservation issues and programs in Nepal from a single species focus toward biodiversity protection. *Mountain Research and Development,* **14**(1), 61–76.

Hough, J.L. and Sherpa, M.N. (1989) Bottom up vs. basic needs: integrating conservation and development in the Annapurna and Michiru Mountain conservation areas of Nepal and Malawi. *Ambio,* **18**(8), 434–41.

Hutt, M. (ed.) (1994) *Nepal in the Nineties: Versions of the Past, Visions of the Future.* Delhi: Oxford University Press.

IIED/ODA (1994) Whose Eden? An overview of community approaches to wildlife management. A report to the ODA, IIED.

KMTNC (1990) *Annapurna Conservation Area Project: Three Year Retrospective Progress Report March 1986–December 1989.* Kathmandu: KMTNC.

KMTNC (1994) *A Decade of Conservation and Development (1984–1994).* Nepal: KMTNC.

Korten, D. (1987) *Community Management: Asian Experiences and Perspectives.* New Delhi: Kumaran Press.

Lama, T.S. and Lipp, J.R. (1994) *Annapurna Conservation Area Project Annual Progress Report, 15 July 1993–14 July 1994.* Katmandu: KMTNC.

Macfarlane, A. (1994) Fatalism and development in Nepal. In M. Hutt (ed.), *Nepal in the Nineties: Versions of the Past, Visions of the Future.* Delhi: Oxford University Press, pp. 106–27.

Messerschmidt, D.A. (1995) *Rapid Appraisal for Community Forestry: The RA Process and Rapid Diagnostic Tools.* London: IIED Participatory Methodology Series.

Metz, J.J. (1991) A reassessment of the causes and severity of Nepal's environmental crisis. *World Development,* **19**(7), 805–20.

168    *Sara Parker*

Midgley, J. (1986) *Community Participation, Social Development and the State.* London, Methuen.

NCS (1993) Environmental education and awareness. *NCS Nepal, Quarterly Newsletter of the National Conservation Strategy Implementation,* no. 4, 6–7.

NCS (1994) Environmental education in Nepal: past and present. *NCS Nepal, Quarterly Newsletter of the National Conservation Strategy Implementation,* no. 2, 1–3.

NPC/IUCN (1991) *Environmental Education in Nepal: A Review.* National Planning Commission, HMG Nepal in collaboration with IUCN – The World Conservation Union.

Oakley, P. and Marsden, D. (1984) *Approaches to Participation in Rural Development.* Geneva: ILO.

Pignéde, B. (1966) *The Gurungs: The Himalayan Population of Nepal.* Nepal: Ratna Pustak Bhandar.

Pimbert, M.P. and Pretty, J.N. (1995a) Beyond conservation ideology and the wilderness myth. *Natural Resources Forum,* 19(1), 5–14.

Pimbert, M.P. and Pretty, J.N. (1995b) Parks, people and professional: putting 'participation' into protected area management. UNRISD Discussion Paper UNRISD/IIED/WWF-International.

Pye-Smith, C. and Feyerbrand, G.B. (1994) *The Wealth of Communities.* London: Earthscan.

Quarrie, J. (ed.) (1992) *Earth Summit '92: The United Nations Conference on Environment and Development, Rio de Janeiro 1992.* London: The Regency Press Corporation.

Rademacher, A. and Tamang, D. (1993) *Democracy Development and NGOs in Nepal Search.* Katmandu, Nepal:

Rahman, M.D. (1993) *People's Self Development: Perspectives on Participatory Action Research.* London: Zed Books.

Seddon, D. (1987) *Nepal: A State of Poverty.* Vikas Publishing House.

Seddon, D. (1994) Democracy and development in Nepal. In M. Hutt (ed.), *Nepal in the Nineties: Versions of the Past, Visions of the Future.* Delhi: Oxford University Press, pp. 128–64.

Shackley, M. (1994) The land of Lo, Nepal/Tibet. The first eight months of tourism. *Tourism Management,* 15(1), 17–26.

Shreshtra, N.K. (1993) An overview of NGOs' agricultural activities in Nepal. In J. Farrington and D. Lewis (eds), *Non Government Organizations and the State in Asia.* London: Routledge, pp. 200–13.

Stiefel, M. and Wolfe, M. (1994) *A Voice for the Excluded: Popular Participation in Development.* London: Zed Books.

Wells, M.P. (1993) Neglect of the biological riches: the economics of nature tourism in Nepal. *Biodiversity and Conservation,* 2(4), 445–64.

Wells, M.P. and Brandon, K. (1992) *People and Parks: Linking Protected Area Management with Local Communities.* Washington, DC: The World Bank/WWF/USAID.

World Bank (1994) *World Development Report 1994.* New York: Oxford University Press.

## 9

# Global Processes and the Politics of Sustainable Development in Colombia and Costa Rica

Philip J. O'Brien

## Introduction

In the last few years, following the United Nations Conference on Environment and Development (UNCED) in 1992, there has emerged in Latin America an interesting attempt to institutionalize the active participation of many groups – business, NGOs, indigenous communities and local communities – in an interactive dialogue with sectors of the state around issues of sustainable development. Many of these initiatives have been actively supported with finance from bilateral and international bodies concerned with development and the environment.

Two countries which have advanced far down the road of participation are Costa Rica and Colombia. Concerns with participation arose for different motives in each case. In Colombia's case a strong discourse for creating a participatory democracy arose with the Constituent Assembly of 1991. This was part of the peace process with sectors of Colombia's guerrillas, and also part of the attempt to stem the ever rising tide of violence from drug, political and social conflict. These concerns were embodied in Colombia's new Constitution in 1991 which enshrined an enormous array of legal rights to enable Colombian citizens and communities to actively participate in the affairs of their country. In Costa Rica, the most stable, peaceful and socially cohesive country in Latin America, the introduction of more participatory forms of democracy arose mainly from Costa Rica's desire to find a development 'ecological niche' for itself and to secure foreign financial assistance.

In both countries concerns about the increasing importance of meeting environmental standards in international trade, and particularly the environmental concerns built into the NAFTA agreements, spurred the business communities to accept participatory structures for issues dealing with the environment. Somewhat surprisingly it was drug-, corruption- and violence-ridden Colombia which found it easier to institutionalize a participatory structure for issues relating to sustainable development than socially stable Costa Rica. In both countries, global processes surrounding sustainable development play a key role in triggering and supporting local initiatives.

## Global Processes

### Development Discourses

Two discourses have dominated the last decade's debate on the challenge of development. The first talks of economic growth through competitive markets, deregulation, privatization and integration into global markets. Particularly in Latin American and other Third World countries neo-liberal policies became a requirement as part of the debt re-negotiations. The second discourse, which was given credibility by UNCED, emphasizes sustainable development, ecological limits, equity and regulation.

Overall the former has more influence, reflecting the consensus view of Washington and the dominant power interests throughout the world. The World Bank's 1991 World Development Report, *The Challenge of Development*, summed it up as follows: 'a consensus is gradually forming in favour of a market friendly approach to development'. Government interventions are considered to do more harm than good, with the following possible exceptions: investments in people; maintenance of macroeconomic stability; integration of the national economy into the world economy; and provision of a competitive climate for private enterprise (World Bank, 1991).

The debt crisis enabled the International Monetary Fund (IMF) and the World Bank (IBRD) together with local elites to push through a series of structural reforms, accelerating the integration of Latin America into global markets and definitively establishing the hegemony of the neo-liberal model of development (O'Brien, 1993). The results in Latin America have been mixed. There have been some positive indicators on growth in the 1990s after years of falling per capita GDP, but lower incomes and services for the majority as well as a severe deterioration in environmental quality for all.

The sustainable development alternative is less coherent and analytically rigorous than the neo-liberal one. As a result of the negotiations leading up to UNCED in 1992 many of its concerns and language have now been co-opted and diluted within the dominant discourse. The World Bank in particular moved quickly to establish its 'green' credentials, introducing environmental impact assessments for all major development projects, playing a key role in the establishment and operation of the Global Environmental Facility (GEF), and establishing itself as an important think-tank on environmentally sound development (World Bank, 1992b, 1994).

Sustainable development however raises problems largely ignored by, and difficult to integrate into, the dominant development model, emphasizing as it has ecological sustainability, the ecological importance of population growth, resource use and ownership, equity and poverty, consumption and production levels and styles, alternative indicators of progress, and democratic participation.

Both politically and practically there are a series of tensions between the neo-liberal recipes for growth and the issues of sustainable development.

## The Emergence of Sustainable Development

Until the Brundtland Report of 1987 (Brundtland, 1987) the debate on environment and development essentially ran along two parallel tracks: one emphasizing the environment and conservation with little analysis of human societies, and the other development and poverty with little analysis of the environment. It was the Brundtland Report which brought together human activity and the environment in a single concept, that of sustainable development',[1] just as it brought together the ideas of environmental management and participation. As Brundtland herself put it, sustainable development is the holistic concept best covering 'the combination of environment and development, the links between economy and ecology, and between poverty and environment' (quoted in Sarre *et al,*. 1991), with her definition emphasizing intergenerational and intragenerational equity, needs and limitations.[2]

## The Complexity of Ecological Problems

Ecological problems as highlighted within the sustainable development discourse focus on three functions of the environment: the provision of resources for human activity; the absorption of wastes from human activity and the provision of services independently of or interdependently with human activity (Hueting, 1992). Excessive and badly conceived human use of the environment has created a series of interrelated global, regional, national and local consequences such as climate change, ozone depletion, acidification, species extinction, deforestation, loss of soil fertility, water depletion, toxic pollution and resource depletion. Ecological change often results from the accumulation of small, almost imperceptible, acts by millions of individuals.

Also it may be impossible to predict its timing, nature and consequences (Gore, 1992). Uncertainty adds to the difficulties faced by political decision-makers, whose time horizon is notoriously short.

In practice the Brundtland Report steered an ambiguous course between the various positions on sustainable development.[3] It did emphasize such things as the need to produce more with less, to reduce population growth, to redistribute income, and to assist poor countries to grow to overcome extreme poverty; but it also stressed the importance of reviving world economic growth as an essential prerequisite for sustainable development which became the source of the idea of sustainable growth (McNeil, 1991).[4] Indeed Brundtland's priorities emphasized reviving growth and changing the quality of growth without clarifying how to reconcile this growth with ecological limits or guidance on how to change the quality of growth.

The definition of sustainable development and its operation became a crucial political problem. The IUCN Report, *Caring for the Earth* (IUCN, 1991), attempted to popularize a shift towards 'sustainable living' and quality of life, based on a respect for ecological integrity and a critique of existing development patterns. But in the end the generally accepted definition world-wide became the first part of Brundtland's definition: 'development which meets the needs of the present without compromising the ability of future generations to meet their own needs'. Most Third World governments and elites were as reluctant as their counterparts in the rich nations to question the nature of economic growth and the distribution of the benefits of that growth. However, although the need for greater equity *now* was lost, as was the emphasis on needs as opposed to wants, fundamental issues of equity and participation became inextricably tied to the debate on sustainable development.

## The United Nations Conference on Environment and Development (UNCED): the Politics of Participation

In 1988 the independent Centre for Our Common Future was established in Geneva to act as the organizer for a network for the follow-up to the Brundtland Report, and in 1989 the United Nations General Assembly called for a United Nations Conference on Environment and Development which was held in Rio de Janeiro in June 1992.[5] Both the Centre and the UNCED Secretariat helped publicize and encourage the truly mammoth amount of meetings and reports, mainly of the independent sectors which made the concept of sustainable development common currency throughout the world.

The politics of sustainable development is thus very much a UN initiative. Recognizing world-wide concerns, it looks for a global strategy which could link down to the local community and even households and individuals as the way forward. In practice 'there are no grand answers', rather, 'sustainable development will be an ongoing cumulative process ... based on millions of right decisions at all levels of management, from the global to the local' (Carley and Christie, 1992).

## The Emergence of Participation

These millions of decisions required an unprecedented process of participation. UNCED occurred at a time when, for a number of interrelated reasons, participation had become widely recognized as an essential ingredient for development. Faced with the inadequacies of its debt strategy, the World Bank had identified 'inadequate participation' as one of the main reasons why aid projects were ineffective (World Bank, 1992a). Good governance, involving greater decentralization, participation and transparency, was also seen as essential for sound development policies (Williams and Young, 1994).

Politically, UNCED also coincided with the collapse of the communist regimes in the former Soviet Union and East Europe, and the world-wide 'retreat' of the interventionist state. The retreat of the state, often imposed through debt-induced structural adjustment programmes in poor countries, led to a crisis in provision of social services to the poor. As a response the neo-liberal discourse began to advocate that the state should create an 'enabling environment' for popular participation and self-help initiatives to cope with the increasing social and political tensions arising from structural adjustment. Self-help community participation and NGO involvement thus became a practical response to economic and social crises among the poor and disadvantaged (Stiefel and Wolfe, 1994). Thus paradoxically the collapse of centralized state planning models, the discrediting of the interventionist state, the failure of aid projects, and the lack of State resources to provide services and goods for the poor led to a wide acceptance of the need for participation. And a neo-liberal version of participation began to co-mingle with an earlier, radical version of empowerment and social transformation (Friedmann, 1992).

## Sustainable Development and Participation

From the beginning it was widely accepted that solutions to environmental problems did indeed require participation.[6] Environmental management demands a long-term, comprehensive and coherent policy approach – something most governments are incapable of delivering. State action in this field could succeed only if local communities were organized to defend and manage their environments and to overcome resistance from other sectors of the bureaucracy and environmentally damaging interests. The environment was also an issue attractive to NGOs who saw a niche for themselves and their participatory action programmes in this field.

One participatory strategy was to ask for each Government to submit a National Report, agreed after widespread consultation. The other strategy was to involve NGOs in the negotiation preparatory process itself.[7] Perhaps more than ever, varying from country to country, NGOs had to move from protest to think politically and strategically at a national and international level.

In practice a politics of sustainable development had also emerged (Roddick and Dodds, 1993). This was still more a politics of process than content: the Rio Agreements reflect the cautious steps of governments who insisted on liberally sprinkling the texts with such phrases as 'where appropriate', 'if possible', and calling for 'better information and scientific research'.

But the texts are also clear that while governments and international bodies have responsibility for setting frameworks, the active participation of their citizens with the right of access to relevant information was also necessary. UNCED took the initiative of moving the participation of just NGOs, already well-established in international environmental negotiations, to the much broader strata of concerned citizen groups.

Agenda 21 devotes a whole section to the actions and the right of nine major groups to be consulted and to actively participate in the process.[8] Each group is both to make its own contribution to sustainable development and to get involved in participatory meetings with government and each other to reach consensus on overcoming blockages to change. This search for consensus through dialogue became known as the spirit of Rio.

Ambiguity lay at the heart of the UNCED agreements. It is possible to interpret UNCED as supporting the primacy of economic growth: Principle 12 of the Rio Declaration on Environment and Development strongly supports an 'open international economic system that would lead to economic growth and sustainable development' (Earth Summit, 1992). On the other hand Chapter 12 of Agenda 21 questions economic growth and calls for 'the need for new concepts of wealth and prosperity which allow for higher standards of living through changed life styles and are less dependent on the earth's finite resources and more in harmony with the Earth's carrying capacity' (Earth Summit, 1992). Participation likewise could be interpreted as involving a radical shift in power and resources or as a technocratic response to declining state investments.

UNCED neither clearly defined sustainable development and participation nor really clarified the various approaches to them. Within limits interpretations of both were to be part of the on-going political process and debate – part of a journey to an as yet unknown destination. There were of course guidelines and sign-posts – particularly Agenda 21.

## Towards a New Participation

UNCED thus marked the move towards a new politics of participation. This new politics signalled the switch away from both state-controlled participation and state-opposed participation to a model where civil society groups maintain their independence, but sit down and negotiate with each other. The way forward was seen as democratic participative planning with free markets. There is frequently a contradiction betweeen the two, and UNCED did little to resolve these contradictions apart from encouraging participation as part of an ongoing political process and debate.

A new spirit of co-operation between the state, private enterprise and NGOs was considered essential for sustainable development.[9] In some countries strategies for national sustainable development were established using a participative approach: in others the participatory approach was cosmetic. Perhaps surprisingly, given their authoritarian political traditions, participation in the search for sustainable development became widespread throughout Latin America: most countries established National Sustainable Development Commissions with genuine participation from civil society (Earth Council, 1994). This was not the case in many developed countries such as the UK.

Both Colombia and Costa Rica established ambitious institutional structures for trying to reach consensus on strategies for sustainable development. And although the political and institutional setting in both varies considerably, the processes for institutionalizing policies for sustainable development have been remarkably similar. What has also been similar has been the difficulties in moving from intentions to implementation.

# Ecology, Development and Conservation in Costa Rica and Colombia

### Ecology and Development

Colombia and Costa Rica are ecologically interesting countries, reflecting their positions as bridges between North and South America, and with Atlantic and Pacific coastlines, with a variety of mountainous ranges leading to heavy rainfall.[10] Colombia has six important natural regions: Andean, Caribbean, Orinoco, Amazon, Pacific, and Inter-Andean (Pombo, 1990). Its people reflect this diversity in their culture and ethnic compositions with about 10 per cent black and about 2 per cent indigenous. It is rich in water and hydrobiology with many coral reefs, mangrove swamps, and underwater meadows. It has a rich store of non-renewable resources in coal, oil and gas, gold, nickel and emeralds, and it has fertile soil for coffee, fruit, cut flowers and other agricultural crops, and pasture for cattle. Over 43 per cent of its land area is still covered with forests. It is one of the richest countries in the world in terms of biodiversity with an estimated 10 per cent of planetary biodiversity in only 0.8 per cent of the world's land mass, second only to Brazil in the total number of species to be found (Andrade *et al.*, 1992).

Within its 20,000 square miles Costa Rica also has a great variety of ecological zones: 12 different sorts of tropical forests, sub-alpine dwarfed vegetation, tropical beaches, corals, mangroves, etc. It has very few non-renewable resources. It has rich agricultural soil particularly for coffee and bananas, and pasture for cattle. In 1950 72 per cent of Costa Rica was covered in forest; in 1985 26 per cent (Carriere, 1991). Costa Rica has little diverse cultural and ethnic mix (about 2 per cent of African-Caribbean descent and 0.5 per cent indigenous).

In the last 50 years the development process in both Colombia and Costa Rica has put great strain on their ecological systems. Colombia's population has increased from 18.5 million 30 years ago to today's 32.3 million. Costa Rica's population increased from 862,000 in 1950 to 2 million in 1975 and 3 million in 1990.[11]

In spite of the damage caused by drugs, corruption, violence and guerrilla wars the pattern of development in Colombia has been one of steady growth, with GNP per capita increasing from $320 in 1962 to $1190 in 1992. In the same period there has been a rapid growth in urban population from 53.5 per cent to 70 per cent of the population, and, for Latin America, an unusual spread of four major cities of over 1 million. The spatial distribution of the population is also unusual with the majority of the population living in the mountainous ecological systems, leaving the Amazon and the Orinoco plains and much of the coast unpopulated. Income distribution has improved in the same period with the top 10 per cent take falling from 53 per cent to 37 per cent of total income and the bottom 20 per cent take increasing from 2 per cent to 4 per cent of total income. Nevertheless, Colombia still has extreme poverty in all the shanty towns of the major cities and in parts of the rural areas. Official Government statistics claim that 22 per cent of Colombians live in extreme poverty (Colombia National Report for UNCED, 1992).

Colombia however, unlike Costa Rica, is still plagued with massive social problems. The armed struggle still dominates large parts of Colombia. Drug-related violence, and violence in general, is endemic. And the shanty towns and parts of the rural areas have generated poverty, social instability and environmental risks. However, Colombia's two-party system remains remarkably stable (Hartlyn, 1989).

Colombia's development pattern, while it is similar to that of many Latin American countries, has been managed more successfully than most. It managed to pay its debt without going into deep recession and it has managed to shift from the import substitution model of centralized state intervention and protection of local industry to a process of economic liberalization, decentralization and privatization of the state with less disturbance than many other Latin American countries. Structural adjustment in Colombia was more a desire by the Colombian elite to open up their economy to the world markets than an IMF- and World Bank-imposed model.

But the development model of the last 50 years has left a heavy toll on Colombia's ecosystems. The uncontrolled growth of all the cities has left a huge legacy of environmental problems: atmospheric and noise pollution and traffic congestion are endemic. Rivers, especially those near big cities, are badly polluted. Degradation of soils due to excessive use of fertilizers and pesticides, especially in the coffee areas where the shade trees have been cut down, is common. Desertification is rising in the fragile Andean ecosystems due to the removal of tree cover, and the often forced migration of the poor into the Andean forest areas. Deforestation is massive, endemic and largely uncontrolled. The recent development of both oil and coal extraction, and their transport to the coast, has led to numerous problems in the areas affected. In general, widespread poverty and economic growth has led to an inefficient and unsustainable use of natural resources (Carrizosa Umana, 1992).

In Costa Rica, reforms begun in the 1940s and consolidated and extended after the 'civil war' of 1948 have allowed the country to avoid extremes of poverty and wealth as well as cycles of violence and repression in pursuit of social cohesion and consensus (Edelman and Kenen, 1989). Nevertheless, Costa Rica's development pattern has been more uneven than Colombia's. There was an active period of agricultural modernization and industrialization between 1960 and 1973. At this time Costa Rica had the fastest rate of deforestation in the world. This was followed by an ecologically destructive period of heavy state intervention in a small scale import substitution model until 1979 (Ramirez and Maldonado, 1988). Thereafter Costa Rica was forced to adjust to one of the highest per capita debts in Latin America.

Structural adjustment has hit Costa Rica badly (Hansen-Kuhn, 1993). It has forced the privatization of many state institutions, led to cuts in social services, and meant the discontinuation of government subsidies, and destruction of small farmers. Costa Rica managed, however, to preserve a state-sponsored health service, one of the best in the Americas, a high standard of education and much of its social consensus. But distribution of both income and land has worsened since the onset of the debt crisis (Lara, 1995). The 1980s were a lost decade for Costa Rica in living standards, and although in the 1990s steady economic growth has resumed, many of the state's social programmes remain severely reduced. Using traditional growth criteria Costa Rica has been described as 'one of the third world's most successful cases of transition toward an export-led growth strategy in the 1980s' (Clark, 1993) based on foreign investment and non-traditional exports. But this transition has widened the gap between the rich and the poor, and put severe strains on Costa Rica's renowned social cohesion and tolerance.

Furthermore the privatization of the state has led to the growth of semi-autonomous and autonomous institutions administering many of Costa Rica's natural assets. Policy on Costa Rica's biodiversity for example is effectively being run by the autonomous National Institute for Biodiversity (INBIO), and programmes such as the Debt for Nature Swap has shifted the decision-making process over Costa Rica's natural resources away from the government to international organizations and autonomous bodies in Costa Rica. In Costa Rica some have called this the creation of a parallel state.

### Conservation Policies in Costa Rica and Colombia prior to UNCED

Costa Rica is probably one of the most advanced countries in Latin America so far as ecologial awareness is concerned, but it was not always that way. The extraordinarily rapid depletion of its forests led to predictions of Costa Rica having to import wood for its saw mills and with no woodlands outside its national parks by the end of this century.[12] After much pressure from Costa Rica's growing environmental movement, and its internationally respected scientific community, the politicians bowed to public pressure, and began to establish national conservation strategies. In 1986 the then government established the Ministry of Mines, Energy and Natural Resources to strengthen the National Parks Service and environmental protection in general. By 1990 30 per cent of Costa Rica's territory was protected, and by 1994 reforestation roughly equalled rates of deforestation. The finance for some of the protected areas came from an aggressive debt for nature swap. And unlike Colombia the parks are well supervised and on the whole popular with, and respected by, the local people – although in one forest preserve, Osa National Park, there have been major conflicts with gold prospectors.

Initially, however, there were problems due to lack of consultation. In 1985 the Barra del Colorado wildlife refuge was created by decree, and the local people informed they could no longer hunt or cut trees. Those without title were expelled. The pure conservationist approach had to give way in the face of the public outcry that ensued (Uttig, 1993).

The lessons were learned: for sustainable development to have any chance of moving forward crucial social issues had to be considered, in particular that of ensuring local sustainable livelihoods.

Even before the UNCED Conference Costa Rica became one of the first countries to produce a sustainable development strategy. With financial assistance from the IUCN, a group of professionals produced a Conservation Strategy for Sustainable Development for Costa Rica. It was a remarkable, even visionary, document (MIRENEM, 1990). What was even more unusual, the document was widely debated in a series of forums culminating in a Congress in 1989 at which the presidential candidates debated the issues. There had emerged a consensus in Costa Rica that the country's development strategy in the past had ignored the environmental impacts at a very high cost. The issues surrounding sustainable development had now become part of the political debate.

Colombia has a long history of environmental legislation, going back to colonial times and legislation passed under Simon Bolivar (Pombo, 1990). Colombia established its first nature reserve in 1948, and in 1959 declared most of its Amazon, Pacific and Andean forests to be reserves. However, there was always the problem of enforcement. Enforcement improved somewhat with the establishment of INDERENA (the agency responsible for renewable natural resources and the environment) as an autonomous sub-unit within the Ministry of Agriculture. After the Stockholm Conference, Colombia passed an ambitious Natural Resources and Environment Code which unfortunately was seldom followed. There were sporadic attempts at popular participation, but in the absence of a clear legislative framework these tended to die away after the initial period of enthusiasm.

To control certain territorities, and to administer the natural resources, Colombia created a number of Regional Autonomous Corporations in imitation of the USA Tennessee Valley Authority (Carrizosa Umana, 1992). In 1978 these Regional Autonomous Corporations came under the Department of Planning which established a separate Environmental Policy Division within Planning – an important boost to integrating environmental considerations within economic planning.

But in general, in spite of an impressive array of legislation, environmental considerations were strictly subordinate to those of the economy. There was little coherence to policies, and there was such a conflicting overlap in institutional responsibilities and lack of resources that Colombia's environment continued to suffer rapid deterioration (Uribe Botero, 1992).

Then a change in attitude, and later a switch in resources occurred following the establishment of a Constituent Assembly to draft a new Constitution for Colombia which became law in 1991 (Ritchey-Vance, 1991). The debate over the new Constitution took place at the time of a high profile for environmental issues, both internationally and locally. Colombia's growing environmental movement, together with demands from indigenous and Afro-Colombian communities, helped to ensure that Colombia's new Constitution enshrined 43 very progressive principles and laws on the relationship between the environment and development (Velasquez, 1992). The new Constitution marks a conceptual break with the 1886 Constitution which saw the environment solely in terms of territoriality and natural resources to be exploited. Sustainable development, quality of life for all, ecological wealth, and the creation of a democracy with popular particpation were some of the key guiding principles in the new Constitution.

Important changes had taken place both in Costa Rica and Colombia prior to the UNCED Conference. What UNCED did was to give a significant international and national boost to institutionalizing and adding to these changes.

## Participation for Sustainable Development in Colombia

Colombia participated fully in the build up to UNCED and at UNCED itself it formed an important alliance with Mexico and Venezuela (the Group of 3), and actively particpated in the newly created UN Commission for Sustainable Development where it strongly criticized the rich countries for failing to assist in clean technology transfer. The experience of participation encouraged contacts and alliances between government officials and NGOs. And although Colombia's Report to UNCED did not conform to the ideal model of an open and transparent process, the Colombian Government did attempt to consult quite widely with selected academics, NGOs and businessmen, sowing the seeds for future co-operation.

In the build up to UNCED, environmental issues received a high international profile. Many co-operative initiatives were announced by the rich nations in an effort to persuade the poorer countries to participate fully in the UNCED process. These initiatives usually involved NGOs, then emerging for many donors as a more cost-effective vehicle for channelling assistance than government bureaucracies. In 1991 the European Union, for example, agreed to exempt 4 per cent of its customs duties on Colombian coffee for a fund for environmental improvements, and shortly after, ex-President Bush's Initiative for the Americas set up the Law for the Conversion of Debt in which national NGOs would have to be the majority in any organizational structures for debt conversion schemes. In response to such initiatives the Colombian Department of Planning and INDERENA called a meeting to discuss with Colombian NGOs the establishment of a new style organization, Ecofondo (Ecofondo, 1994). This organization was defined as a corporation consisting of NGOs concerned with the environment to which social and community organizations could affiliate. Ecofondo's early meetings decided that the organization would be open, democratic and participative with strong regionally based groupings of NGOs. Its Board of Directors consisted of five democratically elected NGO representatives and two Government ones (Ecofondo, 1994).

The first foreign money in a debt for environment swap to Ecofondo came from the Government of Canada. Initial relations with the USA scheme proved more complicated as the USA was unhappy with Ecofondo's open democratic structures, preferring a more 'professional' body, but eventually a compromise was reached, and money from the USA's Initiative for the Americas will be channelled through Ecofondo.

The offer of outside money acted as a catalyst to Colombia's NGO movement which up until then had been under-resourced, fragmented, and in spite of many valiant efforts lacking in strategy and ability to influence policies (Gaviria, 1992). A few NGOs condemned the new processes as a massive exercise of co-optation by the Colombian state and bilateral and international agencies. These NGOs feared that the independence of the

Colombian NGOs would be seriously compromised, and their ability to protest seriously weakened. They argued that the NGOs would become just another bureaucracy, divorced from the common people. However, these were a minority, and in a short space of time over 400 NGOs affiliated to Ecofondo, making it one of the largest participative and democratic environmental organizations in the Americas.

## Community and Ethnic Groups

The new Constitution gave explicit recognition to Colombia's indigenous and Afro-Colombian communities. Even before the new Constitution, Colombia had begun a process of recognizing the territorial rights of its indigenous peoples – some 1.9 per cent of Colombia's population (Artango Ochoa, 1992). The new Constitution went further and gave indigenous territories the status of Territorial Entities in which indigenous communities have autonomy, their own system of government, language and culture, and administer royalties and taxes from resources in their areas. So far some 27 million hectares have been deeded to indigenous communities.[13] One motive behind this unique process was the desire to encourage sustainable development in such areas as the Colombian Amazon.

Relations with the Afro-Colombian communities were more difficult as historically the Colombian legal and political system had never recognized the separate rights of the descendants of black slaves brought to Colombia, even though the black community make up about 10 per cent of Colombia's population. Moreover the black community was less well organized than the indigenous ones with major differences between rural and urban black communities. Nevertheless, after considerable lobbying and political mobilization, the Colombian government finally passed a new law in 1994 which recognized for the first time the existence and rights of the Afro-Colombian black communities, including the right to collective property of black communities who occupy 'vacant' land along river banks (*Revista Esteros*, 1994).

This new legal and participatory structure of the rural black communities is particularly important in Colombia's most biodiverse region, the Pacific Choco, where about 1 million Afro-Colombians and a small number of indigenous people and others live in small municipalities. The Choco is also a favoured area for foreign assistance, receiving finance from the Global Environmental Facility, the World Bank and the Inter-American Development Bank. All three agencies have emphasized the importance of their funds being used for a participative, sustainable and equitable economic and social development of the region.

Thus the legal recognition of indigenous and black communities' collective rights over forests and other natural resources also emphasizes the importance of participatory methods to achieve a pattern of sustainable development in crucial 'hotspots' of planetary biodiversity.

Although urban and other areas of Colombia have received less foreign assistance, the new Constitution and the new Ministry of the Environment have strengthened the rights of ordinary people to use legal instruments in the protection of their local environments. For example local environmental agendas (local Agenda 21s) with local environmental committees have been established in all the districts of Bogota (Viva Bogota Viva, 1994). Recourse to legal rights, including the right of access to information and the accountability of the local authorities, is achieving some success.[14]

However, the use of legal petitions can cause divisions within local communities. In the Caribbean island of San Andres a legal petition to stop all new buildings led to much dispute as many on the island feared this could lead to unemployment.

Overall the strengthened Colombian environmental movement, the invigorated voices of the indigenous and rural black communities, and the new-found confidence of many poor communities have begun to change attitudes and policies in Colombia. These and other interests obtained recognition in Colombia's new Ministry of the Environment and its ambitious National and Regional Sustainable Development Commissions.

## The New Ministry of the Environment

In 1993 Colombia became the first country in the world to establish a new post-UNCED Ministry of the Environment (Ley 99 – Law 99 of December 1993). The first article of the law recognized the role of UNCED.[15] The new ministry has four basic functions: to formulate strategic policies on the environment exclusively and intersectorially with other ministries; to establish regulations on the use, conservation and restoration of renewable natural resources; to administer strategic areas such as the National Parks; to grant, refuse or suspend environmental licences for large strategic projects (Rodriguez Becerra, 1994).

In keeping with Colombia's move towards decentralization, the Autonomous Regional Corporations were reorganized and some new ones created to be responsible for the environment in their areas. Towns of over 1 million people were given their own environmental authority.

Crucially, both the Ministry and the Autonomous Regional Corporations were given special ear-marked funds from new taxes. It is estimated that the new funding system will double the amount of funds going to environmental protection (Rodriguez Becerra, 1994).

In addition the Ministry was designed to be but one key player in the formulation of policies for sustainable development. Colombia recognized the dangers of isolating environmental policies from other policies. To try and reach a wide-spread consensus on policies for sustainable development Colombia established a National Environment System with a National Environmental Council within it, Colombia's equivalent of the National

Sustainable Development Commissions elsewhere (Wilches-Chaux, 1994). The National Environment Council consisted of the Minister of the Environment and eight other Ministers, the Director of Planning, the Controller General and the Procurator General of the Republic (the Ombudsman), the Presidents of Ecopetrol (Colombia's national state oil company), and the National Council of Oceanography, and one representative from each of the following – the governors, mayors, the indigenous and black communities, the NGOs and the universities, and representatives of the business community. The ministers who made up the Cabinet committee on environment and development and who were on the National Environment Council were the Minister of Agriculture, Health, Development, Mines and Energy, Public Works and Transport, Defence, Commerce and Education. Participative structures were also created at the level of the Autonomous Regional Corporations, the Departments and Municipalities, and the large urban centres. In addition five national, but regionally dispersed, scientific environmental research institutes were created or given new roles.

But economic policy making was considered outside the remit of sustainable development. The Department of Planning was encouraged to draw up plans for a new system of national accounts, bringing in environmental costs, and develop sustainable development indicators, and look at Green taxes. But in general the new participative structures do not facilitate the discussion of any contradictions between sustainable development and the neo-liberal development model in Colombia.

The role of the business community was considered critical in the whole process. Colombian businessmen had set up a Colombian Business Council for Sustainable Development as part of the UNCED process, and were willing to participate with others in the search for the best solutions to environmental problems (ANDI, 1993). Businessmen, particularly the large exporters, had followed the NAFTA negotiations closely, and were impressed by the importance given to and the disputes over environmental considerations. They anticipated that to secure a growing market for Colombia's exports they would need to improve environmental and human health conditions.[16] Businessmen on the whole welcomed the new structures – provided their wealth-making activities did not come under frontal attack.

Bringing business on board was important given the weakness of the Colombian state in enforcing its legislation. If businesses were involved in the beginning in helping design environmental policies and legislation, then they might be more willing to abide by the new laws. This proved to be the case in the rules governing the granting of environmental licences for major projects.

## Participation in Action

Colombia is a country famous for the complexity, comprehensiveness and thoroughness of its laws. Its constitution is without doubt one of the most advanced and modern in the world but its citizens are also famous for their ability to disobey and circumvent the constitution and the laws.[17]

In all matters relating to the environment and development there has been a profound change in Colombia. Colombia now has a set of laws, a set of principles in the constitution, and an institutional framework, including a new Ministry of the Environment, for tackling the problems of sustainable development second to none. But the basic question still remains: will all the above make any difference? Or will Colombia still remain a country dominated by corruption and violence, in which the influence of drug money goes right up to the presidency?

It is much too early to pass judgement. However, there are small signs that the combination of advanced legislation and particpation can make a difference. An example of participation in practice is the construction of Ecopetrol's new oil and gas pipeline from Bahia Malaga to Buga in the west of Colombia (*Ecologica*, 1993). The original proposal for the project entailed crossing part of the territory occupied by poor black and indigenous communities in the biodiversity-rich area of Choco. With the new institutional framework, Ecopetrol was obliged to consult the local communities affected by its plans, including informing them about Ecopetrol's own Environmental Impact Assessment of the project. The communities, together with NGOs, objected that the assessment did not adequately deal with the social and cultural impacts and was too short-term in its assessment of impacts. Ecopetrol agreed to halt its operations if the local communities accepted in principle the need for a pipeline. The local communities agreed, and proposed an alternative, less environmentally damaging, but more costly route. Ecopetrol could not agree to the proposed changes, and the dispute went to the courts. The courts decided that Ecopetrol needed an environmental licence as the pipeline crossed a forestry reserve. The Ministry of the Environment refused to grant a licence, and Ecopetrol had to accept an alternative route. Probably for the first time in Colombia's history the social and environmental impact of a major project was opened to debate by all concerned, and as a consequence was altered. Other examples are now occurring all over Colombia. In the light of Colombia's enormous problems of drugs, violence, poverty and corruption, these examples may seem all small items; none the less they are significant steps towards a new more equitable and sustainable Colombia. Also internally Colombia became dominated by the upsurge in guerrilla violence, and the scandals surrounding the drug cartels' financing of the President's election campaign. Faced with a major constitutional crisis, long-run issues of sustainable development tended to fade.

## Participation for Sustainable Development in Costa Rica

By the time of the UNCED negotiations Costa Rica had established an international reputation for itself for its national parks and forestry reserves.[18] It was also beginning to be a model for biodiversity prospecting. Lack of resources limited Costa Rica's role at UNCED, and its efforts to form a negotiating bloc with the rest of Central America never worked. It did manage, however, to play a role in negotiations for the Biodiversity Convention, and furthermore it managed to obtain two key benefits from UNCED: it secured the headquarters of the Earth Council and it signed a mutual sustainable development pact with Holland.

The UNCED Conference coincided with a new government in Costa Rica, that of President Calderon. The strategy produced under the previous government, Conservation Strategy for Sustainable Development for Costa Rica, was considered too ambitious by the incoming government, and was quietly dropped. Instead the new government wanted to publicize Costa Rica's image as a peace-loving, ecologically sustainable country to boost ecological tourism and attract foreign funds for its initiatives on sustainable development.

However, Costa Rica's growing environmental movement was generally hostile to the new government and suspicious of its neo-liberal rhetoric. This attitude persisted throughout the government, and relations between the government and most Costa Rican NGOs were often mutually hostile. This hostility began almost immediately. In response to the UNCED process, the government established a special Cabinet Committee, under the chair of the President to co-ordinate and plan environmental initiatives. It also set up a forum for a 'New Environmental Order of International Cooperation' under the energetic leadership of the wife of the then Minister of Foreign Relations. This forum however was chosen by the government, and many NGOs regarded it with suspicion. Their suspicions seemed to be confirmed when the government asked just two organizations close to the government, the NeoTropica Foundation and the Centre for Environmental Studies and Policies, to draft Costa Rica's Report to UNCED. Other NGOs were furious and they wrote a letter of complaint to UNCED about the lack of genuine consultation and participation.

It was not an auspicious start, and this mutual suspicion dogged the whole period of the Calderon Government. Then an agreement with Holland, the siting of the Earth Council in Costa Rica, and the success of INBIO, the National Institute for Biodiversity, offered the possibilities of bringing about important changes in Costa Rica's approach to sustainable development.

Within Costa Rica there was much talk about 'valuing' Costa Rica's biodiversity, its 'green gold'. To help prospect this 'green gold', the previous government established a non-profit-making autonomous institution, The National Institute for Biodiversity, INBIO, to compile an inventory of Costa

Rica's biodiversity. In 1991 INBIO signed a pioneering agreement with the USA multinational pharmaceutical company, Merck, whereby Merck obtained a monopoly on samples from a particular area in return for a $1million down payment, and an unknown share of the royalties if any sample was turned into a marketable product by Merck. It was a controversial deal even within Costa Rica (Kloppenburg and Rodriguez, 1992). But it brought much-needed cash to Costa Rica for developing its riches in biodiversity, created employment and training for Costa Rican scientists and for local people trained as parataxonomists to collect specimens, and helped towards the conservation of its tropical rainforests. Subsequent deals were negotiated with Merck and other companies, and Costa Rica became something of a model for biodiversity prospecting (Sittenfield, 1994). INBIO also became an important actor in negotiations over participative structures for sustainable development and other relevant matters.

During the UNCED Conference itself Costa Rica was chosen as the site for The Earth Council. This was the brain-child of Maurice Strong, the Secretary General of UNCED, who wanted to create a high-powered non-governmental international organization which would act as both a think tank and a galvanizer for citizen groups to carry forward Agenda 21. The presence of such an organization in Costa Rica would have spin-offs within Costa Rica itself.

The other success was the signing, also during the UNCED Conference, of an outline agreement with Holland for a mutual sustainable development pact.[19] The Dutch idea was to introduce innovative financing for Agenda 21 by encouraging participative processes towards sustainable development, and mutually evaluating each others progress.

The first visit of a Dutch delegation to Costa Rica to begin negotiating a formal agreement immediately created problems for the Costa Rican Government. Part of the agreement was to involve NGOs from the beginning. However the Costa Rican Government wanted to confine NGO participation to a few, carefully selected NGOs. In response the more radical NGOs gate-crashed the meetings, and persuaded the Dutch delegation to visit grassroots organizations to discuss their local problems of environment and development. Thereafter the Dutch politely insisted that the NGO representation should be chosen by the NGOs themselves. Delegations from Costa Rica visited Holland in return.[20]

The Dutch Agreement galvanized the NGOs to organize themselves. The Costa Rican NGOs were fragmented, small, over-reliant on fluctuating foreign finance, and apart from sporadic successful pressure politics, having little impact on legislation and policies. If NGOs were to respond to the Dutch and other foreign initiatives, then they had to organize themselves and develop strategic and political planning. With financial help from the Dutch Government, the Inter American Development Bank and the UNDP, the NGOs organized a series of national forums to agree an organizational and political strategy. The meetings attracted large numbers of organizations, including those from popular social movements. As in Colombia the Costa Rican NGOs established a democratic, participative structure with regionally based NGO structures, hoping to overcome the country's strong centralist tendencies. A few NGOs stayed outside the process, arguing as did some of their counterparts in Colombia that the NGO movement was falling into the trap of co-optation. But most accepted that while still maintaining their tradition of protest and denunciation, they also now had to learn to lobby and negotiate with the government and business.

As in Colombia Costa Rican business responded actively to the new agenda of sustainable development. The Costa Rican Union of Chambers and Associations of Private Firms set up an Environmental Council to respond to the Mutual Sustainable Development Pact with Holland, and the new participative structures emerging in Costa Rica. Businessmen were keen to establish 'ecological niches' for themselves in export markets, aware that they could not compete with their cheap labour rivals in the rest of Central America. They were thus keen to move up market, and to sell their products as quality, ecologically sustainable products. Eco-labelling was something which firms in Costa Rica positively favoured. Most also favoured closer contact with NGOs, provided they were responsible and not anti-business. The increase in contacts between the NGOs and business led to greater mutual understanding between them.

NGO relations with the Calderon Government were never resolved. Some in the government were disposed to accept that any structures to discuss, agree, co-ordinate and administer any monies coming from Holland or elsewhere should be open, participative and representative. Others were unwilling to risk the government opening up the process to radical NGOs and even losing control of the process.

In the end the NGOs were unable to accept the Government's proposals, and withdrew from any agreements, thus delaying the implementation of the Dutch Agreement and any viable National Sustainable Development Commission.

The Calderon Government was also keen to promote tourism in Costa Rica as tourism was rapidly becoming Costa Rica's biggest foreign exchange earner. However, it became caught between its desire to expand tourism as rapidly as possible and to lessen the environmental costs of this huge increase in tourists. It cleverly decided to promote ecological tourism, conducting a massive publicity campaign to portray Costa Rica as *the* ecologically friendly and sustainable country (Budowski, 1992). Tourists flooded in in their thousands. Money from tourism helped persuade local communities that it was worthwhile not cutting down forests and dumping rubbish into the seas and rivers. But the infrastructure was not ready to cope with the influx, and rules and regulations on the building of hotels and the use of the National Parks and protected areas were frequently flouted. Many NGOs became alarmed, and began to conduct hard-hitting campaigns against the government over its failure to protect the environment. This further soured relations between them and the government with government officials accusing some NGOs of being extremist, and a cover for former communists and leftists. The NGOs responded by accusing the government of hypocrisy and greed.

A change in attitude occurred when the opposition party, the PLN, won the elections in May 1994, and immediately promised to resolve the deadlock with the NGOs. The new government of President Figueres went even further, and in the first few days of the government invited the Earth Council, NGOs, bilateral and international aid agencies, and ambassadors and others to discuss with the new ministers a strategy for sustainable development for Costa Rica. A subsequent document, *From the Forest to Society: A New Costa Rican Development Model as Part of an Alliance with Nature*, promised a bold new vision, offering to make Costa Rica a model of sustainable development for the developing countries. There was a clear bid by Costa Rica in all of this to try and attract foreign assistance for environmental projects, particularly as the level of aid to Costa Rica was declining sharply.

President Figueres moved quickly to establish his credentials on the international stage as a promoter of sustainable development. In October 1994 the Presidents of Central America met in Managua to sign a regional Alliance for Sustainable Development with an ambitious programme of action, including the establishment of a joint 'environmental fund'. In the same year during the UN Meeting of the Convention on Climate Change Costa Rica and the USA signed 'The Bilateral Agreement of Cooperation for Sustainable Development and Implementation' whereby the USA promised to invest in a massive programme of reforestation in Costa Rica to compensate for $CO_2$ emissions within the USA.

And as in Colombia the government co-operated with business and the NGOs to establish an ambitious National Sustainable Development Commission with a lead role taken by the Ministry of Planning, after years during which this ministry had lost much of its power. The National Sustainable Development System consists of representative participants from the public and private sectors, the NGOs and the universities in its four components: a National Council for Sustainable Development; the Foundation for Sustainable Development to administer funds; Technical Consultative Committees; and a Sectorial Council for Sustainable Development.

However, this took longer to establish than many NGOs expected, and much of the momentum towards change was lost. All too quickly the new government became dominated by budgetary constraints, and pressures from the IMF and the World Bank to cut government expenditures and maintain its export drive. Sustainable development required long-term decisions, and the government increasingly operated on a monthly basis. Not surprisingly the initial enthusiasm for a strategy for sustainable development faded, and the elaborate structures surrounding the National Sustainable Development Commission became little more than public relations exercises. Equally unsurprisingly the NGOs became frustrated, and began to lose both the initial enthusiasm and a sense of a political strategy. And there is now a danger that many NGOs will revert back to their protest and denunciation activities rather than seeking consensual solutions to the problems.

## Conclusions

Structures for sustainable development require a long-term strategic perspective. It is much too early to decide whether the ambitious structures in Colombia and Costa Rica will work and will make much of an overall difference. Participation in and of itself does not solve problems. But it can help in the search for more sustainable practical solutions to problems arising from growth and human activities. Both Colombia and Costa Rica do seem to have embraced the spirit of Rio. Initially in Colombia this was more marked than in Costa Rica. Years of violence in Colombia had led to willingness on the part of most NGOs to try a less confrontational approach to the problems. Technocrats and others in the state sector, particularly those looking for support within their own ministry and across ministries for the new ideas were willing to encourage the new structures. And businessmen were looking for practical support to engage with the new, largely international, environmental rules of the game. In Costa Rica many NGOs found it more difficult to break with the politics of confrontation – if only to engender some political excitement.

In both countries participation has led to greater mutual understanding, tolerance and transparency. Not all NGOs are pleased: many fearing a massive process of co-optation by the state and international agencies, and the blunting of their protests. Although both the Colombian and Costa Rican NGOs insisted on bringing traditional popular organizations such as trade unions and peasant organizations into the process, neither the state nor the bilateral and international agencies were keen to encourage this and whether participation can really involve the ordinary people in whose name most of the projects are undertaken still remains open.

In both countries bilateral and international aid agencies have played a critical triggering role in finance, advice and training. The NGOs in both countries could not have organized themselves so effectively without external, especially financial, assistance.

But participation has hidden costs: all sides are complaining about the enormous amount of time, endless meetings and discussions are taking up, often at the cost of other work. To participate in regional and international meetings and networks has also been costly. Various groups have dropped out as a consequence. The President of the Association of Small Farmers in Costa Rica for example complained bitterly that he did not have the time and resources to spend days debating the finer points of the meaning of sustainable development as did the middle-class intellectuals running the NGOs.

Also weaknesses soon emerged with the new structures which became widely criticized for being over-elaborate and complex. In Colombia crucial ministries such as Transport and Mines and Energy began to send lower-ranking officials to the National Sustainable Development Commission, and the Ministry of the Environment began to find it increasingly difficult to ensure that transport policies, for example, took full cognizance of environmental and social factors. In Costa Rica the financial crisis of the state, and the often externally imposed pressure to privatize and cut budgets soon overshadowed the government's plans for sustainable development.

In both countries it became clear very quickly that the priorities of the neo-liberal model of development, and the drive to greater integration into the regional and global markets were dominant. Even international agencies were unambiguous about this: the World Bank, for example, took little cognizance of sustainable development in its structural adjustment packages.

Sustainable development still remains the poor sister as a development model. But it remains an alternative, and all participants are gaining in experience in what it can mean in practice.

## Acknowledgement

The author would like to thank the ESRC Global Environmental Change Programme, project L320 25 3032, and the Carnegie Foundation for financial assistance to carry out participative observation and in-depth interviews with key actors concerned with sustainable development in Colombia and Costa Rica.

## Notes

1  Who first conceived the notion of 'sustainable development' is uncertain. But its emergence can be traced back to the rise of both a global environmental movement (McCormick, 1989) after the Second World War (the World Wildlife Fund's original first objective in 1961 talked about 'ensuring that any utilisation of species and ecosystems is sustainable'), and the growing scientific understanding of the seriousness of ecological deterioration (Pickering and Owen, 1994). Mounting concern over the sustainability of ecosystems, in particular the need to deal with transboundary pollution, led to the 1972 UN Stockholm Conference on the Human Environment (Brenton, 1994) which raised the world's awareness, and which set up the United Nations Environment Programme (UNEP) to monitor environmental change. UNEP together with the WWF and the IUCN published in 1980 the landmark *World Conservation Strategy Report* which emphasized the importance of environmental education and public participation to ensure the sustainable utilization of species and ecosystems.

2   The full definition of sustainable development offered in the Brundtland Report is: 'development which meets the needs of the present without compromising the ability of future generations to meet their own needs. It contains within it two key concepts: the concept of needs, in particular the essential needs of the world's poor, to which overriding priority should be given; and the idea of limitations imposed by the state of technology and social organisation in the environment's ability to meet present and future needs'.

3   Views on what should be done have varied enormously from radical doomsday prophets, but we can still change in time approach (Meadows *et al.*, 1992). Political opinions may stress the need for a radical change in social habits as in the ideology of the Green Parties (Dobson, 1992), advocate market-based solutions (Pearce, 1990) or emphasize the need for 'steady state economies' (Daly, 1992). We see cautious managerialism e.g. most governments and international agencies (World Bank, 1992), technological optimists and narrow cost/benefit analysis (Nordhaus, 1991). In the last few years there has emerged a fierce counterattack against the 'green lobby's' analysis and proposed solutions of environmental problems (North, 1993).

4   Whether development and the environment are necessarily in contradiction remains an open question. The conventional view is that human welfare or utility or happiness depend on a series of links: welfare depending on the material standard of living which is proportional to consumption, and thus is inseparable from production, which requires resource throughput i.e. material input and waste output which causes environmental damage.
     If this were necessarily the case then development and the environment would be in contradiction. There may come a point when it is. But it is still possible to both break the links in the above chain, and even devote an increasing share of resources to environmental repair, maintenance and regeneration such that environmental improvements overtake environmental degeneration (Mikesell, 1992).

5   UNCED's remit was to 'elaborate strategies and measures to halt and reverse the effects of environmental degradation in the context of strengthened national and international efforts to promote sustainable and environmentally sound development in all countries'.

6   The UNCED process even at the early preparatory stage emphasized participation by: business (leading multinational companies set up the Business Council for Sustainable Development); NGOs; local government; professional bodies; religious organizations; communities and individuals.

7   This spurred NGOs to try and get their own act together, hold national and regional meetings, international meetings, and eventually to sign their own treaties in Rio where they held a Global Forum.

8   These nine major groups are: women; youth; indigenous peoples; business; trade unions; local authorities; farmers; scientists and professsionals, and campaign groups.

9   For that co-operation to work, NGO finances and organization had to be strengthened in many countries. If NGOs were to play an intermediary role between state and civil society then NGOs had to scale up their organizations by creating national co-ordinating NGO structures with international links and local and regional bases.

10  Both countries are particularly worried about the impact of climate change and ozone depletion on their ecosystems, and both have begun studies on how to cope. Both countries are particularly interested in the Biodiversity Convention, wanting to protect and gain from the obvious riches they both have in biodiversity.

11    Colombia's population is estimated to reach 38 million in the year 2000 and 54 million in the year 2025. Costa Rica's population is expected to stabilize around 7 million in 2080.

12    Deforestation was estimated to cause the loss of about 680 million tons of soil per annum causing serious erosion particularly on the Pacific coast, silting of reservoirs, and watershed deterioration, threatening hydroelectric schemes (Ramirez and Maldonado, 1988).

13    As one commentator has written: 'the scale of land entitlement' and 'the commitment of the government to recognise indigenous rights in the full sense that they are entitled and encouraged to retain their own cultures and traditions must surely have little precedent in recent times' (Bunyard, 1992).

14    In one case children won a legal petition to remove a police building constructed in a run-down park where they were accustomed to play.

15    '... the process of economic and social development of the country will be oriented according to the universal principles of sustainable development contained in the Declaration of Rio de Janeiro of June 1992 on the environment and development' (Article 1i).

16    On the whole Colombian businessmen are uneasy about 'green labelling', but are aware that their cut-flower exports, for example, could face consumer boycotts in Europe and elsewhere unless Colombian pesticide regulations are tightened up and enforced.

17    Colombia's most famous novelist, Gabriel Garcia Marquez, put it thus: 'The Constitution, the Law ... everything in Colombia is magnificent, everything on paper' (quoted in Pearce, 1990).

18    Costa Rica's reputation for ecological sustainability has always been exaggerated. Its rapid deforestation of old forest, indiscriminate and dangerous use of pesticides, uncontrolled dumping of wastes into its rivers, soil erosion, and air, noise and traffic pollution in San José are on a par with much of Latin America.

19    Holland signed similar pacts with Benin and Bhutan.

20    Many of the Costa Rican delegates were personally highly critical of many aspects of the Dutch unsustainable life-style. But, with Holland footing the bills for the Sustainable Development Agreement between Holland and Costa Rica, they were not going to publicly criticize the Dutch. This became even less likely as strong efforts were made to cut the finances for the programme within the Dutch Parliament. Mutuality in the end was not that mutual.

# References

ANDI (Asociación Nacional de Industriales) (1993) *El Pliego de Modificaciones al Proyecto No 129 de Creacion del Ministerio del Ambiente.* Bogota.

Andrade, G. with J. Pablo Ruiz and R. Gomez (1992) *Biodoversidad Conservación y Uso de Recursos Naturales – Colombia en el Contexto Internacional.* Bogota: CEREC Y FESCOL.

Artango Ochoa, R. (1992) Situacion territorial y tratamiento legal de las areas indigenas del litoral pacifico y la Amazonia de Colombia. In *Derechos Territoriales Indigenas y Ecologia en las Selvas Tropicales de America.* Bogota: Fundacion GAIA and CEREC.

Brenton, T. (1994) *The Greening of Machiavelli: The Evolution of Environmental Politics.* London: Earthscan.

Brundtland Report, World Commission on Environment and Development (1987) *Our Common Future.* London: Oxford University Press.

Budowski, T. (1992) Ecotourism Costa Rican style. In V. Barzetti and Y. Rovinski (eds), *Towards a Green Central America.* West Hartford, CT: Kumarian Press.

Bunyard, P. (1992) Colombia. In *Amazonia: Cause and Case for International Cooperation.*

Amsterdam, Netherlands: IUCN and Brussels: Environment and Development Resource Centre.
Carley, M. and Christie, I. (1992) *Managing Sustainable Development*. London: Earthscan.
Carriere, J. (1991) The crisis in Costa Rica: an ecological perspective. In D. Goodman and M. Redclift (eds), *Environment and Development in Latin America: The Politics of Sustainability*. Manchester: Manchester University Press.
Carrizosa Umana, J. (1992) *La Politica Ambiental en Colombia*. Bogota: CEREC.
Clark, M.A. (1993) *Transnational Alliances and Development Strategies: The Transition to Export-led Growth in Costa Rica, 1983 to 1990*. Madison: University of Wisconsin Press.
Colombia National Report for UNCED (1992) *Colombia*. Bogota.
Daly, H. (1992) *Steady-State Economics*. London: Earthscan.
Dobson, A. (1992) *Green Political Thought*. London: Routledge.
Earth Council (1994) *International Forum 'From Forest to Society': The Challenge Can Be Met*. San Jose, CA: Earth Council.
Earth Council, Natural Resources Defence Council and World Resources Institute (1994) *Directory of National Commissions on Sustainable Development*. San Jose, CA: Earth Council.
*Earth Summit '92* (1992) London: The Regency Press.
Ecofondo (1993) *Corporación Ecofondo Documentos*. Bogota: Ecofondo.
Ecofondo (1994) *Edicion Especial*. Bogota.
*Ecologica* (1993) Proyecto Biopacifico, Poliducto: una ruta de Concertacion. No. 15/16, May–October. Bogota.
Edelman, J. and Kenen, J. (eds) (1989) *The Costa Rica Reader*. New York: Grove Weidenfield.
Friedmann, J. (1992) *Empowerment: The Politics of Alternative Development*. Oxford: Blackwell.
Gaviria, B. (1992) The Colombian environmental movement – social actor or space for participation. In M. Garcia-Guadilla and J. Blauert (eds), *Environmental Social Movements in Latin America and Europe: Challenging Development and Democracy*. London: Barmarick.
Gore, A. (1992) *Earth in Balance*. New York: Houghton Mifflin.
Hansen-Kuhn (1993) *Structural Adjustment in Central America: The Case of Costa Rica*. Washington, DC: The Development Group for Alternative Policy.
Hartlyn, J. (1989), Colombia: the politics of violence and accommodation. In L. Diamond, J. Linz and S. Martin Lipset (eds), *Democracy in Developing Countries: Latin America*. Boulder, CO: Lynne Rienner.
Hueting, R. (1992) The economic functions of the environment. In P. Ekins and M. Max Neef (eds), *Real Life Economics*. London: Routledge.
IUCN (1991) *World Conservation Strategy*. Zurich: Gland.
Kloppenburg, J. and Rodriguez, S. (1992) Conservationists or corsairs. *Seedling*.
Lara, S. (1995) *Inside Costa Rica*. Albuquerque, NM: Resource Center Press.
McCormick, J. (1989) *The Global Environmental Movement*. London: Belhaven Press.
McNeil, J. (1991) The growth imperative and sustainable development. In J. McNeil, P. Winsemius and T. Yakushiji, *Beyond Interdependence*. Oxford: Oxford University Press.
Meadows, D., Meadows, D. and Randers, J. (1992) *Beyond the Limits*. London: Earthscan.
Mikesell, R. (1992) *Economic Development and the Environment*. London: Mansell.
Ministerio del Medio Ambiente (1994) *Ley 99 de 1993*. Bogota.
MIRENEM (1990) *Estrategia de Conservacion para el Desarrollo Sostenible de Costa Rica*. San José.

Nordhaus, W. (1991) To slow or not to slow: the economists of the greenhouse effect. *The Economic Journal*, **101**.

North, R. (1993) *Life on a Modern Planet*. Manchester: Manchester University Press.

*Nueva Constitucion Politica de Colombia* (1991) Texto Official, Editorial Esquilo.

O'Brien, P. (1993) The Latin American debt crisis. In S. Riley (ed.), *The Politics of Global Debt*. London and New York: St Martin's Press and Macmillan Press.

Pearce, D., Markandya, A. and Barbier, E. (1989) *Blueprint for a Green Economy*. London: Earthscan.

Pearce, J. (1990) *Colombia: Inside the Labyrinth*. London: Latin America Bureau.

Pickering, K. and Owen, L. (1994) *An Introduction to Global Environmental Issues*. London: Routledge.

Pombo, D. (ed.) (1990) *Perfil Ambiental de Colombia*. Bogota: Editorial Escala.

Ramirez, A. and Maldonado, T. (eds) (1988) *Desarrollo Socioeconomico y el Ambiente Natural de Costa Rica*. San José: Fundacion NeoTropica.

*Revista Esteros* (1994) Ley de Communidades Negras – Ley 70. Medellin.

Ritchey-Vance, M. (1991) *The Art of Association: NGOs and Civil Society in Colombia*. Rosslyn: Inter-American Foundation.

Roddick, J.F. and Dodds, F. (1993) Agenda 21's political strategy. *Environmental Politics*, **2**(4).

Rodriguez Becerra, M. (1994) *Crisis Ambiental y Relaciones Internacionales – Hacia un Estrategia Colombiana*. Bogota: Fescol.

Sarre, P., Smith, P. and Morris, E. (1991) *One World for One Earth*. London: Earthscan.

Sittenfield, A. (1994) Biodiversity prospecting frameworks: the INBIO experience in Costa Rica. Paper presented to Biological Diversity: Exploring the Complexities. University of Arizona, Tucson.

Stiefel, M. and Wolfe, M. (1994) *A Voice for the Excluded: Popular Participation in Development*. London: Zed Books.

Uribe Botero, E. (1992) Politica ambiental para Colombia. *Planeacion y Desarrollo*, **23**(1).

Uttig, P. (1993) *Trees, People and Power*. London: Earthscan.

Velasquez, F. (1992) La nueva constitucion y la participacion. In M. Jursisch Duran (ed.), *Colombia, una Democracia en Construccion*. Bogota: Ediciones Foro Nacional por Colombia.

*Viva Bogota Viva* (1994) *Agendas Locales Ambientals*. Bogota: Programa de Educacion Ambiental Masiva.

Wilches-Chaux, G. (1994) El sistema del ambiente: el papel de la corporacion y de sus socios. *Ecofondo* (edicion especial).

Williams, D. and Young, T. (1994) Governance, the World Bank and liberal theory. *Political Studies*, **42**.

World Bank (1991) *World Development Report 1991*. New York: Oxford University Press.

World Bank (1992a) *Governance and Development*. Washington, DC: World Bank.

World Bank (1992b) *World Development Report 1992*. New York and Oxford: Oxford University Press.

World Bank (1994) *Making Development Sustainable*. Washington, DC: World Bank.

World Bank (1995) *World Development Report 1995*. New York: Oxford University Press.

# IV
## Coping with Industrialization and Pollution

# 10

# Sustaining Mineral-driven Development: Chile and Jamaica

## Richard M. Auty

## Introduction

Following on from Hamilton (Chapter 2), this chapter compares progress towards sustainable development in two mineral economies, Chile and Jamaica. These countries provide instructive contrasts not only between bauxite mining and copper mining but also between countries which have differing absorptive capacity for mine effluent (which reflects differences in population density and climate) as well as between a successful and an unsuccessful economic adjuster.

The chapter evaluates the two countries in terms of three basic requirements for sustainable development which are (Auty and Warhurst, 1993): appropriate macro-economic policy; compensation for the depletion of the ore asset (and the adequacy of genuine saving) and measures to minimize the environmental damage from mine effluent disposal. However, the environmental conditions are examined in greater depth than macro policy because the latter has been analysed elsewhere (Auty, 1993).

More specifically, after briefly considering macro policy reform, the provision for the depleting mineral asset is examined. The pollution shadows cast by mining in Jamaica and Chile are compared, and then the three main pollution issues (land degradation, air-borne emissions and water-borne emissions) are each analysed separately. The final section summarizes the main differences between the two countries and draws some general conclusions. It stresses the practical problems faced by environmental accounting which have arisen in the absence of a consensus on the measurement of key indices of environmental damage.

## Sound Macro Management: An Essential Condition for Sustainable Development

One of the more robust conclusions to emerge from development economics over the past two decades is the fundamental importance of sound macro-economic policy to the success of other policy objectives. A wide range of studies attests to the strength of pragmatic orthodox economic policies. Such policies have been pursued by, among others, the East Asian 'miracle' countries (including the oil-exporting mineral economies of Indonesia and Malaysia). A critical feature of orthodox macro-economic policy is the creation of two hard constraints, namely, a commitment to fiscal balance and to a competitive exchange rate (Pinto, 1987).

Within such a macro-economic framework, the governments of mineral economies also need sensible policies for taxing the mining sector and for deploying the mineral revenues. A pre-determined and profit-sensitive tax system is required which is designed to capture a large proportion of any rents (defined as revenues minus costs, including a normal return on capital). Such a resource rent tax secures for the government that portion of the mining companies' total discounted cash flow which is in excess of the level required to yield a return on capital commensurate with the risk of the investment (Daniel, 1992).

As for the deployment of the mineral tax revenues, they should first be placed in a mineral stabilization fund (MSF). The prime function of an MSF is to ensure an orderly injection of the mineral rents into the economy. It may be desirable to 'sterilize' the rents by accumulating them abroad in order to mute their potential inflationary impact on the domestic economy. This is especially necessary where the rents are large in relation to GDP. Such a situation is associated with the youthful expansionary stage of the mineral-driven cycle or after very large positive price shocks, as in the case of the oil-exporters after 1973 and 1979.

When rents are high in relation to GDP, the danger arises that political pressure for the government to spend the mineral revenues rapidly will be difficult to resist. But such rapid spending will amplify the boom stage of the mineral boom/bust cycle (Gelb, 1988). The overrapid absorption of the rents takes the form of some combination of inflationary investments (which exceed physical implementation capacity) and unsustainable expansion of consumption. Overrapid rent absorption triggers a strengthening in the real exchange rate and intensifies the Dutch Disease effects (the weakening of the non-mining tradables sectors, principally agriculture and manufacturing).

A key advantage of using an MSF to dampen down such exchange-rate fluctuations is that it subsequently facilitates the economic diversification which is necessary for *mature* mineral economies whose mineral sectors have ceased to expand strongly. The MSF is also a useful policy instrument for achieving the second sustainability condition, namely, making investments in alternative wealth-generating activity to substitute for the depleting ore asset. Such investments may be conceptualized as substituting produced (man-made) capital and/or human capital (education) for the depleting natural capital (i.e. the mineral resource).

In this context, Chile embarked on orthodox economic reforms in the mid-1970s and rapid economic growth was eventually established, but only after a serious set-back in 1979–82 when policy-makers became too doctrinaire and neglected emerging strains in manufacturing and banking and allowed the exchange rate to over-strengthen. An MSF was adopted after the 1979–82 set-back which subsequently helped to sterilize the massive revenue inflow associated with the late-1980s copper boom and therefore to maintain the pace of economic diversification. Importantly, Chile also tightened the regulation of capital flows in the aftermath of the 1979–82 debacle in order to limit the macro-economic damage which abrupt movements in capital can cause.

In contrast, Jamaica postponed macro-reform until the mid-1980s and maintained until 1988 a tax regime which was not profit-sensitive. As in Zambia, where economic reform was also long-delayed (Auty, 1993), the cumulative damage has proved hard to reverse. The inevitable structural adjustment of the late 1980s produced some symptoms in Jamaica of the 'disease' it was meant to cure. This is because it entailed high rates of interest which attracted a large capital inflow without adding to long-term wealth-creating investment (Brewster, 1994). Inflation was not curbed, the exchange rate appreciated, economic diversification was retarded and economic growth remained low (Table 10.1). This, in turn, perpetuated uncertainty over the political commitment of the government to reform, further slowing economic improvement.

Fortunately, the inherent characteristics of bauxite mining and the pattern of multinational corporate (MNC) mine ownership (as opposed to state ownership) have limited the extent to which the Jamaican economic problems retarded expenditure on environmental improvement. In other mineral economies such as Zambia, Bolivia and Peru where state ownership

**Table 10.1** Comparative economic performance, Chile and Jamaica

|  | Chile | Jamaica |
|---|---|---|
| GDP per capita 1973 (US$) | 1180 | 1040 |
| GDP per capita 1993 (US$) | 3170 | 1440 |
| GDP growth 1984–93 (%/yr) | 7.2 | 2.2 |
| Investment 1984–93 (% GDP) | 22.7 | 26.2 |
| ICOR | 3.2 | 11.9 |
| Minerals/total exports (%) | 47.2 | 60.2† |

*Note*: † CEPAL (1993) 1988–91 for Jamaica; 1988–92 for Chile.
*Source*: World Bank (1995).

dominated the mining sector, macro mismanagement was associated with the decapitalization of the state mining firms (Auty, 1993) which severely curtailed defensive environmental expenditure.

## Accounting for Ore Depletion

This section examines both the practical problems and the economic consequences of incorporating the depletion of environmental capital, here the mineral asset, into the national accounts. The value of the depletion component is estimated for 1990 only, the peak year of a mineral boom. This implies that the depletion component will be at its largest. This is appropriate for the purpose in hand because the principal concern here is to determine the maximum scale of the required adjustment to the national accounts and the sensitivity of such adjustments to the different conventions on measurement. Moreover, as will be demonstrated, the absence of a consensus on the measurement of key parameters makes a more detailed time series analysis of the depletion component somewhat premature.

### Adjusting for Ore Depletion

The most common measure of mineral depletion is the net price method which takes the mineral rent as the depletion component. The rent is defined as the difference between the total extraction costs, including a normal return on capital, and the revenue generated. The net price method is one of three approaches (along with the present value and replacement cost) which all contain biases towards the overestimation of the depletion component (Bartelmus and van Tongeren, 1994).

A fourth measure of the natural resource depletion component is provided by the 'user cost' approach (El Serafy, 1989) which allocates only a part of the rents to depletion. The user cost method subdivides the rent into two components: an income component and a capital (i.e. depletion) component. The capital component is defined as the amount which must be saved annually from the net revenue in order to accumulate a sufficient sum over the life of the mine which, when invested at the prevailing rate of interest provides, after the exhaustion of the asset, an annual income equivalent to that earned during the extraction phase (Mikesell, 1992). In this way, consumption by the present generation does not occur at the expense of future generations. The capital component is subtracted from the net domestic product (NDP, which is GDP minus the cost of the depletion of produced (man-made) assets) and saved/invested, whereas, as its name implies, the income component is available for consumption by the present generation.

Some indication of the scale of the difference between the net price and user cost approaches to natural resource depletion can be gained from earlier calculations made for Papua New Guinea which suggest that the net price depletion calculation is three to seven times that of the user cost figure (Bartelmus *et al.*, 1992). The net price method also exhibits greater volatility from year-to-year than the user cost does.

## Jamaican Bauxite Rent and Depletion Estimates 1990

Hamilton (Chapter 2) uses Bureau of Mines data from the mid-1980s in his broader study which produce rents which tend to comprise around half the mineral revenues. While a rent of this magnitude may be not untypical for hydrocarbons, it is far too high a fraction of revenues for most hard minerals. A different approach is therefore adopted here to measure the rents, the first step of which is to determine the long-run marginal cost of global production. The long-run marginal cost of global production is defined as the price required for a new entrant to embark on production. The average cost of production for the country under study is subtracted from that figure to derive the rent.

The alumina price required in 1990 to justify investment by a new entrant was $320/tonne and that figure sets the marginal cost. Data provided by the International Bauxite Association suggest that the cost of alumina production for the four Jamaican refineries ranged from $165 to $199/tonne, with an average of $181. The subtraction of the average Jamaican cost from the marginal cost yields a figure for the *potential* rent of $139/tonne of alumina.

The potential rent figure does not take account of the capacity of consumers and workers to capture the rents. The consumers may do so in terms of a cheaper price for alumina and the workers through wages above market-clearing levels (Crowson, 1994). The actual realized average price for Jamaican alumina in 1990 was $222/tonne (Planning Institute of Jamaica, 1994) which yields an average rent of $41/tonne of alumina, an amount one-third of the potential rent. This gap between the actual and potential rent implies that consumers had captured two-thirds of the *potential* rent in terms of lower alumina prices. This occurred because excess global alumina capacity was installed prior to the 1973 oil shock which provided many subsequent opportunities for cheap brown-field capacity expansion. This, in turn, deterred new entrants whose capital charges and total production costs would have been much higher. The actual total rent for Jamaica in 1990, expressed in aggregate terms, was $181 million (Table 10.2) and this is the value of the depletion component under the net price method. The aggregate figure is based on a total production of 10.9 million tonnes of bauxite (3.9 million tonnes of which were shipped as crude ore and the rest as alumina).

The user cost method yields a lower depletion component. It is sensitive to the longevity of the mine and, therefore, to the size of the ore reserves. The JBI (1991) estimates Jamaican bauxite reserves at 2 billion tonnes in 1990, a figure which has not been reduced since mining commenced in 1952

Table 10.2 Estimated potential and actual rent on Jamaica bauxite, 1990

| Refinery/Mine | Output | Cost (US$/tonne) | | | Rent (US$/tonne) | | Σ Rent ($ million) | |
|---|---|---|---|---|---|---|---|---|
| | (million t) | Operating | Capital | Total | Price $320 | $222 | Price $320 | $222 |
| *Refinery data* | | | | | | | | |
| Alcan Ewarton } | 0.975 | 133 | 39 | 172 | 148 | 50 | | |
| Alcan Kirkvine } | | | | | | | | |
| Alcoa | 0.706 | 126 | 39 | 165 | 155 | 57 | | |
| Alpart | 1.188 | 160 | 39 | 199 | 121 | 23 | | |
| *Sectoral data* | | | | | | | | |
| Total/average | 2.869 | 142 | 39 | 181 | 139 | 41 | 399 | 118 |
| Kaiser Bauxite mine | 3.911 | n.a. | n.a. | 20 | 56 | 16 | 219 | 63 |
| Total: bauxite/alumina | 10.921 | | | | | | 618 | 181 |

*Sources:* Planning Institute of Jamaica; International Bauxite Association, Kingston, Jamaica (1994), Cost estimates, mimeo.

**Table 10.3** True income as a percentage of net receipts

| Life expectancy of reserve (years) | Discount rate (%) | | |
|---|---|---|---|
| | 2 | 5 | 10 |
| 2 | 6 | 14 | 25 |
| 5 | 11 | 25 | 44 |
| 10 | 20 | 42 | 65 |
| 20 | 34 | 64 | 86 |
| 50 | 64 | 92 | 99 |
| 100 | 86 | 99 | 100 |

*Source*: El Serafy and Lutz (1989).

despite the fact that 324.4 million tonnes of bauxite have been mined (annual bauxite production averaged 8.3 million tonnes and peaked at 15 million tonnes in the early 1970s). This outcome is not unusual and it is consistent with the tendency of ore reserves to expand in line with on-going exploration activity.

If it is assumed for the purpose of estimating the remaining life of the mineral reserves that Jamaican output returns to its peak level and stabilizes, then the remaining bauxite reserves would last 133 years. According to Table 10.3, under the user cost principle, the fraction of the rent which is true income is 99 per cent or more at interest rates over 5 per cent. The true income is still 86 per cent if an interest rate close to the social rate of time preference is selected. For 1990, using the social rate of time preference the depletion component would be $2.24/tonne of bauxite ($24.46 million in aggregate) of the actual rent, and $7.84/tonne ($85.6 million) of the potential rent. These figures are approximately one-seventh those calculated under the net price method.

Table 10.4 uses aggregate data to adjust the Jamaican National Accounts by estimating Environmental Domestic Product 1 (which is NDP minus the natural asset depletion component) for Jamaica in 1990 under the differing assumptions. The results suggest that even if the net price method is used to estimate the depletion coefficient, the correction required to the national accounts is a very modest one of around 2 per cent of GDP. This is well short of the adjustments made for a group of non-fuel primary product exporters by Hamilton and O'Connor (1994) and reported in Chapter 2 which used the net price method and assumed that around half the revenues comprised rents. The figures in Table 10.4 underline the sensitivity of the depletion calculation to variations in both the data and the assumptions. Unless, or until, a consensus emerges in regard to environmental accounting, the benefits envisaged by Hamilton will remain only partially realized.

**Table 10.4**   Adjustment to Jamaican national accounts for bauxite depletion, 1990 (US$ million)

| Identity | GDP | NDP | EDP1 user cost | EDP1 net price |
|---|---|---|---|---|
| Total economy | 4242 | 3945[1] | n.a. | n.a. |
| Bauxite/alumina sector | 390 | 351[2] | 326 | 265 |
| Memo item: saving | | | | |
| gross saving | 1164 | 867 | 842[3] | 781[3] |
| % GDP | 27 | 20 | 20 | 18 |

*Notes:*
[1] Assumes 7 per cent depreciation of GDP as advised by SIJ.
[2] Actual sector figure of US$39.52 million supplied by SIJ.
[3] Saving rate corrected for bauxite depletion only (not all natural capital depletion).
*Source*: Statistical Institute of Jamaica (1994) and text.

## Chilean Copper Rent and Depletion Estimates 1990

The copper price required in 1990 to justify investment by an efficient new producer was $0.99/lb. This estimate is based on more recent (and realistic) production costs from the Bureau of Mines (1991). It assumes an investment of $5190 per tonne of mining, smelting and refining capacity; 15 per cent for capital recovery (which includes tax at 33.3 per cent); straight line capital depreciation at 10 per cent over 15 years; and efficient production (implying operating costs of $0.41/lb, after deducting by-product credits).

The average cost of copper production in Chile in 1990 can be derived from Table 10.5 which summarizes the costs of Codelco which produced 70

**Table 10.5**   Estimated Chilean copper production costs and rents, 1990

| Item | cents/lb |
|---|---|
| *Operating cost* | |
| Mining | 0.17 |
| Milling | 0.18 |
| Smelting | 0.11 |
| Local tax | 0.01 |
| By-product credit | (0.05) |
| Subtotal | 0.41 |
| *Capital charge* (assumed assets of $4400/tonne) | |
| Depreciation | 0.11 |
| Normal return (share assets = $3085/tonne) | 0.14 |
| Corporation tax | 0.06† |
| Subtotal | 0.31 |
| *Total cost* | 0.72 |
| *Potential rent* (at 99¢/lb copper price) | 0.27 |
| *Actual rent* (at $1.08/lb realized copper price) | 0.36† |
| *Total rent* (at $1.08/lb on 1.5584 million tonnes national output, in $ million) | $1.281 |

*Note*: † Actual tax paid by Codelco 1990 = $915 million (37¢/lb).
*Sources*: Bureau of Mines (1991); Codelco (1991).

**Table 10.6** Adjustment to Chilean national accounts for ore-depletion, 1990 (US$ billion)[1]

| Item | GDP | NDP | EDP1 user cost | | Net price |
|---|---|---|---|---|---|
| | | | 10% | 20% | |
| Total output | 30.17 | 28.06 | 28.02 | 27.49 | 26.78 |
| Mining output | 2.20 | 1.82[2] | 1.78[3] | 1.25[4] | 0.54[5] |
| Gross saving | 7.46 | 5.35 | 5.32 | 4.78 | 4.07 |
| (% GDP) | 24.73 | 19.1 | 19.00 | 17.39 | 15.08 |

*Notes:*
[1] Exchange rate: P305/US$1 (World Bank, 1995), with mining at 7.3 per cent of GDP in constant price data.
[2] Assuming Codelco depreciation rate for total industry.
[3] 3% net revenue = depletion charge (0.018¢/lb).
[4] 45% net revenue = depletion charge (16¢/lb).
[5] 100% net revenue = depletion charge (36¢/lb).
*Source:* ECLA (1994).

per cent of the country's output in that year. The average cost was 72¢/lb and subtracting that from the marginal cost yields a figure for the *potential* rent of 27¢/lb. When adjusted for the actual realized price of copper, the rent *increases* to 36¢/lb (reflecting, in contrast to alumina, a shortage of global supply relative to demand in that year). The depletion component is $915 million in aggregate terms.

Turning to the user cost method, data on Chilean copper reserves are provided by CEPAL (1991) which estimated them at 107 million tonnes in 1990 on a base reserve basis (i.e. all known reserves currently viable or likely to be viable). There are sufficient copper reserves for 40 years of extraction if annual production expands to stabilize at 2.5 million tonnes. Table 10.3 indicates that with such reserves, the fraction of the rent which is true income is over 97 per cent using the private discount rate. This yields a depletion component which is very small, barely 0.1 per cent of GDP (Table 10.6).

But as already noted with regard to Jamaica, the depletion figure is sensitive to the assumptions used. For example, true income falls to 55 per cent of net revenue if an interest rate close to the social rate of time preference is selected in calculating the user cost. For 1990, using the social rate of time preference the depletion component would be 16¢/lb and would depress NDP by 1.62 per cent (Table 10.6). Finally, using the net price method, the adjustment to the national accounts more than doubles to 4.02 per cent of GDP.

In aggregate terms the depletion component for Chilean copper in 1990 amounts to $1.28 billion with the net price depletion method. It falls to $569 million under the user cost method with a social preference interest rate. Yet even the user cost method may over-state the adjustment for ore depletion because, as noted earlier, official mineral reserve figures are invariably under-estimated.

# The Environmental Impact of Bauxite and Copper Refining

## Costing Environmental Impacts of Mining

There are few studies of the cost of environmental damage and abatement from mining in general, let alone for specific countries (Hamilton and Atkinson, 1995). Among the methods available for assessing damage, contingent valuation might produce useful results. But alternative measurements of the environmental impact, such as hedonistic pricing or costing the production loss in environmentally-sensitive livelihoods such as farming and fishing which is attributable to mining, are easier to undertake and seem likely to be effective.

Hedonistic pricing generates surrogate prices by comparing the cost of similar goods (e.g. housing or labour) in polluted and unpolluted locations (Barde and Pearce, 1991). For example, the workforce in mining typically captures a fraction of the rents in terms of wages above the market-clearing rate. But the capture of rents by labour can also be regarded as a true cost to the mining sector which, historically, has been required to compensate workers for hazardous job conditions. For example, in the case of Jamaica in 1990, if mining wages are assumed to be 50 per cent above the shadow rate, the workforce would capture 4 per cent of the total sector revenues as compensation (Statistical Institute of Jamaica, 1994). The production loss calculations estimate the value of the reductions in output attributable to pollution (Crosson and Haas, 1983).

The approach adopted here is to assess the extent to which mining companies are internalizing environmental impacts through compensation payments and defensive expenditures. No attempt is made, however, to incorporate the estimates into the national accounts because there is presently even less agreement on how best to achieve that than there is over the measurement of mineral depletion.

## Contrasting Pollution Shadows

Bauxite occurs extensively in the earth's crust, so that the commercial reserves tend to be much more accessible than copper reserves. Most bauxite is strip-mined, a process which typically requires the removal of the topsoil and only a modest amount of overburden (Martyn, 1992). The principal environmental impacts of bauxite *mining* are, therefore, a relatively small disturbance of the landscape, emissions of dust (which is not believed to have chemical effects, although it may trigger latent respiratory problems (Bell, 1986)) and the disposal of water where it has been used to control dust levels.

The *refining* of bauxite into alumina halves the input weight. Refining uses caustic soda to separate out the alumina from the red mud waste which comprises mostly tiny particles of iron oxide from which it is quite difficult to detach the caustic soda (Bell, 1986). Red mud has a very high pH value of between 12.5 and 13 and requires careful storage to avoid contamination of the water-table.

The airborne emissions from alumina refining include crystals of carbonate and bicarbonate that are produced from the red mud ponds in dry weather by the reaction of caustic soda and $CO_2$. The refinery stack emissions include suspended particulates and $SO_2$. The caustic soda corrodes metal and damages plant life. The smelting of alumina into aluminium ingot is not undertaken in Jamaica and so it is not considered further here.

Copper mining creates considerable solid waste, especially if the mine is open cast: each tonne of copper mined typically results in some 35 to 140 tonnes of material being discarded. The low purity of copper requires concentration before shipping. This is a fermentation process which involves heat and large volumes of water. The concentrator enriches the ore to 30 per cent copper content prior to transport by slurry pipeline to the refinery. The tailings are usually held in liquid suspension and deposited in ponds which must be sealed behind dams to prevent ground water contamination.

Where copper concentrate is refined before export, as in most cases in Chile, considerable air pollution occurs. The refinery produces waste gases as well as slag. The gases include $SO_2$ (due to the oxidization of sulphur-bearing minerals), particulates and impurities like arsenic. The gases are vented via stacks into the atmosphere but they are also released within the smelter.

# Land Degradation

### Jamaica Land Reclamation

This section focuses on Jamaica because land is not sufficiently scarce in Chile to justify the restoration of the mined areas which lie in remote unpopulated areas on the flanks of the Andes. In contrast, the high population density of Jamaica and the scarcity of land have meant that since mining commenced in 1952, the juxtaposition of mines, refineries and farms has drawn government attention to land restoration. Formal measures to deal with airborne and waterborne emissions (including tailings) have lagged, however, and the sanctions against companies have been modest (JBI, 1992). Corporate pride and self-interest have, therefore, acted as more important spurs to pollution control (IBA, 1992).

Jamaican bauxite occurs in pockets within a large number of small basins in the limestone bedrock (unlike the extensive bauxite reserves of Latin America, West Africa and Australia). Jamaican ore deposits vary in shape and size with an average depth of 3 to 20 m and an area ranging from 65 × 65 m up to 130 × 500 m. The smaller bauxite pockets contain 50,000 tonnes of ore while the larger ones may hold more than 1 million tonnes (IBA, 1992). The area mined in any one year in order to supply a 700,000-tonne alumina refinery is typically 16 ha, while a further 20 ha of land are required for tailings disposal.

Bauxite soils occupy two-thirds of the Jamaican surface area and are relatively infertile, with a low humus content and high risk of erosion where slopes exceed 5° (Wellington, 1986). Crop yields are, therefore, inherently low although they can be improved with scientific farming. Early land restoration rarely left yields as high as previously. This is because the pH levels are higher on restored bauxite land (7.7 compared with 6.1) while organic content is lower (1.1 per cent compared with 3.5 per cent) and water-retention capacity is diminished (World Bank, 1993). Even pastoral activity is sensitive to mining, with productivity reduced by up to one-third on reclaimed lands, although more typically by 5 to 15 per cent (Wellington, 1986). Yet such shortfalls may overstate the actual loss of farm output because the bulk of the land acquired by the mining companies was previously under pasture on large estates which, unlike peasant farms, do not utilize the land extensively (Salmon, 1987).

An improvement in the quality of the reclamation of mined-out bauxite land occurred in the late 1980s (Neufville, 1993). Previously, soil was restored only to the bottom of the mined-out pit and the vegetation was left to recover on its own. As a result, rain erosion prior to vegetative regeneration sometimes removed half the restored topsoil. Such practices restricted subsequent land use because soil of 15 cm depth will usually only support pasture whereas 45 cm are required for cropping and 60 cm for fruit trees (Weir, 1982).

Under the new practice, at least 30 cm of topsoil are restored and in order to improve the organic structure, grasses are planted during the first two years and both chemical and organic nutrients (such as chicken manure) are added. In addition, the landscape is graded so that sheer drops are removed through either terracing or greater smoothing of the mined-out area. When combined with instruction in farming methods, the reclaimed land provides higher yields, so that Kaiser Bauxite now receives requests from displaced farmers for resettlement on the dry pasture land of the north coast (Figure 10.1) in preference to 'better' unmined land acquired by the company elsewhere in Jamaica.

## Costs of Jamaican Land Reclamation

Alcoa estimates the costs of land rehabilitation at around $25,000 per ha. This figure is based on charges for earth-moving equipment (which with a usage rate of 50 hours per ha comprise around two-thirds of the cost) and the costs of crop restoration. But such a figure may be 30 to 40 per cent below the 'full cost' due to the exclusion of any overhead charge. Even with an

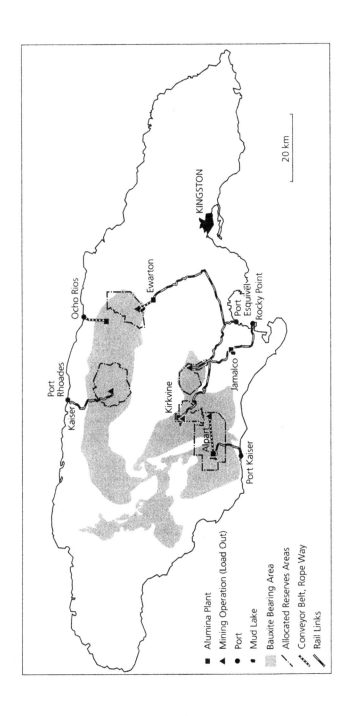

**Figure 10.1  Location of Jamaican bauxite reserves, mines and alumina refineries**

overhead charge of 30 per cent, however, the reclamation cost is still modest at 16¢/tonne bauxite (which is around 37¢/tonne of alumina and less than $1/tonne of aluminium). The 16¢/tonne figure for land reclamation is significantly smaller than the sum of 59¢/tonne of bauxite which the MNCs pay to the government as a royalty (IBA, 1992). Moreover, prior to the recent adoption of higher reclamation standards the cost of land restoration was one-third lower still.

An estimate of the total cost of land reclamation can now be made for the Jamaican bauxite sector as a whole. Assuming 200 ha of mined-out land are restored annually, the total cost per annum is only $5 million. This is barely 1 per cent of the total sector revenues, which normally exceed $500 million annually (Planning Institute of Jamaica, 1994).

# Water-borne Emissions

### Jamaican Water-borne Emissions

Government legislation for air-borne and water-borne emissions in both Chile and Jamaica lagged behind the industrial countries. Jamaica began to strengthen its formal regulatory regime in 1991 with the establishment of the Natural Resource Conservation Authority (NRCA). Under the new system, any physical development in the mining/refinery sector requires a permit from the NRCA and permits are also needed for discharges (Government of Jamaica, 1991). The Jamaica Bauxite Institute (JBI) is responsible for monitoring the environmental performance of the sector on behalf of the NRCA.

Caustic soda is expensive, so that the relatively large amounts required to process Jamaican bauxite provide an incentive to recycle it. For example, Alcoa already recycles around 50 per cent of its process water in order to capture caustic soda for re-use as well as to curb caustic soda emissions. In addition to improved recycling, new *dry* disposal methods for red mud (the tailings from bauxite mining) are also being explored. There is, however, evidence from early tailing ponds that they dry out and revegetate. Nevertheless, where insufficient attention is given to lining the ponds, there is a threat to water supplies which requires compensation, as with Alpart in southwest Jamaica (Figure 10.1).

As well as incurring costs either to reduce environmental damage or to compensate for its adverse impacts, the bauxite companies also make outlays on public relations. Such outlays might be viewed as further compensation to the local (and in some instances, national) community for the presence of the mine. The public relations programmes provide assistance with community centres, clinics, schools and basic services such as electricity and water when they move in to a new area. There is, however, a risk that when a mine starts up local people are likely to view such public relations spending as a new resource to be exploited, thereby heightening their dependence on finite mining activity.

## Chilean Experience

Mining in northern Chile has resulted in ocean pollution and water shortages. Coastal pollution has been especially severe in the vicinity of Antofagasta (Figure 10.2). It resulted historically from tailings from six copper mines being dumped directly into the sea. This dumping has ceased but not before it changed the acidity levels in the sea-water with serious local consequences for the marine flora and fauna.

To the south, within the Central Valley, the principal threat from water-borne mine effluent is to farming. But the costs are being internalized by the mines. For example, experimental work with tailings water irrigation has been undertaken by El Teniente mine. Since 1987, the mine tailings have been transported 87 km by an open concrete channel to Caren, which has 80 years of storage capacity at present production. The new Caren dam stores mine tailings, provides the region's farmers with a reliable non-toxic supply of recycled water (which is checked for safety) and also prevents winter flooding.

Although the water at Caren is highly alkaline and also has levels of molybdenum and sulphate which exceed official levels (requiring special government dispensation), it has been used successfully to grow crops and to nurture animals on a 10-ha farm owned by Codelco (Codelco, 1991). The crops grown include wheat, maize, asparagus, grapes, beans, tomatoes, melons, citruses, peaches, while the animals reared include sheep, cattle and rabbits. Where effluent exceeds permissible levels Codelco compensates farmers by buying the rights to surface water and then supplying them with unpolluted underground water (Munoz, 1994).

The feasibility of using recycled tailings water for agricultural purposes has also been demonstrated by an Exxon subsidiary, Chagres. Recycled water is used on corporate farmland and will be supplied to adjacent farmers (Smith, 1993). It can be argued that, far from depressing productivity, the provision by the mining companies of such recycled irrigation water to local farmers effectively *enhances* the productivity of otherwise arid and unproductive land. Sulphates carried in recycled water pose few problems compared with molybdenum because sulphates become trapped in the soil and have no effects on plants. But molybdenum forms molecules with other materials in the surface soil layers. Care must, therefore, be taken to guard against the contamination of the water table. Irrigation must be restricted to no more than 1 m of soil depth in order to ensure that the impact of pollutants is local and minimal (Valenzuela, 1994).

**Figure 10.2**   Location of Chilean copper mines and processing plants

# Air-borne Emissions

## Jamaican Emissions

Compared with copper refining, alumina refining has relatively minor impacts on ambient standards and any adverse effects cost little to compensate. For example, in 1989 Alcan paid $2 million in compensation to householders for roof damage as part of a new initiative while also paying $100,000 to third parties for more general damage effects. Elsewhere, Kaiser investigated complaints about health effects around its north coast mine (Figure 10.1). Most complaints relating to aggravated sinus trouble were of dubious merit, being triggered by other causes such as pollen and dusty pre-mine roads.

Noise is a more serious grievance than atmospheric particles and Kaiser introduced a compensation scheme in 1993. The new scheme paid $55/ quarter in compensation to those living within 100 m of a bauxite road and $23 for those living between 100 and 130 m from the road. Those living within 800 m of the loading area (where bauxite is dumped from trucks onto trains) were eligible for compensation of $36/quarter. An interesting experiment designed to use compensation to raise incomes in a self-sustaining fashion involves the option to participate in a broiler farm business in lieu of noise compensation payments. Kaiser estimates that those who join can earn an extra $227 per year above their compensation payments, on a lasting basis.

## Chilean Ambient Standards

Overall, air pollution from bauxite mining is a very modest problem in Jamaica compared with Chile. The remainder of this section, therefore, concentrates on Chile where, by 1989, copper smelters were responsible for 93 per cent of the country's $SO_2$ emissions. The latter comprised some 922,000 tonnes of sulphur, making Chile the world's fourth largest emitter of sulphur from point sources – after the USA, China and Russia. But two years later, by 1991, defensive expenditures had cut the level of emissions by 15 per cent and projected improvements should cut them by a further two-thirds to 250,000 tonnes by the year 2000 (despite an expected 20 per cent increase in copper production). This improvement will, however, entail around $1 billion in investment and still more capital will be required in order to cut arsenic emissions (Lagos and Velesco, 1993).

Chile experienced strong pressure in the early 1990s to adopt North American environmental standards. For example, US producers of farm products cited mining pollution as grounds for banning Chilean produce. This caused Chilean farmers to lobby their government to tighten mining emission restrictions. Similarly, US copper producers accused their Chilean counterparts of environmental dumping because they failed to meet North American environmental standards. But the courts dismissed such charges on the grounds that low population densities in Chile make EPA standards excessively stringent when applied to that country. Another way of conceptualizing this is to say that the Chilean environment has a higher absorptive capacity for mine emissions.

Chile's Decree 185 sets a uniform standard of $SO_2$ emissions across the country for human health. The decree specifies daily and annual (but not hourly) maximum levels. It sets the national health emission limit for sulphur at an annual daily average of 80 mgm/m$^3$ (0.028 ppm) with a limit of 365 mgm (0.13 ppm) in any single day. In the case of particulates the standard is set at a maximum daily average of 150 mgm/m$^3$.

A separate and more stringent standard for air-borne emissions exists for agriculture which not only includes a third (*hourly*) limit but also imposes tighter requirements in the productive central region than the barren north (Figure 10.2). The north has greater absorptive capacity because it comprises the Atacama desert, which is one of the driest places on earth and is, in consequence, very sparsely populated, so that competition for land and water resources is minimal. Moreover, air pollution abatement is aided by the 'natural' ventilation of the prevailing south-westerly winds. The arid climate also cuts the incidence of acid rain damage (*Diario Official*, 1992).

### Air Pollution Abatement in Chile

Current demands for improved pollution abatement in developing countries imply substantial cost penalties for long-established producers. For example, whereas most smelters in the industrial countries now use the latest flash smelting technology which typically captures 97 to 99 per cent of sulphur from effluent gas, many plants in developing countries only capture 50 per cent of such gases or less (World Bank, 1994). Although large investments in sulphuric acid plants can boost the gas capture level to between 50 and 70 per cent, in order to match best practice the production process must be expensively converted from the traditional reverbatory furnace technology. In contrast, new refineries are able to incorporate pollution abatement technology in the original plant design *and* to operate at significantly lower cost.

Investment to reduce environmental damage dominates abatement costs in Chile. The ratio between environmental investment and total investment observed for Ventanas and Disputada has been one-fifth and this appears representative for the industry as a whole (Lagos and Velesco, 1993). Expressed in terms of average production costs, one estimate puts the overall cost of environmental compliance at around 8¢/lb for Chile, some 11 per cent of total costs (Munoz, 1994). There are, however, complications in measurement which probably overstate the true environmental expenditure.

This is because many environmental investments, especially those associated with reducing gas emissions, often yield improvements in productivity which lower total production costs.

The main negative impact of copper refinery emissions appears to be in terms of the health of the workforce and their families. For example, there are reports of a high incidence of birth defects, lung cancers, etc. in the vicinity of Chuquicamata but there are as yet no scientific studies. However, it can be argued (and is by the workforce, anxious to preserve their jobs) that the costs of impaired health are already reflected in the higher wages paid by the copper mining industry. In 1990 the pay of mine workers at Chuquicamata averaged $1000 per month compared with $275 for coal miners in the south (*Financial Times*, 1990). In line with hedonistic pricing, such higher wages can be seen as the additional remuneration required to compensate for the more hazardous working conditions. However, such a view provides no grounds for complacency, and investments are being made to curb emissions.

The multinational mining firms in Chile have adopted their own (usually North American) corporate codes in setting desirable abatement targets, working with *ad hoc* committees prior to the provision of a practical legal environmental framework. But the state firms, which until recently dominated Chilean production, lagged behind. As a consequence, it was estimated in 1991 that the cost to Chile's five state-owned smelters of complying with Decree 185 would be $1 billion, but this still excluded the costs of compliance for arsenic emissions (Lagos, 1994).

Of the estimated total investment cost to Chilean state firms for environmental standard compliance, the largest Codelco unit, Chuquicamata, will alone account for $500 million (Fluckiger, 1994). Meanwhile, the cost pressures which compliance places on the older state-owned Chilean mines and refineries are being intensified by the expansion of new, cleaner low-cost producers, a process which is likely to intensify.

In the more densely settled regions like the Central Valley, the refinery emissions do occur in farming areas. But there is little evidence that farm productivity is reduced by smelter emissions – other than within the smelter emission 'hot spot' adjacent to a plant like Chagres which is located directly within a farming area. The 'background' levels of toxic metal in the soil around Chagres are naturally high, but they are especially high in the general vicinity of the smelter. Away from the immediate vicinity of the smelter and its 'hot spot' plume, concentrations are not critical for many plants which have a low take-up of toxic materials. Moreover, the naturally high metal content and alkalinity of Chilean soils make EPA standards unrealistic and inappropriate.

It would seem that any loss of land productivity attributable to smelter emissions is minimal, provided that some restriction of crops is accepted. The range of crops which are not adversely affected by the take-up of minerals (which concentrate in the green leaves of plants) is wide and includes grains, pulses and fruits. Where substantial crop damage is incurred, it usually reflects abuse of compensation schemes by local farmers. For example, farmers near the Chagres smelter deliberately plant crops like tomatoes which are sensitive to plant emissions. This is because the compensation which they receive provides a more secure income than is 'normally' provided by farming which is subject to the vagaries of the weather and pests.

Overall, the Chilean copper industry is well on the way to internalizing the costs of its environmental impact at a *national* level. This is reflected in the relatively high wage level within copper mining; potential improvements in land productivity through irrigation and crop compensation schemes; and the capital investments in plant and machinery being made to conform to tightening environmental standards. In contrast, the costs imposed by Chilean mine pollution on to the *international* community is still neglected due to reliance on 'natural' ventilation to remove some air pollutants.

## Conclusion

The experience of Chile and Jamaica suggests that the mineral economies may be moving faster towards attaining the three basic requirements for sustainable development than initially thought, although measurement problems are proving more contentious than expected. Chile has acquired a reputation for Latin American 'best practice' in economic management, but although Jamaica has also embarked on economic reform, it has made less progress. Yet the potential threat which economic weakness poses to Jamaican efforts to improve its environment is fortunately offset by the fact that the mining sector is dominated by MNCs who adopt 'best practice' corporate environmental standards, and also by the fact that the pollution shadow associated with bauxite mining is less pronounced than that of, for example, copper in Chile.

The overall cost of making allowance for the depletion of the bauxite ore requires little modification to the Jamaican national accounts. It reduces the level of true saving by only 2 per cent of GDP even if the upwardly biased net price approach to depletion is adopted. Nor is the depletion component especially large in Chile. Even employing the net price method to calculate depletion would depress NDP by around 4 per cent, still leaving a healthy rate of genuine saving.

As with asset depletion, the cost of curbing environmental degradation from Jamaican bauxite mining is low in relation to both the sector's total costs of production and to the GDP. The major Jamaican costs entail some modest loss of scarce farmland and some risk of water supply contamination. Air-borne emissions from Jamaican alumina refineries tend to be within international standards and occasional pollution episodes are a highly localized problem. The mining MNCs have long relied on *ad hoc* agreements to deal with environmental impacts in the absence of an effective national environmental policy for the bauxite sector.

The principal damage in copper mining appears to be to the health of copper sector workers from smelter emissions, and to farm productivity. The costs of both are being internalized by the industry, led by the private foreign-owned mines, in terms of: high wages; investments in pollution abatement technology; and the provision of irrigation water supplies/crop compensation schemes. A rule of thumb suggests that around one-fifth of all investment by established Chilean copper producers since the 1970s has gone towards curbing environmental damage. But the difficulty of attributing investment benefits to specific tasks, like pollution abatement, means that the one-fifth investment rule almost certainly overstates the environmental charge.

Overall, although considerable progress has been made in internalizing the costs of environmental damage, both the technical problems of measuring impacts and of assigning costs, and the lack of a consensus on calculating a depletion coefficient, are retarding the development of environmental accounting. Consequently, the signals for resource use efficiency at the macro level which environmental accounting has the potential to provide are as yet less clear than was initially hoped.

# Acknowledgement

The financial assistance of RTZ with field work is gratefully acknowledged.

# References

Ahmad, Y.J., El Serafy, S. and Lutz, E. (eds) (1989) *Environmental Accounting for Sustainable Development.* Washington, DC: World Bank.

Auty, R.M. (1993) *Sustaining Development in Mineral Economies.* London: Routledge.

Auty, R.M. and Warhurst, A. (1993) Sustaining development in mineral economies. *Resources Policy,* **19**, 14–29.

Barde, J.P. and Pearce, D.W. (1991) *Valuing the Environment.* London: Earthscan.

Bartelmus, P., Lutz, E. and Schweinfest, S. (1992) Integrated environmental and economic accounting: a case study for PNG. Environment Working Paper No. 54. Washington, DC: World Bank.

Bartelmus, P. and van Tongeren, J. (1994) Environmental accounting: an operational perspective. Working Paper No. 1, Department for Economic and Social Information and Policy Analysis, New York: United Nations.

Bell, J. (1986) Caustic waste menaces Jamaica. *New Scientist,* 3 April, 33–7.

Brewster, H. Dutch Disease in the age of adjustment. Paper presented to the UNCTAD Conference on Development, Environment and Mining, 1–3 June. Washington, DC: World Bank.

Bureau of Mines (1991) *Copper.* Washington, DC: Bureau of Mines.

CEPAL (1991) *La Mineria in Chile.* LC/R. 1020. Santiago: CEPAL.

CEPAL (1993) *Statistical Yearbook for Latin America and the Caribbean.* Santiago: CEPAL.

Clarendon Alumina Production Limited (1990) *Annual Report 1989–90.* Kingston: United Co-op Printers.

Codelco (1991) *Codelco: Making a Future*. Rancagua: Codelco.

Crosson, P.R. and Haas, R.B. (1983) Agricultural land. In P.R. Portney (ed.), *Current Issues in Natural Resource Policy*. Washington, DC: Resources For the Future, pp. 253–82.

Crowson, P.C.F. (1994) Mineral rents, taxation and sustainability. Paper presented to the UNCTAD International Conference on Development, Environment and Mining, 1–3 June. Washington, DC: World Bank.

Daniel, P. (1992) Economic policy in mineral-exporting countries: what have we learned? In J.E. Tilton (ed.) *Mineral Wealth and Economic Development*. Washington, DC: Resources for the Future, pp. 81–121.

*Diario Official* (1992) Reglamenta funcionamiento de establecimentos emisores de anhidrido sulfuroso, material particulado y arsenico in todo el territoria de la republica. *Diario Official de la Republic de Chile*, 18 January, Santiago.

ECLA (1994) *Statistical Yearbook for Latin America and the Caribbean 1993*. Santiago: ECLA.

El Serafy, S. (1989) The proper calculation of income from depletable natural resources. In Y.J. Ahmad, S. El Serafy and E. Lutz (eds), *Environmental Accounting for Sustainable Development*. Washington, DC: World Bank, pp. 10–18.

Fields, R.M. (1987) *Jamaica: Country Environmental Profile*. Kingston: R.M. Fields and Associates.

*Financial Times* (1990) Chilean miners have to dig in stony ground. 10 August.

Fluckiger, M. (1994) Interview. Santiago: Comision del Cobre Chilena.

Gelb, A. (1988) *Oil Windfalls: Blessing or Curse?* New York: Oxford University Press.

Government of Jamaica (1991) *The Natural Resources Conservation Authority Act 1991*. Kingston: Government Printer.

Hamilton, K. and Atkinson, G. (1995) Valuing air pollution in the National Accounts. Paper presented for the London Group on National Accounts and the Environment, Washington, DC.

Hamilton, K. and O'Connor, J. (1994) Genuine saving and the financing of investment. Working Paper. Washington, DC: Environment Division, World Bank.

IBA (1992) Bauxite mining and environment management at Kirkvine. Kingston: IBA/EB/LIII/07/92.

JBI (1992) *The Bauxite/Alumina Industry and the Environment*. Kingston: Jamaica Bauxite Institute.

Lagos, G.E. (1994) Developing national policies in Chile. In R.G. Eggert (ed.), *Mining and the Environment*. Washington, DC: Resources for the Future, pp. 85–109.

Lagos, G.E. and Velesco, P. (1993) *Environmental Policies and Priorities of Selected Mining Companies in Chile: A Case Study*. Santiago: CESCO.

Martyn, P. (1992) *Bauxite Mine Rehabilitation Survey*. London: International Primary Aluminium Institute.

Mikesell, R.F. (1992) *Economic Development and the Environment*. London: Mansell.

Ministry of Production Mining and Commerce (1994) Kingston: Commissioner of Lands Office.

Munoz, G. (1994) Interview. Santiago: Codelco.

Neufville, L.N. (1993) The impact of mining on occupational safety and health and the environment. Paper presented at Mining-Tech 1993, Lulea.

Pinto, B. (1987) Nigeria during and after the oil boom: a policy comparison with Indonesia. *World Bank Economic Review*, 1, 419–25.

Planning Institute of Jamaica (1994) *Economic and Social Survey Jamaica 1993*. Kingston: Government of Jamaica.

Salmon, M. (1987) Land utilization within Jamaica's bauxite land economy. *Social and Economic Studies*, 36, 57–92.

Smith, W.S. (1993) Chile and copper. *The Lamp*, 75 (2), 1–9.

Statistical Institute of Jamaica (1994) *National Income and Product 1992*. Kingston: Statistical Institute of Jamaica.

Valenzuela, L.F. (1994) Interview. Santiago: Compania Minera Disputada de las Condes.

Weir (1982) Impact of bauxite alumina industries on the Jamaican environment. Kingston: Weir Consulting Services Ltd.

Wellington, K.E. (1986) Utilization of bauxite lands for agriculture. *Journal of the Geological Society of Jamaica*, March, 49–54.

World Bank (1989) *World Bank Tables 1988–89*. Baltimore: Johns Hopkins University Press.

World Bank (1993) *Jamaica: Economic Issues and Environmental Management*. Washington, DC: World Bank.

World Bank (1994) *Market Outlook for Major Energy Products, Metals and Minerals*. Washington, DC: World Bank.

World Bank (1995) *World Tables 1995*. Baltimore: Johns Hopkins University Press.

# 11

# Pollution Patterns in the Industrialization Process

## Richard M. Auty and Michael Tribe

## Introduction

This chapter addresses the issue of whether there are observable systematic patterns in the development of industrial pollution during the process of industrialization. The topic can be broken down into four sub-issues:

- First, whether over time, with rising per capita incomes and the increasing share of industry in national product, the overall level of pollution changes in a systematic way.
- Second, associated with the first, whether, with the commodity composition of industrial production changing over time, the environmental pollution profile changes during the process of industrialization. This second sub-issue includes the distinction between different types of pollution (air-borne, water-borne and solid matter).
- Third, within the context of the product cycle, whether there is a systematic transfer of 'dirty industries' from the developed market economies (DMEs) to the less-developed countries (LDCs).
- Fourth, associated with the third, whether industrial production in the LDCs is systematically more pollution intensive than in the DMEs due to the nature of the socio-economic structures of the LDCs with less developed environmental controls, and with significantly less capacity to enforce those controls which are in place.

The discussion of these sub-issues which follows does not adhere rigidly to the above sequence. To some extent the chapter investigates the factors affecting the nature of the 'elasticity of industrial pollution' with respect to economic development. Related to this concern is the question of whether the same patterns of pollution which have been observed in the industrial development of the DMEs are likely to be replicated in the LDCs, or whether these 'late-industrializers' will trace a different trajectory.

In making this broad comparison it has to be recognized explicitly that the global economy is divided in a much more complex manner than might be suggested by the simple 'dual' region approach suggested above. Instead of being reduced to the DMEs and LDCs, the world might be divided into (i) the DMEs, (ii) the transitional economies of Eastern Europe and the former USSR, (iii) the semi-industrialized nations of Latin America, (iv) the newly industrializing economies of Southeast Asia, (v) the large low-income economies of South Asia and (vi) the low-income countries of sub-Saharan Africa. Even these broad groupings each contain considerable diversity.

This chapter concentrates on the manufacturing sub-sector and so excludes consideration of mineral extraction, construction, water purification and distribution, public sewage/sanitation provision and electricity production and distribution – all of which are included in the industrial sector in the UN System of National Accounts (World Bank, 1995, p. 232). The chapter also excludes consideration of energy and resource depletion/recycling, concentrating on the specific questions associated with environmental pollution through manufacturing activity. Another issue which is only indirectly linked to the concerns of the chapter, but which is also important, is the health and safety aspect of manufacturing production and of product characteristics.

The chapter has been divided into two main sections. In the first we attempt to set out some of the broad questions relating to environmental pollution and industrial development. In the second we set out some evidence from individual countries as a basis for preliminary testing of some of the hypotheses which can be established on the basis of the broader issues outlined in the first section. The chapter ends with a summary involving an overview of the conclusions arising from the discussion.

## The Product Cycle and Pollution Patterns

Raymond Vernon's original article putting forward the concept of the product cycle appeared in 1966 (Vernon, 1966). In 1979 he published a reconsideration and a partial retraction of the original arguments (Vernon, 1979). The basic proposition is that in the process of industrial innovation, particularly concerning the introduction of significantly new products in industrially developed countries (which necessarily involve new production technologies), the production of established products becomes 'routinized' and is transferred to countries with a lower level of industrial development (usually with lower wage levels), with an associated 'reverse flow' of trade in finished products from the latter to the former. The industrial sector in more developed countries replaces the production of 'routinized' products with the production of new products, retaining a degree of dynamism in this process. The fact that industrial research and development tends to be centralized in the more developed countries reinforces their market dominance. This approach fits well, in general, with a process of industrialization in which MNCs are major actors. While the detailed evidence relating to this model is open to endless wrangling, there is a certain attraction in its simplicity, and it certainly contains a sufficient germ of truth to be a useful concept to use in the analysis of global industrial development in the second half of the twentieth century (Williamson and Milner, 1991, pp. 73–5).

However, it is not the intention of this chapter to review the overall validity of the concept of the product cycle as applied to industrial development. But, one way in which such a broader application might work involves a reformulation of the product cycle model as an income and market structure-driven process rather than a technology-driven process (see Auty, 1993). Rather the question here is whether the product cycle approach is in any way applicable to the relationship between industrial development and patterns of environmental pollution. Specifically, we wish to ask whether there is any systematic transfer of 'dirty industries' from DMEs (with increasingly stringent environmental protection legislation which is equally increasingly effectively implemented) to 'pollution havens' in LDCs, together with an associated reverse flow of trade in manufactures from LDCs to DMEs, as with the basic product cycle model. If the process of industrialization is principally driven by other factors such as technology, external economies and demand within LDCs, then the 'pollution haven' thesis may be an insignificant factor.

Our interest in this issue has been partly activated by developments in the literature which emphasize the question of international trade and the environment (Cropper and Oates, 1992; Low, 1992) rather than the broader and more interesting question of industrial development and the environment. Earlier discussion of some associated aspects may be found in Tribe (1994). Cropper and Oates state part of the argument very clearly:

> In particular, there has been a concern that the less developed countries, with their emphasis on economic development rather than environmental protection, will tend over time to develop a comparative advantage in pollution-intensive industries. In consequence they will become the 'havens' for the world's dirty industries, this concern has become known as the 'pollution haven hypothesis' .... Why have domestic environmental measures not induced 'industrial flight', and the development of 'pollution havens'? The primary reason seems to be that the costs of pollution control have not, in fact, loomed very large even in heavily polluting industries. Existing estimates suggest that control costs have run in the order of only 1 to 2.5 per cent of total costs in most pollution intensive industries .... There seems not to have been a discernible movement in investment in these industries to the less developed countries because major political and economic uncertainties have

apparently loomed much larger in location decisions than have the modest savings from less stringent environmental controls. (1992, pp. 697–9)

Casual observation might suggest that there has been a process of transfer of 'dirty industries' and 'dirty technologies' from DMEs to LDCs (to retain the simplicity of the bifocal approach). It is not necessary, however, to argue that these industries and technologies have been transferred *because* the investors are endeavouring to avoid the pollution control regulations which are enforced in the DMEs (together with their associated costs). In many cases, it is likely that other factors have led to the transfer of a particular line of industrial production. These factors include technology transfer in response to changes in dynamic comparative advantage; the development of external economies; the availability of low-cost inputs in the LDCs; and growth in demand within the LDCs (for example, in the case of the NICs, the rapidly increasing levels of per capita income in the Pacific Rim region imply the development of a much more significant focus of purchasing power than has existed at any time before in that region).

It is not even necessary that the entire production process is transferred from the DMEs to the LDCs for a model akin to the product cycle to be appealing. It is sufficient that a significant amount of industrial capacity be established in the LDC category economy, so that the proportional balance of global industrial production changes in favour of the LDCs. Examples of industries where such a change has occurred, and where pollution is a significant issue, include iron, steel and other metallic processing, petroleum refining, chemicals and fertilizers, and leather manufacture (World Bank, 1991).

The process of developing outward-oriented industries, as opposed to import-substituting industries, in LDCs necessarily involves increasing the value-added associated with exports of previously unprocessed or semi-processed raw materials, or increasing the value-added associated with domestic raw materials which have not been previously exported. This implies that many of the export-oriented industries are likely to be at the 'lower-end' of the International Standard Industrial Classification (ISIC), an area of production which is more likely to involve a more significant risk of pollution as compared with the 'higher end' ISIC. The lower end of the ISIC includes many agro-industries, for example, which tend to dominate the manufacturing sector in the least developed economies. This industrial dynamic would then be based on a tendency towards the transfer of production capacity from DMEs to LDCs not caused by a process of technological and new product development, and not caused by 'push' factors emanating from the DMEs, but rather by 'pull' factors originating in the desire of LDCs to expand their manufacturing sectors and to do this through a resource-based and outward-oriented, industrialization strategy (Roemer, 1979).

Another factor which could account for a high level of 'pollution intensity' of the manufacturing sector in LDCs is associated with the nature of evolving consumption and production patterns in the process of economic growth and development. First, if there is any tendency for consumption patterns at lower levels of per capita income to include products which have a greater tendency to pollute the environment when they are being produced, so that the proportion of 'pollution-intensive' products consumed falls as per capita income rises, this will reinforce the industrial pollution problem in LDCs. Second, if the nature of industrial production changes with increasing per capita income levels, so that at lower levels a higher proportion of manufactured goods are produced in smaller establishments using technologies which have a higher 'pollution intensity' than those which become the norm as the scale of production and sophistication of production technology increases with per capita income levels, then industrial pollution will be worse in LDCs. Third, the nature of consumption technology (including product packaging) changes in the process of economic growth and development and this itself impinges on the polluting effect of manufactured goods. At different levels of per capita income/consumption and of industrial development, the interaction between waste-creation, waste-disposal and waste-recycling changes. However, the interaction may be indeterminate, so that there would be no systematic trend over time.

In analysing the relationship between industrial development and environmental pollution it is necessary to make some distinctions. DMEs might have lighter 'pollution shadows' because industries are subject to more stringent environmental controls and penalties, and have, therefore, adopted production technologies which avoid higher levels of pollution – either intrinsically cleaner technologies or dirtier technologies with 'environmental add-ons'. LDCs might have denser 'pollution shadows' either because the industries which are predominant are by their nature more 'pollution intensive' on average than industries in the DMEs, or because dirty industries have not adopted cleaner technologies or 'environmental add-ons' due to the slacker nature of environmental controls and penalties. This is the type of reasoning which lends itself to the establishment, and testing, of hypotheses, so that empirical verification is a realistic possibility. However, it might not be possible to test whether similar, or the same, industries in DMEs are less environmentally hazardous than those in LDCs simply because some industries are just not present in both categories of country. The testing would have to be undertaken in carefully selected individual, or groups of, industries.

The 'pollution haven' thesis (analogous to 'tax havens') mentioned above implies either that dirtier industries re-locate to LDCs, or that industries which re-locate (or are originally located) in LDCs do not adopt environmentally clean technologies or 'add-ons'. Again, this should be an empirically verifiable thesis. However, there are some other issues involved which may be interesting to explore in the context of the product cycle approach to industrial pollution. First, is the fact that as industries in DMEs find themselves under greater pressure to conform to ever tighter environmental controls, production technologies are being developed which are inherently less polluting and which do not necessarily depend on 'add-ons'. This implies that the industrial technologies which are 'bought off the shelf' by LDC industrial investors are increasingly up to date in terms of their environmental characteristics, so that production equipment 'without add-ons' of the older, more polluting, technology is likely not to be available. Thus the technological determinism which is so often criticized on the grounds that inappropriate modern capital-intensive technologies are transferred to LDCs might be praised in the sense that modern less-pollution-intensive technologies are now being transferred. This factor is the more likely to be the case for MNCs and the joint-ventures involving MNCs. Second, there has been a tendency for industrial production processes to be re-designed in the light of more stringent environmental controls, and in some cases this has led to efficiency gains because of the re-design, as reported in the *Guardian* newspaper and in the Annual Report of Her Majesty's Inspectorate of Pollution:

> Regulations imposed on industry to cut pollution have provided an unexpected bonus. Being forced to rethink methods had led to savings of millions of pounds because the greener processes were cheaper, the Inspectorate of Pollution said yesterday in its annual report. An example was a joint study by the Inspectorate and the Bradford chemical company Allied Colloids, which had cut pollution and also increased efficiency. (*Guardian*, 22 July 1995)

> A study undertaken to look at emissions, efficiencies and economics concluded that the company would make operating savings of some £300,000 a year while also reducing pollution emissions for a one-off investment of £100,000. (HM Inspectorate of Pollution, 1995, p. 91)

If this phenomenon is at all common, as is suggested by the remainder of the newspaper article, this is further evidence that the cost handicap associated with environmental controls is unlikely to lead to transfers of industrial pollution to 'pollution havens'.

Another factor which might reinforce the pollution intensity of manufacturing activity (and other economic activity) in LDCs is not the intrinsic technological characteristics of the production processes, but rather the general level of competence of the workforce which is expected to operate the process. For example, in the case of the Bhopal disaster in India it is understood that the accident occurred less due to design failings and more due to operational shortcomings. In many cases environmental problems might arise because of a mix of design and operational factors, each reinforcing the other — for which the Chernobyl disaster might qualify from a quite highly developed country.

# The Evidence for Systematic Pollution Patterns

## Per Capita Income and the Structure of Manufacturing

Over the last 20 years Chenery and Syrquin have made a comprehensive study of structural change during the industrialization process which provides a framework within which to analyse the relationship between economic development and pollution. In their World Bank Discussion Paper (Syrquin and Chenery, 1989), they use data derived from more than 100 countries over three decades to trace not only how the structure of the economy changes with rising per capita income, but most usefully for this study also how the composition of manufacturing changes.

Table 11.1 summarizes the Syrquin and Chenery figures for the aggregate pattern of a 'large' country, meaning one with a population of 20 million or more. This shows that the historical pattern for such countries has been one in which manufacturing raises its share of GDP from just under 12 per cent at $300 (1980 $) per capita income to more than 24 per cent at $4000, with the mid-point (i.e. when manufacturing reaches 18 per cent of GDP) occurring at $1000. Heavy industry (defined as ISIC sectors 35–38) overtakes light industry (31–34 and 39) in importance at just over $1200.

Syrquin and Chenery also identify 'early', 'middle' and 'late' manufacturing sub-sectors. The early group comprises agro-processing (food, beverages and tobacco) and textiles and clothing. It accounts for more than half of all manufacturing value added below $300 per capita income and remains dominant up to an income level of $500. The growth in its share of GDP ceases above $1000 and its share declines slightly above the $2000 income level. Table 11.1 also confirms that within the early cluster of manufacturing, agro-processing is the dominant sub-component.

The middle group of industries is more capital-intensive in nature: it comprises wood products, non-metallic minerals (mainly cement and ceramics), chemicals and rubber. Its share of GDP almost doubles as per capita income rises from $300 to $2000. From the outset, chemicals and rubber between them dominate output in the middle group (accounting for two-thirds).

The late group of industries comprises paper and printing, basic metals, and metals products and machinery. Broadly, it combines capital-intensive sub-sectors with skill-intensive ones. The late sub-group outstrips the middle group in size by $1100 per capita income and overtakes the early group at around $2600. It almost equals the size of the early and middle groups combined above the $5000 income level.

Syrquin and Chenery do not investigate trends at income levels above $5000 so that in order to trace changes in the structure of the DME economies, it is necessary to turn to other sources. The evidence points to a relative decline in the manufacturing sector's share of GDP, although with

**Table 11.1** Average variation in industrial structure with level of development (Population = 20 million)

| Sector | ISIC code | Income per capita (1980 US$) | | | | | | | Total change | Income at mid-point |
|---|---|---|---|---|---|---|---|---|---|---|
| | | Mean under $300 | $300 | $500 | $1000 | $2000 | $4000 | Mean over $5000 | | |
| Manufacturing | 3 | 0.119 | 0.120 | 0.151 | 0.188 | 0.219 | 0.244 | 0.269 | 0.150 | 1200 |
| Food, beverages and tobacco | 31 | 0.028 | 0.042 | 0.045 | 0.047 | 0.046 | 0.042 | 0.040 | 0.012 | – |
| Textiles and clothing | 32 | 0.034 | 0.026 | 0.030 | 0.033 | 0.034 | 0.032 | 0.029 | – | – |
| Wood and products | 33 | 0.002 | 0.004 | 0.005 | 0.006 | 0.008 | 0.010 | 0.014 | 0.012 | 2000 |
| Paper and printing | 34 | 0.005 | 0.003 | 0.004 | 0.007 | 0.011 | 0.016 | 0.025 | 0.020 | 3000 |
| Chemicals and rubber | 35 | 0.018 | 0.024 | 0.030 | 0.036 | 0.040 | 0.042 | 0.034 | 0.016 | 400 |
| Non-metallic minerals | 36 | 0.005 | 0.005 | 0.008 | 0.011 | 0.012 | 0.013 | 0.014 | 0.009 | 700 |
| Basic metals | 37 | 0.006 | 0.005 | 0.009 | 0.013 | 0.017 | 0.019 | 0.020 | 0.014 | 1000 |
| Metal products and machinery | 38 | 0.018 | 0.010 | 0.019 | 0.032 | 0.048 | 0.066 | 0.087 | 0.069 | 2500 |
| Other | 39 | 0.003 | 0.001 | 0.001 | 0.003 | 0.003 | 0.004 | 0.006 | – | – |
| Light industry | 31–34,39 | 0.072 | 0.076 | 0.085 | 0.096 | 0.102 | 0.104 | 0.114 | 0.042 | 900 |
| Heavy industry | 35–38 | 0.047 | 0.044 | 0.066 | 0.092 | 0.117 | 0.140 | 0.155 | 0.108 | 1500 |
| Early | 31,32,39 | 0.066 | 0.069 | 0.076 | 0.083 | 0.083 | 0.078 | 0.074 | – | – |
| Middle | 33,35,36 | 0.024 | 0.033 | 0.043 | 0.053 | 0.060 | 0.065 | 0.062 | 0.038 | 500 |
| Late | 34,37,38 | 0.029 | 0.018 | 0.032 | 0.052 | 0.076 | 0.101 | 0.132 | 0.103 | 2500 |

Source: Syrquin and Chenery (1989, Table 6, p. 32).

some lag in the more successful industrial exporting countries. Wolf (1991) shows that the share of manufacturing in the GDP of the largest industrial economies is declining and that by 1987 it ranged downwards from 31 per cent in Germany through 29 per cent in Japan, 23 per cent in Italy, 21 per cent in France and Britain, to just over 19 per cent in the US. Respected international secondary data sources confirm this trend, but United States data are systematically unavailable for the particular years selected (e.g. World Bank, 1995, Table 3, p. 167). Brown and Julius (1994) use *employment* data to predict a further long-term contraction in manufacturing's share in the DMEs' output (halving to 10 per cent between 1990 and 2020). In a more detailed analysis of the US economy, Krugman and Lawrence (1994) show that the share of manufacturing in GDP fell between 1970 and 1990 from 25 to 18.4 per cent of GDP. An important cause of the decline is the fact that the prices of manufactured goods fell relative to the prices of services by over one-fifth due to sustained high productivity growth in the former.

Such long-term changes in the ratio of manufacturing to services appear to occur slowly and changes in the composition of manufacturing may proceed faster, and therefore, have considerable significance for pollution. For example, Lawrence (1984, p. 64) calculated that between 1969 and 1980, high-technology sub-sectors in the US expanded their share of manufacturing output from 27 to 38 per cent. Offsetting this, the contribution of capital-intensive industry fell from 32 to 27 per cent, agro-processing also fell from 28 to 23 per cent while labour-intensive manufacturing held steady at 13 to 14 per cent. These trends suggest that the composition of manufacturing may be as important a determinant of the pollution-intensity of GDP as the relative size of the manufacturing sector.

Some caution is required in interpreting the figures. For example, the Syrquin and Chenery trends are based on historical data and patterns of both consumption and of manufacturing technology are constantly changing. Moreover, the aggregate data necessarily mask significant variations among countries which are attributable to differences in natural resource endowment (Lal, 1992) and development strategy (discussed further below). These limitations should be borne in mind when making both projections of the aggregate data into the future and inferences about specific countries. These issues are addressed in later sections of the chapter, but first the link between per capita income, the composition of manufacturing and pollution is explored.

**Pollution Patterns and the Structure of Manufacturing**

This section draws on research by the World Bank on East Asia, a region which has experienced rapid industrial growth in recent years, to examine the pollutants associated with each of the three income-related groupings of manufacturing recognized by Syrquin and Chenery, and characterized as early, middle and late stages of industrialization. The evidence suggests that the three basic categories of emissions (water-borne, air-borne and solid waste) do vary systematically with changing per capita income and related industrial structure, but that there are substantial variations about the mean for each category.

*Early industries impact water pollution*

Organic waste is the prime industrial emission problem in the early stages of industrialization, rather than gaseous discharges or toxic wastes (World Bank, 1994a). This reflects the dominance of agro-processing in the early industry group noted above. Although locally, high concentrations of such effluent may be severe, such early industrial pollutants are not usually health-threatening and their total bio-chemical oxygen demand (BOD) is likely to be significantly less (below one-third) than that made by household sewage, for example.

Data for Thailand in 1991, when the country was entering the middle stages of industrialization, provide some quantitative evidence. Thailand then had a per capita income of $1600 (in current US dollars), and its pre-treated industrial BOD totalled 852,000 tonnes in that year, or about 19 kg/$1000 of GDP. Just over half of this discharge emanated from the food-processing sector (with sugar milling prominent) and slightly more than two-fifths from beverage production. This left textiles and pulp and paper with around 2.5 per cent of the share each (World Bank, 1994a). The dominance of food and beverages in early industry is confirmed in Indonesia, whose per capita income is less than half that of Thailand (World Bank, 1994b).

Data for Malaysia (World Bank, 1993), already in the middle stage of industrialization, show that early industry continues to dominate industrial *water* pollution. Food and beverages, palm oil, raw rubber and textiles and leather still accounted for 70 per cent of such emissions. But Malaysia also shows that while in the aggregate the early industries may continue to dominate water pollution, the middle industries tend to have a much higher pollution intensity (expressed in pounds of BOD per day per million dollars of value added). For example, whereas early industries like food products and beverages display BOD demands of 79 lb and 26 lb per million dollars of value added, respectively, middle industries such as 'other chemicals' and pulp and paper create a BOD demand of 360 lb and 114 lb, respectively, per million dollars of output. This implies that the middle industries have the potential to rapidly intensify water pollution. It may also account for the observed lag (discussed at greater length below) in reducing water-borne pollution compared with air-borne pollution (Grossman, 1995).

*Middle industry intensifies water and air emissions*

Although the early industries continue to expand through the middle stage both absolutely and in terms of their share of GDP (albeit modestly), the middle industries grow faster. Table 11.1 shows that the middle set comprises chemicals, ceramics, cement and wood processing. Such sub-sectors not only exhibit high BOD demand, as noted above, they also accelerate the build-up of solid and hazardous wastes and their most significant environmental effect is to boost air-borne pollution.

Among the air-borne emissions, suspended particulates are a major problem. For example, in the late 1980s such emissions exceeded recommended levels by more than 50 per cent in Kuala Lumpur, by 250 per cent in Bangkok and almost 300 per cent in Jakarta (World Bank, 1993). But this inverse correlation with per capita income is not consistent with the projection based on the changing industrial structure. This is because the data are for the leading cities rather than the industrial sector as such so that other factors become important, notably the contribution of motor vehicles and individual city size (with Kuala Lumpur much the smaller city). For example, Thai industry's share of suspended particulates expanded from 26 to 36 per cent between 1983 and 1992, but the figures are for the Bangkok Metropolitan Area only, a region where three-quarters of Thai manufacturing is concentrated (World Bank, 1994a). The Thai data suggest that, for other important air-borne pollutants, the contribution of the industrial sector falls as per capita income rises: in the case of $SO_2$ easing from 36 to 28 per cent between 1983 and 1992 and for nitrogen oxides from 13 to 11 per cent. Consistent with this conclusion, Malaysia also experienced some decline in the contribution which industry made to air-borne particulates – and from a lower initial base (a fact in line with the country's higher per capita income level) – from 16 to 14 per cent over the period 1987–91 (World Bank, 1993).

*Late industry intensifies toxic waste*

In the late stage of industrialization hazardous waste is likely to become the major pollution problem. Although hazardous wastes may be vented into the waterways and the atmosphere, they are most likely to be disposed of on land and, therefore, to have localized and potentially severe adverse health effects. UN data for the late-1980s show solid waste, measured in kg/head/day rising from 0.75 in Manila through 0.88 in Bangkok and 1.29 in Kuala Lumpur to 2.8 in Seoul (World Bank, 1993).

According to estimates made for Thailand in the early-1990s, approximating the middle stage of industrialization, toxic solid waste displayed considerable potential for rapid expansion and manufacturing was responsible for most of it (around 80 per cent of the annual total of 1 million tonnes). The scale of increase in toxic solid waste in Thailand was projected to be three-fold within a decade, due to the projected rapid expansion of base metals, chemicals and machinery. Much of the material emitted has a high health risk. In the case of Thailand in the early-1990s, heavy metals sludge and solids accounted for almost half of these emissions; acid wastes for one-eighth; and infectious waste for one-twelfth.

But if toxic waste becomes a leading problem at higher income levels and is concentrated in the cities, even at low income levels the rural areas still suffer from its impact. The composition of toxic waste in lower middle-income countries like Indonesia is dominated by emissions from rural activity. World Bank (1994b) data reveal that agricultural chemicals remain the largest source of toxic waste (almost 30 per cent) in Indonesia, followed by wood products and steel (with 10 per cent each), basic industrial chemicals (7 per cent) and spinning and weaving (6 per cent).

Summarizing, southeast Asian case studies provide some evidence that systematic changes do occur in emission problems as per capita incomes rise. Such changes have an important spatial dimension because with rising per capita income the relative importance of rural activity declines in relation to urban activity. At low income levels the predominantly rural and resource-based nature of industrial activity is less geographically concentrated and its main impact is on water bodies (such dispersal reduces emission density and aids the bio-chemical breakdown of pollutants). As per capita incomes rise and industrial activity becomes more localized in cities, so the problem of industrial pollution is compounded by other emissions. The concentration of population and vehicles renders human waste an increasing source of water pollution and vehicle exhausts a major source of atmospheric pollution. Consequently, the changing composition of industrial pollution takes place against such 'background noise' and is a part only, albeit a major one, of the broader picture.

## Long-Term Pollution Trends

This section seeks to generalize about the broad relationship between industrial pollution and rising per capita income. It does so in two stages. First, the evidence is examined in support of the theory that, as per capita income rises, the pollution intensity of GDP traces an inverted U-shape whose crest has historically shown a declining trend. Second, the principal causes of deviations from the underlying trend are explored.

### *The inverted U-shape*

There is evidence to suggest that as market economies industrialize, the intensity with which they use energy and materials, and the rate at which they emit pollutants, first increases and then declines (Bernstam, 1991). The 'inverted U-shape', illustrated in the top section of Figure 11.1, reflects, as

The theory

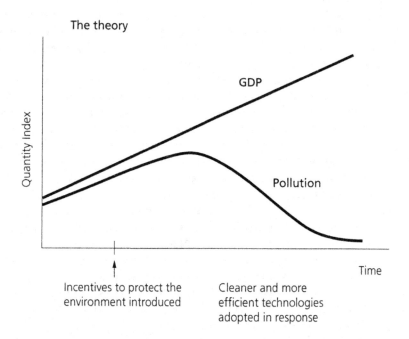

Incentives to protect the
environment introduced

Cleaner and more
efficient technologies
adopted in response

The practice: GDP and emissions in OECD countries

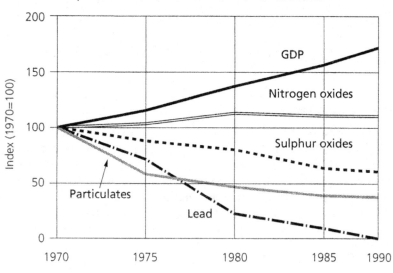

**Figure 11.1**   Breaking the link between growth in GDP and pollution (*Source:* World Bank, 1992, p. 40)

discussed earlier, the changing structure of the economy (as countries first build up the infrastructure of a modern economy and then spend an increasing fraction of their income on services). It also reflects technological change and a growing preference for a cleaner environment.

As noted in the previous section, the intensity of pollution of middle industry tends to be higher than that of early industry. Moreover, the rate of growth in the size of the manufacturing sector relative to GDP, and also its growth in aggregate terms, further boosts the volume of pollution. For example, the Indonesian manufacturing sector expanded eight-fold between 1970 and 1980 and is projected to increase a further thirteen-fold by 2020, when the country will still be in the 'middle' stage of industrialization (World Bank, 1994b).

But at higher income levels there is a decline not only in the emissions-intensity of GDP but also in the absolute volume of most, but not all, pollutants. Several recent studies corroborate the downward trend. Bernstam (1991) measured pollution trends in the DMEs for the period 1970–85 and found a declining trend in the absolute volume of most pollutants, as shown in Table 11.2, especially from stationary sources (down by one-quarter to one-third with the exception of Canada). These results are broadly confirmed by the World Bank (1992), based on data for the industrial countries over a slightly longer period spanning the years 1970–88, as shown in Figure 11.1.

A recent study by Grossman (1995) also records the downturn of the inverted U-shape for the pollution intensity of GDP. For example, the downturn in suspended particulate and $SO_2$ emissions occurs around the per capita income level of $5000 (measured in 1985 US dollars at purchasing power parity). This approximates to the average per capita income of countries like Malaysia and Mexico in the early 1990s. Other atmospheric pollutants, such as carbon monoxide, carbon dioxide and nitrogen oxides, appear to peak at somewhat higher per capita income levels. The turning-point for water pollution also appears to occur later at between $8500 and $11,500 per capita income. Over that range the levels of faecal coliform counts, dissolved oxygen, BOD and nitrate all begin to improve. The inverted U-shape pattern is not universal, however: for example, the levels of toxic metals in rivers appear to fall steeply to around $5000 per capita income before levelling out or rising slightly and then falling again at $14,000.

The inverted U-shape may be explained by the combination of changing demand (linked to changes in the structure of GDP and the composition of manufacturing outlined in earlier sections) and a higher preference as incomes rise for pollution abatement. A recent World Bank study speculates that it may be possible to de-link GDP from natural resource use (World Bank, 1992, p. 40). It notes that, historically, reductions in the use intensity in *market* economies (but not socialist economies) have *preceded* the increase in government concern for the environment. The subsequent adoption of

**Table 11.2** Trends in emission of air pollutants in market economies by source, for selected countries, 1970–85 (in thousand metric tonnes)

| | 1970 | | | 1975 | | | 1980 | | | 1985 | | | Ratio 1985/1970 (%) | | |
|---|---|---|---|---|---|---|---|---|---|---|---|---|---|---|---|
| | A | S | T | A | S | T | A | S | T | A | S | T | A | S | T |
| Canada | 10,078 | 12,068 | 22,146 | 10,519 | 11,089 | 21,078 | 9975 | 10,552 | 20,527 | 9340 | 10,260 | 19,600 | 92.7 | 85.0 | 88.5 |
| USA | 93,600 | 96,700 | 190,300 | 83,100 | 76,400 | 159,500 | 72,200 | 79,600 | 151,800 | 63,000 | 70,000 | 133,000 | 76.3 | 72.4 | 69.9 |
| Germany | 11,189 | 12,858 | 24,047 | 12,802 | 9427 | 22,229 | 11,822 | 9190 | 21,012 | 9379 | 7641 | 17,020 | 83.8 | 59.4 | 70.8 |
| France | 5451 | 7889 | 13,340 | 5805 | 8184 | 13,989 | 6472 | 7976 | 14,448 | 6882[a] | 4830[a] | 11,712[a] | 126.3[a] | 61.2[a] | 87.8[a] |
| UK | 4395 | 11,435 | 15,830 | 4942 | 9547 | 14,489 | 5722 | 8908 | 14,630 | 5636 | 7574 | 13,210 | 128.2 | 66.2 | 83.4 |
| Italy | 6590 | 5552 | 12,142 | 6680 | 4633 | 11,313 | 6666 | 4699 | 11,365 | 6674 | 3511 | 10,185 | 101.3 | 63.2 | 83.9 |
| Norway | n.a. | n.a. | n.a. | 671 | 402 | 1073 | 712 | 436 | 1148 | 736 | 382 | 1118 | n.a. | n.a. | n.a. |
| Sweden | 1997 | 1397 | 3394 | 1853 | 1139 | 2992 | 1690 | 960 | 2650 | 1921 | 1021 | 2942 | 96.2 | 73.1 | 86.7 |
| Netherlands | 2096 | 1822 | 3918 | 2097 | 1342 | 3439 | 1673 | 1447 | 3120 | 1417 | 1280 | 2697 | 67.6 | 70.3 | 68.8 |

*Notes:* A = emissions from transportation; S = emissions from stationary sources; T = total emissions

[a] For France, the data are from 1987 rather than 1985.

In some cases, the data are missing on emissions from one of the five major emission sources in a given year. The data for a previous or subsequent year were then added, assuming no change for a given source of emissions over a five-year period.

The data for sources of discharges do not add to the total in the table because emissions from solid wastes and miscellaneous uncontrolled sources are not included.

*Source:* Bernstam (1991, p. 17).

policies to correct the market failure (which had under-valued the natural resources used to absorb pollutants) then served to accelerate this process (see Figure 11.1).

There is also evidence that cost pressures have systematically encouraged technological innovation to curb resource use (and, therefore, emissions), even before efforts to cost out fully the use of natural capital intensified that trend. In line with the product cycle model, there is evidence that most products experience an S-shaped demand cycle (albeit of very varied speeds and durations) which exerts a constant squeeze on profits that feeds through to all inputs, including natural resources. The research suggests that almost irrespective of the industrial product studied, real margins (measured as a fraction of real value added per tonne) fall by around 30 per cent with each cumulative doubling in demand (Hochgraf, 1983). The resulting squeeze on margins encourages producers to do two things. First, to economize on *all* inputs (including energy and materials) in order to maintain market share and, second, to find new high-growth products which initially yield high profit margins. Such pressures on margins show up in product miniaturization and falling ratios of materials volumes to weight which yield increased energy efficiency and lower pollution.

Reddy and Goldenberg (1990) provide evidence of the scale of such a long-term technological improvement with reference to the energy-intensity of GDP (Figure 11.2), which might be used as a proxy for the pollution-intensity of GDP. They plot the energy intensity trend of the five largest DMEs and show that whereas the UK, as the first industrial nation, experienced a peak of 1.03 tonnes of oil equivalent per $1000 of GDP around 1880, Germany peaked around 1920 at 80 per cent of that level whereas Japan peaked at two-fifths of the UK level around 1940. Reddy and Goldenberg go on to suggest that the less developed countries may expect to at least match the Japanese level if not improve on it. There are, however, factors which work to deflect countries from the standard 'best practice' pattern.

*Deviations from the 'best practice' pollution trajectory*

The main causes of country deviations from the 'best practice' pollution trajectory are associated with differences in their natural resource endowment (of which, following Myint (1964, pp. 30–1), country size is a key component), aggregate purchasing power, development strategy and institutional capability.

Syrquin and Chenery (1989) provide empirical evidence of the relationship between natural resource endowment and industrial structure. Figure 11.3 identifies four variations associated with different types of economy, which Syrquin and Chenery identify on the basis of country size (it may be recalled that 'small' implies a population below 20 million) and the relative

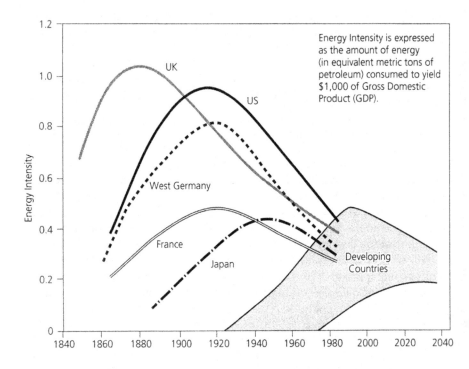

**Figure 11.2** Historical trends in the energy-efficiency of GDP (*Source*: Reddy and Goldenberg, 1990, p. 64)

importance of the primary and the manufacturing sectors. These differences broadly correspond with differences in the natural resource endowment. For example, with reference to East and South Asia, the small primary group of countries includes Nepal, Papua New Guinea and Sri Lanka; the large primary group comprises Burma, Indonesia, the Philippines and Thailand; the small manufacturing countries include resource-deficient and market-deficient Hong Kong, Singapore and Taiwan; while the group of large manufacturing (market-rich and resource-deficient) countries comprises Bangladesh, China, India, Korea and Pakistan.

The main deviations from the industrialization pattern traced by the Syrquin and Chenery aggregated norm (described earlier) are now outlined. The large manufacturing country starts the industrialization process with all three sectors (early, middle and late) somewhat larger than the aggregate norms, but the late group of industries expands much faster (compare Tables 11.1 and 11.3 and Figure 11.3a). Perkins and Syrquin (1989) attribute this to the greater ability of large, market-rich countries to capture economies of scale. They also find that large countries are likely to be more self-sufficient

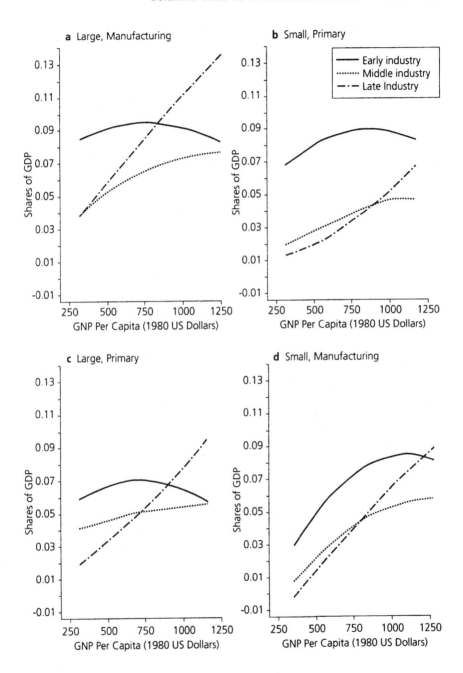

**Figure 11.3** Structure of value added in manufacturing, by country type (*Source*: Syrquin and Chenery, 1989, pp. 58–9)

**Table 11.3**    Structure of manufacturing, 1991, selected countries

| Country | Per capita income (US$) | Food, beverages, tobacco | Textiles, apparel | Machinery, transport | Chemicals | Other |
|---|---|---|---|---|---|---|
| Uganda | 170 | 61 | 12 | 3 | 6 | 19 |
| Ghana* | 450 | 34 | 16 | 4 | 4 | 41 |
| China | 470 | 15 | 14 | 25 | 13 | 34 |
| Indonesia | 670 | 24 | 16 | 12 | 7 | 40 |
| Philippines | 770 | 36 | 11 | 8 | 12 | 25 |
| Thailand | 1840 | 28 | 24 | 14 | 3 | 36 |
| Malaysia | 2790 | 11 | 6 | 35 | 12 | 37 |
| Korea | 6790 | 11 | 11 | 33 | 9 | 36 |

*Note:** The data for the structure of Ghanaian manufacturing are for 1970.
*Source*: World Bank (1994c, Table 1, p. 162 and Table 6, p. 172; 1995, Table 6, p. 172).

(autarkic) than small and medium-sized countries. This has, historically, had important negative implications for the adoption of resource-conserving technology.

The large primary countries have significantly less reliance on the early group of industries throughout the industrialization process (suggesting, for example, that agro-processing and textiles may be less significant). For these countries, the middle group of industries begin with a lower share of GDP to the early group, but increase that share modestly to parity with the early group. The share of the late group of industries in these countries starts from a lower base and rises strongly but not to the same extent as in the large manufacturing countries.

Turning to the small primary countries, the agro-processing group retains its dominance of the early group of industries throughout the process of industrialization: the expansion of the middle and late group of industries commences later than in the larger countries and proceeds at a much slower pace. Finally, in the small manufacturing countries, the early industries have less initial dominance, and both the middle and late categories achieve less importance than in the aggregate pattern (presumably reflecting an earlier switch into service activities).

Evidence is emerging that, in line with Syrquin and Chenery, significant deviations in economic structure and resource use efficiency are linked to differences in the natural resource endowment and choice of development strategy. For example, large manufacturing countries favour high levels of autarky. Bernstam (1991) has analysed the implications of industrial autarky for resource-intensity: a combination of insulation from market-sensitive technology and inaccurate signals concerning resource scarcity is likely to arrest, and even reverse, the historical trend to declining resource-intensity and pollution-intensity of GDP. Bernstam shows further that steel and energy are used far more efficiently in the DMEs compared to the centrally planned economies. Birdsall and Wheeler (1992) also link weak performance in pollution abatement with protected slow-growth economies. The above findings suggest that a development strategy which is in line with a country's resource endowment and implemented within a market-sensitive economic policy is a prerequisite for improving the efficiency of resource use and lowering pollution. However, within such a framework there is still scope for deviation from best practice pollution abatement if inappropriate environmental policies are adopted. Even well-managed LDC economies have failed in this respect, often by establishing over-elaborate environmental requirements which they lack the financial and/or technical resources to implement. For example, Thailand established an emission limit for BOD (over 5 days at 20°C) of 20 to 60 mg/litre (depending on location) with a 100 mg/litre maximum. These standards proved difficult to enforce so that heavy reliance was placed upon self-monitoring. The standards also proved too stringent so that industrial polluters were required to remove 95 to 100 per cent of the BOD prior to discharge when the cost of shifting from 80 to 90 per cent removal raises costs five-fold (World Bank, 1994a) and cannot be justified by the benefits secured. Moreover, a common reaction by polluters to stringent standards is to dilute liquid waste emissions by making much greater use of (under-priced) clean water.

The World Bank (1994a) recommends that such command and control systems for industrial water pollution should be replaced by presumptive charges. The latter are levied on emissions under the assumption of a given technology and, therefore, of an expected ratio between the volume of production and the level of emissions. Firms achieving cleaner production become eligible for a rebate. Unlike the regulatory scheme, the presumptive charge facilitates the reduction of pollution at least cost. This is because the individual firm is left to decide whether it is cheapest for it to pay the charge; to invest in equipment to curb emissions; or to sub-contract waste-water treatment to specialist firms (as occurs in Export Processing Zones in Thailand, for example). Similarly, air-borne emissions could be reduced through presumptive charges on larger firms and also by the adoption of a more rational price structure. For example, Thai fuel taxes were much lower on domestic lignite and imported coal as compared with fuel oil and diesel. The readjustment of taxes to remove the price distortion enhances the incentive both to conserve energy and to use cleaner fuels.

The benefits of market-driven environmental policies are maximized in relation to the administrative input required if such charges are initially applied to the largest firms only, using data collected about the output volumes and treatment levels of such firms. For example, research from the Philippines suggests that around 100 large plants account for 60 per cent of pollution. A charge of $500/tonne of BOD has been proposed for Thailand with rebates paid if firms can demonstrate superior performance. The adoption of such a scheme was expected to halve total BOD demand.

Recognizing the lack of trained personnel as a constraint, NGOs can be co-opted to assist in emission monitoring while the training of special environmental police can also help improve enforcement.

The targeting of larger firms can be expected to induce some trickle-down of improved practice. For example, where large firms assemble supplies from small plants, they can be made responsible for the presumed aggregate pollution and so be given an incentive to encourage improved practice among suppliers. Such a system appears to be especially suitable for dealing with hazardous waste in the metal-finishing and the electronics sectors, for example. Other measures to reduce emissions from small firms include making local authorities responsible for their emission levels and subsidizing technical assistance for abatement reduction (World Bank, 1993).

A further problem arises with low-income countries because a clean environment may appear to warrant lower priority than the provision of basic needs to eliminate absolute poverty. Such delay may be imprudent, however. Taking Indonesia as an example, although BOD intensity per $1000 output is expected to decline by 20 per cent between 1980 and 2020, the volume of total emissions will grow twenty-fold with no policy change. Total suspended particulates will increase 30 per cent in emission intensity and grow 35-fold in volume (World Bank, 1994b). Sanctioning such expansions in emissions by postponing abatement measures is short-sighted. Rather, the late industrializers can turn their late start to advantage by providing incentives to adopt the cleanest technology now. In the case of Indonesia, historical growth rates indicate that by 2010 some 85 per cent of manufacturing capacity will be of post-present vintage and therefore pollution-abating − if appropriate incentives are given (Brandon and Raman Kutty, 1993). Unfortunately, this would also require a strengthening of market pressures by further reducing import protection, a move likely to engender strong political opposition.

### Evidence from Late Industrializers

It is extremely difficult to obtain completely consistent comparable data from late industrializers (at a lower per capita income level than, for example, Indonesia), partly due to the limited extent of the published material which is in circulation. However, two recent volumes from the relevant Ghanaian and Ugandan authorities are clearly positive responses to the increased international concern with the environment in recent years. One notable feature is the extent to which the industries which are the principal sources of pollution are unrelated to any type of 'pollution haven' development or to the inward transfer of pollution-intensive activities from the DMEs.

A UNIDO study which investigated the sources of industrial effluents and their probable pollutant inputs reported that for the zone between Cote d'Ivoire and Benin, the main producer of industrial pollutants by weight is the textile industry whose wastes contain 30% of all polluting substances. The manufacture of food products constitutes 25% while petroleum refining and handling contribute 20%. Mineral exploration and processing are also responsible for about 10%. Thus these four activities contribute up to 85% of the pollution load. (Ghana Environmental Protection Council, 1994, p. 3)

If this experience is typical, then a high proportion of industrial pollution in early industrializing countries is related to the types of industrial activities which (a) form an essential part of an import substitution/basic needs industrial strategy, and (b) form an integral element of an export processing/resource-based type of development.

Further supporting evidence for this pattern is provided from the Ugandan report, demonstrating that some of the most serious industrial pollution arises in sectors that would usually be regarded as 'traditional' and which are related to long-standing agricultural processing activities:

A survey of 22 of these [coffee processing] factories including the CMB-CPSU was carried out from 1989 to 1991. Respirable dust concentrations were measured, and a medical examination carried out on 1,200 workers and 200 control subjects. Dust concentrations ranged between 1 to 25 mg/m$^3$ with higher values registered in older factories. This pollution was accompanied by a high incidence of lung disorders of which the worst were occupational asthma, rhinitis and allergic alveolitis. The permissible exposure of toxic organic dust is 0.2 mg/m$^3$. This has been far exceeded in the Uganda coffee industry. Over 50,000 coffee industry workers are being exposed to this health hazard in Uganda. (Uganda Ministry of Natural Resources, 1994, p. 201)

It should be noted that the measurements cited in this quotation are plant-specific rather than for a broader geographical area as cited earlier for East Asia.

A second notable feature of the early industrializers is the recording of appallingly bad pollution experiences for some of the industries for which information is available. Apart from the respirable dust in the Ugandan coffee processing industry the main problems are summarized as follows:

Some industries which had some form of effluent treatment facilities have failed to maintain them, e.g. textile industries. Most industries have old technology which may not meet environmental challenges of the day. Given the low performance levels of our small-scale manufacturers, many cannot afford the new technology. By law, the National Water and Sewerage Corporation is responsible for industrial sewage treatment. Will the corporation remain viable if it extends its services to cover these many smaller industries? (Uganda Ministry of Natural Resources, 1994, p. 202)

A third feature is a lack of consistent environmental controls and an even more patchy implementation of such controls:

No laws exist for controlling industrial pollution. Waste water is discharged either into rivers or into open drains which in effect serve as sewers. Air emissions are uncontrolled. Disposal of solids and effluents from industry including toxic and hazardous wastes is similarly uncontrolled. There is no legislation regulating the problem of wastes from factories and industrial installations. (Ghana Environmental Protection Council, 1994, pp. 47-8)

A fourth (and perhaps the most important) common feature of the two country reports is the absence of effective monitoring and lack of facilities for regular testing of environmental pollution by industries. The Ghana report states the situation clearly:

There is a general paucity of information in Ghana on studies and/or monitoring of factors affecting the environment due to industrial activities and the use of hazardous chemicals. Insufficient institutional support for sustained *research and monitoring* of the environment has meant that baseline data for virtually all the monitoring indicators are non-existent in this country. (Ghana Environmental Protection Council, 1994, p. 3)

The Uganda report is equally clear:

These Acts, however, are not a meaningful way to regulate industry in the absence of standards against which to judge pollution and health status. The situation is worsened by the absence of regular environmental monitoring and audits. (Uganda Ministry of Natural Resources, 1994, p. 206)

There are three public testing laboratories in the country. These are operated by the National Water and Sewerage Corporation, the Water Development Department (of the Ministry of Natural Resources) and the Government Chemist (of the Ministry of Internal Affairs). The first is reasonably well equipped, while the other two are in desperate need of facilities. (Uganda Ministry of Natural Resources, 1994, p. 205)

The evidence assembled from Ghana and Uganda is sufficient to confirm that the principal problem associated with industrial pollution in these two late industrializers is simply that of creating the basic infrastructure of legislation, monitoring and control. In these circumstances even those data which are patchily available cannot be regarded as sufficiently comprehensive to permit a balanced view of the overall gravity of the situation.

## Conclusions

Table 11.4 summarizes some of the major conclusions from this review. During the process of industrialization, the structure of manufacturing diversifies from resource-processing to capital-intensive intermediates and then skill-intensive engineering and hi-tech products. This broad pattern of structural change means that emissions are initially dominated by organic pollutants but then rapid growth occurs first in air-borne emissions and then in solid waste pollutants, followed later by the rapid build-up in hazardous materials.

**Table 11.4** Typology of industrial development and industrial pollution

| | Late industrializers/ early industry | Large LDCs | NICs/middle industry | DMEs/ late/mature industry |
|---|---|---|---|---|
| Examples of countries | Sub-Saharan Africa, Oceania | India, China, Pakistan | Korea, Malaysia, Indonesia, Mexico, Brazil, Thailand | United States, west and north Europe, Japan |
| Per capita income | Low | Low | Middle | High |
| Manufacturing sector | Small | Moderate | High | High |
| Predominant industries | Primary processing (agro-industry) | Primary processing, chemical, capital goods | Full range | Full range |
| Major pollution hazards | Water/organic emissions | Water–air/organic–inorganic emissions | Higher intensity of water–air/organic–inorganic emissions | Higher intensity of water–air/organic–inorganic toxic emissions |
| Level of pollution control legislation | Low | Low | Moderate | High |
| Effectiveness of pollution control measures | Low | Low | Moderate | High |
| Level of pollution monitoring | Low | Low | Moderate | High |
| Overall incidence of industrial pollution | Low | Moderate | Moderate | Low |
| Industrial scale/technology type | High proportion of SMEs/ pollution-intensive technology | High proportion of SMEs/ pollution-intensive technology | Mixture of SMEs and LSEs/ mixture of high and low pollution-intensive technology | High proportion of LSEs/ low pollution-intensive technology |

*Notes:* LDC – less developed country; NIC – newly industrializing country; DME – developed market economy; SME – small and medium-scale enterprises; LSE – large-scale enterprise.
*Source:* This table represents a tentative suggestion of an approximate typology.

In aggregate terms, the build-up of pollution traces an inverted U-shape with rising per capita income. This trend reflects both the changing composition of demand at higher per capita incomes (as expenditure on services expands *vis-à-vis* expenditure on food and manufactured goods) and also the tightening of environmental policies. There is also evidence of a historical trend towards lower levels of materials use, energy use and pollution as per capita incomes rise. But such trends are not automatic, and deterioration may occur during periods of prolonged economic stagnation or decline, as is perhaps suggested by the African examples.

Deviations from the general pattern are caused by differences in the natural resource endowments of countries, with larger countries historically tending to be more self-sufficient and, therefore, experiencing more rapid industrialization. The choice of industrial and environmental policies can also cause significant deviations from the general pattern. Historically, the most significant adverse deviations have occurred under the autarkic policies of the more centrally-planned economies.

Evidence which is available in the less-developed late industrializers suggests that industrial pollution is a problem due to the underdeveloped nature of the environmental legislation and control system, and is based largely on the dynamics of internal industrial development rather than on a process of transfer of 'dirty industries' from the DMEs in a form of modified 'product cycle'. It is unlikely that they will develop into 'pollution havens' since new larger scale investments tend to be subject to fairly stringent perusal and control, so that the most serious problems tend to be associated with older technologies and with small and medium-scale industry. To the extent that new industrial development in these late industrializers is likely to be environmentally more acceptable, this conclusion may be viewed optimistically in terms of the future.

If the post-1970s consensus on macro and industrial policy holds and welfare-maximizing environmental policies are effectively deployed, then the late-starting industrializers should trace a less pollution-intensive trajectory than the historical trend. It is not clear, however, that industrial policies should be adopted which discriminate against high-polluting industries (ISIS, 1992). This is because such policies will distort the mix of industries with likely unforeseen ramifications. For most sectors of industry the cost of adopting pollution abatement technology is modest relative to total production costs (for example, under 1 per cent for most industrial sectors in the US and rarely over 3 per cent (Low, 1992, p. 107)). But demands for rapid implementation are likely to impose significantly higher costs which, in the case of Japan during the mid-1970s pushed investment expenditure on environmental improvement up from 5 per cent to almost 18 per cent over a three-year period before falling back to the original level (World Bank, 1993).

# References

Auty, R.M. (1993) Emerging competitiveness of NICs in heavy and chemical industry: effects of the product cycle and technological change, *Tijdschrift voor Economische en Sociale Geografie*, **84**, 185–97.

Bernstam, M. (1991) *The Wealth of Nations and the Environment*. IEA Occasional Paper 85. London: Institute of Economic Affairs.

Birdsall, N. and Wheeler, D. (1992) Trade policy and industrial pollution in Latin America: where are the pollution havens? In P. Low (ed.), *International Trade and the Environment*. World Bank Discussion Papers no. 159. Washington, DC: World Bank.

Brandon, C. and Raman Kutty, R. (1993) *Toward an Environmental Strategy for Asia*. Washington, DC: World Bank.

Brown, R. and Julius, D. (1994) Manufacturing in the New World Order. *Finance and the International Economy*, **7**.

Cropper, M.L. and Oates, W.E. (1992) Environmental economics: a survey. *Journal of Economic Literature*, **30**, 675–740.

Ghana Environmental Protection Council (1994) *Ghana Environmental Action Plan Volume 2: Technical Background Papers*. Accra: Ghana Environmental Protection Council.

Grossman, G. (1995) Pollution and growth: what do we know? In I. Goldin and L.A. Winters (eds), *The Economics of Sustainable Development*. Cambridge: Cambridge University Press, pp. 19–46.

Her Majesty's Inspectorate of Pollution (1995) *1994–95 Annual Report*. London: Department of the Environment/HMSO.

Hochgraf, N.N. (1983) The future technological environment. Paper presented to the Eleventh World Petroleum Conference, London, Panel PD-9, pp. 1–10.

ISIS (1992) *Managing Manufacturing Pollution: The Experiences of Malaysia, Thailand and Indonesia*. Malaysia: Institute of Strategic Studies.

Krugman, P.R. and Lawrence, R.Z. (1994) Trade, jobs and wages. *Scientific American*, **270** (4), 22–7.

Lal, D. (1992) Why growth rates differ. The political economy of social capability in 21 less developed countries. KDI 20th Anniversary Symposium on Economic Growth and Social Capability, KDI, Seoul.

Lawrence, R.Z. (1984) *Can America Compete?* Washington, DC: Brookings Institution.

Low, P. (1992) *International Trade and the Environment*. World Bank Discussion Papers no. 159. Washington, DC: World Bank.

Myint, H. (1964) *The Economics of the Developing Countries*. London: Hutchinson.

Perkins, D. and Syrquin, M. (1989) Large countries: the influence of size. In H. Chenery and T.N. Srinivasan (eds), *Handbook of Development Economics, Volume 2*. Amsterdam: North-Holland, pp. 1691–1753.

Reddy, A.K.N. and Goldenberg, J. (1990) Energy for the developing world. *Scientific American*, **263**(3), 63–72.

Roemer, M. (1979) Resource-based industrialization in the developing countries: a survey. *Journal of Development Economics*, **6**, 162–202.

Syrquin, M. and Chenery, H.B. (1989) *Patterns of Development, 1950 to 1983*. World Bank Discussion Paper no. 41. Washington, DC: World Bank.

Tribe, M.A. (1994) Environmental policy, projects and economic analysis for the industrial sector in less developed countries. Paper presented to the Development Studies Association Conference, University of Lancaster, Lancaster.

Uganda Ministry of Natural Resources (1994) *State of the Environment: Report for Uganda 1994*. Kampala: National Environment Information Centre.

Vernon, R. (1966) International investment and international trade in the product cycle. *Quarterly Journal of Economics*, **80**, 190–207.

Vernon, R. (1979) The product cycle hypothesis in the new international environment. *Oxford Bulletin of Economics and Statistics*, **41**, 255–67.

Williamson, J. and Milner, C. (1991) *The World Economy: A Textbook in International Economics*. Hemel Hempstead: Harvester-Wheatsheaf.

Wolf, M. (1991) On the (un)importance of manufacturing. *Financial Times*, 1 July.

World Bank (1991) *Environmental Source Book – Volume III: Guidelines for Environmental Assessment of Energy and Industry Projects*. World Bank Technical Paper no. 151. Washinton, DC: Environment Department, World Bank.

World Bank (1992) *World Development Report 1992*. Washington, DC: World Bank.

World Bank (1993) *Malaysia: Managing Costs of Urban Pollution*. Report 11764-MA. Washington, DC: World Bank.

World Bank (1994a) *Thailand: Mitigating Pollution and Congestion Impacts in a High-growth Economy*. Report 11770-TH. Washington, DC: World Bank.

World Bank (1994b) *Indonesia: Environment and Development*. Report 12083-IND. Washington, DC: World Bank.

World Bank (1994c) *World Development Report 1994*. Washington, DC: World Bank.

World Bank (1995) *World Development Report 1995*. Washington, DC: World Bank.

## 12

# Industrialization in Vietnam: Social Change and Environment in Transitional Developing Countries

## Tim Forsyth

## Introduction

This chapter assesses progress to sustainable development in the rapidly industrializing, transitional economy of Vietnam. Since the United Nations Conference on Environment and Development (UNCED), held in Rio de Janeiro in 1992, environmental policy in many countries has aimed to represent different sections of society, and to regulate or employ industry in environmental protection (Jänicke, 1992; Munasinghe, 1993). Yet in rapidly industrializing countries such aims may neglect the comparative power of industry compared with environmental concerns in society (Middleton *et al.*, 1993; Rosendal, 1995). Consequently, much environmental legislation may not represent all society, nor even effectively regulate industry.

This dilemma has immense implications for economies in debt, or undergoing transition from communist regimes to democracy or a market economy (Rau, 1991; van Brabant, 1992). Such countries need industrialization and investment in order to generate funds for modernization and development. Some researchers have argued that foreign investment may enable the development of better environmental regulations and democracy (Osaghae, 1994; Munslow and Ekoku, 1995; Payne, 1995). However, others have stated that industrialization may result in further authoritarianism if business is allied with the state (Peluso, 1993; Schroeder and Neumann, 1995). This may also lead to resistance against trade unions or environmental regulation.

Effective environmental policies, formulated in consultation with international aid agencies, may enable governments to implement industrialization with adequate environmental protection (see Auty and Tribe this volume). However, in some countries, public concern about environmental damage or industrialization has led to civil society activity which may regulate state policy. Yet the development of such civil society depends on relaxation of totalitarianism, and on the perception of environment, or reforming ideology, within domestic society.

The first part of this chapter discusses theoretical relationships between industrialization and the formulation of civil society and environmental policy. Particular reference is then given to socialist developing countries in transition. Later sections then describe recent developments in Vietnam concerning industrialization and environmental policy. The discussion and conclusion assess what lessons may be learnt concerning social transition and sustainable industrialization in transitional developing countries.

## Civil Society and Environment in Industrializing Countries

Many scholars have used the concept of 'civil society' to explain the influence of public groups on government policy. Civil society is the emergence of political voice within society, as distinct from state. Classically, it has been divided into groups favouring business, and groups favouring liberal reform (Urry, 1981; Cohen and Arato, 1992; Tester, 1992; Hall, 1995). Environmentalism may be considered a reforming or liberal ideology, and is often opposed to industrial groups because it seeks to impose restrictions on business.

Much early discussion of civil society was based on Western European experience, and on the ability of new business elites to regulate militaristic regimes in favour of democracy (Huntingdon, 1968, 1984; Urry, 1981). Such ideas of a gradual transition from authoritarianism to liberal democracy have influenced recent debates about the influence of industrialization or foreign-direct-investment (FDI) on developing countries. Some have argued that FDI in developing countries may enhance democracy, as well as improve environmental regulation by imposing international standards (Osaghae, 1994; Payne, 1995).

However, others have challenged this interpretation by arguing that authoritarianism may continue even after industrialization or political reform. This may take the form of clientelism (Roniger and Günes-Ayata, 1994), or the establishment of alliances between state and industry to produce favourable conditions for industrialization (Browett, 1986; White, 1995). It may also inhibit environmental protection by suppressing public concern for environment or trade unions. In addition, states may oppose the adoption of science and technology associated with environmental protection through lack of funds or fear of reform (Basi, 1995; Vu Cao Dam, 1995).

Alliances between industry and state have been cited as a reason underlying the rapid industrialization and economic prosperity of newly industrialized countries (NICs) in East and Southeast Asia. Countries such as Singapore, South Korea, and Taiwan have experienced some of the world's highest rates of economic growth in recent years, yet have also maintained authoritarian states (Sharma, 1984; Hawes and Hong Liu, 1993; Hewison *et al.*, 1993; Robison *et al.*, 1993; Wilkinson, 1994; Bowen and Leinbach, 1995). Such states partly attracted FDI by keeping cheap labour costs, and implementing few environmental regulations. States may argue that such alliances are necessary in order to attract investment, and to prevent an exodus of large employers to cheaper countries (Bergstø and Endresen, 1992; Amirahmadi and Wu, 1994).

However, in more recently developing countries such as Thailand and Malaysia, industrialization has also been associated with a rise in public concern about environmental impacts. These have also been associated with pro-democracy movements, and with the growing importance of previously powerless groups in society such as female factory workers or rural farmers (Hirsch and Lohmann, 1989).

In addition, the growing importance of environmental civil society has emphasized the ways in which environmental perception varies between different groups of society (Nash, 1982; Munasinghe, 1993; Redclift and Woodgate, 1994; Howarth, 1995). As a consequence, environmental policy may not represent all sectors of society. However, under-represented groups may ally with each other against the state. At times, the motivation for environmental activism has also been linked to underlying philosophies or ideologies in society, such as Buddhism (Taylor, 1993; Bryant, 1995; Lohmann, 1995; Pedersen, 1995).

Such civil society activity may lead to democratization if it forces government to change policy to reflect new viewpoints. However, such changes may be opposed by the government, who may consider it a greater priority to attract FDI and industrialization. As a result of this, some have argued that some recent environmental legislation in developing countries such as Thailand has given the appearance of protecting the environment, but in reality has not challenged existing power bases of pro-industry sections of government (Forsyth, 1996, 1997).

## Environment in Post-socialist Transition and Development

Environmental protection against industry is of immense significance in transitional socialist economies who may be now attracting new FDI, or need to renovate antiquated state enterprises renowned for pollution or inefficiency (DeBardelben, 1985). The change to greater sustainability is also associated with a growth, or return to, democracy, and the rise of new industrial elites within societies.

Much research since the spectacular collapse of the Soviet Union and Eastern European communist regimes in 1988–91 has assumed that there will be a transition from state socialism to democratic capitalism (Dallago *et al.*, 1992; Berend, 1994). However, this has been criticized by many writers who have said that this transition is neither proven, nor desirable (Brzeski, 1994; Meadwell, 1995). Similarly, western approaches to sustainable development and environmental regulation in such countries may also be based in western experiences rather than reflective of indigenous perceptions (DuBois, 1991; Howarth, 1995).

Environmental protection in transitional developing countries may aim to regulate FDI to prevent the attraction of pollution-intensive industries or inadequate waste treatment facilities (Hesselberg, 1992). This may mean the implementation of regulations or penalties, such as the 'polluter pays principle' (Smets, 1994), in order to internalize economic costs of environmental protection into industrialization. Alternatively, it can also mean employing private enterprise to construct badly needed environmental infrastructure such as waste or water-treatment plants. Such schemes have been attempted in the Soviet Union and China (Ward and Jinan Li, 1993; Bater, 1994).

However, such economic transition may lead to resentment by local populations who see it as a betrayal of old socialist values, or who have experienced little benefit to date of the transition. In Poland and Russia this has been marked by the ironic rebirth in popularity for communist parties under democracy, and a concern about perceived corruption among state officials (Kornai, 1992, p. 104; Ishiyama, 1995). Debates concerning 'market socialism' often focus on the use of private ownership of industry in order to maximize efficiency, or on the means to allocate business surpluses in an equitable way (Roemer, 1992). In China, for example, economic liberalization has reduced the amounts of funds collected by the state in revenue. Between 1983 and 1992, China experienced extremely high GNP growth of an average 9.7 per cent per year. However, state revenue fell from 34 per cent of GNP in 1978 to just 19 per cent in 1989 (Aage, 1994, pp. 18–24).

Public dissent, or civil society activity, has traditionally been suppressed in communist regimes because of totalitarianism. However, in Eastern Europe, civil society may be emerging as a result of resentment against corruption, or poor political reform (Keane, 1988; Nowak, 1991; Fish, 1994). In China, civil society has been identified among urban migrants, or between lower sections of the state with business (Whiting, 1991; Nathan, 1993; Solinger, 1993, 1995; Wank, 1995). However, regulation of authoritarian states may also be achieved through inter-state factionalism, or regionalism, as observed in Taiwan (Fang Wang, 1994).

There are only a few transitional, developing countries in East and Southeast Asia, including Vietnam, China, North Korea, Mongolia, Myanmar (Burma), Laos, and Cambodia. The experience of transition varies between

**Table 12.1** Vietnam: average annual growth rate, 1981–93 (%)

|  | *1981–85* | *1986–90* | *1991* | *1992* | *1993* |
|---|---|---|---|---|---|
| GDP | 5.2 | 5.9 | 8.6 | 8.1 | n/a |
| Industrial output | 0.6 | 9.5 | 5.9 | 5.3 | 15.3 |
| Agricultural output | 1.9 | 5.3 | 3.6 | −0.1 | 4.4 |
| Exports | 15.6 | 28.0 | −8.1 | 18.6 | 21.2 |
| Imports | 7.2 | 8.2 | −8.7 | 7.1 | 31.5 |
| State sector industry | n/a | n/a | 11.8 | 19.5 | 10.75* |
| Non-state sector industry | n/a | n/a | 7.4 | 6.0 | 8.0* |

*Note*: * Estimated data
*Source*: Adapted from *Statistical Yearbooks of Vietnam*, 1986–93, in Vu Tuan Anh (1994, p. 101; 1995, p. 58).

different countries. In Myanmar, for example, economic transition is hampered by vast ethnic diversity and continued war within the country. International agencies see diversification of the domestic manufacturing base to be a priority, although observers have commented that economic reform need not be related to political reform (UNIDO, 1987; Cook and Minogue, 1993). In Mongolia, virtually all of the agricultural sector is now in private hands, and large-scale industrial enterprises are being passed to the private sector. However, as in Laos, geographical isolation and lack of transport infrastructure still hamper development (UNIDO, 1993, 1994). Such countries are likely to experience industrialization at different rates to Vietnam. Yet each may undergo similar transitions in society resulting from industrialization and privatization.

# Vietnam: Economy and Society in Transition

Vietnam is undergoing immense economic and social changes as the result of industrialization. In 1995 Vietnam joined ASEAN and normalized diplomatic ties with the United States – just 20 years after North Vietnamese forces overran Saigon to unite the country under communism. During the early 1990s, Vietnam's GDP grew at over 8 per cent a year (Table 12.1), and its population reached 70 million, of which 22 per cent was urban. Ho Chi Minh City (Saigon), Hanoi and Haiphong are its largest cities (Pham Binh Quyen *et al.*, 1995, p. 383).

Vietnam is still politically communist. However, planning was always more diversified between different regions than was the practice of European communism (Mallon, 1993, p. 205). This was because of the difficulties in communication between regions, and because of the need for regional self-sufficiency during wartime. Today, regions are still relatively autonomous and occasionally show reluctance to follow directives from central government based in Hanoi. Ironically, despite its militaristic image, the state of Vietnam is weak because of this regionalism (Thrift and Forbes, 1985; Beresford and McFarlane, 1995).

Early communist economic policies for the united Vietnam resulted in opposition from inhabitants of the south, and in food shortages and galloping inflation (Beresford, 1993, p. 216). As a consequence of these, the government of Vietnam introduced a programme of economic liberalization in 1986 known as *Doi Moi* ('renovation') (Fforde and de Vylder, 1988; Reinhardt, 1993; Vu Tuan Anh, 1994, p. 110).

*Doi Moi* addressed three main problems. First was the clarification of relationships between state and state enterprises, in order to identify what role each enterprise should play in wider, national economic management. Second, reform aimed to provide greater autonomy for enterprises to use market forces in management. Third, *Doi Moi* aimed to restructure the state in order to increase efficiency (Vo Nhan Tri, 1990; Dan Ton That, 1993; Dang Duc Dam, 1995, p. 21). Practices adopted included equitization – the transformation of state enterprises to share-holding companies, and the establishment of pricing mechanisms which reflected demand and supply (Spoor, 1988; Dinh, 1993; de Vylder, 1995; Gates and Truong, 1995; Irvin, 1995; Kolko, 1995).

Most significantly, the state has had to reduce subsidies to state enterprises and local co-operatives. As a result, the numbers of state enterprises have fallen from 12,084 to 6264 between 1990 and 1994 (*Vietnam Investment Review* – hereafter *VIR* – 14–20 November 1994; Dang Duc Dam, 1995, p. 21). Over 60 per cent of the remaining enterprises are small, employing less than 200 people each. However, centrally managed state enterprises still control key areas of the economy, such as cement, heavy industry, forestry, mining and chemical production.

There is also an occasional lack of co-ordination between state and non-state enterprises. Between 1993 and 1994, the Vietnamese state lost millions of dollars of potential income by selling rubber on the international market at a below-market price. Officials blamed this on regulations that made the state unable to intervene in the marketing carried out by new companies (*VIR*, 4–10 July 1994). Table 12.2 lists changes in numbers of state, private and co-operative industrial enterprises, showing the rapid decline in locally based co-operatives as the result of cuts in subsidies, and the gradual rise in numbers of private enterprises which have partly absorbed old co-operatives (*VIR*, 26 December 1994–1 January 1995).

Today, badly needed funds come from FDI, which is attracted to Vietnam on account of its comparatively cheap labour, and excellent proximity to expanding markets in southern China, mainland Southeast Asia, and insular Southeast Asia. Key industries so far include oil and gas exploration and refining; aquaculture; textiles, and other light manufacturing (Table 12.3). The government has encouraged investors by establishing Export Processing Zones (EPZs) in which factories manufacturing exports may be established

**Table 12.2** State, co-operative, and private industrial activities in Vietnam

| | 1985 | | | 1990 | | | 1992 | | |
|---|---|---|---|---|---|---|---|---|---|
| | State | Co-op | Private | State | Co-op | Private | State | Co-op | Private |
| Total | 3050 | 35,629 | 920 | 2762 | 13,086 | 770 | 2268 | 5723 | 1114 |
| Electricity | 75 | 8 | — | 82 | 11 | — | 13 | 30 | — |
| Fuels | 41 | 26 | — | 33 | 11 | — | 24 | 7 | — |
| Ferrous metallurgy | 15 | 51 | — | 8 | 40 | 1 | 9 | 38 | 2 |
| Non-ferrous metallurgy | 13 | 38 | — | 1 | 30 | — | 41 | 11 | 1 |
| Equipment and machinery | 416 | 1455 | 45 | 377 | 530 | 26 | 287 | 305 | 21 |
| Electric and electronic | 79 | 209 | 7 | 61 | 109 | 14 | 67 | 49 | 10 |
| Other metallic products | 144 | 3895 | 5 | 136 | 1205 | 20 | 88 | 624 | 22 |
| Chemicals, fertilizers, rubber | 242 | 2012 | 24 | 210 | 794 | 28 | 197 | 4743 | 29 |
| Material construction | 526 | 6414 | 64 | 492 | 2802 | 106 | 375 | 1161 | 262 |
| Wood, wood products | 280 | 3800 | 60 | 200 | 1436 | 131 | 140 | 535 | 207 |
| Cellulose and paper | 60 | 222 | 5 | 53 | 188 | 11 | 43 | 141 | 30 |
| Glass, earthware, porcelain | 89 | 402 | 125 | 91 | 219 | 9 | 63 | 125 | 49 |
| Food | 103 | 4140 | 320 | 70 | 955 | 223 | 47 | 208 | 86 |
| Foodstuff | 531 | 6682 | 246 | 447 | 2588 | 130 | 427 | 1050 | 154 |
| Textiles | 113 | 2971 | 1 | 118 | 1224 | 17 | 110 | 474 | 83 |
| Sewing products | 67 | 1574 | — | 96 | 296 | 26 | 92 | 262 | 114 |
| Tanning and leather | 10 | 222 | 1 | 30 | 82 | 2 | 27 | 53 | 3 |
| Printing | 87 | 74 | 5 | 101 | 17 | 2 | 102 | 19 | 4 |
| Others | 159 | 1434 | 12 | 145 | 549 | 24 | 116 | 158 | 37 |
| Total for 3 categories each year | 39,599 | | | 16,618 | | | 9105 | | |
| Percentage of yearly total | 7.7 | 90.0 | 2.3 | 16.6 | 78.7 | 4.7 | 25.0 | 62.8 | 12.2 |

*Source:* Adapted from National Statistical Office, in Dang Duc Dam (1995, pp. 177–80).

Table 12.3   Foreign investment in Vietnam, 1988–93

| | Projects | % | Registered capital ($USm) | % |
|---|---|---|---|---|
| Hotels, tourism | 113 | 13.0 | 1905.8 | 20.9 |
| Light industry | 221 | 25.5 | 1414.9 | 15.5 |
| Oil and gas | 25 | 2.9 | 1281.1 | 14.0 |
| Heavy industry | 127 | 14.6 | 1247.5 | 13.6 |
| Transport and communications | 57 | 6.6 | 759.3 | 9.3 |
| Construction | 65 | 7.5 | 744.9 | 9.1 |
| Services | 73 | 8.4 | 728.3 | 8.0 |
| Agriculture and forestry | 117 | 13.5 | 446.6 | 5.0 |
| Building EPZs | 5 · | 0.6 | 306.8 | 3.3 |
| Finance, banking | 16 | 1.8 | 152.9 | 1.6 |
| Fishery | 27 | 3.1 | 94.3 | 1.0 |
| Culture, education and health care | 21 | 2.4 | 36.2 | 0.3 |
| Export–Import | 1 | 0.0 | 0.3 | 0.0 |
| Total | 868 | 100.0 | 9139.3 | 100.0 |

Source: SCCI (1994) in Vu Tuan Anh (1995, p. 50).

quickly and efficiently. The average size of these in 1994 was 195 ha compared with 64 ha in Taiwan, and one ha was estimated to create an average US$4.7 m worth of exports, and 192 jobs (*VIR*, 24–30 January 1994).

Historically, economic power and manufacturing lay in South, rather than North, Vietnam. During the 1970s, the failure of southern Vietnam to commit itself to the communist reforms originating from Hanoi contributed to their failure (Beresford, 1993, p. 216), and today, Ho Chi Minh City has 22 and 50 times more registered private enterprises than Hanoi and Haiphong respectively (*VIR*, 7–13 March 1994). However, this commercial culture was weakened by the exodus of many pro-capitalist entrepreneurs from southern Vietnam before and after the communist victory. Furthermore, many ethnic Chinese − so effective as entrepreneurs in other Asian countries − fled following persecution by the Vietnamese state during the 1970s and 1980s.

The absence of such groups from the new Vietnam meant that the society was somewhat more uniform than before, but also lacking many members who could have emerged to become part of a new business elite. However, overseas Chinese and Vietnamese (the *Viet Kieu*) are largely involved in foreign investment in Vietnam, and so have an economic, if not political, interest in domestic change. Indeed, Taiwan, Hong Kong, and Singapore have been the most active foreign investors (Dang Duc Dam, 1995, p. 166).

In addition, industrialization is also controlled by political cadres, or the lower echelons of state. In particular, the army is emerging as a new business force. During wartime, the Corps 11 of the army's General Industrial Department constructed tunnels along the Ho Chi Minh Trail, and repaired bombed bridges. Today, it is one of Vietnam's most prominent construction contractors, claiming to have turned over US$12.7 million in 1994, and planning to compete for airport, schools and housing projects in the future (*VIR*, 23–29 January 1995). In 1995, the military were also the first group to break the national monopoly on the supply of telephones (*VIR*, 26 June–2 July 1995). As such, the military are emerging to be part of the new business elite in Vietnam. Politically, however, such groups are unlikely to challenge the state's authority because they are already part of the state.

The emphasis on foreign or state-based investment in government industrial policy has angered many indigenous entrepreneurs who feel excluded from trade opportunities, or the victims of corruption (*VIR*, 16–22 May 1994; *Asia Inc*, 1995a, b). Such perceived corruption may take place in the self-declared autonomy from national directives by regions in the attraction of investment, or in the misuse of state privileges for personal gain. The prime minister has already reprimanded the Hanoi and Ho Chi Minh City People's Committees for apparent profiteering or favouritism in land allocation (*VIR*, 23–29 May 1994; 27 February–5 March 1995).

Furthermore, there has been an increase in industrial strikes since the beginning of *Doi Moi*, with over 100 counted between 1989 and 1994, of which half were in foreign-invested factories (*VIR*, 18–24 July 1994 and 10–16 July 1995). Vietnam introduced new labour codes in 1994, which stated that all enterprises should have a trade union. Although Vietnam's minimum wage of US$30 to 35 per month in 1994–95 compares well with China (US$27) or Indonesia (US$28), research has shown that 8 per cent of foreign-invested enterprises in Vietnam pay less than this, and many others only pay it to trained workers. The law, therefore, aimed to gain a fairer deal for Vietnamese workers, but also to provide for a regulated investment environment where strikes would be rare. However, after the codes had been passed, the Vietnamese Minister of Labour claimed that 80 per cent of foreign-invested enterprises still had no trade union, and that grievances with employers were going unanswered (Jerneck and Nguyen Thanh Ha, 1995; *VIR*, 3–9 July 1995).

## Environmental Policy and Industry in Vietnam

Following industrialization and the increase in FDI, Vietnam is now facing new threats of urban and industrial pollution (Beresford and Fraser, 1992; Huynh and Stengel, 1993; Jamison and Baark, 1995; Pham Ngoc Dang and Tran Hieu Nhue, 1995). The volume of urban and solid waste in Vietnam amounts to 9100 cu m per day, of which only 400 cu m is collected (Pham Binh Queyn *et al.*, 1995, p. 383). Furthermore, degradation of surface and subsurface water supplies through industrial waste is an increasing hazard. Unplanned urbanization has brought industries closer to residential areas and vice versa.

International organizations such as UNDP, IUCN and WWF are undertaking projects in Vietnam to co-ordinate environmental protection on a broad range of topics (UNDP, 1994, 1995). Some initial discussion of environmental objectives was undertaken following the publication of a National Conservation Strategy in 1986, and a National Plan for Environmental and Sustainable Development in 1991 (SCS *et al.*, 1991; Beresford and Fraser, 1992, p. 8).

In 1992 the Vietnamese restructured the State Committee for Sciences to form the Ministry of Science, Technology and Environment (MOSTE). In 1994, a national law on Environment Protection (NLEP) became effective. An existing department was renamed the National Environment Agency (NEA) as the key enforcer and representative of environmental policy within government. In addition, smaller representatives of MOSTE were established within each other government ministry and regional government. Also, some provinces formed their own Environment Committees (ECs) as part of the provincial government, or so-called People's Committee (Nguyen Dac Hy, 1995; World Bank, 1995, p. 102).

The new law on environment was wide-reaching and forward-looking, drawing attention to potential risks from nuclear contamination and importation of waste, as well as conservationist issues like provision for national parks. Regarding industry, the law stated that all potential FDI should submit an environmental-impact assessment (EIA), which was to be conducted by the NEA, before factory construction or manufacturing could begin. Additionally, the state has begun using economic instruments to internalize costs of environmental protection into industry. Currently, for example, the highest water tariffs have been introduced in Hanoi and Ho Chi Minh City for foreign institutions (World Bank, 1995, p. 76). Further research into these techniques is currently being carried out (UNDP, 1994).

Furthermore, private enterprise has been approached to construct badly needed environmental infrastructure through the so-called Build–Operate–Transfer (BOT) process. In Vietnam to date, there have been two such BOT projects: a water-treatment plant constructed by a Malaysian consortium, and an urban-waste treatment plant, which also generates electricity and manufacturers organic fertilizer, operated by an Indian group (*Asia Inc.*, 1995c; *VIR*, 27 March–2 April 1995). Both are located in Ho Chi Minh City. The scheme allows companies to build a plant and then operate it tax-free for the first four years, and then at half the standard rate of tax for the next four years. After a total of 20 years, the company is then contracted to sell the plant back to the state at the nominal fee of one US dollar.

However, these attempts to regulate industrialization have been challenged by activities of regions outside Hanoi. In Ho Chi Minh City, for example, the local Environmental Committee increased environmental regulation by compiling a 'Black Book' of 43 major polluting companies in 1994. This was partly because they considered the reliance on EIA to be ineffective (Environmental Committee of Ho Chi Minh City, 1995; *VIR*, 10–16 July 1995). In addition, several provincial governments have shown autonomy by planning their own EPZs, thus increasing the numbers of sites available to FDI. The proliferation of EPZs and probable local variations in evaluation of proposed investment suggest that the weakness of the state may make the NLEP difficult to enforce (FIAS, 1994). Indeed, newspapers have reported that the high level of FDI received by Dong Nai province in the south of some 57 projects, including 33 that are 100 per cent foreign-owned by April 1994, has reduced its capacity to implement the NLEP (*VIR*, 4–10 April 1994).

Within government, the new NEA is weak compared with agencies supporting industrialization, such as the State Committee for Co-operation and Investment (SCCI). Late in 1995, the NEA had approximately 40 staff compared with some hundreds for the SCCI, and development workers considered it likely that the SCCI would merge with the State Planning Committee (SPC), the central administration of government, thus making it more powerful within government, and, therefore, likely to be more influential than MOSTE or the NEA (*VIR*, 20–26 March 1995).

There has also been a limited public outcry against environmental degradation when it is seen to result from unregulated or foreign business activity. In Quang Ninh province, in the far north of Vietnam, local government and concerned communities complained about the environmental impacts of unregulated coal-mining activities in a region with huge tourism potential based on limestone scenery in Halong Bay (Bach Tan Sinh, 1995). The result was a letter from the Prime Minister, Vo Van Kiet, to the entire population of the province, urging them to support state and provincial administrators in implementing directives controlling coal mining (*VIR*, 8–14 August 1994). A new mining law is being drafted to regulate exploitation (*VIR*, 6–12 March 1995).

In Ho Chi Minh City, two incidences of oil spills from ships on the Saigon River in 1994 led to damage to local aquaculture and water supplies. Residents claimed for compensation, resulting in a settlement from a Singaporean ship owner (*VIR*, 26 December–1 January 1995). Such outcries have also been supported by attention in Vietnam's growing media (Phuc Tien, 1995). In 1993, the *Lao Dong Chu Nhat* ('Labour Sunday') newspaper, a Hanoi-based representative of the labour movement, published a damning criticism of the People's Committee of Nghe An province for apparent corruption in selling the protected timber species, *pomu (Fokendia hodginsii)*, for export when this had been restricted by state decree (*Lao Dong Chu Nhat*, 10 October 1993).

## Discussion

Environmental policy in Vietnam has been developed quickly and in response to FDI. As a result of this, Vietnam may achieve industrialization with considerably less pollution than experienced by the first wave of industrial countries (Auty and Tribe, this volume). In addition, private enterprise has been used imaginatively to provide badly needed environmental infra-structure such as waste-treatment centres.

However, there are apparent problems within the policy as it currently stands which may favour investors rather than environmental management. Also, there is evidence to suggest that government industrial and environmental policy may be undermined by the apparent neglect of domestic viewpoints.

The effectiveness of the new environment law is questioned by the weakness of the NEA compared with the pro-industry sections of government such as the SCCI. Also, the construction of new, unauthorized EPZs by provinces weakens the power of central authority, and reduces the resources available to local governments to enforce environmental standards. In addition, the dependency on EIA as the main means of assessment may allow investors to conceal certain impacts which may occur after construction (World Bank, 1995, p. 114).

The relevance of the law for existing, or state industry is less clear. State enterprises may be forced to reduce waste of resources by cuts in public subsidies. Joint ventures with foreign investors may also allow these enterprises to adopt international environmental standards. However, there is, to date, no evidence to indicate if such joint ventures have resulted in an improvement in environmental performance. Also, the shortage of funds to state enterprises does not encourage the adoption of new science and technology for environmental purposes (Jamison and Baark, 1995; Vu Cao Dam, 1995).

Public response to the law is also unclear. There is much obedience to its directives, for example, Article 28 of the law stated that the government would prohibit the production or firing of firecrackers as they cause noise and air pollution and are hazardous to health (MOSTE, 1994, p. 40). Firecrackers have been used for centuries by Vietnamese culture in festivals or religious ceremonies. However, following the restrictions introduced for Tet (New Year) 1995, there was an almost total abandonment of firecrackers (*VIR*, 17–23 January 1994; Denis Fenton UNDP, Hans Friedrich, IUCN, personal communication, 1995). However, this apparent obedience may also indicate general unpopularity of firecrackers in society. Indeed, in Tet 1994, firecracker-related accidents killed 71 people and injured 465 (*VIR*, 26 December–1 January 1995). A more telling test could be the so-called 'Campaign for Urban Civilization'. This, started in 1995, is an attempt by central government to make streets more passable by removing such obstacles as street-side stalls, advertising placards and unnecessarily long doorsteps (*VIR*, 22–28 May 1995). These measures may interfere with day-to-day life to a much greater extent than banning firecrackers, and so may eventually result in civil disobedience. Yet there is clear public dissent when state or business is perceived to be corrupt, or betraying old principles of socialism. This has been observed in other post-communist, or transitional societies (Kornai, 1992, p. 104). This is related to the varying fortunes of domestic society and foreign investment in Vietnam, while many local co-operatives have closed because of shortage of funding (Ronnås, 1992).

Environmentally, this has been reflected in disputes over natural-resource allocation, or threatened damage to livelihoods resulting from pollution or unregulated business activity. This is, therefore, different to many other public initiatives undertaken by elites within society concerning reforestation or conservation of biodiversity. There are still only a few independent Vietnamese environmental non-governmental organizations (NGOs), and they are generally dominated by educated elite members of society. The Institute of Ecological Economy (sometimes called 'Eco Eco'), for example, was established in 1990 to establish ten sustainable villages in ecologically fragile agricultural zones, rather than confront industry or state over industrialization (Nguyen Van Truong, 1992; Jamison and Baark, 1995, p. 281).

It is, therefore, arguable that current environmental policy in Vietnam does not reflect domestic perceptions of environmental problems. Such perceptions relate to old socialist principles of equitable allocation of resources and surpluses, rather than more Western concerns such as biodiversity conservation (DuBois, 1991; Howarth, 1995), or the need to regulate industry (Hesselberg, 1992; Wapner, 1995). The willingness of the public on one hand to criticize the state for corruption, yet on the other to obey new state restrictions on firecrackers, suggest that such actions may result from a basic ideology within society, rather than the effects of totalitarianism.

The result is a dilemma. Regulating foreign investment is important to enable Vietnam to industrialize and protect the environment at the same time. However, the avoidance of non-elite visions of environmental problems may lead to public dissent which undermines policy. Greater concern needs to be shown for the domestic industrial sector concurrently with FDI. But this is likely to be opposed by the Vietnam state in case this develops an autonomous business elite which may threaten its power. It may also require funds which can only be achieved once FDI is in operation (Jänicke, 1992).

The state in Vietnam is, therefore, developing industrialization and environmental policy while it holds on to power. Environmental policy reflects this power by representing only elitist viewpoints, and by the relative weakness, so far, of the environmental agencies in government compared with pro-industry agencies, and the reliance on EIAs alone for environmental assessment. However, the state is already experiencing challenges to authority by the autonomous actions of regions, and by the greater success, to date, of the south in attracting industrialization (Beresford and McFarlane, 1995). Civil society forms a controlling influence on the new business elite by opposing corruption. However, this could regulate state as well as industry if state members are seen to benefit unfairly from economic liberalization, or if domestic society feels under-represented in policy.

Transitional, developing countries may, therefore, be undergoing a process of proletarianization because of industrialization. Yet, the new labour force, in Vietnam, is united by a strong socialist ideology, and has political skills by being able to ally with the media. This close association of modern political techniques with opposition to inequity in industrialization may be a distinguishing feature of late twentieth-century civil society in industrializing countries, compared with historic examples from Europe (Meadwell, 1995; Mouzelis, 1995).

Future approaches to environmental policy in transitional developing countries may, therefore, need to acknowledge the ability of non-elite groups to activate on environment and development topics. However, the perspectives they offer on environmental problems may be different to those proposed by international or middle-class groups. Similarly, an overt concentration on regulating FDI alone may result in reduced pollution. But there is a need to assess how far groups in favour of environment are represented in government. Unbalanced power relations between pro-industry and pro-environment groups in government may result in toothless legislation.

## Conclusions

This chapter has examined sustainable development and industrialization in the transitional developing economy of Vietnam. The ability of the state to protect environment against pollution was discussed in relation to recent legislation and involvement of private enterprise. Public participation and opposition to environmental policy and industrialization was also reviewed. It was argued that recent policy changes do not represent much of domestic society. However, Vietnam requires industrialization to generate funds for development.

Evidence suggests that Vietnam has made a solid institutional start to environmental policy through the 1994 National Law on Environment Protection, and the creation of the National Environment Agency within the new Ministry of Science, Technology and Environment. This has accelerated environmental protection by requiring foreign-direct investment to submit environmental-impact assessments, and providing a political structure to implement environmental policy. In addition, foreign companies have been contracted to build environmental infrastructure such as waste-treatment centres in build-operate-transfer projects. There are also plans to implement economic-pricing instruments to internalize the costs of environmental protection into the industrialization process. Such achievements may enable Vietnam to undergo industrialization with comparatively less pollution than the first wave of industrializing countries. However, this progress in environmental protection is countered by the unequal distribution of the benefits of economic liberalization, and the lack of representation of all perspectives on environmental problems in environmental policy. Industrialization to date has mainly benefited foreign investors and state members. Domestic society has experienced a rapid fall in the number of state-sponsored industrial co-operatives. The transition from state socialism to a market economy in Vietnam has, therefore, not seen an associated rise of democracy and political liberalism. The state is still holding on to power, and foreign investors have little interest in democratization or trade unions.

As a consequence, environmental policy may reflect the relative power of the pro-industry agencies of government such as the State Committee for Co-operation and Investment, rather than the newer and smaller National Environment Agency. The 1994 law has also been criticized for depending too heavily on Environmental Impact Assessments as the main means of monitoring. Also, lower echelons of the state, such as local governments in provinces or parts of the army, are emerging as a form of new business elite by allying with investors, or by establishing industrial zones and trade in contravention of state directives. This weakens the power of the new environmental policy, and reflects the general weakness of the Hanoi State because of regionalism. Nevertheless, in Ho Chi Minh City, the local Environment Committee has actually improved restrictions on pollution by taking its own initiative.

Transitional developing countries may, therefore, experience problems or regionalism, and conflicts between state and new business elites in the implementation of sustainable development. In addition, they also need to reflect domestic perceptions about natural resource allocation and management. In common with other transitional societies, Vietnam is experiencing public dissent against perceived corruption among members of the state and foreign investors. Such perceptions do not always match western priorities for environmental protection because they are concerned with more basic aspects of livelihood rather than concerns discussed at UNCED such as biodiversity conservation or climatic change. However, these perceptions are held by a group with a deep-seated ideology in socialism, and the ability to ally with media.

Other transitional developing countries, such as Myanmar and Laos, will experience different patterns of industrialization because of unequal populations, resources, and proximity to markets. However, the experience of Vietnam indicates that authoritarian states may encounter problems in keeping power when regions have historic differences and are industrializing quickly. This is similar to the differences developing between the Chinese state in Beijing and the rapidly industrializing provinces of Guangdong and Guanxi in the south of China. In the long term, conflict may be avoided by representing different sections of society in policy, and by adhering to ideology held within society.

However, the alliance of domestic business elites with the state may mean an effective transfer of power eventually from the old military regime to an authoritarian business regime which opposes environmental regulation, but may favour environmental entrepreneurialism. Research may then focus on making environmental protection through private enterprise more effective, and on the alliances formed between local civil society and international environmental groups.

## Acknowledgements

The author would like to thank Bach Tan Sinh (MOSTE), Do Thi Minh Duc (University of Hanoi), Hans Friedrich (IUCN) and Yannick Glemarec (UNDP) for guidance. This research was financed by the Geography and Anthropology Research Division of the London School of Economics.

## References

Aage, H. (1994) Sustainable transition. In R.W. Campbell (ed.), *The Postcommunist Economic Transformation: Essays in Honor of Gregory Grossman*. Boulder, San Francisco and Oxford: Westview Press, pp. 15–41.

Amirahmadi, H. and Wu, W. (1994) Foreign direct investment in developing countries. *Journal of Developing Areas*, **28**(1), 167–90.

Bach Tan Sinh (1995) *Environmental Policy in Vietnam: Conflicting Interests in Quang Ninh Province – Coal Mining, Tourism and Livelihoods*. Hanoi: Ministry of Science, Technology and Environment.

Basi, R. (1995) Pravda and priority: environmental regulation in post-Soviet Russia. *International Environmental Affairs*, **7**(1), 3–21.

Bater, J.H. (1994) Privatization in Moscow. *Geographical Review*, **84**(2), 201–15.

Berend, I.T. (1994) Self-regulating or regulated market economy? On the model of east-central European transformation. In R.W. Campbell (ed.), *The Postcommunist Economic Transformation: Essays in Honor of Gregory Grossman*. Boulder, San Francisco and Oxford: Westview Press, pp. 43–64.

Beresford, M. (1993) The political economy of dismantling the 'bureaucratic centralism and subsidy system' in Vietnam. In K. Hewison, R. Robison and G. Rodan (eds), *Southeast Asia in the 1990s: Authoritarianism, Democracy and Capitalism*. St. Leonard's, Australia: Allen and Unwin, pp. 213–36.

Beresford, M. and Fraser, L. (1992) Political economy of environment in Vietnam. *Journal of Contemporary Asia*, **22**(1), 3–19.

Beresford, M. and McFarlane, B. (1995) Regional inequality and regionalism in Vietnam and China. *Journal of Contemporary Asia*, **25**(1), 50–72.

Bergstø, B. and Endresen, S.B. (1992) From north to south: a locational shift in industrial pollution? *Norsk Geografisk Tidsskrift [Norwegian Journal of Geography]*, **46**(4), 175–82.

Bowen, J.T. Jr and Leinbach, T.R. (1995) The state and liberalization: the airline industry in the East Asian NICs. *Annals of the Association of American Geographers*, **85**(3), 468–93.

Browett, J.G. (1986) Industrialization in the global periphery: the significance of the newly industrialising countries of East and Southeast Asia. *Environment and Planning D: Society and Space*, **4**, 401–18.

Bryant, C.G.A. (1995) Civic nation, civil society, civil religion. In J.A. Hall (ed.), *Civil Society: Theory, History, Comparison*. Cambridge: Polity Press, pp. 136–57.

Brzeski, A. (1994) Postcommunist transformation: between accident and design. In R. Campbell (ed.), *The Postcommunist Economic Transformation: Essays in Honor of Gregory Grossman*. Boulder, San Francisco and Oxford: Westview Press, pp. 3–13.

Cao Van Sung (ed.) (1995) *Environment and Bioresources of Vietnam: Present Situation and Solutions*. Hanoi: The Gioi Publishers, pp. 3–13.

Cohen, J.L. and Arato, A. (1992) *Civil Society and Political Theory*. Cambridge, MA: MIT Press.

Cook, P. and Minogue, M. (1993) Economic reform and political change in Myanmar (Burma). *World Development*, **21**(7), 1151–61.

Dallago, B., Ajani, G. and Grancelli, B. (eds) (1992) *Privatization and Entrepreneurship in Post-Socialist Countries: Economy, Law and Society*. London: St Martin's Press.

Dan Ton That (1993) The role of the state and economic development in the reconstruction of Vietnam. In Mya Than and J.L.H. Tan (eds), *Vietnam's Dilemmas and Options: The Challenge of Economic Transition in the 1990s*. Singapore: ASEAN Economic Research Unit, Institute of Southeast Asia Studies, pp. 22–50.

Dang Duc Dam (1995) *Vietnam's Economy 1986–1995*. Hanoi: The Gioi Publishers.

DeBardelben, J. (1985) *The Environment and Marxism-Leninism: The Soviet and East German Experience*. Westview Special Studies on the Soviet Union and Eastern Europe. Boulder and London: Westview Press.

de Vylder, S. (1995) State and market in Vietnam: some issues for an economy in transition. In I. Nørund, C.L. Gates and Vu Cao Dam (eds), *Vietnam in a Changing World*. Richmond, Surrey: Curzon Press, pp. 31–70.

Dinh, Q. (1993) Vietnam's policy reforms and its future. *Journal of Contemporary Asia*, **23**(4), 532–53.

DuBois, M. (1991) The governance of the third world: a Foucauldian perspective on power relations in development. *Alternatives*, **16**, 1–30.

Environment Committee of Ho Chi Minh City (1995) *Environment Protection Activities in Ho Chi Minh City*. Ho Chi Minh City: People's Committee of Ho Chi Minh City, Environment Committee.

FIAS (Foreign Investment Advisory Service) (1994) *Screening and Approval of Foreign Direct Investment and Coordination of Investment Promotion Activities in Vietnam*. Hanoi: International Finance Corporation, Multilateral Investment Guarantee Agency, and the World Bank.

Fang Wang (1994) The political economy of authoritarian clientelism in Taiwan. In L. Roniger and A. Günes-Ayata (eds), *Democracy, Clientelism, and Civil Society*. Boulder and London: Lynne Rienner, pp. 181–206.

Fforde, A. and de Vylder, S. (1988) *Vietnam: An Economy in Transition*. Stockholm: Swedish International Development Authority.

Fish, M.S. (1994) Russia's fourth transition. *Journal of Democracy*, **5**(3), 31–42.

Forsyth, T. (1996) Industrial pollution and government policy in Thailand: rhetoric versus reality. Working paper, Department of Geography, London School of Economics.

Forsyth, T. (1997) The politics of environmental health: industrialization and suspected poisoning in Thailand. Working paper, Department of Geography, London School of Economics.

Gates, C. and Truong, D. (1995) Development strategy and trade and investment policies for structural change. In I. Nørlund, C.L. Gates and Vu Cao Dam (eds), *Vietnam in a Changing World*. Richmond, Surrey: Curzon Press, pp. 85–108.

Günes-Ayata, A. (1994) Clientelism: premodern, modern, and postmodern. In L. Roniger and A. Günes-Ayata (eds), *Democracy, Clientelism, and Civil Society*. Boulder and London: Lynne Rienner, pp. 19–28.

Hall, J.A. (1995) In search of civil society. In J.A. Hall (ed.), *Civil Society: Theory, History, Comparison*. Cambridge: Polity Press, pp. 1–31.

Hawes, G. and Hong Liu (1993) Explaining the dynamics of the Southeast Asian political economy: state, society, and the search for economic growth. *World Politics*, **45**, 629–60.

Hesselberg, J. (1992) Exports of pollution-intensive industries to the South. *Norsk Geografisk Tidsskrift [Norwegian Journal of Geography]*, **46**(4), 171–4.

Hewison, K. and Brown, A. (1994) Labor and unions in an industrializing Thailand. *Journal of Contemporary Asia*, **24**(4), 483–514.

Hewison, K., Robison, R. and Rodan, G. (eds) (1993) *Southeast Asia in the 1990s: Authoritarianism, Democracy and Capitalism*. St Leonard's, Australia: Allen and Unwin.

Hirsch, P. and Lohmann, L. (1989) Contemporary politics of environment in Thailand. *Asian Survey*, **89**(4), 439–53.

Howarth, J.M. (1995) Ecology: modern hero or post-modern villain? From scientific trees to phenomenological wood. *Biodiversity and Conservation*, **4**, 786–97.

Huntingdon, S. (1968) *Political Order in Developing Societies*. New Haven: Yale.

Huntingdon, S. (1984) Will more states become democratic? *Political Science Quarterly*, **99**(2), 193–218.

Huynh, F. and Stengel, H. (1993) Sustainable development: challenges to a developing country. In Mya Than and J.L.H. Tan (eds), *Vietnam's Dilemmas and Options: The Challenge of Economic Transition in the 1990s*. Singapore: ASEAN Economic Research Unit, Institute of Southeast Asia Studies, pp. 259–84.

Irvin, G. (1995) Vietnam: assessing the achievements of *Doi Moi*. *Journal of Development Studies*, **31**(5), 725–50.

Ishiyama, J.T. (1995) Communist parties in transition: structures, leaders, and processes of democratization in Eastern Europe. *Comparative Politics*, **27**(2), 147–66.

Jamison, A. and Baark, E. (1995) From market reforms to sustainable development: the cultural dimensions of science and technology policy in Vietnam and China. In I. Nørund, C.L. Gates and Vu Cao Dam (eds), *Vietnam in a Changing World*. Richmond, Surrey: Curzon Press, pp. 269–92.

Jänicke, M. (1992) Conditions for environmental policy success: an international comparison. In M. Jachtenfuchs and M. Strübel (eds), *Environmental Policy in Europe: Assessments, Challenges, and Perspectives*. Baden-Baden: Nomos Verlagsgesellschaft, pp. 71–97.

Jerneck, A. and Nguyen Thanh Ha (1995) The role of the enterprise unions in the shift from central planning to market orientation. In I. Nørlund, C.L. Gates and Vu Cao Dam (eds), *Vietnam in a Changing World*. Richmond, Surrey: Curzon Press, pp. 159–80.

Keane, J. (1988) *Democracy and Society: On the Predicaments of European Socialism, the Prospects for Democracy, and the Problem of Controlling Social and Political Power*. London and New York: Verso.

Kolko, G. (1995) Vietnam since 1975: winning a war and losing the peace. *Journal of Contemporary Asia*, **25**(1), 3–49.

Kornai, J. (1992) The affinity between ownership and coordination mechanisms: the common experience of reform in socialist countries. In K.Z. Poznanski (ed.), *Constructing Capitalism: the Reemergence of Civil Society and Liberal Economy in the Post-communist World*. Boulder, San Francisco and Oxford: Westview Press, pp. 97–116.

Lohmann, R.A. (1995) Buddhist commons and the question of a third sector in Asia. *Voluntas*, **6**(2), 140–58.

Mallon, R.L. (1993) Vietnam: image and reality. In J. Heath (ed.), *Revitalizing Socialist Enterprise: A Race Against Time*. London and New York: Routledge, pp. 204–21.

Meadwell, H. (1995) Post-Marxism, no friend of civil society. In J.A. Hall (ed.), *Civil Society: Theory, History, Comparison*. Cambridge: Polity Press, pp. 183–99.

Middleton, N., O'Keefe, P. and Moyo, S. (1993) *Tears of the Crocodile: From Rio to Reality in the Developing World*. Boulder, CO and London: Pluto Press.

MOSTE (Ministry of Science, Technology, and Environment, Vietnam) (1994) *Law on Environmental Protection*. Hanoi: MOSTE (in Vietnamese, English, and French).

Mouzelis, N. (1995) Modernity, late development and civil society. In J.A.Hall (ed.), *Civil Society: Theory, History, Comparison*. Cambridge: Polity Press, pp. 224–49.

Munasinghe, M. (1993) Environmental issues and economic decisions in developing countries. *World Development*, **21**(11), 1729–48.

Munslow, B. and Ekoku, F.E. (1995) Is democracy necessary for sustainable development? *Democratization*, **2**(2), 158–78.

Mya Than and Tan, J.L.H. (eds) (1993) *Vietnam's Dilemmas and Options: The Challenge of Economic Transition in the 1990s*. Singapore: ASEAN Economic Research Unit, Institute of Southeast Asia Studies.

Nash, R.F. (1982) (3rd ed. revised) *Wilderness and the American Mind*. New Haven: Yale University Press.

Nathan, A. (1993) China's path from communism. *Journal of Democracy*, **4**(2), 30–42.

Nguyen Dac Hy (1995) Discussions on environmental protection laws. In Cao Van Sung (ed.), *Environment and Bioresources of Vietnam: Present Situation and Solutions*. Hanoi: The Gioi Publishers, pp. 226–35.

Nguyen Van Truong (1992) *An Approach to the Ecological Economy of Vietnam*. Hanoi: Institute of Ecological Economy.

Nowak, L. (1991) *Power and Civil Society: Toward a Dynamic Theory of Real Socialism*. Contributions in Political Science, no. 271. New York, Westport, and London: Greenwood Press.

Osaghae, E. (ed.) (1994) *Between State and Civil Society in Africa: Perspectives on Development*. Dakar, Senegal: Codesria Book Series.

Payne, R.A. (1995) Freedom and the environment. *Journal of Democracy*, **6**(3), 41–55.

Pedersen, P. (1995) Nature, religion and cultural identity: the religious environmentalist paradigm. In O. Brun and A. Kalland (eds), *Asian Perspectives of Nature*. Richmond, Surrey: Curzon Press, pp. 258–76.

Peluso, N.L. (1993) Coercing conservation: the politics of state resource control. In R.D. Lipshutz and K. Conca (eds), *The State and Social Power in Global Environmental Politics*. New York: Columbia University Press.

Pham Binh Quyen, Dang Duc Nhan and Nguyen Van San (1995) Environmental pollution in Vietnam: analytical estimation and environmental priorities. *Trends in Analytical Chemistry*, **14**(8), 383–8.

Pham Ngoc Dang and Tran Hieu Nhue (1995) Environmental pollution in Vietnam. In Cao Van Sung (ed.), *Environment and Bioresources of Vietnam: Present Situation and Solutions*. Hanoi: The Gioi Publishers, pp. 129–200.

Phuc Tien (1995) Vietnamese media: general trends in 1994. *Annals of Ho Chi Minh City University A: Social Sciences*, **2**, 42–6.

Rau, Z. (ed.) (1991) *The Reemergence of Civil Society in Eastern Europe and the Soviet Union*. Boulder, San Francisco and Oxford: Westview Press.

Redclift, M. and Woodgate, G. (1994) Sociology and the environment: discordant discourse? In M. Redclift and T. Benton (eds), *Social Theory and the Global Environment*. London and New York: Routledge, pp. 51–66.

Reinhardt, J. (1993) Industrial restructuring and industrial policy in Vietnam. In Mya Than and J.L.H. Tan (eds), *Vietnam's Dilemmas and Options: The Challenge of Economic Transition in the 1990s*. Singapore: ASEAN Economic Research Unit, Institute of Southeast Asia Studies, pp. 71–96.

Robison, R., Hewison, K. and Rodan, G. (1993) Political power in industrialising capitalist societies: theoretical approaches. In K. Hewison, R. Robison and G. Rodan (eds), *Southeast Asia in the 1990s: Authoritarianism, Democracy and Capitalism*. St. Leonard's, Australia: Allen and Unwin, pp. 9–38.

Roemer, J.E. (1992) Can there be socialism after communism? *Politics and Society*, **20**(3), 261–76.

Roniger, L. (1994) The comparative study of clientelism and the changing nature of civil society in the contemporary world. In L. Roniger and A. Günes-Ayata (eds), *Democracy, Clientelism, and Civil Society*. Boulder and London: Lynne Rienner, pp. 1–18.

Roniger, L. and Günes-Ayata, A. (1994) (eds), *Democracy, Clientelism, and Civil Society*. Boulder and London: Lynne Rienner.

Ronnås, P. (1992) *Employment Generation Through Private Entrepreneurship in Vietnam*. Geneva: Swedish International Development Authority and International Labor Organization Asian Regional Team for Employment Promotion.

Rosendal, G.K. (1995) The forest issue in post-UNCED international negotiations: conflicting interests and fora for reconciliation. *Biodiversity and Conservation*, **4**, 91–107.

SCS (State Committee for Sciences); UNDP; (SIDA) Swedish International Development Authority, UNEP and IUCN (1991) *Vietnam National Plan for Environment and Sustainable Development 1991–2000: Framework for Action*. Hanoi: SCS Project VIE/89/021.

Schroeder, R.A. and Neumann, R.P. (1995) Manifest ecological destinies: local rights and global environmental agendas. *Antipode*, **27**(4), 321–4.

Sharma, B. (1984) Multinational corporations and industrialisation in Southeast and East Asia. *Contemporary Southeast Asia*, **6**(2), 159–71.

Smets, H. (1994) The polluter pays principle. In L. Campiglio, L. Pineschi, D. Siniscalco and T. Treves (eds), *The Environment after Rio: International Law and Economics*. London/Dordrecht/Boston: Graham and Trotman/Martinus Nijhof Publishers/International Environmental Law and Policy Series, pp. 131–48.

Solinger, D.J. (1993) China's transients and the state: a form of civil society? *Politics and Society*, **21**(1), 91–122.

Solinger, D.J. (1995) China's urban transients in the transition from socialism and the collapse of the communist 'urban public goods regime'. *Comparative Politics*, **27**(2), 127–46.

Spoor, M. (1988) Reforming state finance in post-1975 Vietnam. *Journal of Development Studies*, **24**(4), 102–14.

Taylor, J.L. (1993) Buddhist revitalization, modernization and social change in contemporary Thailand. *Sojourn*, **8**(1), 62–81.

Tester, K. (1992) *Civil Society*. London and New York: Routledge.

Thrift, N.J. and Forbes, D.K. (1985) Cities, socialism and war: Hanoi, Saigon and the Vietnamese experience of urbanization. *Environment and Planning D: Society and Space*, **3**, 279–308.

UNDP (1994) *Strengthening National Capacities to Integrate the Environment into Investment Planning and Public Policy Making*. Hanoi: UNDP Capacity 21 Project.

UNDP (1995) (2nd ed.) *Environment and Natural Resource Management: Strategy and Action Plan for UNDP Vietnam*. Hanoi: UNDP.

UNESCO (1994) *Environmental Awareness Programme Framework in Vietnam: Proposed Strategy and Projects*. Hanoi: UNESCO.

UNIDO (1987) *Burma: Transition to Agro-based Industrial Economy*. Rome: UNIDO Industrial Development Review Series.

UNIDO (1993) *Mongolia: Restructuring for a Market Economy*. Rome: UNIDO Industrial Development Review Series.

UNIDO (1994) *Lao People's Democratic Republic: Industrial Transition*. Rome: UNIDO Industrial Development Review Series.

Urry, J. (1981) *The Anatomy of Capitalist Societies: The Economy, Civil Society and the State*. London: Macmillan.

van Brabant, J.M. (1992) *Privatising Eastern Europe: The Role of Markets and Ownership in the Transition.* Dordrecht, Boston, and London: Kluwer Academic Publishers.

Vo Nhan Tri (1990) *Vietnam's Economic Policy Since 1975.* Singapore: ASEAN Economic Research Unit, Institute of Southeast Asian Studies.

Vu Cao Dam (1995) Vietnam's science and technology policy in the market economy reforms: a political perspective. In I. Nørlund, C.L. Gates and Vu Cao Dam (eds), *Vietnam in a Changing World.* Richmond, Surrey: Curzon Press.

Vu Tuan Anh (ed.) (1994) *Vietnam's Economic Reform: Results and Problems.* Hanoi: National Center for Social and Human Sciences, Institute of Economics, Social Science Publishing House.

Vu Tuan Anh (ed.) (1995) *Economic Reform and Development in Vietnam.* Hanoi: National Center for Social and Human Sciences, Institute of Economics, Social Science Publishing House.

Wank, D.L. (1995) Civil society in communist China? Private business and political alliance, 1989. In J.A. Hall (ed.), *Civil Society: Theory, History, Comparison.* Cambridge: Polity Press, pp. 56–79.

Wapner, P. (1995) Politics beyond the state: environmental activism and world civic politics. *World Politics,* **47**, 311–40.

Ward, R.M. and Jinan Li (1993) Solid-waste disposal in Shanghai. *Geographical Review,* **83**(1), 29–42.

Weigle, M.A. and Butterfield, J. (1992) Civil society in reforming communist regimes: the logic of emergence. *Comparative Politics,* **25**(1), 3–30.

Weisberg, B. and Schell, O. (1979) *Ecocide in Indochina.* San Francisco: Canfield Press.

White, G. (1995) Civil society, democratization and development (II): two country cases. *Democratization,* **2**(2), 56–84.

Whiting, S.H. (1991) The politics of NGO development in China. *Voluntas,* **2**(2), 16–48.

Wilkinson, B. (1994) *Labor and Industry in the Asia-Pacific: Lessons from the Newly-Industrialized Countries.* Berlin and New York: Walter de Gruyter.

World Bank (1994) Vietnam Public Sector Management and Private Sector Initiatives: An Economic Report. 26 September. Country Operations Division, Country Department 1, East Asia and Pacific Region, Report no. 13143-VN, World Bank, Hanoi.

World Bank (1995) *Vietnam Environmental Program and Policy Priorities for a Socialist Economy in Transition,* in two volumes: *1: Executive Summary and Main Report: The Supporting Annexes.* Report no. 13200-VN, Agriculture and Environment Operations Division, Country Department 1, East Asia and Pacific Region. Hanoi: World Bank.

## Magazine and newspaper articles

*Asia Inc.*
January 1995a: David DeVoss, *Déjà vu* for the *Viet Kieu*, 4(1), 40–45.
January 1995b: John Colmey, Left behind in the rush, 4(1), 46–7.
April 1995c: Salil Tripathi, The last dragon, 4(4), 24–31.

*Lao Dong Chu Nhat [Labour Sunday]*
10 October 1993: Tran Duy Phuong and Tran Quang Lam, Disobeying the government decree, Nghe An has sold Pomu (*Fokendia hodginsii*) to overseas buyers (translated by WWF, Hanoi).

*VIR (Vietnam Investment Review)*
3–9 January 1994: Van Phu, Minister proposes measures to curtail regionalism, 4(116), p. 11.
17–23 January: Reuter, Less firecrackers and drinks during Tet, Premier orders, 4(118), p. 8.
24–30 January 1994: Tran Dinh Thanh, Equitization: some pros and cons, 4(119), p. 14.
7–20 February 1994: Philippe Agret (AFP), Quiet Tet festival for firecracker capital, 4(121–22), p. 20.
7–13 March 1994: Tran Thanh, Swelling private sector needs incentives to grow, 4(124), p. 12.
14–20 March 1994: Hoang Van Huan, EPZs account for 14pc of all foreign investment, 4(126), p. 12.
4–10 April 1994: Nguyen Anh Tuan, Investment in Dong Nai province outpacing management capacity, 4(129), p. 23.
2–8 May 1994: (no author), First waste treatment JV signed, 4(133), p. 4.
16–22 May 1994: Nguyen Van Phu, Cry of unfair play – local investors say foreigners get first priority, 4(135), p. 19.
23–29 May 1994: Nguyen Tri Dung, Power abusers fall under reform puch, 4(136), p. 1.
4–10 July 1994: AFP, Millions lost over pricing error, 4(142), p. 19.
18–24 July 1994: Hai Hung, Provinces gain right to capitalise land, 4(144), p. 21.
8–14 August 1994: Cong Thanh, PM gets tough on coal exploitation, 4(147), p. 19.
26 December 1994–1 January 1995: (no author), Compensation terms agreed for Neptune Aries oil spill in Saigon, 4(167), p. 1.
26 December 1994–1 January 1995: Ngoc Phu, Village stockpiling for Tet as firecracking ban nears, 4(167), p. 28.
16–22 January 1995: Robert Templer, Hai Phong struggling to realise EPZ ambitions, 5(169), p. 28.
23–29 January 1995: Le Hao, Military flexes muscles on business scene, 5(172), p. 16.
30 January–5 February 1995: Nguyen Anh Tuan, Slow growth at export zones suggests policy shortfall, 5(173), p. 222.
27 February–5 March 1995: Nguyen Tri Dung, Premier demands dyke prosecutions, 5(176), p. 1.
27 February–5 March 1995: (no author), Cities strangled by rising pollution, 5(176), p. 27.
6–12 March 1995: Wilhelm Popp, New mining law could bring order to the industry, 5(177), p. 26.
13–19 March 1995: An Khong, Environment week raises new awareness, 5(178), p. 8.
20–26 March 1995: (no author), SCCI faces merger in ministries review, 5(179), p. 2.
27 March–2 April 1995: Cong Thanh, Water treatment plant ushers in the BOT age, 5(180), p. 16.
22–28 May 1995: (no author), Billboards to come down at newly built intersection, 5(188), p. 27.

3–9 July 1995: (no author), Pollution deadline for city factories, **5**(194), p. 14.
10–16 July 1995: Ha Thang, Government backs 'green initiative', **5**(195), p. 7.
10–16 July 1995: Trinh Thi, Trouble strike at foreign enterprises, **5**(195), p. 26.

# 13

# The International Dimensions of Sustainable Development: Rio Reconsidered

## Andrew Jordan and Katrina Brown

The real measure of our success will be in what happens when we leave here, in our own countries, in our own organisations in our own lives. Will this Summit merely be a high point in our expressions of good intentions and enthusiasm and excitement, or will it really be the start of a process of a fundamental change which we absolutely need?

(Maurice Strong, 14 June 1992).[1]

## Introduction

This chapter discusses the international dimensions of sustainable development and explores how the current debate on environment and development issues is constructed in the context of various international institutions. It takes the United Nations Conference on Environment and Development (UNCED) in 1992 (the so-called Earth Summit, held in Rio) as its starting-point. The Rio Summit was itself part of an ongoing process that had started with the Brundtland Report in 1987, but which can be traced back to the 1972 Stockholm environment conference (see Chapter 1). This chapter examines how the agreements negotiated at Rio have fared and how some of the issues which emerged during the Summit, especially those concerning North–South relations, have evolved in the last five years. We consider whether the international and trans-generational conflicts which manifested

1 Secretary-General of the UNCED. Closing speech to the plenary session of the UNCED. Reprinted in Johnson (1993, pp. 519–23).

themselves so clearly at Rio have proved to be serious impediments to sustainable development at an international level.

The chapter first reviews what was achieved at Rio and outlines the themes which were revealed during negotiations. The evolving institutions for sustainable development are examined, namely the nascent Commission on Sustainable Development and the World Bank's Global Environment Facility (GEF), both of which have a role in implementing 'Agenda 21', a vast blueprint for implementing sustainable development into the twenty-first century, and the other Rio agreements. The progress towards sustainable development is then explored through the implementation of two binding agreements signed at Rio, the Conventions on Climate Change and Biological Diversity.

## What Did Rio Achieve?

In the first two weeks of June 1992, the world's leaders, journalists and foreign diplomats met in Rio at the UNCED Earth Summit to chart the course to a more environmentally sustainable future. UNCED was itself a reflection of a wider awareness of the serious environmental and developmental challenges facing humanity. Leaders duly acknowledged this seriousness and pledged to reverse the trends that threatened sustainability, signed international agreements and promised significant amounts of new money. But, five years on, what exactly did the meeting achieve? Was it, as Strong hoped, the start of a process of fundamental change or merely a temporary surge of awareness that has since subsided? Writing just after the close of the UNCED, the Deputy-General of the Conference, Nintin Desai, suggested that it had secured four important achievements.

> First, it has secured a set of agreements between Governments which mark a significant advance in international co-operation on development and environment issues. Second, it has secured political commitment to these agreements at the highest level and placed the issue of sustainable development at the heart of the international diplomatic agenda. Third, it has opened new pathways for communication and co-operation between official and non-official organisations working towards developmental and environmental ends. Fourth, it has led to an enormous increase in public awareness of the issues that were tackled in the process .... All these elements are interlinked .... Together they constitute a significant first step in the transition to sustainable development. (Quoted in Grubb *et al.*, 1993, p. 49)

The agreements are outlined in Table 13.1, which shows their respective objectives and characteristics. They each have an important bearing on different aspects of sustainable development. However, only the Framework Convention on Climate Change and the Convention on Biological Diversity are binding under international law. Agenda 21, the Rio Declaration and the

**Table 13.1**  The UNCED agreements

---

**The Framework Convention on Climate Change**
- climate change is a serious problem
- action cannot wait until resolution of scientific uncertainties
- developed countries should take the lead
- compensation paid to developing countries for additional costs of implementing Convention
- developed countries aim to return to 1990 emission levels by 2000
- reporting process established

**Convention on Biological Diversity**
- conservation and sustainable use of biodiversity and components
- states have sovereign rights over biological resources in their territories
- benefits of development of biological resources to be shared in fair and equitable way on mutually agreed terms
- countries to develop national plans
- funding arrangements under GEF

**Agenda 21**
- 40 chapters outlining an action plan for sustainable development
- integrates environment and development concerns in the UN
- strongly orientated towards bottom-up participatory and community-based approaches
- acceptance of market principles, within appropriate regulatory framework
- performance targets mostly limited to those previously agreed elsewhere

**Rio Declaration**
- 27 principles for guiding action on environment and development
- stresses right to and need for development and poverty alleviation
- principles concerning trade and environment are ambiguous and in some tension
- rights and roles of special groups

**Forest Principles**
- represents blocked attempt to negotiate convention on forests
- emphasizes sovereign rights to exploit forests
- general principles of forest protection and sustainable management

---

*Source*: Adapted from Grubb *et al.* (1993).

Forest Principles are non-binding statements of intent, sometimes termed 'soft law', which provide guidelines or frameworks for future development.

More critical voices pointed out that try as it might, the UNCED simply could not paper over the huge disagreements between North and South which had become steadily more glaring in the run-up to the Conference. Rather than a short and punchy 'Earth Charter' that Strong had promised, UNCED delivered a Declaration so bland as to 'provide ... something for everybody' (Holmberg *et al.*, 1993, p. 7). The length and unwieldiness of Agenda 21 reflected the political difficulty of achieving consensus: 'an immense document of good intentions, made toothless by the rigid exclusion of timetables, serious financial targets, consideration of the terms of international trade and, above all, the role and accountability of the internationals' (Middleton *et al.*, 1993, p. 2). The USA, meanwhile, was so worried about the financial implications of the Biodiversity Convention that it refused to sign it, and only agreed to the Climate Convention after furious last-minute deals were brokered. Rather than global partnership, there was mutual suspicion and deep controversies over very basic questions. In many respects, Rio was a product of the rising tide of public concern for the environment in the late 1980s, which gave rise to high-profile debates about the term 'sustainable development' as set out in the landmark UN report by Gro Harlem Brundtland, *Our Common Future* (WCED, 1987). By the time Rio took place, that wave of anxiety and concern had already begun to ebb. Since 1992 it has been difficult for NGOs and pressure groups, and for governments themselves, to sustain interest in 'global' environmental issues.

Rio, however, also needs to be seen as part of an ongoing process which uses Agenda 21 as a focus and a means by which sustainable development becomes ingrained into the UN system (Grubb *et al.*, 1993). Post-Rio conferences have addressed development and environment issues covered by Agenda 21, for example, those on women (Beijing); on population and development (Cairo); and on urban environments (Habitat II in Istanbul). However, few real new commitments have come from these fora. Since Rio a Convention on Desertification has been negotiated and agreed (in Paris 1995), although it seems unlikely that a convention on forests will be developed, despite the convening of an Intergovernmental Panel on Forests (IPF). This *ad hoc* forum had completed two meetings up to mid-1996 and was mandated to report to the Commission on Sustainable Development (CSD) in 1997. Follow-up meetings of the CSD will review progress on sustainable development, and the Conventions will be strengthened through meetings of the respective Conference of the Parties (COP).

Some of these initiatives are reviewed here in the light of the key themes or points of conflict and debate, which emerged and became prominent during the UNCED. They are:

- equity concerns, both intra- and inter-generational;
- states' common but differentiated responsibility for causing environmental change;
- sovereignty and governance; and
- economics and finance.

There are many conflicts and trade-offs between these themes, many of which go to the heart of the functioning of the international political economy. One need only read through the 27 principles of the Rio Declaration to identify some of the basic ones.

## Institutional Developments since Rio

The United Nations is, at the same time, the best and the worst place to address the challenges thrown up by the concept of sustainability. The underlying paradox is that, while the UN is the only feasible international forum in which states can meet to decide new international rules and conventions, it actively excludes participation by non-state actors such as non-governmental groups, indigenous peoples, and even entire nations who do not enjoy the formal attributes of statehood. The UN is a creature of state control. It is a supra-national body but its ability to intervene, at least in the environmental affairs of individual states, is weak. It has to cajole and negotiate rather than bully and coerce. Then there are the well-known accusations of wastage, corruption, bureaucratic infighting and institutional inertia (Henry, 1996). Like all bureaucracies, the UN is organized into different sectors, each with specialized functions and remits in order to achieve efficient administrative performance. A perennial problem is finding ways to improve the co-ordination between different units. The underlying message of sustainable development – that environmental concerns must be integrated into development priorities – has in many ways reinforced this and made the need for co-ordination more pressing.

### The Commission on Sustainable Development

Brundtland's *Our Common Future* (WCED, 1987) is always worth re-visiting. From page 316 onwards, it seeks to establish leadership and co-ordination within the UN. Using diplomatic language, it was clearly irritated by the failure of most, if not all, UN initiatives to promote sustainability and to establish high-level centres of leadership and expertise linked to the much-manipulated programme and budget allocation process. The Commission saw the need for a powerful supervisory function for all this co-ordination at the very apex of the UN, and it recommended a UN Board of Sustainable Development (p. 318) with the capacity to assess, advise, assist and report on progress made and needed on sustainable development. The Board should be chaired by the Secretary-General, with supreme powers to create inter-agency commitment to and co-ordination for sustainable development.

In the event, the Rio conference fudged this issue. The CSD is a lower-rank body, linked to the Economic and Social Council (ECOSOC) rather than the General Assembly, with limited powers to coerce and cajole the cumbersome UN process. That said, no other new organization was created at Rio and some consider the CSD to be one of the 'more surprising and significant achievements' of the UNCED (Imber, 1994, p. 55). In many respects, however, it is a creature of state control, unable to inspect activities at the sub-national level directly for itself or do more than accept what states themselves report. Although it consists of high-level representatives, including ministers, from 53 countries and meets in full once a year, with various inter-sessional assemblies, many feared that the CSD would become a talking shop – a forum for sterile debate and political rhetoric. Its central task is to oversee the implementation of Agenda 21, which it does by reviewing reports submitted by governments, to culminate in a special session of the General Assembly in June 1997, five years on from the UNCED. The main products of this meeting are likely to be some form of political declaration on the value of the CSD, a new work programme, and a statement on areas requiring further attention. Environmental groups can be expected to use the occasion to try and strengthen the CSD's role beyond that of simply monitoring and discussing issues.

So how well has the CSD actually performed? As the most concrete institutional achievement to arise from Rio, it has always been burdened with the expectation that it would co-ordinate the many disparate parts of the UN and reduce duplication. A series of agencies have been given this task in the past and few have made an impact (Imber, 1994). The UN system is simply too balkanized and states too wary of providing it with the extra resources it demands. Critics contend that the CSD has spent too much time debating Agenda 21 at length. In trying to cover every chapter in depth it has simply dissipated its efforts and duplicated work carried out elsewhere. At first, it chose a number of focus areas but these were too broad, and it is now concentrating on specific issues, such as forests, sustainability indicators and techniques for monitoring the activities of states. One of its chief successes has been the setting up of an Intergovernmental Panel on Forests.

The fact, however, that government representatives at CSD sessions are predominantly from environment ministries, with little influence over their more powerful colleagues in trade and industry departments, has undoubtedly lessened its impact. So too has the ignorance shown by the green lobby. Aside from a hard core of environmental activists, some of its meetings are very poorly attended. The chief problem though is a lack of clarity on what the whole reporting process is meant to achieve and the best means to get there. In the rush to 'do something' at Rio, many feel the criteria for assessment were neglected. What, for example, does the CSD do when it has received reports from every country? Beyond these procedural issues, others question whom the CSD is actually meant to be representing. Gordon (1994), for example, points out that it remains essentially inter-governmental and that it has made limited efforts to incorporate local environmental groups in its proceedings or even canvass their opinions. Yet their participation, he believes, is crucial if the process is to have legitimacy.

## Wider Reform of the UN System

During the UNCED, a number of existing UN agencies committed themselves to the goal of sustainable development. There was much talk about strengthening the co-ordinating and catalytic roles of the UN Environment Programme (UNEP), while the UN Development Programme (UNDP) was expected to extend its capacity-building activities, particularly through its stake in the GEF, and to help generate national sustainability plans. In practice, UNEP remains marginal to the UN system and faces continued demands from states for it to be streamlined in spite of its impressive achievements in promoting international co-operation on issues such as ozone. Now that all UN agencies have environmental issues included in their remit, the UNEP, which was meant to co-ordinate the UN system, has been left with a 'continuing identity crisis' (von Moltke, 1996, p. 56). Some UN agencies have also shown an inclination to return to the practices by which they operated before Rio. The UNDP, for example, has a long history of resisting attempts to green its activities and operations (von Moltke, 1992). If pressure is to be maintained on governments and inter-governmental institutions to ensure that they do not renege on the commitments and processes established at Rio, NGOs will have to do what they can to support existing mechanisms.

Meanwhile, the ability of the UN to act as a global problem-solver is being increasingly called into question. Rather than offering a showcase for its achievements, the UN's fiftieth birthday celebrations in 1995 were used by many states as an opportunity to re-state their calls for reform and renewal. Anti-UN sentiments are especially strong in the USA, which continues to ignore a large portion of its long-standing arrears, although they also exist in other parts of the OECD. Recent events in Rwanda, Somalia and the former Yugoslavia have exposed many of the UN's internal weaknesses to the full, damaging its image still further. When so many of its political and financial resources are being used to undertake peace-keeping activities, it is questionable how much more effective it can be at promoting development and environment activities. In fact, since Rio demands for internal reforms in these two areas have measurably grown.

### Financing Sustainable Development: The GEF

If there is one issue guaranteed to stimulate heated international debate, it is finance. It goes to the heart of the North–South debate and shows no signs of being resolved (Jordan, 1994a). Galbraith (1958, p. 91) explains why:

> Few things have been more productive of controversy over the ages than the suggestion that the rich should, by one device or another, share their wealth with those who are not. With comparatively rare and usually eccentric exceptions the rich have been opposed. The grounds have been many and varied and have been principally noted for the rigorous exclusion of the most important reason, which is the simple unwillingness to give up the enjoyment of what they have. The poor have generally been in favour of greater equality.

Some of the grand sums mooted by the UN prior to Rio as the cost of implementing sustainable development in the developing world (such as $125 billion each year between 1992 and 2000) were plainly fanciful. But of the money actually pledged at Rio, much simply did not materialize. The EU, for example, has been unable to agree upon new mechanisms for realizing the ECU 3 billion it pledged, while many other potential donor states such as the UK and the USA have used rising private capital flows as an excuse to cut back on their aid donations. Even the normally reliable Norwegians have reduced their aid-giving in recent years. The President of the World Bank's offer of an additional 'Earth Increment' to the International Development Agency's tenth tranche also did not materialize, while the famous 0.7 per cent of Gross Domestic Product aid target remains a distant hope. Otherwise, the North and South remain locked into the same unproductive debate whereby the South calls for long-standing aid commitments to be met, while the North insists that developing countries create domestic conditions that facilitate private financial flows (Jordan, 1994b).

Cynics will probably point out that only in relation to global environmental issues have the South's demands, or 'greenmail' as they are sometimes termed, carried any weight, namely the payment of funds to meet the incremental costs of international conventions. This may reflect the *realpolitik* of a world in which the North needs the South to realize its global environmental objectives. On this matter, Tariq Osman Hyder (1992), who was the spokesperson for the G77 coalition and China during the climate negotiations, offers the following:

> the industrialised countries must realise that the rules of the game in the North/South dialogue have changed. In the past, the concept of an interdependent world was mainly a humanitarian ideal expressed in terms of rhetoric rather than practice. The Southern world was seen in terms of 'lifeboat' and 'triage' theories where the weak might have to be left behind. It is now clear that ... we are all in the same lifeboat. If developing countries are not given the trade opportunities, debt relief, credit facilities, financial assistance and the technology flows that they require for their development, we will all eventually pay the price.

For some, an appreciation of growing economic and environmental interdependence will encourage mutually beneficial compacts that cut across the North–South divide (MacNeill *et al.*, 1991). In some respects the Global Environment Facility (GEF) was set up in recognition of this interdependence. Established in 1991, the GEF funds projects in the developing world which realize 'global environmental benefits' such as biodiversity protection and reduction of greenhouse gas emissions. Donations are voluntary and are meant to be new and in addition to existing flows of aid. In practice they have not always been (Jordan, 1994b).

The GEF was one of the main 'winners' at Rio. It arrived as a short-term pilot operation depleted of funds and left with the imprimatur of world leaders and large pledges of new and additional money. In the period since Rio it has been accepted as the financial instrument for the conventions on ozone depletion, climate change and biodiversity, but only on the condition that it be restructured and 'democratized' (i.e., moved away from the World Bank and into the orbit of the UN system, where voting arrangements give the developing countries more power). The donors underlined their support by pledging a further £2 billion for the period 1994–97 (approximately double the size of the 'pilot' GEF (1991–94). In spite of these changes, the GEF's role remains in dispute. Envisaged as a 'new' response to a set of new problems, the GEF has, to a large degree, only provided an extra forum within which old and by now sterile debates about finance can be played out. The GEF's critics contend that it has adopted many of the supposed failings of its administrative parent, the World Bank (Rich, 1994). However, many environmentalists are concerned that the struggle between North and South for control of the reins of the GEF will prevent serious discussion of both the democratization of projects through public consultation, participation and 'ownership' and wider finance-related issues such as debt and trade.

The focus of attention in the future is likely to be the links between the GEF and the conventions, which currently make North–South flows of finance a necessary condition for continuing developing country support. Put crudely, without the offer of additional resources, the developing world simply would not have signed up, although its participation is none the less perceived to be vital to the success of the whole endeavour (Jordan and Werksman, 1995). The idea that the Rio Summit resolved the issue of how to finance the transition to sustainable development is simply erroneous. Beneath the rhetorical support for the GEF by both North and South, there are very profound discrepancies in the way that each side perceives the need for, likely role of and scope of additional financial transfers. The industrialized states tend towards a *minimal* interpretation, transfers being the price (to be minimized wherever possible) paid for enlisting the support of the South in tackling common problems. Meanwhile developing states seek perpetually to advance a *maximal* interpretation of additionality and incrementality, arguing that 'new' environmentally related transfers are a rightful and legitimate means to address the inequities inherent in the operation of the world economy. These represent very different standpoints and do not appear to be easily reconcilable. In the short term, the task of balancing these has been delegated to the COPs of the respective conventions and the GEF. The pathways through which these two bodies evolve in the coming years will offer a fascinating test case of how well international institutions can adapt to the challenge of sustainable development.

## The Climate Convention since Rio: An Evolving International Regime

The signing of the climate convention by 155 countries was very much the highlight of the Earth Summit (Victor and Salt, 1994; Bodansky, 1993). Climate change had emerged as a significant issue in industrialized countries in the late 1980s (see Table 13.2) and negotiations for an international agreement were instigated in 1991 despite the lack of consensus among

**Table 13.2** A chronology of climate politics

| | |
|---|---|
| 1988 | A hot summer in the industrialized world fuels fears of climate change. |
| 1988 | An international conference in Toronto advocates 20 per cent cut in emissions by 2005. |
| 1990 | First IPCC report indicates that a 60 per cent cut in emissions is required to stabilize atmospheric concentrations. |
| 1991 | International negotiations commence. |
| 1992 | Climate Convention signed at Rio. |
| 1993 | Having been ratified, the Convention enters into force. |
| 1995 | Second IPCC report published. Suggests that humans are discernibly altering the climate. |
| 1995 | First meeting of the COP in Berlin adopts a 'mandate'. |
| 1996 | Second meeting of the COP in Geneva agrees to reduce emissions after 2000. |
| 1997 | Third COP in Kyoto to adopt a Protocol limiting emissions beyond 2000. |
| 2001 | IPCC to report; climate change expected to be identifiable and measurable. |

scientists about the seriousness of the problem (see Jäger and O'Riordan, 1996, for a review). Fifteen months later a framework document was agreed in time to be signed by world leaders at the conference. This was a remarkably short space of time given the complexity of the problem and the enormous political and scientific uncertainties involved (Mintzer and Leonard, 1996). In many respects, climate change is the ultimate environmental problem: the time scales involved go well beyond the normal electoral cycle; the activities which produce global warming are central to modern life; all countries are implicated, although some have a greater responsibility than others. Compromises and trade-offs are required over these and a whole mass of other issues for progress to be made. For leaders in a country such as the USA, which is the world's largest emitter, the dilemmas surrounding the problem are enormous: most loss of life is *predicted* to occur in the developing world, while cuts in emissions are almost certain to threaten jobs in domestic fossil-fuel industries; predictions of a multi-billion-dollar business in alternative technologies are at best speculative, while the current lobbying efforts of the fossil-fuel lobbies are intensive and carefully targeted. Critics were quick to point out that the price of consensus was an agreement stripped of binding commitments and timetables for compliance. The political reality, however, was that something had to be agreed in time for Rio: it would have been unthinkable to have had nothing for world leaders to sign.

So rather than the fixed commitment to reduce emissions of greenhouse gases sought by environmentalists, states agreed only to enact policies and programmes with the 'aim' individually or jointly of returning to their 1990 levels those emissions of anthropogenic greenhouse gases not controlled by the Montreal Protocol (e.g., CFCs and HCFCs) by the year 2000. The ultimate objective was 'the stabilization of greenhouse gas concentrations in the atmosphere at a level that prevents dangerous anthropogenic interference with the climate system'. The key word is *dangerous*. At the moment scientists disagree about what is a dangerous level of climate change, although the Convention implies it is a level which prevents ecosystems adapting naturally, which does not threaten food production and which enables economic development to proceed in a sustainable manner (Parry *et al.*, 1996).

Industrialized countries also undertook to meet the incremental costs incurred by developing countries in meeting their commitments under the Convention. Resource transfers are to be managed by the GEF. States also accepted the principle that industrialized countries could meet their commitments jointly with developing countries via a process of 'joint implementation'. This has commonly been interpreted to mean that industrialized countries can invest in developing countries (e.g., in forestry or energy efficiency measures) and claim 'credit' to offset their targets under the Convention. Supporters of joint implementation argue that it is economically efficient and politically advantageous to tie countries together, but its implementation has proved to be a political minefield, raising complex questions of sovereignty and legality. Meanwhile the exact meaning of the term 'incremental cost' was left tantalizingly open. However, in political and institutional terms, the term provides an important recognition that the overall responsibility for causing climate change is common but very clearly *differentiated*.

### Emission Targets: Hit and Miss?

Judged against the Intergovernmental Panel on Climate Change's (IPCC) earlier assessment (Houghton *et al.*, 1990) that a 60 per cent reduction in carbon dioxide emissions was necessary simply to stabilize atmospheric concentrations in the atmosphere, the commitments made at Rio did indeed seem extremely cautious and limited. But optimists felt that through a process of continuous negotiation and re-consideration a more cohesive regime could be constructed. On the face of it, progress since Rio has been encouraging. The Convention was adopted and fully ratified in December 1993, a remarkably short space of time for a treaty of its scope (Bodansky, 1995). New advisory bodies have been formed and a Secretariat has been established in Bonn. Most signatory countries have produced detailed plans covering their emission reduction strategies as demanded by the Convention and small amounts of new money have begun to flow through the GEF, although not without controversy.

Economic recession in many parts of the industrialized world in the mid-1990s has severely dented the enthusiasm for tighter controls displayed before and during Rio. Yet, ironically, it has also assisted some countries in their attempts to reduce emissions. However, unless immediate steps are taken the EU, several other European countries and in all probability the USA, Canada and New Zealand will fail to stabilize emissions and many will overshoot, some spectacularly so. Even well-renowned 'leaders' in the environmental field such as Norway and Finland look set to break their promises unless they institute immediate measures to address the problem. In early 1996, for example, Sweden decided to double a tax on carbon first introduced in 1990, although it will be accompanied by an offsetting reduction in other taxes to keep the measure revenue-neutral. Meanwhile, recent estimates by the Commission, based on returns from the Member States of the EU, suggest that the Community may overshoot by as much as 5 per cent, although others suggest it may be much higher (CEC, 1996). The situation would have been much worse had not the two largest emitters – Germany and the UK – achieved substantial cuts largely as a result of accidental 'one-off' events: in Germany's case the incorporation of the former East Germany and in Britain's, the collapse of the domestic coal industry and the 'dash' for less-polluting gas power stations (O'Riordan and Jäger, 1996). Crippled by squabbles about internal burden-sharing and the competence of Community institutions, the EU has yet to show that it can summon the political will to bridge the likely gap. Repeated attempts by the Commission to introduce a carbon tax have been consistently blocked by Member States and the energy industry, whose lobby was reported to have been 'probably the most powerful offensive against an EC proposal' (*The Economist*, 9 May 1991, p. 91).

Meanwhile, global $CO_2$ emissions continue to increase. Although future emission scenarios are notoriously inaccurate, 'best estimates' suggest emissions 15 to 20 per cent higher in 2000 than in 1990 and as much as 42 per cent higher by 2010, with more than half the total emissions originating in the developed world (International Energy Agency, 1995). Behind these trends lies a deeper sense of political unwillingness to address the proximate source of greenhouse gases, fossil-fuel use, that is such a mainstay of western lifestyles. The industrialized world has still to address seriously the problem of rising emissions from the transport sector, or to take steps to improve the efficiency of energy use. For most governments, the problem is perceived to be too far in the future to warrant expensive and politically painful action, in spite of constantly made claims that climate change offers an opportunity to improve the efficiency of energy use, promote new technologies and reduce the dependency on ultimately finite stocks of fossil fuel. These are the elusive 'win-win' strategies advocated by the World Bank.

## Re-assessing Commitments – Negotiations in the COP

Be that as it may, the focus of debate is increasingly on prospects beyond 2000, including the introduction of cuts and the equity question of when and how far commitments should be extended to developing countries, which continue to hold an enormous potential for growth in emissions. Portents of how the debate on these two most crucial of issues will develop emerged at the first full meeting of the Conference of the Parties in Berlin in March 1995; the first opportunity to review, assess and re-negotiate measures after Rio. In the event, countries agreed that something more should be done but conspicuously failed to decide on what it should be. As the host, Germany, with support from a number of EU Member States, pressed for substantive new commitments embodied in a binding protocol, while the Alliance of Small Island States (AOSIS), who are most susceptible to flooding should sea levels rise, surprised no one by calling for 20 per cent cuts by 2005. A compromise in the form of a broad 'mandate' agreed at Berlin admits that existing commitments are inadequate and commits the parties to 'begin a process to enable [them] to take appropriate action for the period beyond 2000, including the strengthening of the commitments' of industrialized countries. It is generally assumed that this will culminate in the signing of a protocol at the third Conference of the Parties in 1997; there is no assurance that it will be. Set against the high hopes of Rio, the outcome was indeed disappointing. Despite three years of negotiation, the only agreement in the international community was the need for further discussion. Realists, however, pointed out that this is the way international summitry proceeds, particularly on such a complex and divisive problem as global warming. Given the slump in public interest and the persistent chorus of dissenting voices on climate change (Beckerman, 1995; North, 1995; Emsley, 1996), some saw the mandate as being 'quite an accomplishment' (Rowlands, 1995).

At Berlin a coalition of greener developing countries moved from the largely non-committal position adopted at Rio, to side with the AOSIS proposal (Rowlands, 1995). They also firmly refused to promise to accept any new commitments, on the grounds that the problem was and remains one for the industrialized world to deal with. The once-united G77 coalition was left in tatters, with the oil-producing states of the Middle East isolated in their opposition to any advance on the position adopted at Rio. Disagreements even prevented the adoption of procedural rules on voting within the COP. The vast majority of developing countries led by India, however, now believe that climate change is a problem and not a veiled attempt by the North to limit their development or erect trade barriers. The point has been made more eloquently by Tariq Osman Hyder (1992, p. 333):

> It is difficult for most of the developing countries to accept the proposition that they should enter into new commitments which would adversely bind them either now or later on, for the sake of a problem caused by the developed countries – who neither wish to equitably share the remaining emission reserves in the atmosphere, nor to share (even in a small way) the benefits and resources they have built up by plundering the world's greenhouse gas reservoir.

In many respects, the shifting canvas of coalitions, which are even more complicated in their geometry than in the period before Rio (Paterson and Grubb, 1992), reflects a gradual maturing of the debate and the fact that individual states are beginning to more accurately define their own positions within it rather than simply following the pack. The climate change issue is no longer (if it ever was) a North–South dichotomy as the Convention itself seems to imply, for there are now important differences within these two blocks (Grubb and Anderson, 1995). Industrialized states are becoming increasingly differentiated in terms of how they line up on the issue. Around these state positions revolve an increasingly variegated pattern of industrial lobbies, some of which have strong vested interests in promoting tighter controls. On the one hand is the powerful fossil-fuel lobby sailing under the banner of the Global Climate Coalition, which includes major oil and coal producers. On the other are those interests who stand to benefit from controls: renewable sources such as solar power, energy-efficiency industries and natural gas suppliers. The most recent entrant is the insurance industry, which, after much prodding by environmental groups, has recently emerged as a significant force for tighter controls.

However, the runes are that the international community will not resolve its internal political differences in time for the third COP in 1997. The developing countries are too suspicious and unsure about the issue to enter into more intensive negotiations, while the industrialized world still seems unwilling to make the necessary changes to place its energy strategies on more sustainable paths, especially as it becomes clearer that a significant number of countries will not meet even their present commitment. Yet at some point early in the next century the developing countries will have to commit themselves to some form of control to reciprocate the activities undertaken by the industrialized world. A successful climate regime demands trust between states and institutional mechanisms that are seen to be legitimate by all involved. At present, this is far from being the case.

The main hope lies in developments in the cognitive basis of the agreement informed, first and foremost, by the deliberations of the IPCC. Its Second Assessment Report, published in 1996, marks a watershed in the development of the climate regime. In it, scientists concluded that 'the balance of evidence suggests a discernible human influence on global climate' (IPCC, 1996). This statement represents a ground-swell of scientific opinion that climate change not only is occurring but is a threat. Much more scientific research is required to link shifting patterns of climate with specific impacts. The indications, however, are that a 50 per cent cut in current emissions is required to stabilize atmospheric concentrations at merely double their pre-industrial level.

The most recent round of talks took place in Geneva in July 1996. The meeting was vital because, without an agreement to adopt binding controls, a Protocol would not be ready in time for 1997. Despite strong lobbying by the fossil-fuel lobby, which tried to water down and obscure the main points in the latest IPCC report, states agreed to adopt binding limits and achieved significant overall reductions in greenhouse gas emissions, although they stopped short of specifying actual amounts and timescales. Key to the deal was a last-minute *volte-face* by the US government, which threw its weight behind the IPCC's findings. After five years of negotiation, it was a small move but possibly a decisive one. Very tough political decisions lie ahead in the industrialized countries, while scientists must come forward with a better idea of what constitutes a 'dangerous' level of change.

## The Convention on Biological Diversity: Conservationist Charter or Grand Bargain?

As in the case of the Climate Change Convention, the need for an international agreement on the conservation of biological diversity was driven by science rather than by an understanding of the economic and social ramifications of global changes. Since the Stockholm conference, there had been calls to move beyond the species-by-species approach of most existing agreements such as CITES (Convention on International Trade in Endangered Species of Wild Fauna and Flora). Although a number of different international and regional agreements were in existence prior to the Convention on Biological Diversity (CBD), they essentially constituted a piecemeal approach to addressing what was now considered a problem of global proportions requiring co-ordinated policy and action (McConnell, 1996). Their general tenet is that biodiversity is being lost on a global scale and at an alarming rate, such that the world is currently experiencing the highest rates of loss in planetary history, the so-called 'sixth mass extinction crisis' (Raup, 1988; Leakey and Lewin, 1996). However, there are sceptical views on the validity of scientific extrapolations of species extinction, such as those of Julian Simon (see Simon and Wildavsky, 1984; Myers and Simon, 1994), and the science of biodiversity is relatively immature. The term 'biodiversity' — an abbreviation of 'biological diversity' — has only become common parlance in the 1990s; it first reached a wide audience through the publication in 1988 by the US National Science Academy of an influential volume edited by E.O. Wilson, the Harvard entomologist and socio-biologist (Wilson, 1988). After Rio, UNEP co-ordinated a world-wide assessment and state-of-the art review which aimed to produce 'the IPCC of biodiversity' and resulted in the publication of the Global Biodiversity Assessment in 1995 (Heywood and Watson, 1995).

Despite this scientific effort, the scale and rate of loss of biodiversity remain uncertain. This uncertainty is exacerbated by the complexity of biodiversity as a concept — it covers genetic, species and ecosystem diversity. There are scale and disciplinary problems in the definition of the term and its measurement, even before effective strategies for conservation can be formulated (Brown *et al.*, 1993). And the different emphases on aspects of diversity reflect the political nature of the issue: what conservation priorities are chosen, and at what cost, depends entirely on the formulation of the term, as discussed below (and see Chapter 5).

## Negotiating the CBD: North–South Perspectives

Different interpretations of biodiversity and the 'biodiversity problem' were also crudely caricatured along North–South lines at the time of the Rio Summit. The North on the one hand viewed biodiversity conservation as being primarily concerned with the preservation of rare and endangered species and habitats, the major means of achieving this being the effective designation, implementation and enforcement of protected areas. The South, on the other hand, recognized the biodiversity problem to be essentially one of the erosion and overexploitation of genetic resources, and particularly the extraction of these resources from southern countries and their utilization by Northern industries. The North was seen to have profited for many centuries by exploiting Southern biodiversity and to have re-invested little of the huge profits it enjoyed (see Kloppenburg, 1988; Juma, 1989). While developing countries in tropical regions contain much of the world's remaining biological diversity, the developed countries are dependent on these sources of genetic material, because of the links to their agriculture and other systems. For example, 98 per cent of crop production in the USA is based on non-indigenous species (McNeely, 1988), and a recent survey of the UK agricultural research and development industry indicates that they need to replace 7 per cent of germplasm from new sources each year (Swanson, 1996). The means identified by Southern countries to overcome this erosion and overexploitation and hence to conserve biological resources were to strengthen first intellectual property rights, and second the terms on which genetic resources could be used and benefits shared. These two stances resulted in a carefully worded convention, again tackling a very complex issue and negotiated in a relatively short time (Johnson, 1993, p. 81). Fears that northern interests would produce a 'conservationist charter' were tempered by the inclusion in most clauses of the Convention of the phrase 'conservation and *sustainable use* of biodiversity and its components'.

An additional reason for the North–South divide at Rio and in the negotiations for the Convention on Biological Diversity centred on the responsibilities of developing countries. Most of the world's remaining biological diversity exists in developing countries (WCMC, 1992; Heywood and Watson, 1995). This is because species richness increases towards the equator, so that tropical areas generally have greater diversity than temperate regions, and because there are larger areas of relatively unmodified habitats in poorer countries. The protection of global biodiversity was therefore perceived as something which had to be undertaken within the tropical developing countries; hence these countries would bear the main costs. The issue of conservation in the CBD is thus implicitly one of offsetting 'development', so that developing countries would bear the cost of implementation, particularly in terms of development opportunities forgone. This is in contrast to the Climate Change Convention, where developing countries were not expected initially to take a leading role (Brenton, 1994).

## CBD Commitments

The CBD commits signatories to develop national plans for conservation and the sustainable use of biological diversity; to identify and monitor resources, especially those at risk, and to establish a system of protected areas where necessary. This includes, where applicable, respecting and preserving indigenous knowledge, innovations and practices. There are also clauses on research and training, on public education and awareness, on impact assessment and, very importantly, on access to genetic resources and technology. However, there is clear recognition of the social and economic development and poverty eradication priorities of the developing countries.

Perhaps the most controversial issue in the CBD – and that assumed to have prevented the US from signing at Rio – concerns intellectual property rights (IPRs) and access to genetic resources. This recognizes the sovereign rights of states over their natural resources and that authority to determine access to genetic resources rests with the national governments and is subject to national legislation. Further, the CBD stipulates (Article 15.7) that the results of research and development and the benefits arising from the commercial and other utilization of genetic resources must be shared in a fair and equitable way with the contracting party providing such resources.

Measures for the transfer of resources (both financial and technological) from developed to developing countries are agreed in Article 20.2:

> The developed countries Parties shall provide new and additional financial resources to enable developing country Parties to meet the agreed full incremental costs to them of implementing measures which fulfil the obligations of this convention and to benefit from its provisions and which costs are agreed between a developing country Party and the institutional structure referred to in Article 21.

The CBD provides a framework for negotiating a fair exchange between these two aspects, and aims to facilitate a more equitable sharing of the benefits of biodiversity exploitation between countries. Hence Reid *et al.* (1993) describe the CBD as setting the stage for a 'grand bargain'. Few 'grand bargains' have been undertaken to date, but this is an important future facilitating role for the Convention.

## Implementing the CBD – Developments in the COP

The CBD came into force in December 1993, and since then more than 140 countries have ratified the agreement. There have been two meetings of the Conferences of the Parties (COP). The first, in the Bahamas in November 1994, was concerned with establishing institutional mechanisms and procedures, and the second, in Jakarta in November 1995, concentrated on implementation (Bragdon, 1996). The decisions made include:

- a clearing-house mechanism should be established for scientific and technical co-operation that will encourage and facilitate exchange of relevant research and technology;
- a protocol on biosafety should be negotiated (see Munson, 1995);
- the GEF continues to serve as the interim funding mechanism, to survey measures taken by governments to regulate access to genetic resources under Article 15;
- the relationship between the CBD and the Uruguay Round agreement on Trade Related Aspects of Intellectual Property Rights (TRIPS) should be examined in conjunction with the secretariat of the World Trade Organization (WTO); and
- the possibility of co-ordinating the respective work programmes of the secretariats of other biodiversity-related conventions should be explored.

Amongst the issues yet to be resolved is that of forests, and whether they should be the subject of a protocol under the CBD. Tropical forests are the major repository of biodiversity globally, and moist tropical forests are the most species-rich ecosystems known. Given the failure to negotiate any kind of binding agreement on forests at Rio (the Statement of Forest Principles being the compromise document produced, but with no legal clout), there is much suspicion from forest-rich tropical countries, particularly Brazil and Malaysia, on what kind of international undertaking can be made. Provision of a protocol under the CBD would imply that the primary function of forests is for biodiversity conservation, and this is an anathema to countries who see economically productive forests and their harvest and conversion as the means to economic prosperity. The CSD has established an Intergovernmental Panel on Forests to explore the opportunities for international action, and this is due to report to the CSD in 1997. It looks increasingly unlikely that any binding international agreement will be forthcoming, although forests will remain on the agenda of the CBD. As Raustiala and Victor (1996, p. 42) comment, 'Failing to address forests within the CBD is akin to failing to address coal within the Convention on Climate Change'.

In addition, pressure from NGOs calling for a protocol to the CBD on agricultural biodiversity (agro-diversity) have also fallen by the wayside. The issue was negotiated at the Technical Conference on Plant Genetic Resources in mid-1996 and included in the International Undertaking produced from the meeting. Again no legally binding agreement looks likely. This issue is considered especially important by Southern NGOs, who want the role played by developing country farmers in managing and conserving biodiversity on their land acknowledged globally.

Many of the key issues concerning the implementation of the CBD centre on the resolution of intellectual property rights, encompassing a range of very contentious topics. These include *inter alia* the rights of traditional and indigenous people; patenting of life forms and genomes; and farmers' rights and plant breeders' rights. This has been voiced most publicly in concerns about the operation and implications of the Human Genome Diversity Project, referred to as the 'Human Vampire Project' by some NGOs after one programme which collects tribal peoples' blood for analysis of human genetic diversity. The IPR issue is therefore where the interests of the CBD and other international institutions both converge and diverge.

IPRs are also an issue upon which NGOs have focused. There is general agreement that the CBD does not go far enough and that the wording is at best ambiguous and at worst constitutes the 'biggest rip-off since 1492' (Crucible Group, 1994, p. 32). There are two main criticisms. First, the CBD does not cover *ex situ* gene-bank and botanical garden material collected before it came into force. Yet it is this material, which represents most of the genetic material currently known to exist, that is most likely to be commercialized in the near future. The second is the lack of clarification of Farmers' Rights and the apparent acceptance of an IPR system based on patents and copyright agreements, on similar lines to TRIPS. Such rights are based on the concept of novel discoveries by individuals or private companies, with the attendant commercial costs and finance that such action requires. They are thus biased against knowledge developed incrementally over the years and by different generations, or held collectively by communities or groups of people, so they do not recognize innovation by farmers in development of traditional crop varieties, or the use of plants with active alkaloids as drugs in traditional medicine. They therefore enable multinational companies with expertise in genetic engineering to take advantage of indigenous knowledge without paying for the commodity (see, for example, WWF, 1995).

As well as amplifying the dichotomy between North and South, and between traditional and indigenous groups and commercial interests, the provisions on access to genetic resources represent the tension between notions of sovereignty and recognition of common concerns (Imber, 1994, p. 60; Sánchez and Juma, 1994; Bragdon, 1996). Despite its recognition of a global concern for biodiversity loss, the CBD's provisions on access reaffirm a nation's sovereignty over these resources. This issue, of course, was central to the whole UNCED process and is being played out in each of the Rio agreements. This will continue in various international fora for years to come and forms one of the main stumbling-blocks to the successful transition to sustainable development.

Many of the impediments to the successful implementation of the CBD and how effective it will be in meeting its objectives can be traced to its lack of focus and the ambiguity of its wording. This ambiguity was considered necessary in order to ensure global acceptance and ratification. The treaty initially had a lukewarm reception from international legal and environmental groups (Raustiala and Victor, 1996), and there appears to be consensus that much work needs to be done to overcome these difficulties. There are persistent problems over the definition of biodiversity as such an all-encompassing concept, so that priority-setting is difficult because of the different hierarchical scales and the many competing different interests. These difficulties also mean that reporting and monitoring, to which Parties to the Convention are committed, are problematic, and complicate the allocation of funds. The current requirement to define 'incremental costs' of implementation in order to qualify for funding from the GEF is another controversial issue. Whilst incremental cost may be possible to define and quantify for climate change, there are many conceptual problems in applying it to biodiversity projects.

Whether the treaty can overcome these many problematic issues and avoid the endless conflicts experienced in some other international agreements remains to be seen. It requires not only a genuine commitment by the parties, but also skilled and experienced negotiators and diplomacy.

## Appraising Rio

This chapter has illustrated the four issues central to international co-operative action on sustainable development: equity; differential responsibility; sovereignty; and finance and funding. These form the basis of negotiation and dispute and are inherently not open to easy or simple 'solutions'. Equity issues have been largely sidelined in the agreements, although Agenda 21 and other Rio documents have highlighted equitable treatment of minorities and marginalized groups and nations. However, indicators of poverty remain as skewed as in the last decade and the gap between the world's richest and poorest nations, and in many countries the gap between the haves and the have-nots, is ever widening. Between 1960 and 1989, the share of global GNP of the countries with the richest 20 per cent of the world population grew from 70 per cent to 73 per cent, while the share of the countries with the poorest 20 per cent fell from 2.3 per cent to just 1.2 per cent (UNDP, 1992). The UNDP's latest Human Development Report (UNDP, 1996) indicates that the situation continues to worsen. In 1996, 1.6 million people in 100 countries had a lower standard of living than in the 1980s, while the wealth of the world's 358 billionaires is greater than the combined annual incomes of the nearly half the world's people; in 70 countries average incomes are less than they were in 1980, and in 43 less than in 1970. Overall economic growth failed for a quarter of the world's population, while a dozen or so Asian countries experienced a dramatic surge in growth. Two million children die of intestinal diseases due to unclean water each year (World Bank, 1992)

The experience of the Climate Change Convention has highlighted the difficulties in implementing the principle of 'common but differentiated responsibility'. Although some industrialized countries are leading the way in urging reductions in greenhouse gas emissions, many others do not accept their responsibility even to comply with the Convention which they have ratified. The consequences of these actions are already apparent, with the geographical distribution of impacts of climate change so unevenly distributed that those areas of the world least able to cope are likely to be hardest hit. Within these areas, people already impoverished and marginalized are also most vulnerable to adverse impacts of climate change.

Although attitudes to sovereignty have eased somewhat since the polarized debates of the early 1970s, sovereignty issues were highlighted in particular under the Biodiversity Convention. There has been a definite shift in the agenda of the CBD since Rio towards those aspects of the world's biodiversity of direct benefit to nations with diverse biological resources and which are more directly dependent on them. But the conflicts between the CBD and the WTO rules are prime examples of how sovereignty issues are overruled by the drive for economic growth. A definitive and widely adopted interpretation of Farmers' Rights is necessary in order to reverse the current trend towards a wholesale adoption of the TRIPS model. Concerns about sovereignty remain central to ongoing debates about divisive issues such as population growth, consumption patterns and resource use (particularly in the North).

So how then should we appraise Rio? Much depends on what was expected of it. Clearly the world's environmental and development problems cannot be solved at costly and cumbersome international conferences, even high-profile ones like the UNCED. Some see the environmental crisis as symptomatic of a deeper crisis in the international political system, which is still organized around independent nation-states. For Hurrell (1994, p. 146), the fundamental problem is that the nation-state is at once 'too big for the task of devising viable strategies of sustainable development which can only be developed from the bottom up ... and too small for the effective management of global problems ... which by their nature demand increasingly wide-ranging forms of international co-operation.' Thomas (1993, p. 24), for example, cogently observes that states are themselves limited in their *capacity* to bring about changes in a rapidly globalizing world economy. Hopes of implementing the Climate Convention will be strongly affected by shifts in the global economy. Although sustainable development carries responsibilities for powerful organizations like the Catholic Church, the IMF, the GATT and NATO, not to mention trans-national business corporations, none of them were legally bound by anything agreed at Rio. At the same time, the state is seen as too large to deal effectively with the challenge of sustainability at the local level, involving local communities and knowledge systems.

If Rio was expected merely to raise awareness, generate public concern and capture the world's attention, then it would be fair to declare the event a success. Hurrell (1994) believes that it helped to strengthen attitudes to environmental protection and, however varied the level of public concern, 'it is now very difficult to imagine environmental concerns disappearing completely from the agenda of governments'. Through the signing of Conventions and Protocols, states have helped to weave environmental issues into the legal and institutional fabric of international society. The world has at least begun to make a start on translating the fine words of the Brundtland Report into concrete institutional structures. If nothing else, Rio defined a lot more clearly the issues and disagreements still to be addressed.

But others, and not just committed environmentalists, hoped for much more – new diplomatic and financial mechanisms for solving shared problems, and an equitable and sustainable new international order (Hecht and Cockburn, 1992; Middleton *et al.*, 1993; Thomas, 1993). Politicians were not prepared to make such commitments, although they initiated a number of cautious and potentially far-reaching reforms. On this analysis, the Rio event inevitably tinkered at the margins of a much bigger set of problems. What emerged was not the 'spirit of global partnership' mentioned in the Rio Declaration, nor indeed measures which recognize that the world does in fact share a 'Common Future' born of increasing and more complex forms of global interdependence, but national defensiveness – Hardin's 'lifeboat' writ large:

> The rich and powerful will simply not simply cede their advantages, nor will the force majeure of a wounded environment compel change, because catastrophe will be cumulative and strike in little bits. The rich world with its obsessive concern with immigration controls is already reacting to the pressures exerted by an increasingly impoverished South and will dig in yet further. Once again the process will be gradual, but inexorably a fortified and isolated developed world is emerging. (Middleton *et al.*, 1993, p. 10)

At the root of many of these problems is the deep chasm that separates the short-term interests of the developed and the developing states. For many, Rio merely reaffirmed the South's suspicion that the North was not prepared to redefine the international division of labour or its economic, social and political relationship with the rest of the world. The governments of the North can sell the idea of small increases of aid for global environmental assistance to their electorates, but changes which strike at the Western lifestyle or impinge upon individual freedoms will be far more unpopular, even politically suicidal. In contrast, implementing sustainable development will be a far more tortuous and challenging task: intellectually challenging because it is still difficult to envision the structural form of a sustainable society; scientifically challenging, because there are enormous uncertainties in defining and measuring sustainability; but most of all politically challenging, because it questions the existing geopolitical *status quo*. Any transition from non-sustainable to sustainable development will imply an enormous change in the distribution of winners and losers in society – for this reason Johnston (1989, p. 199) considers that it will *never* be a viable item on the international agenda. Of course, this assumes a basic level of agreement on what is being sought: i.e., sustainable development. In fact the very ambiguity of the term helps to paper over enormous differences of perceptions within and between different social groups. As Lele (1991, p. 613) notes:

> Sustainable development is a 'meta-fix' that will unite everybody from the profit-minded industrialist and risk minimising subsistence farmer to the equity seeking social worker, the pollution concerned or wildlife loving First Worlder, the growth maximising policy maker, the goal oriented bureaucrat and, therefore, the vote counting politician.

With the above in mind, some of the conflicts and contentions which arose at the UNCED become slightly more easy to interpret: the disjunction between the fine words of the Rio declaration and Agenda 21, and the unwillingness of the North to make wholesale adjustments to the international systems of trade and finance, or to produce significant quantities of new money; the contrast between the donor-dominated and well-funded GEF and the relatively lowly and toothless Commission on Sustainable Development; the agreement to make modest changes to the governance of the GEF set against a deep resistance to democratize the rest of the Bretton Woods organizations. All of this suggests that the world may have done something for the global environment at Rio, but it did very little to shift the engine of worldwide development onto a more sustainable track. Many of the morally important principles enshrined in the Rio agreements are therefore essentially undermined by the structure of the global economy, by the drive for economic growth, which is recognized in Agenda 21 as the prime contributor to unsustainability, and by the reluctance of the industrialized countries to provide additional financing. Whether these impediments can be overcome or whether they will eclipse any hopes of success for the wider agenda of sustainability – as promoted by the Brundtland Commission and enshrined in Agenda 21 – will be seen in the next few years. The reports to the CSD in 1997 may give us an insight into progress so far.

# References

Beckerman, W. (1995) *Small Is Stupid*. London: Duckworth.

Bodansky, D. (1993) The UN Framework Convention on Climate Change: a commentary. *Yale Journal of International Law*, **18**(2), 451–558.

Bodansky, D. (1995) The emerging climate regime. *Annual Review of Energy and the Environment*, **20**, 425–61.

Bragdon (1996) The United Nations Convention on Biological Diversity. *Global Environmental Change*, **6**(2), 177–9.

Brenton, A. (1994) *The Greening of Machiavelli: The Evolution of International Environmental Politics*. London: RIIA and Earthscan.

Brown, K., Pearce, D.W., Perrings, C. and Swanson, T. (1993) *Economics and the Conservation of Global Biological Diversity*. Working Paper No. 2. Washington, DC: Global Environment Facility.

CEC (1996) *Second Evaluation of National Programmes under the Monitoring Mechanism of Community CO2 and Other Greenhouse Gas Emissions*. COM (96) 91, 14 March 1996.

Crucible Group (1994) *People, Plants and Patents*. Ottawa: IDRC.

Emsley, J. (ed.) (1996) *The Global Warming Debate*. Bournemouth: Bourne Press.

Galbraith, J.K. (1958) *The Affluent Society*. London: Hamish Hamilton.

Gordon, J. (1994) Letting the genie out: local government and the UNCED. *Environmental Politics*, **2**(4), 137–55.

Grubb, M. and Anderson, D. (eds) (1995) *The Emerging International Regime for Climate Change*. London: Earthscan.

Grubb, M., Koch, M., Munson, A., Sullivan, F. and Thomson, K. (1993) *The Earth Summit Agreements: A Guide and Assessment*. London: Earthscan and RIIA.

Hecht, S. and Cockburn, A. (1992) Realpolitik, reality and rhetoric in Rio. *Environment and Planning D*, **10**, 367–75.

Henry, R. (1996) Adapting UN agencies for Agenda 21. *Environmental Politics*, **5**(1), 1–24.

Heywood, V. and Watson, R. (eds) (1995) *Global Biodiversity Assessment*. Cambridge: Cambridge University Press.

Holmberg, J., Thomson, K. and Timberlake, L. (1993) *Facing the Future: Beyond the Earth Summit*. London: Earthscan.

Houghton, J.T., Jenkins, G.J. and Ephraums, J.J. (eds.) (1990) *Climate Change: The IPCC Scientific Assessment*. Cambridge: Cambridge University Press.

Hurrell, A. (1994) A crisis of ecological viability? Global environmental change and the nation state. *Political Studies*, **42**, 146–65.

Hyder, T.O. (1992) Climate negotiations: the North/South perspective. In I. Mintzer (ed.), *Confronting Climate Change*. Cambridge: Cambridge University Press.

Imber, M.F. (1994) *Environmental Security and UN Reform*. London: Macmillan.

Intergovernmental Panel on Climate Change (1996) *Climate Change 1995: Scientific Assessment: Summary for Policy Makers*. Geneva: IPCC.

International Energy Agency (1995) *World Energy Outlook*. Paris: IEA.

Jäger, J. and O'Riordan, T. (1996) The history of climate change science and politics. In T. O'Riordan and J. Jäger (eds), *Politics of Climate Change*. London: Routledge, pp. 1–31.

Johnson, S. (1993) *The Earth Summit*. London: Graham and Trotman.

Johnston, R. (1989) *Nature, Economy and State*. Chichester: John Wiley.

Jordan, A.J. (1994a) Financing the UNCED agenda: the controversy over additionality. *Environment*, **36**(3), 16–20 and 26–34.

Jordan, A.J. (1994b) The politics of incremental cost financing: the evolving role of the Global Environment Facility. *Environment*, **36**(6), 12–20 and 31–36.

Jordan, A.J. and Werksman, J. (1995) Financing global environmental protection. In J. Cameron, J. Werksman and P. Roderick (eds), *Improving Compliance with International Environmental Law*. London: Earthscan.

Juma, C. (1989) *The Gene Hunters: Biotechnology and the Scramble for Seeds*. London: Zed Books/Princeton, NJ: Princeton University Press.

Kloppenburg, J.R., Jr (1988) *First the Seed: The Political Economy of Plant Biotechnology 1492–2000*. Cambridge: Cambridge University Press.

Leakey, R. and Lewin, R. (1996) *The Sixth Extinction: Biodiversity and Its Survival*. London: Weidenfeld and Nicolson.

Lele, S. (1991) Sustainable development: a critical review. *World Development*, **19**(6), 607–21.

McConnell, F. (1996) *The Biodiversity Convention: A Negotiating History*. The Hague: Kluwer International.

McNeely, J.A. (ed.) (1988) *Economics and Conservation of Biodiversity: Developing and Using Economic Incentives*. Gland, Switzerland: IUCN.

MacNeill, J., Winsemius, P. and Yakushiji, T. (1991) *Beyond Interdependence: The Meshing of the World's Economy and the Earth's Ecology*. Oxford: Oxford University Press.

Middleton, N., O'Keefe, P. and Moyo, S. (1993) *Tears of the Crocodile: From Rio to Reality in the Developing World*. London: Pluto Press.

Mintzer, I. and Leonard, J. (1996) *Negotiating Climate Change: The Inside Story of the Rio Convention*. Cambridge: Cambridge University Press.

Munson, A. (1995) Should a biosafety protocol be negotiated as part of the Biodiversity Convention? *Global Environmental Change*, **5**(1), 7–26.

Myers, N. and Simon, J. L. (1994) *Scarcity or Abundance? A Debate on the Environment*. New York: W.W. Norton.

North, R. (1995) *Life on a Modern Planet*. Manchester: Manchester University Press.

O'Riordan, T. and Jäger, J. (eds) (1996) *Politics of Climate Change*. London: Routledge.

Parry, M., Carter, T. and Hulme, M. (1996) What is dangerous climate change? *Global Environmental Change*, **6**(1), 1–6.

Paterson, M. and Grubb, M. (1992) The international politics of climate change. *International Affairs*, **68**, 293–310.

Raustiala, K. and Victor, D.G. (1996) Biodiversity since Rio: the future of the Convention on Biological Diversity. *Environment* **38** (April), 17–20 and 37–45.

Raup, D.M. (1988) Diversity crises in the geological past. In E.O. Wilson (ed.), *Biodiversity*. Washington, DC: National Academy Press, pp. 51–7.

Reid, W.V., Laird, S.A., Meyer, C.A., Gamez, R., Sittenfeld, A., Janzen, D., Gollin, M. and Juma, C. (1993) *Biodiversity Prospecting: Using Genetic Resources for Sustainable Development*. Washington, DC: World Resources Institute.

Rich, B. (1994) *Mortgaging the Earth*. London: Earthscan.

Rowlands, I. (1995) *The Climate Negotiations: Berlin and Beyond*. The Centre for the Study of Global Governance, Discussion Paper 17. London: London School of Economics.

Sánchez, V. and Juma, C. (1994) *Biodiplomacy: Genetic Resources and International Relations*. Nairobi: Acts Press.

Simon, J.L. and Wildavsky, A. (1984) On species loss, the absence of data, and risks to humanity. In J.L. Simon and H. Kahn (eds), *The Resourceful Earth*. Oxford: Blackwell.

Swanson, T. (1996) The reliance of northern economies in southern biodiversity: biodiversity as information. *Ecological Economics*, **17**(1), 1–8.

Thomas, C. (1993) Rio: unravelling the consequences. *Environmental Politics*, special issue.

UNDP (1992) *The Human Development Report*. Oxford: Oxford University Press.

UNDP (1996) *The Human Development Report*. Oxford: Oxford University Press.

United Nations (1992) *Convention on Biological Diversity*. Nairobi: UNEP.

Victor, D. and Salt, J. (1994) From Rio to Berlin ... managing climate change. *Environment*, **36**(10), 6–15 and 22–32.

von Moltke, K. (1992) The United Nations development system and environmental management. *World Development*, **20**(4), 619–26.

von Moltke, K. (1996) Why UNEP matters. In H. Bergesen and G. Parman (eds), *Green Globe Yearbook 1996*. Oxford: Oxford University Press.

Wilson, E.O. (1988) *Biodiversity*. Washington, DC: National Academy Press.

World Bank, (1992) *World Development Report*. Washington, DC: World Bank.

World Commission on Environment and Development (WCED) (1987) *Our Common Future*. Oxford: Oxford University Press.

World Conservation Monitoring Centre (WCMC) (1992) *Global Biodiversity: Status of the Earth's Living Resources*. London: Chapman and Hall.

World Wide Fund for Nature (WWF) (1995) *The UN Biodiversity Convention and the WTO TRIPS Agreement*. Gland, Switzerland: WWF.

## 14

# Sustainable Development: Taking Stock

## Richard M. Auty and Katrina Brown

The chapters in this volume attest to the complexity of devising and implementing policies to achieve sustainable development. The weak sustainability approach, as outlined for example in the 1992 World Development Report (World Bank, 1992), has proved too sanguine. That approach assumes, in effect, that the flow of scientific information on the environment will inform a rational policy debate which will, in turn, lead to actions that bring about appropriate adjustments in prices so that they more accurately reflect the relative scarcity of factors of production (including environmental services). It anticipates that rapid improvements in sustainability will come initially from behavioural adjustments to the new prices, and more long-term, from the design of resource-conserving technology whose incorporation into the capital stock will bring further environmental improvements.

In practice, it has proved difficult to implement each of the three principal steps which the weak green approach prescribes (indeed, many scholars conclude that the weak green approach is too flawed to provide a useful starting-point for such an exercise in the first place). First, in the absence of scientific data which are beyond reasonable dispute, agreement over the appropriate policy response is difficult to achieve. Under these circumstances, sceptical negotiators on environmental issues are likely to find it all too easy to postpone unwelcome changes, especially if the groups which they represent must bear a substantial part of the adjustment costs. Second, the philosophical debate about the purposes of sustainable development compounds the problems of reaching a policy consensus that arise from the resistance of those adversely affected by policy changes at all levels (global, regional, national and local). There are also difficult conflicts to resolve between the various tiers of government. Third, even after an agreed environmental policy has been thrashed out, policy instruments must be designed which can ensure that the policy objectives can be achieved. Moreover, whatever policy instruments are selected, adequate resources must be secured for their effective implementation, something which the low-income countries have found especially problematic (as, for example, revealed in the discussion of industrial pollution in Uganda and Kenya in Chapter 11).

The remainder of this chapter draws upon the insights provided by the authors of this book, supplemented where appropriate by other sources, in order to explore the obstacles to the successful implementation of sustainable development. More specifically, the chapter discusses: the incorporation of physical parameters into the analysis of sustainable development (including the problems of quantifying 'environmental services'); the institutional mechanisms for achieving an informed consensus on policy (such as the bottom-up strategies for political empowerment); and ways of implementing policies, especially in the low-income countries (of South Asia, sub-Saharan Africa and the transitional economies of southeast Asia).

## Incorporating Physical Parameters

Much of the scepticism over sustainable development of critics like Beckerman arises from exaggerated claims of the imminence of environmental catastrophe and, therefore, of the importance of environmental issues compared with other welfare concerns. Beckerman reports that ill-informed and irresponsible claims prompted both his major sorties into the environmental debate, first in the early 1970s and again in the mid-1990s (see Beckerman, 1974 and 1995, respectively). Such exaggeration thrives where information is inadequate, as is the case with a whole range of environmental concerns from the rate of global deforestation to the magnitude and causes of climatic change. A clear example at the micro level has been provided in Chapter 5 with reference to the changing characterization of ecosystem dynamics.

To Beckerman (1995), global climate change over the next century can be seen as a minor constraint on development (a matter of 'putting on a lighter shirt'), whereas to others it is a major catastrophe. The disagreements between these two extremes are based on perceptions and analysis of such phenomena as adaptation and resilience, as well as policy responsiveness. These phenomena are informed by analysis at the micro level and are further informed not by a set of inalienable laws, but by historical analysis. Yet the scenarios of global-scale impacts are also dependent on projections of global population trends and rates of economic growth which are notoriously unreliable, as Timothy Dyson warns in making his projections of food consumption and supply for South Asia in Chapter 6. Such projections are also susceptible to fashions in modelling and the modes of analysis (see Rosenweig and Parry, 1994; Homewood, 1995; Pittock, 1995).

A comprehensive range of physical measurements is still, therefore, required which will help to quantify the degree of real concern so that policy-makers can draw up appropriate goals and then specify meaningful targets for achieving improvements (World Bank, 1995). In Chapter 2 of this book, Kirk Hamilton demonstrates the potential utility of genuine saving as an index of progress towards sustainability. But in illustrating his thesis with reference to natural capital consumption, he is forced by data limitations to use estimates about the value of mineral resources (and, therefore, of natural asset consumption) which, when set against the data for Chile and Jamaica presented by Richard Auty in Chapter 10, appear to be considerably over-estimated. Auty shows how the different approaches to estimating mineral asset depletion produce very different results, underlining the difficulty of drawing policy conclusions in the absence of agreement on the most appropriate index.

The two mineral economy case studies in Chapter 10 also show the difficulty of estimating the extent to which the mining sector's use of environmental services can be quantified and valued. Similar problems are identified by James Winpenny in Chapter 3, who notes a plethora of approaches to measuring the value of water and a disconcerting lack of standardization. There is clearly scope for physical geographers, ecologists, economists and other specialists to co-operate in the definition and measurement of more specific environmental indices.

There are also sharp divisions of opinion over whether such environ-mental indices are most appropriately addressed in monetary or non-monetary terms. A compromise might be to make use of both sets of indicators. For example, attempts to measure land resources as part of an assessment of the distribution of natural capital have used not only the commercial value of land but also a natural capital index (NCI) which is applied to value non-commercial land. The NCI is derived by multiplying the area of 'natural' (undeveloped) land by an index of biodiversity. Composite estimates of natural capital suggest that monetary and non-monetary measures perform complementary, rather than competing, functions. For example, whereas conventional monetary accounting fails to include biodiversity (unlike the NCI), the NCI excludes the subsoil assets (minerals, for example) which are included by monetary approaches (World Bank, 1995).

Using such measurements, preliminary attempts have been made to measure the distribution of global wealth. The findings carry important policy implications but their utility is once more blunted by disputes over the appropriateness of the methodology used. A recent study (World Bank, 1995) claims to confirm that traditional approaches have overstated the role of produced capital and neglected natural capital. More surprisingly, it points to the very great importance which human capital contributes to wealth (two-thirds at the global level). As Chapter 2 in this book notes, human capital has received even less attention in the sustainability research agenda than the measurement and valuation of environmental services.

Meanwhile, in discussing measurement of the principal forms of capital, the World Bank (1995) notes the existence of a fourth category (along with produced, natural and human capital) – social infrastructure, which according to the Bank is even more neglected. This is described as the 'institutional and cultural bases required for a society to function'. The definition and measurement of social infrastructure capital does indeed present a major challenge but it is one which disciplines like sociology, politics and anthropology have long been deeply concerned with. Such 'discoveries' underline the importance of inter-disciplinary research.

## Institutional Mechanisms for Policy Formulation

A common complaint levelled by environmental critics at the evolving global economy concerns the overbearing role of science and, more especially, of the solutions for environmental problems proposed by its practitioners (Norgaard, 1994). One frequently cited example of this excessive faith in science has been the way governments of developing countries dismiss the environmental wisdom accumulated by peasant farmers and pastoralists. Disdain for traditional approaches was initially associated with colonial regimes but was often perpetuated by newly independent governments. In Chapter 7 Oriel Kenny has documented one such instance with reference to pastoralists in the Marsabit region of Kenya. She describes how colonial and post-colonial central government intervention undermined traditional practices and prevented what was an inherently flexible system from adapting through its own efforts to growing population pressure. The result, in Oriel Kenny's view, is an outcome which is anything but sustainable.

Such disappointing policy outcomes, when coupled with the inability of many governments (notably in sub-Saharan Africa and Latin America) to cope adequately with the proliferation of tasks which they assumed through the 1960s and 1970s, has created the necessity and opportunity for a fresh start. Participatory approaches are proposed which 'empower' people at the grassroots level and provide a 'bottom-up' approach to environmental and other development issues. The NGOs are seen as a vital catalyst for the diffusion of this approach. The insight into rural livelihoods provided elsewhere (Chapter 4) underlines the difficulties of trying to evolve effective institutions which can not only accommodate the wide range of divergent interests, but do so without seriously impairing the essential flexibility of response to severe and mounting pressures for change.

Case studies at the national and sub-national level stress the need for new institutions if sustainable development is to operationalized. In the case of

Nepal, for example, two chapters (5 and 8) focus on the role of institutions in supporting the conservation of biodiversity. The case of the Annapurna Conservation Area Project (ACAP), described in Chapter 8, shows how efforts to conserve the natural resources of the mountains, the main tourist attraction (and thus important in maintaining the tourism industry, the largest generator of foreign exchange in the country), can also be combined with supporting local people's livelihoods. Indeed the ACAP is implemented on the basis that only by involving local people and giving them a stake in conservation will such a project be in any way sustainable. Yet a dilemma is noted in regard to the ACAP as to when the instigators of participatory change should withdraw. As Oriel Kenny notes (Chapter 7) with reference to the Marsabit pastoralists, if agencies remain too long they risk embedding a culture of dependency, a risk which is readily recognized by mining firms in Jamaica and Chile.

In Chapter 9 Philip O'Brien describes two of the more ambitious attempts to build new institutions at a national level. The Colombian approach is strongly prescriptive in character and seeks to implement some of the policies which are part of the 'spirit of UNCED'. O'Brien reports some promising signs, in both Colombia and Costa Rica, in terms of the compromises reached between the central government and various 'minority' interests and the readiness of a wide range of pressure groups to be involved. But although the re-routing of a large hydrocarbon pipeline in Colombia is hailed as an instance of the ability to ensure that major projects can be forced to take full note of environmental and social concerns, the experience of PNG warns how quickly severe conflicts *within* initially successful grassroots coalitions can quickly develop (Duncan *et al.*, 1995). Moreover, the enormous amounts of time which participants must put into the environmental negotiations is emerging as a major limitation of the approach. It is still too early as yet to evaluate the viability of these approaches to empowerment and their utility for other countries.

Other local-level analyses of institutions highlight the role of property rights. Chapters 5 and 7 show that complex property rights have frequently evolved to manage diverse resources in dynamic environments, and that just as often neither state nor private regimes have the flexibility required to utilize biological resources in a sustainable manner. In addition, these two studies demonstrate that government policies are often based on rather simplistic assumptions about the functioning of fragile ecosystems and the role of human intervention. Such assumptions are now being challenged within ecological and biological science, with new insights which stress processes such as resilience and adaptation of different ecosystems and their components. Individual land management and resource utilization strategies are often adapted to the variability of such systems. However, that is not to say that all that is 'traditional' is necessarily good or sustainable. With changes in the wider political and economic – and perhaps also the physical –

environment, flexible approaches are needed which can build on the best of both local, and outside, experience and knowledge.

Such policy-making problems manifest themselves at a global level as well as the grassroots. Chapter 13 reviews how tensions which were apparent at the UNCED in 1992 have been played out as the institutions and agreements initiated at Rio are implemented. The key issues – the push for economic growth versus environmental concerns; national sovereignty against global interests; inter- and intra-generational equity; responsibility and financing – are gradually being addressed within the different agreements and institutions. It remains to be seen whether any effective progress towards sustainable development can be achieved through such means, but the need for international co-ordinated efforts to address pressing transboundary problems is none the less necessary.

## Implementation Problems

Even when agreed policies have been formulated and given the required legal backing, their execution may still encounter formidable problems. For example, strongly centralized governments like those of the former centrally planned economies, now re-designated the 'transitional economies', have encountered acute problems in seeking to move towards sustainable development. The basic fear is that the state, in seeking to accelerate economic growth by attracting foreign direct investment, will neglect local interests, including a wide range of environmental concerns. In Chapter 12, Tim Forsyth notes how environmental concerns have augmented the long-running and deep-seated political tensions between regional governments and the central government in such economies.

Elsewhere, rainforest management provides another illustration of implementation problems. This is one issue (like pollution monitoring) in which the scale and nature of the terrain requiring surveillance, whether in Papua New Guinea or the Amazon, calls for more substantial financial resources than have tended to be forthcoming. There is also the risk that if policing programmes are underfunded, the officials involved may abuse their authority in order to augment their incomes and thereby make a grave situation worse. Ironically, such a disappointing outcome may sow the seeds of a solution: for example, Philip O'Brien attributes part of the Colombian enthusiasm for a national participatory approach to environmental issues to a reaction against the problems created by the drug trade.

But effective policy implementation also calls for a knowledge of household dynamics. Policies which range from promoting agricultural change in sub-Saharan Africa to compensating farmers for the social and environmental disruption caused by mining in Irian Jaya have proved disappointing because they have tended to ignore the effects of social obligations and household survival strategies. John Cameron has shown in

Chapter 4 how policies which are targeted at specific sectors can run into unexpected obstacles which emanate from the diversity of income sources of the hard-pressed rural resident. Yet the existence of such complex livelihoods only serves to reinforce the wisdom of involving grassroots communities in policy formulation – and of securing a sound understanding of environmental processes.

The chapters in this book document the halting and differentiated progress which has been made in moving from the diagnosis of environmental problems to both prescription and remedy. They highlight the need to monitor the diverse range of institutional and policy experiments currently under way and they also stress the role which multi-level, cross-cultural, interdisciplinary research must play in interpreting the results of such experiments and in distilling the appropriate policy lessons from them.

# References

Beckerman, W. (1974) *In Defence of Economic Growth*. London: Jonathan Cape.

Beckerman, W. (1995) *Small Is Stupid: Blowing the Whistle on the Greens*. London: Duckworth.

Duncan, R., Warner, R. and Temu, I. (1995) *The Papua New Guinea Economy: Improving the Investment Climate*. Canberra: AusAID.

Homewood, K. (1995) Climate change and vulnerable groups. Mimeo, Department of Anthropology, University College London.

Norgaard, R.B. (1994) *Development Betrayed: The End of Progress and a Coevolutionary Revisioning of the Future*. London: Routledge.

Pittock, A.B. (1995) Climate change and world food supply: report on reports. *Environment*, **38**(9), 25–50.

Rosenweig, C. and Parry, M.L. (1994) Potential impact of climatic change on world food supply. *Nature*, **367**, 133–8.

World Bank (1992) *World Development Report 1992*. Washington, DC: World Bank.

World Bank (1995) *Monitoring Environmental Progress: A Report on Work in Progress*. Washington, DC: Environmentally Sustainable Development, World Bank.

# Name Index

Adger, N.   97; *see also* Brown, K. *et al.*
Agrawal, A.N. *et al.*   112
Ahamed, C.S.   74
Ahmad, A.   55
Ajani, G., *see* Dallago, B. *et al.*
Alam, M.M.   53, 62, 65, 70, 73
Allan, T.   32
Amirahmadi, H.   249
Anderson, D.   283
Andrade, G.   175
Annis, S.   151, 164
Arato, A.   248
Arrow, K. *et al.*   4, 12
Artango Ochoa, R.   181
Atkinson, G.   23, 24, 206
Auty, R.M.   15, 197, 199–200, 222, 248, 258, 298

Baark, E.   255, 258–9
Bach Tan Sinh   257, 262
Bajracharya, S.   166
Bakht, Z.   66
Barde, J.-P.   206
Barnett, A.S.   51
Bartelmus, P.   200; *et al.* 201
Basi, R.   248
Bateman, I., *see* Turner, R.K. *et al.*
Bater, J.H.   250
Baxter, P.T.W.   130
Beckerman, W.   96, 282, 297
Beer, C., *see* Repetto, R. *et al.*
Behrens, W., *see* Meadows, D.H. *et al.*
Bell, J.   160, 206–7
Benton, T.   13
Berend, I.T.   250
Beresford, M.   252, 254, 255–6, 259
Bergstø, B.   249
Berkes, F.   12–13
Bernstam, M.   231, 233, 238
Bilsborrow, R.E.   51
Birdsall, N.   239
Bista, 154
Blaike, P. *et al.*   144
Bodansky, D.   278, 280
Bolin, B. *see* Arrow, K. *et al.*

Bose, A.   112
Bowen, J.T., Jr   249
Bragdon   286, 288
Brandon, C.   240
Brandon, K.   159–60
Brenton, A.   286
Brewster, H.   199
Bromley, D.   13
Browett, J.G.   248
Brown, K.   14–15, 86, 93–4, 96–7; *et al.*   11, 284
Brown, L.R.   119
Brown, M.   153, 159–60, 165
Brown, R.   228
Brundtland, Gro Harlem   273
Bryant, C.G.A.   249
Brzeski, A.   250
Budowski, T.   187
Burkey, S.   153–4
Bush, J.   139

Cameron, J.   14, 302; *see also* Blaike, P. *et al.*
Campbell, D.J.   133
Carley, M.   173
Carr, M.   78
Carriere, J.   176
Carrizosa Umana, J.   179
Carter, T., *see* Parry, M. *et al.*
Chambers, R.   12, 153, 160
Chaudhuri, S.   79
Chenery, H.B.   226, 228, 235–6, 238
Chowdhury, N.   65, 73
Christie, I.   173
Clark, M.A.   177
Clark, W.C., *see* Turner, B.L. *et al.*
Cline, W.   7
Cobb, J.B.   8
Cockburn, A.   291
Cohen, J.L.   248
Cohen and Uphoff   153–4
Constanza, R.   12; *see also* Arrow, K. *et al.*
Conway, G.   12
Cook, P.   251
Cox, T.   87
Croll, E.   13

Cropper, M.L.   222
Crosson, P.R.   206
Crowson, P.C.F.   201
Crucible Group   288

Dallago, B. *et al.*   250
Daly, H.E.   4, 8
Dan Ton That   252
Dang Duc Dam   252, 254
Dang Duc Nhan, *see* Pham Binh Quyen *et al.*
Daniel, P.   198
Dasgupta, P.   10; *see also* Arrow, K. *et al.*
De Coursey, M.   148, 152, 159
de Vylder, S.   252
DeBardelben, J.   249
Desai, N.   271
Dinerstein, E.   89
Dinh, Q.   252
Do Thi Minh Duc   262
Dodds, F.   174
Dovers, S.R.   97
DuBois, M.   250, 259
Dubourg, W.R.   32
Duffus, D.   96
Duncan, R. *et al.*   300
Dyson, T.   14, 297

Eber, S.   148, 159
Edelman, J.   177
Edwards, M.   151, 164
Ekins, P.   11
Ekoku, F.E.   247
El Serafy, S.   25, 200
Elbadawi, I.   25
Ellis, J.   134
Emsley, J.   282
Endresen, S.B.   249
Ephraums, J.J., *see* Houghton, J.T. *et al.*

Fairhead, J.   95
Fang Wang   250
Farid, S.M.   66, 74
Farrington, J.   154–5
Fenton, D.   258
Feyerbrand, G.B.   159
Fforde, A.   252
Fish, M.S.   250
Fisher, R.L.   154–5
Fluckiger, M.   215
Folke, C., *see* Arrow, K. *et al.*
Forbes, D.K.   252
Forsyth, T.   15, 249, 301
Fowler, A.   151, 154, 164
Fraser, L.   255–6
Fratkin, E.   139
Freire, P.   154
Friedrich, H.   258, 262
Friedman, J.   173

Furer-Haimendorf, C.   154

Galbraith, J.K.   276
Galvin, K.A.   134
Gamez, R., *see* Reid, W.V. *et al.*
Gates, C.   252
Gaviria, B.   180
Gelb, A.   26, 198
Ghai, D.   13
Ghimire, K.   51
Gibbons, D.C.   42, 44–5
Gilmour, D.   154–5
Glemarec, Y.   262
Goldenberg, J.   235–6
Gollin, M., *see* Reid, W.V. *et al.*
Gomez, R., *see* Andrade, G. *et al.*
Gomez Pompa, A.   95
Gordon, J.   275
Gore, A.   172
Goulet, D.   154
Grancelli, B., *see* Dallago, B. *et al.*
Gray, S.L.   43, 44
Grossman, G.   229, 233
Grubb, M.   283; *et al.* 273
Grzybowski, C.   52
Guha, R.   52
Gunaratnam, D.J., *see* Kutcher, G. *et al.*
Günes-Ayata, A.   248
Gupta, R.C., *see* Agrawal, A.N. *et al.*
Gurung, C.P.   148, 152, 157, 159
Gurung, D.   166
Gurung, N.   166

Haas, R.B.   206
Hageman, A.   10
Hall, J.A.   248
Hamilton, K.   14, 22–7, 197, 201, 203, 206, 298
Hansen-Kuhn,   177
Harrison, S.   155
Hartlyn, J.   176
Hartwick, J.   10, 22
Hawes, G.   249
Hecht, S.   291
Heinen, J.T.   89, 145–6, 159–60
Henry, R.   274
Herbon, D.   78
Hesselberg, J.   250, 259
Hewison, K. *et al.*   249; *see also* Robison, R. *et al.*
Heywood, V.   85, 284–5
Hguyen Van San, *see* Pham Binh Quyen *et al.*
Hilborn, R.   12, 97; *see also* Arrow, K. *et al.*, Ludwig, D. *et al.*
Hirsch, F.   5
Hirsch, P.   249
Hobart, M.   13
Hochgraf, N.N.   235

Hogg, R.   129, 130, 133
Holling, C.S.   4
Holmberg, J. *et al.*   272
Homewood, K.   298
Hong Liu   249
Hossain, M.   71; *et al.* 61
Hough, J.L.   159
Houghton, J.T. *et al.*   280
Howarth, J.   12, 97, 249–50, 259
Hueting, R.   171
Hulme, D.   151, 164
Hulme, M., *see* Parry, M. *et al.*
Huntingdon, S.   248
Hurrell, A.   290–1
Hutt, M.   147
Huynh, F.   255
Hyder, T.O.   277

Imber, M.F.   274–5, 288
Irvin, G.   252
Ishiyama, J.T.   250
Islam, L.   79
Islam, M.N., *see* Hossain, M. *et al.*
Islam, R.   62, 65, 70–1, 73

Jacobs, M.   13
Jaeger, W.K.   84
Jagannathan, N.V.   50
Jäger, J.   279, 281
Jamison, A.   255, 258–9
Jänicke, M.   247, 259
Jansson, B.-O., *see* Arrow, K. *et al.*
Janzen, D., *see* Reid, W.V. *et al.*
Jenkins, G.J., *see* Houghton, J.T. *et al.*
Jerneck, A.   255
Jinan Li   250
Johnson, S.   285
Johnston, R.   292
Jordan, A.   15, 276–7, 278
Julius, D.   228
Juma, C.   285, 288; *see also* Reid, W.V. *et al.*

Karki   97
Kates, R.W., *see* Turner, B.L. *et al.*
Kattel, B.   97, 145–6, 159–60
Kaus, A.   95
Keane, J.   251
Kenen, J.   177
Kenny, O.   14, 133, 140, 299–300
Khatri, T.   97
Kloppenburg, J.R.   186, 285
Koch, M., *see* Grubb, M. *et al.*
Kolko, G.   252
Kornai, J.   250, 259
Korten, D.   153
Krugman, P.R.   228
Kutcher, G. *et al.*   49

Lagos, G.E.   213–14, 215
Laird, S.A., *see* Reid, W.V. *et al.*
Lal, D.   228
Lama, T.S.   148, 150, 155–6, 163
Lara, S.   177
Lawrence, R.Z.   228
Leach, M.   95
Leakey, R.   284
Lehmkuhl, J.F. *et al.*   93
Leinbach, T.R.   249
Lele, S.   292
Leonard, J.   279
Levin, S., *see* Arrow, K. *et al.*
Lewin, R.   284
Lipp, J.R.   148, 150, 155–6, 163
Lohmann, L.   249
Lohmann, R.A.   249
Lovins, A.B.   5
Low, P.   222
Ludwig, D.   12, 97; *et al.* 12, 85
Lugo, A.   95
Lutz, E., *see* Bartelmus, P. *et al.*

McCabe, J.T. *et al.*   136
McConnell, F.   284
Mace, R.   141
Macfarlane, A.   155
McFarlane, B.   252, 259
McGuirk, S., *see* Kutcher, G. *et al.*
McNeely, J.A.   285
McNeil, J.   172
MacNeill, J. *et al.*   277
Magrath, W., *see* Repetto, R. *et al.*
Mahato, Ram Din   97
Mahmud, W.   67
Maldonado, T.   177
Maler, K.-G.   22; *see also* Arrow, K. *et al.*
Mallon, R.L.   251
Malthus, Thomas Robert   103, 123
Mankiw, N.G.   10
Marsden, D.   153, 160
Martyn, P.   206
Mathews, J.T., *see* Turner, B.L. *et al.*
Meadows, D.H. *et al.*   11
Meadows, D.L., *see* Meadows, D.H. *et al.*
Meadwell, H.   250, 260
Messerschmidt, D.A.   160
Metz, J.J.   144
Meyer, C.A., *see* Reid, W.V. *et al.*
Meyer, S.   4
Meyer, W.B., *see* Turner, B.L. *et al.*
Middleton, N. *et al.*   247, 272, 291
Midgley, J.   153
Mikesell, R.F.   10, 200
Milner, C.   222
Minogue, M.   251
Mintzer, I.   279
Mishra, H.R.   89

Morris, E., *see* Sarre, P. *et al.*
Mott MacDonald   65
Mouzelis, N.   260
Moyo, S., *see* Middleton, N. *et al.*
Munasinghe, M.   247, 249
Munoz, G.   211, 214
Munslow, B.   247
Munson, A.   286; *see also* Grubb, M. *et al.*
Muqtada, M.   53, 62, 65, 70, 73, 74
Myers, N.   284
Myint, H.   235

Nash, R.F.   249
Nathan, A.   250
Ndulu, B.   25
Nepal, S.K.   89
Neufville, L.N.   208
Neumann, R.P.   247
Nguyen Dac Hy   255
Nguyen Thanh Ha   255
Nguyen Van Truong   259
Nordhaus, W.D.   9–10
Norgaard, R.   4, 13, 299
North, R.   282
Nowak, L.   250

Oakley, P.   153, 160
Oates, W.E.   222
Oba, G.   133
O'Brien, Philip J.   14, 170, 300–1
O'Connor, J.   203
O'Keefe, P., *see* Middleton, N. *et al.*
O'Leary, M.   137, 139
O'Riordan, T.   3, 5, 279, 281
Osaghae, E.   247–8
Ostrom, E.   13
Owens, S.   4

Parker, S.   14
Parkin, D.   13
Parry, M.   298; *et al.* 280
Paterson, M.   283
Pathak, B.   97
Payne, R.A.   247–8
Pearce, D.W.   24, 206; *see also* Brown, K. *et al.*; Turner, R.K. *et al.*
Pedersen, P.   249
Peet, N.   90, 97
Peluso, N.L.   247
Perkins, S., *see* McCabe, J.T. *et al.*
Perkins, D.   236
Perrings, C.   12; *see also* Arrow, K. *et al.*; Brown, K. *et al.*; wa-Githinji, M.
Peskin, H.M.   9
Pezzey, J.   21
Pham Binh Quyen *et al.*   251, 255
Pham Ngoc Dang   255
Phuc Tien   257

Pignéde, B.   155
Pimbert, M.P.   145–6
Pimental, D., *see* Arrow, K. *et al.*
Pinto, B.   198
Pittock, A.B.   298
Pokharel, S.K.   87, 89, 92
Pombo, D.   175, 179
Pretty, J.N.   145–6
Pye-Smith, C.   159

Quarrie, J.   154
Quasem, M.A.   55, 70

Rademacher, A.   147
Rahman, A.   54, 62, 65, 70–1, 73, 74
Rahman, M.D.   153
Rahman, M.H., *see* Hossain, M. *et al.*
Raman Kutty, R.   240
Ramirez, A.   177
Randers, J., *see* Meadows, D.H. *et al.*
Rashid, M.A.   72
Rau, Z.   247
Raup, D.M.   284
Raustiala, K.   287, 289
Redclift, M.   13, 249
Reddy, A.K.N.   235–6
Reid, W.V. *et al.*   286
Reinhardt, J.   252
Repetto, R. *et al.*   21
Rich, B.   278
Ritchey-Vance, M.   179
Robison, R. *et al.*   249; *see also* Hewison, K. *et al.*
Rodan, G., *see* Hewison, K. *et al.*; Robison, R. *et al.*
Roddick, J.F.   174
Rodriguez, S.   186
Rodriguez Becerra, M.   182
Roemer, J.E.   250
Roemer, M.   223
Roniger, L.   248
Ronnås, P.   259
Rosendal, G.K.   247
Rosenweig, C.   298
Rossini, F., *see* Repetto, R. *et al.*
Rowlands, I.   282
Ruiz, J.P., *see* Andrade, G. *et al.*
Runge   132
Runords, J.F., *see* Turner, B.L. *et al.*

Sachs, W.   4
Sage, C.   13
Salmon, M.   208
Salt, J.   278
Sánchez, V.   288
Sandford, S.   136
Sarre, P. *et al.*   171
Schofield, C., *see* McCabe, J.T. *et al.*

Schroeder, R.A. 247
Schweinfest, S., *see* Bartelmus, P. *et al.*
Scoones, I. 130, 140
Scott, G.L. 78
Seddon, D. 144, 147, 154–5; *see also*
Blaike, P. *et al.*
Shackley, M. 148
Sharma, G. 97
Sharma, U. 89, 97; *see also* Lehmkuhl, J.F.
*et al.*
Shaw, R.P. 51
Sherpa, M.N. 159
Shreshtra, N.K. 147, 154–5
Simon, J. 284
Sittenfield, A. 186; *see also* Reid, W.V. *et al.*
Skeldon, R. 51
Smets, H. 250
Smith, P., *see* Sarre, P. *et al.*
Smith, W.S. 211
Solinger, D.J. 250
Spencer, Paul 133
Spoor, M. 252
Stengel, H. 255
Stiefel, M. 153–4, 173
Strong, M. 186, 270–2
Sukhatme, P.V. 104
Sullivan, F., *see* Grubb, M. *et al.*
Summers, L.H. 8
Swanson, T. 285; *see also* Brown, K. *et al.*
Swift, J. 134, 142
Symanski, R. 95
Syrquin, M. 226, 228, 235–6, 238

Tamang, D. 147
Taslim, M.A. 74
Taylor, J.L. 249
Temu, I., *see* Duncan, R. *et al.*
Tester, K. 248
Thakali, S. 160, 164–5
Thomas, C. 290–1
Thomson, K., *see* Grubb, M. *et al.*; Holmberg,
J. *et al.*
Thrift, N.J. 252
Timberlake, L., *see* Holmberg, J. *et al.*
Tisdell, C. 52
Toulmin, C. 141
Tran Hieu Nhue 255
Tribe, M. 15, 222, 248, 258
Truong, D. 252
Turner, B.L. *et al.* 3
Turner, R.K. *et al.* 5, 7; *see also* Brown, K. *et al.*

Uphoff 153–4
Upreti, R.K., *see* Lehmkuhl, J.F. *et al.*
Uribe Botero, E. 179
Urry, J. 248

Uttig, P. 178

Valenzuela, L.F. 211
van Brabant, J.M. 247
van Tongeren, J. 200
Varma, H.O., *see* Agrawal, A.N. *et al.*
Velasquez, F. 179
Velesco, P. 213–14
Venturino 138
Vernon, R. 221
Victor, D. 278, 287, 289
Vijverberg, W.P.M. 52
Vo Nhan Tri 252
von Moltke, K. 276
Vu Cao Dam 248, 258
Vu Tuan Anh 252

wa–Githinji, M. 12
Walters, C., *see* Ludwig, D. *et al.*
Wank, D.L. 250
Wapner, P. 259
Ward, R.M. 250
Warford, J. 37
Warhurst, A. 197
Warner, R., *see* Duncan, R. *et al.*
Watson, R.T. 85, 284–5
Weber, K.E. 89
Weir 208
Weitzman, M.L. 22, 27
Well, M., *see* Repetto, R. *et al.*
Wellington, K.E. 208
Wells, M.P. 144, 146, 159–60
Werksman, J. 278
Wheeler, D. 239
White, G. 248
Whiting, S.H. 250
Wilches-Chaux, G. 183
Wildavsky, A. 284
Wilkinson, B. 249
Williams, D. 173
Williamson, J. 222
Wilson, E.O. 284
Winpenny, J.T. 14, 298
Winsemius, P., *see* MacNeill, J. *et al.*
Wolfe, M. 153–4, 173, 228
Woodgate, G. 249
Wu, W. 249
Wyckoff Baird, B. 153, 159–60, 165
Wynne, B. 4

Yakushiji, T., *see* MacNeill, J. *et al.*
Yonzon 145–6
Young, R.A. 43, 44
Young, T. 173

Zimmerer, K.S. 12, 95

# Subject Index

Afghanistan 104–14, 118–25
Africa 25
  see also sub-Saharan Africa and individual
    countries
Agenda 21 154, 174, 186, 271–5, 289, 292
agro-processing 226, 228–9, 238, 241
aid 277
  see also food aid
air pollution 213–16, 230–1
Alliance of Small Island States (AOSIS) 282
Annapurna Conservation Area 14, 144–66,
  300
arable land, potential 117, 120, 125
autarky 238, 244
authoritarianism 247–50, 261
average incremental cost (AIC) 38–9

Bangladesh 14, 52–80, 104–25
bauxite production 201–17
'best practice' in pollution control 216,
  235–6, 239
Bhopal 225
bio-chemical oxygen demand (BOD)
  229–30, 233, 239–40
biodiversity 83–7, 93–5, 144, 146, 148,
  157, 175–8, 181, 185–6
  prospecting 186
Biological Diversity, UN Convention
  on 85, 93, 271–2, 277, 284–90
Bolivia 199
'bottom-up' approaches 14, 154, 290, 297,
  299
Brazil 175, 287
British Geological Survey 36, 42
Brundtland Commission and Report 3, 11,
  21, 171–2, 270, 274, 291–2
burning of grassland 89, 94–5
Burundi 26
business organizations, involvement
  of 183, 187–8

calorie intake 104–6
Canada 180, 233, 280
carbon dioxide emissions and carbon
  tax 25, 28, 280–1
carrying capacity 95, 130, 134, 174

casualization of employment 65–6
censuses
  of employment 66–7
  of population 53, 60, 70
cereal production in South Asia 106–16
  and consumption 110
  projections of 115–16, 120–3
Chernobyl 225
Chile 15, 122, 197–8, 204–7, 211–16, 298,
  300
China 60, 117, 119, 213, 250, 252, 255,
  261, 277
  see also Yellow River
Chitwan National Park 162
CITES (Convention on International Trade in
  Endangered Species) 284
civil society 248–50, 259–60
climate change 124, 297
  see also rainfall
Climate Change, UN Convention on
  271–2, 277–84, 287, 290
collective farming 138
Colombia 14, 169–70, 175–84, 189–90,
  300–1
communism 250–2, 254, 259
compensation payments 213, 216–17, 257
Conferences of the Parties (to UN
  conventions) 282–3, 287
conservation policies 83–7, 94, 144–8, 157,
  178–9, 182, 285–6
copper production 204–7, 211–17
'cornucopian' view of development 5–6
corruption 250, 255–61, 274
Costa Rica 169–70, 175–9, 185–90, 300
costs of pollution control 214–16, 222–3,
  244
critical natural capital 4, 84

debt repayment 170, 173, 177, 180, 278
'deep ecology' 5–6
degradation of land 137, 146, 148, 152,
  207–10, 216
democracy 248–9
dependency, culture of 140, 300
depletion premium 37
  see also mineral depletion

desertification   132, 177, 273
disasters, environmental   225
discount rate   7–9, 39–40
discouraged withdrawal from the labour
  market   78–9
disequilibrium analysis   95, 140–1
diversification, economic   198–9
drought   26, 130–2, 136–42
drought-resistant crops   135

Earth Council   185–6, 188
Earth Summit, *see* Rio Conference
Ecofondo   180–1
ecology   3–5, 12, 51, 95
  *see also* 'deep ecology'; 'new ecology'
economic approaches to sustainability   4–5,
  14
economic growth   172, 174, 224, 292, 310
  *see also* growth theory
education   29, 58–62, 138, 140
  *see also* environmental education
efficiency and pollution   225
Egypt   32, 120
elasticity
  of demand for food with respect to
    income   116–17
  of employment with respect to
    growth   72–7
  of industrial pollution with respect to
    economic development   220
elephant damage   90, 135
endangered species and habitats   86, 89, 96,
  148, 284
energy, use of   235–6, 238, 281
Environment and Development
  UN Conference and Declaration on, *see*
    Rio Declaration
  World Commission on, *see* Brundtland
    Commission
environmental capital   4–8
environmental education   156–63
environmental impact assessments   171,
  184, 256, 260–1, 286
environmental indices   298
equity   83, 289, 301
  within and between generations   8–10,
    84, 96, 171, 273
ethnic diversity   148, 175, 251
European Community/Union   33, 113, 180,
  276, 280–2
evaluation of development projects   160–1,
  164–5

famine   110–11, 115, 123–4, 139
Farmers' Rights   288, 290
fertilizers, use of   119, 124
  pollution from   231
Finland   281

fisheries management   85
food aid   113, 125, 132, 135–6, 139
Food for the Hungry   132, 135
food production per capita
  FAO index of   112–13
  in South Asia, *see* South Asia
foreign direct investment (FDI)   247–61
forests, clearance of   177–8
Forests, Intergovernmental Panel on
  272–3, 275, 287
France   228
funding of programmes   164–5, 180, 182

genetic resources   285–8
'genuine saving'   23–9, 298
Germany   228, 235, 281–2
Ghana   240–2
Ghandruk   150, 159–60
Global Climate Coalition   283
Global Environment Facility   171, 181, 271,
  275–8, 280, 287, 289, 292
Global Environmental Change
  Programme   126
global environmental problems and
  solutions   4, 171, 290
global warming   7, 69, 279, 282
grassland habitats   88–96
grazing regimes   132–4, 137, 141
green revolution   51, 107, 111, 119, 125
greenhouse gases   51, 277–84, 290
growth theory   10, 27, 29

Hangu Region   36
health risks   215, 217, 221, 230–1, 241, 258,
  290
hedonistic pricing   206, 215
high-technology industries   228, 242
high-yielding varieties (HYVs)   107, 111,
  117, 119
Holland   185–7
Hong Kong   254
human capital   8, 29, 299
human error   225
Human Genome Diversity Project   288
human-induced changes in habitats   95
hydropower   42, 44, 46, 163

income per capita, effects of changes
  in   116–17, 226, 230–1
  *see also* inverted U-shape
India   103–26, 282
indigenous communities   96, 133–4, 150,
  152, 155–6, 169, 181, 183–4, 274
indivisibilities in production   35–6, 38
Indonesia   122, 198, 229–30, 233, 240, 255
industrialization   15, 220, 226–9, 242–3
  in Vietnam   247–51, 257–61
  *see also* late industrializers

inequality 125, 177, 289
  see also wealth
infrastructure
  environmental 256, 258, 260
  social 299
Integrated Project in Arid Lands
  (IPAL) 132–7
intellectual property rights 285–8
Inter-American Development Bank 181
Interaid 132
International Bank for Reconstruction and
  Development, see World Bank
International Development Agency 277
International Monetary Fund 170, 188, 290
inverted U-shape (relating pollution to
  income) 231–3, 244
irreversible damage to the environment 34
irrigation 45–8, 73–4, 110, 112, 117, 124,
  133, 140, 142, 211
Italy 228

Jamaica 15, 197–216, 298, 300
Japan 228, 235, 244

Kenya 26, 297
  see also Marsabit District
Kenyan Agricultural Research Institute
  (KARI) 130–1, 134, 137–8
King Mahendra Trust for Nature
  Conservation 147–52, 160, 164
Kosi Tappu National Reserve 89
Kuznets Curve, Environmental 33

labour force statistics 53–73, 80
labour shortages 58–9, 65, 70
land restoration 207–10
  see also degradation of land
Laos 250–1, 261
large and small firms, pollution control
  in 239–40
late industrializers 240–4
Latin America 14, 25, 60, 169–70, 175, 299
legislation and regulation,
  environmental 179, 181–4, 220, 222–
  5, 239, 242, 244, 247–50, 256–60
Lesotho 32
liberalization
  economic 125, 176, 250, 252, 258–61
  political 248, 261
Libya 32
Limits to Growth 11
literacy programmes 158, 163
livelihood analysis 51–80

macro-economic policy 198–9
malaria, eradication of 110–11
Malawi 25–6
Malaysia 198, 229–30, 249, 287

manufacturing 221, 227–8, 233, 237–8
  'early', 'middle' and 'late' stages of 226
  value added in 237
marginal cost of mineral production 201
marginal cost pricing 31, 35–41, 49
  instability associated with 38
market-driven policies 52, 170, 239
Marsabit District 14, 129–41, 299–300
Mexico 180
Middle East 25, 32
migration flows 51–2, 59–60, 67–70, 79–
  80, 124, 126
mineral depletion, measurement of 200–5,
  298
mineral economies 197–9, 216, 298
mineral stabilization funds 198–9
Mongolia 250–1
Montreal Protocol 279
multinational corporations 188, 216, 222,
  288, 290–1
multiple cropping 112, 119–20, 124–5
mutual sustainable development
  pacts 185–7
Myanmar 251, 261

Nairobi Conference (1976) 132
national accounts 14, 21–9, 52, 183, 200,
  203–6, 216–17, 221
national parks 145–6, 148, 178, 185, 188,
  256
  see also Royal Bardia; Royal Chitwan
National Parks and Protected Areas,
  Congress on 145
'neo-liberal' model of development 170–1,
  173, 183, 185, 190
Nepal 104–25, 300
  see also Annapurna Conservation Area;
  Royal Bardia National Park
'net price' measure of mineral
  depletion 200–1, 203, 205, 216
'new ecology' 12, 95–6
new products and technologies 221
New Zealand 280
newly industrialized countries (NICs) 25,
  221, 223, 249
Niger 26
Nigeria 26
nomadic pastoralism 14, 129–42
non-governmental organizations
  (NGOs) 15, 132, 146–7, 151, 153–4,
  169, 173–5, 180–90, 240, 259, 273, 274,
  276, 287–8, 299
  'scaling up' by 150, 164
non-renewable resources 11, 14, 27–8
North America Free Trade Agreement
  (NAFTA) 170, 183
North–South divisions 13, 15, 272, 277–91
Norway 277, 281

opportunity cost of water supplies 40–1, 49
*Our Common Future*, *see* Brundtland
    Commission and Report
overexploitation 154–5, 285
    *see also* carrying capacity
overpopulation 103
ownership of resources 4, 12, 96, 129–36,
    141, 300

Pakistan 104–25
panchayat system 155
Papua New Guinea 201, 300
participation rates 53–6
participatory approaches 145–7, 150–63,
    169–70, 173–4, 181–9, 299, 301–2
permits
    for exploitation of natural resources 90–
    2, 210
    for tourists and trekkers 152, 157, 164
Peru 199
Philippines, the 239
Poland 250
politics of development 172–5
pollution 15, 28, 33–4, 197, 206–7, 210–
    17, 220–44
    systematic changes in level of 220, 229,
    231–5, 244
    in Vietnam 255–7
pollution havens 222, 224–5, 240, 244
pollution intensity 224–40
pollution shadows 197, 206–7, 216, 224
population estimates and projections 104,
    115
postponement of pollution control
    measures 240
poverty and destitution 7–8, 12, 50, 139–
    40, 176–7, 240, 289
'poverty traps' 29
precautionary principle, the 34
present value, *see* discount rate
preservationist approach to
    conservation 85
presumptive charges for pollution 239
privatization 66–8
process- and target-orientation 165
product cycle, the 221, 223–5, 235, 244
project appraisal techniques 52
proletarianization 260
property rights, *see* ownership of resources
protected areas 144–5, 148–50, 179, 285–6
    *see also* national parks
public opinion 248–9, 258–61, 273, 291
public relations 210–11

quality of life 55, 172, 179

rainfall, distribution of 134–5
recycling 210–11

renewable natural resources 83
rents from mineral extraction 198, 201–6
Rio Conference on Environment and
    Development 11–12, 15, 21, 52, 169–
    75, 179–86, 189, 247, 261, 270–92,
    300–1
    achievements of 271–2, 290
Rio Declaration 174, 271–3, 291–2
Royal Bardia National Park 83–4, 86–94
Royal Chitwan National Park 89, 93
royalties from natural resources 28
Russia 213, 250
Rwanda 26, 276

science, faith in 299
sedentarization 130, 137–9, 141
self-sufficiency in food 110, 113, 125
Singapore 249, 254
SNA (System of National Accounts) 21,
    221
social approach to sustainable
    development 4–5, 12, 93, 96
social problems 176, 184
Somalia 124, 276
South Africa 26, 32, 60, 297
South Korea 249
South and Southeast Asia 14, 25, 228,
    250–2
    food supplies 103–26
    *see also individual countries*
Soviet Union, *see* Russia
Sri Lanka 104–25
standards, environmental 214–16
    international 248, 258
    *see also* legislation
Stockholm Conference (1972) 270, 284
'strong' and 'weak' sustainability 4–11, 84–
    5, 93, 296
structural change during
    industrialization 226
sub-Saharan Africa 14, 25–7, 29, 60, 104,
    221, 297, 299
substitution of technology or resources 37,
    199
'success stories' 164
sustainable development
    definitions of 3, 5, 21
    obstacles to success of 170, 297–302
    scepticism about 9–13, 96, 292
Sustainable Development
    Alliance for 188
    UN Commission for 180, 271, 273–5,
    292
sustainable utilization of resources 83–6,
    93–6
    definition of 85
sustained yield, concept of 85–6, 96
Sweden 281

Taiwan 249–50, 254
Tall Grasslands Research Project 97
targets for use of natural resources 5
taxation of rents 198–9
Thailand 229–31, 239, 249
Thames, River 33
total capital stock 8
tourism 144, 148, 150, 152, 164, 185, 187,
    257, 300
    ecological 187
traditional practices and institutions 13, 96,
    299–300
tragedy of the commons 136
transition economies 15, 177, 221, 247–51,
    259–61, 301
tribal divisions 133–4

Uganda 240–2, 297
uncertainty about ecological systems 97
underemployment 56–7, 70–2, 78
undernutrition 105–6, 124
unemployment rates 69
UNESCO 132
United Kingdom 33, 175, 225, 228, 235,
    281, 285
United Nations
    conferences on women, population and
        urban environment 273
    Development Programme (UNDP) 255–
        6, 275–6, 289
    Environment Programme (UNEP) 275–6,
        284
    Organization 273–6
    Research Institute for Social Development
        (UNRISD) 50, 154
    *see also* Biological Diversity; Climate
        Change; population estimates; Rio
        Conference; Rio Declaration;
        Sustainable Development; UNESCO
United States 33, 43–5, 113, 170, 180, 188,
    213, 228, 251, 272, 276, 279–80, 284–6
Uruguay Round 287

user cost' 36–9, 200–1, 203, 205
utility functions 22–3

Venezuela 180
Vietnam 15, 247–8, 250–62

warfare 111, 113, 133, 176, 251, 254
water pollution 33–4, 210–11, 229–30
water resources, management of 31–49
    pricing policy 35–41, 49
    sustainability rule for 31–2, 34–5, 49
    valuation of supplies 41–9, 298
    water quality 32–4
'weak' sustainability, *see* 'strong' and 'weak'
    sustainability
wealth 21, 298–9
welfare, maximization of 8–10, 21–3
willingness-to-pay 42, 47
women's employment 53, 56
women's and mothers' groups 140, 156,
    158, 162
work-sharing 78
working time 55–7, 62–5, 69–71
World Bank 24, 50, 71, 73, 75, 77, 116,
    144, 170–1, 173, 181, 188, 190, 208,
    214, 223, 226, 228–33, 239–40, 244,
    277–8, 281, 290, 296, 298–9
World Food Programme 113
World Trade Organization 287, 290
Worldwatch Institute 119

Yellow River 36, 47–8
yields, agricultural 112, 119–21, 124–5,
    208
    *see also* high-yielding varieties
young people, labour force participation
    of 53–6
Yugoslavia 276

Zaire 26–7
Zambia 199
Zimbabwe 26

Printed in the United States
by Baker & Taylor Publisher Services